The Who FAQ

Series Editor: Robert Rodriguez

The Who FAQ

All That's Left to Know About Fifty Years of Maximum R&B

Mike Segretto

Backbeat
Books

An Imprint of Hal Leonard Corporation

Published in 2014 by Backbeat Books
An Imprint of Hal Leonard Corporation
7777 West Bluemound Road
Milwaukee, WI 53213

Trade Book Division Editorial Offices
33 Plymouth St., Montclair, NJ 07042

The FAQ series was conceived by Robert Rodriguez and developed with Stuart Shea.

Printed in the United States of America

Book design by Snow Creative Services

Library of Congress Cataloging-in-Publication Data is available upon request.

ISBN 978-1-48036-103-4

www.backbeatbooks.com

For Desmond Elvis Segretto

Contents

Foreword

The High Numbers opened for the Kinks at Goldhawk Social Club Shepherd's Bush in 1964. I remember how focused and aggressive they sounded. Pete Townshend with his cutting amphetamine stride looked comedic at first with his big nose, a bit like our bass player Pete Quaife, but then I realized how unique and cool he looked and sounded. Roger Daltrey wore the corniest clothes; he didn't know how to make his hair flat enough. It looked like he had it ironed with tufts sticking out at the edges. His voice fitted the songs perfectly, but I was irritated that he sang with an American accent, which I thought was really strange for a band that was from Shepherd's Bush. Seemed to me like he didn't quite get it. John Entwistle looked like he was always blocked (blocked meant stoned), but he looked the coolest of them all. I always suspected he was a shy guy putting on a tough exterior, but unfortunately, I never got to know him that well. What was so noticeable was the drummer who looked like a teenage version of Robert Newton—the actor from the movies *Hatter's Castle* and *Treasure Island*—with a mad gleam in his eye. Keith Moon didn't belong on Earth. He was an alien from another world. He was classic: a perfect rock drummer, perfect loony, funny, and inspirational. He always made me laugh. They were young, for fuck's sake, but so were we. I remember thinking at the time, "Those cheeky sods; they're really good, aren't they?" How dare they be that good when they were *our* support band and it was the Kinks' show! They had something, which I sensed would have a phenomenal impact in the world of popular music. The High Numbers would soon come to be known as the Who.

Me and Pete Quaife loved the Who. I always thought Pete Quaife was a true mod. He would drive to the Kinks' shows on his Vespa with his parka stained with lorry fumes from driving behind trucks. The mods were all about a sharp dress sense, attitude, and amphetamines. I used to meet with Keith Moon on *Ready Steady Go* and divvy up the drugs before the show. In the beginning we used to do purple hearts, which were used for heart patients in hospitals. Later on we moved on to other types of amphetamines. A close friend of mine worked in the clothes shops on Carnaby St., and he would score for me. We used to get so blocked that it was hard to smile. I loved the amphetamine stutter on "My Generation." Other songs I liked from that period included "I Can See for Miles," "Pictures of Lily," and "Substitute." John Entwistle was a great bass player: really lyrical and musical and had a great tone. I met him a few times at the TV studios and on tours. I reckon that he and Pete Quaife were way ahead of their time. They had to be the best bass players of that period.

After we were banned from the United States from 1966 until 1969, we had to virtually start all over again in the seventies. During this period, we were opening for the Who on a few shows in America. Although Ray never said much, I think he had a sneaking respect for the Who. I was a bit irritated, because it was obvious they were inspired by the Kinks. Pete Townshend and Ray and me had a mutual friend called Barry Fantoni, a singer, writer, and journalist. I think he used to cross relate information backwards and forwards from one camp to the other; not a spy exactly or a secret agent. I don't know, but something was going on. Barry once asked if his friend Pete Townshend could have access to our multi tracks so he could listen to them. Of course, we wouldn't let them out of our hands. "Pretty cheeky," we thought! But in interviews, Pete Townshend was always forthcoming in giving the Kinks credit as a major influence on their work. I had to admit that back in the day I knew that the Who were gonna be huge. It was inevitable. Their music sounds as poignant and immediate today as it did back then. They had a magic or charisma that has lasted them through the years and will continue long into the future.

—Dave Davies, July 2013

Guitarist **Dave Davies** cofounded the Kinks with his brother Ray. With the Who, the Kinks helped form the backbone of British pop, and Dave wrote some of their best-loved songs, including "Death of a Clown," "Susannah's Still Alive," and "Living on a Thin Line." Dave is still very active in music, having released his most recent solo album, *I Will Be Me*, in 2013. You'll be reading a lot more about Dave and the Kinks throughout this book, since they had such a profound influence on the Who. You can also see what Dave's up to on his website, davedavies.com.

Acknowledgments

The *Who FAQ* was a great, big bastard of a research project, and the only way I was able to maintain my sanity while putting it all together was by leaning on the generosity, talents, and two cents of a lot of groovy people. I must give pride of place to Robert Rodriguez, the inventor of the FAQ series and a fab writer in his own right (you must read his *Revolver: How the Beatles Reimagined Rock 'n' Roll*. You must). Robert is the cat who dug my bloggy babblings about the Who enough to stalk me down on the Internet and ask if I wanted to submit a proposal for this book. Following so close I couldn't even call it second place is my genius wife, Elise Nussbaum, who edited my proposal to ensure it was fit for human eyes, a chore I appreciate all the more because she doesn't particularly like the Who. I promise that when you write *The Magnetic Fields FAQ*, I'll do you the same favor, Elise.

A kinky, kolossal thanks to Dave Davies for contributing the foreword to this book, and a gallon of gratitude to writer Rebecca G. Wilson for introducing me to him. Getting to chat with Dave was the absolute highlight of my career.

A zillion thanks to all who humored me enough to respond to my geeky questions or put me in touch with those who could, including Jon Astley, Chris Huston, Jill Bussey, Henry Scott-Irvine, Chris Holmes, Alan McKendree, and Stefani Kelly. Additional slobbering gratitude goes to those who helped shape the finished product with their sharp edits, advice, and questions, particularly my official Backbeat editor, Bernadette Malavarca, but also my friends who donated their time and valuable feedback. Many thanks and much love to Phil Ryan for double-checking my analysis of Keith Moon's drumming and Matt Marshall for doing the same for my analysis of John Entwistle's songwriting technique. I also want to shower some sincere appreciation on Jeffrey Dinsmore, Steve Mirek, and Uncle Rob Busch for their notes, questions, and corrections. Thanks to my parents, who inadvertently sparked my Who curiosity when they gave me Nicholas Schaffner's *The British Invasion* as a Christmas gift quite a number of years ago . . . and of course my cat, Ms. Boris Karloff, who wrote the chapter about Roger Daltrey's nipples.

Finally, I'd like to thank you, reader, and not just because you paid your few bucks for this book or had the gumption to shoplift it in an age when there are barely any bookstores left to shoplift from. Fans such as yourself—or perhaps fans *including* yourself—helped me complete this book by responding to my online polls and queries. The Who has always been the ultimate fans' band; the rare group that actually cared what their devotees' thought and felt. What other band would allow an audience member to fill in for an "ailing" bandmate, as the Who did at the Cow Palace in 1973? What other band would have considered including their audience in the making of their music, as the Who did while trying to create *Lifehouse*? So I would have been remiss not to get your input when writing the chapters on the Who's most underrated songs and essential solo albums. Now let's hope this goes a little smoother than *Lifehouse*.

Welcome!

Introduction
Welcome

Who?

The band itself is a question, its name an interrogative pronoun begging for an answer. Who are the Who, and how did these four guys—with their penchant for violence and almost uncomfortably raw confessionals, their cartoony comedy and unashamedly intellectual projects, their curmudgeonly leader who conspicuously lacks the qualities of a classic pop idol—become one of the most famous, most influential, most powerful rock 'n' roll bands in the world?

Attempting to answer those broad questions births countless more queries, because nothing about the Who is simple. Just look at the most basic product of this (or any) band: their music. The Who had hit songs in their UK homeland about sci-fi cross-dressers and masturbation. Their breakthrough in the States was a psychotically cheerful ditty about kids bullying a geek named Happy Jack. Their worldwide breakthrough on LP was a double-disc "rock opera" about a deaf, dumb, and blind pinball fanatic who becomes a teen messiah. What? Is this a joke?

Nope. And this is only a whiff of the weirdness wafting around the Who.

The first time I really took notice of my other favorite bands moved me to make declarative statements. My reaction to the Beatles shaking their mop tops and exuding pure pop joy: "Wow!" Seeing Jagger in the "Start Me Up" video after MTV *finally* started broadcasting in New York: "That guy has some bad pit stains." But the Who provoked a question: "What the fuck is he doing?"

It was early 1989, and I was flicking through channels hunting for something to stab away the boredom of being a teenager on suburban Long Island. I stopped on one of the music channels, MTV or VH-1. Tommy Smothers was marching up and down the stage, asking canned questions of a bunch of antsy cretins in frilly shirts. Tommy traded scripted quips with a guitarist who looked like a flamingo with laser-lit blue eyes, a diminutive singer with a fluffy perm who held himself tighter than a boxer backed in a corner, and a dour bass player clad in gangster black who looked like he'd rather be in a grave than exchanging words with the host, or I assumed, anyone. Then Tommy moved on to an impishly grinning drummer with basset hound eyes. This guy clearly had no intention of staying on script. Still catching his breath after the manic, lip-synched pantomime that had just ended, the drummer cheerily insulted the host, dropped a casual fart joke, and set an unpredictable mood for a performance that would end with him setting off enough nonsanctioned explosives in his bass drum to set the guitarist's hair on fire and blow himself off his drum riser.

But that massive boom wasn't even the moment in *The Kids Are Alright* that inspired me to ask, "What the fuck is he doing?" My question came a bit earlier while the Who were faking their way through a prerecorded version of "My Generation." Obviously, I'd heard this song before, even owned it on an "As Seen on TV" various artists compilation called *Brits Blitz*, so I'd already heard the mid-song solo. However, I'd never *seen* it. At the time, I was a fledgling bass player, just two years into taking my weekly lessons, studying my scales, and learning how to stay in the deep background so that I might one day have the skills to lend modest support to a lead guitarist. Because that's what bass players do. Only, that's not what the bass player in the Who was doing. He was playing the fucking solo. When I'd heard that solo in the past, I always assumed it was just a standard electric guitar with a lot of low end. Big deal. As it turns out, it was a bass, and this guy wasn't cheating by using a pick. He was tapping out the solo with fingers moving with the velocity of hummingbird wings. Had the drummer picked up his floor tom and blown through it like it was a trombone, I wouldn't have been any more floored.

"What the fuck is he doing?"

Well, what John Entwistle was doing was wiping his arse with the rock 'n' roll bassist's rulebook, showing off how he'd invented a completely new way to play his instrument (the fact that he looked so bored doing it just made his achievement cooler). Since I was studying the bass, I thought this was the most audacious and inventive thing in *The Kids Are Alright*, but it was really just one of many audacious occurrences, because the entire band had equal contempt for the rules. Really, I could have asked myself any number of questions over the next two hours. Why isn't Keith Moon keeping time on his snare and hi-hat like a proper drummer? Why are those nuts smashing their expensive instruments? What's with all this pretentious rock opera horseshit?

These are the kinds of questions a Who novice frequently asks. After I became curious enough to buy *Meaty, Beaty, Big, and Bouncy* a month or so after I first saw *The Kids Are Alright*, and I became a Who freak for good, the questions never stopped coming. They just got more and more specific. Who really completed the first rock opera? What did the mods and the punks *really* think of the Who? Which of their recordings are still unavailable? Who were their wives and girlfriends? Who were their most important influences, and which artists were their most loyal followers? Where do the guys stand on the issues: politics, religion, philanthropy? Just how many mixes of "Magic Bus" are there, and what's with that long one on *Meaty, Beaty*? Who's the model on the back cover of *The Who Sell Out*? Why did Pete Townshend include what sounds like a barking seal on "The Dirty Jobs," and why is it missing from every remix of *Quadrophenia*?

Since that first viewing of *The Kids Are Alright*, I've spent *way* too much time seeking answers to questions such as these, reading every book and article about the Who I could scrounge, watching every interview, scrutinizing every song over and over and over. So, in a sense, I've been researching the book you're now perusing for the past twenty-five years. In putting it together, I tried to answer enough basic questions to acclimate the Who novice and enough obscure ones to satisfy my fellow obsessive geeks. I know that there are a few hardcore Wholigans out there who could read a book like this from cover to cover, spike it on the floor, and sneer, "*Pfft*, I already knew all that." So I've expanded the band's orbit a bit further to address some questions few fans may have ever even thought to ask: "What TV shows should the Who fan check out?" or "What records did the Who exclusively release in the Philippines?"

You might think these kinds of questions are, errr, *a bit much*. What kind of loony needs to know such minutiae? You might just want to know which outside musicians guest-starred on the Who's records or which compilations you need to pick up in order to own every studio recording the band officially released. Although I did try to assemble them in a sensible and readable order, the chapters are essentially stand-alone articles addressing various aspects of Who history, so feel free to violate the most basic rule of book reading and hop around from chapter to chapter according to your own particular curiosities. After all, as John Entwistle's performance in *The Kids Are Alright* taught me, violating rules is the essence of the Who.

The Who FAQ

Four Faces

Who's Who in the Who

There are but four faces in the World's Greatest Rock 'n' Roll Band. Others have come and gone through their ranks (sit tight; we'll get to those guys in the next chapter), but Who fans will forever see them as Roger, John, Pete, and Keith. Why? The obvious answer is that this was the lineup during their greatest period. Duh. However, these are also the Who's archetypal members because each man is such an archetype. Only the Beatles—who had their own heartthrob, quiet one, caustic deep thinker, and clown—boasted such distinct and contrasting members.

Yet the guys in the Who were very different from the Beatles, which may account for why they stir such personal feelings in their fans after all these years, why they connect on such an intimate level with their followers that it almost seems at odds with their bombastic music. For all their personality quirks, their violence, their silliness, their pretentions, their seemingly inhuman triumphs and failures, Roger, John, Pete, and Keith are so adored because they are such distinct reflections of their audience. They are so *human*. While Led Zeppelin was rampaging like gods and monsters through Middle Earth, while the Rolling Stones were luxuriating in mythic decadence, while the Beatles were beaming down from some other galaxy where everyone has more wit, talent, charisma, and imagination than any earthling deserves to possess, the Who were down at the pub getting pissed.

Roger Daltrey: the terse tough guy at the end of the bar, knackered from laboring all day, staking out his territory, his knuckles ready to dish out rebuke to anyone who's got a problem with that.

Pete Townshend: the soused intellectual endlessly pontificating to everyone in earshot, his verbiage spiced with enough humor, insight, and self-effacing honesty to keep everyone listening.

Keith Moon: the incorrigible, attention-starved clown, drunkenly capering and dropping his drawers to the amusement—and often the annoyance—of the crowd.

John Entwistle: the shadow figure, quietly egging on his mate Moon from a table at the back of the room, secretly harboring a talent that holds all the chaos together.

Who fans can see themselves in their favorite band. Are you a Pete or a Keith? Are you more likely to wax philosophical or fart to get a cheap laugh? By asking, "Who's who in the Who?," we are also asking the band's favorite question of all: "Who Are You?"

The Rock: Roger Daltrey

The stereotype is easy to formulate. Take one look at the singer baring his taut torso beneath a mane of golden ringlets, twirling his microphone lead as if it's a weapon. His stance is uncompromising. He does not hide behind a guitar drawn up to his chest like Lennon. He does not wiggle his ass coyly like Jagger. He marches in place. He thrusts his fist. He's at war. His voice bears out the bearishness of his posture: deep, growly, it detonates into a terrifying scream. Jagger's or Little Richard's are the sexy yowls of a panther. Roger Daltrey's scream is the roar of a grizzly bear before it mauls a camper into mush.

Roger Daltrey fostered this persona, and stories of how he'd bully his bandmates, even smack them around when he felt it was deserved, supported the stereotype that the guy was a brute. Even Pete Townshend thought Rog was a

On the cover of disc two of the *Thirty Years of Maximum R&B* box set, art director Roger Evans superimposed Roger Daltrey looking sharp and Beatlesque in 1966 next to his far curlier incarnation in 1975.   *Author's collection*

"yobbo," British parlance for a young thug. Because his talent wasn't as striking and landscape altering as those of Pete, John, or Keith, Roger's value has often been downplayed. The truth is there would have been no Who if not for him.

Roger Harry Daltrey came screaming into the world on March 1, 1944. Outside Hammersmith Hospital, the Nazis were blitzing East London. After three months in this precarious environment, Irene Daltrey, baby Roger, and some forty-one thousand other Brits were evacuated. Mother and son sat out World War II's remaining fifteen months in virtual isolation on a farm in Stranraer, Scotland. There they suffered serious deprivations, subsisting mostly on potatoes. Meanwhile, father Harry was serving in the Royal Artillery.

After the war, the Daltreys returned to bomb-ravaged Shepherd's Bush. Despite a childhood of health issues brought on by his malnourishment in Scotland and an attempt to nourish himself by swallowing a rusty nail when he was three, Roger thrived amidst the Bush's wrecked buildings and working-class denizens. When the family moved to Bedford Park in 1957, and he was placed in Acton County Grammar, a boys' school populated by upper-class kids from Acton, Chiswick, and Ealing, Roger changed. Self-conscious about his working-class background and Cockney accent, wary of the upper crust, and feeling hopelessly displaced, his grades started slipping and he began acting out with a local gang of similarly disgruntled "Teddy Boys": lads who wore drape jackets and chunky shoes, teased their hair up into pompadours, and dug the sounds of American singers such as Elvis Presley and Eddie Cochran. In other words, the future front man of the flagship mod band was a rocker.

While Roger seemed as though he was becoming increasingly wayward, he was actually finding a unique direction. The same year the Daltreys settled in Bedford Park, he went to work on building his first guitar and met schoolmate Pete Townshend. Roger was beating up one of Pete's friends at the time.

After being expelled from Acton County Grammar for accumulated crimes (smoking in the boy's room, mocking his teachers, wearing his Teddy Boy getup on school photo day), Roger gave up on school and went to work, first as an electrician's assistant, then in a sheet metal factory, where he often stayed late to use the equipment to build guitars and amplifiers for his band the Detours.

And so, Roger Daltrey would recruit John Entwistle, who would recruit Pete Townshend, who would all have a fateful meeting with one Keith Moon in the spring of 1964. Having founded the band that would become the Who, Daltrey may have been justified in his belief that it was his to rule. His belligerent methods were another matter, and the singer often found himself close to being expelled from his own band throughout much of the sixties. Only the fear of losing the thing that mattered most to him, the Who, got him to mend his ways.

Daltrey's fits of rage became rare after that, though they did not fade completely. Still, he would never enjoy a totally cozy relationship with his bandmates. As he was at Acton County Grammar, he remained the Who's odd man out. Watch the "Who Are You" sequence in *The Kids Are Alright* for an illustration of his place in the band: Townshend, Entwistle, and Moon are apparently tipsy as they goof around a microphone while recording their handclap track; Daltrey is isolated in a sound booth cutting his vocals, making faces or giggling when he flubs a line, but not visibly sharing those light moments with his coworkers. Townshend would later sneer at Daltrey's attempts to buddy up to him onstage while duetting on "Sister Disco."

Despite such rebuffs, Roger Daltrey has never been reluctant to voice his love for his bandmates or his adoration of Townshend's songwriting gifts. He has been incredibly generous with his time and money (see chapter 33), cares deeply about young people, the working class, and the environment. In 2012, Middlesex University bestowed an honorary degree on the high school dropout for his decades of service as a dedicated entertainer and philanthropist. For a supposed "yobbo," Roger Daltrey is a pretty admirable guy.

The Quiet One: John Entwistle

Now let's dim the spotlight on the singer, slide our glance to stage right. Watch closely, because this cat is not going to wow you with any glitzy moves, though he will astound your eardrums and possibly puncture them with his incomparable bass playing. Call him John Johns. Call him John Allison or John Browne. Call him The Ox or Thunderfingers. It doesn't matter what you call him, because once the stationary bass man's fingers start fluttering, there is no question that you are listening to John Alec Entwistle.

Seven months after Roger Daltrey made his debut, John Entwistle too was born at Hammersmith Hospital. On October 9, 1944, Maud "Queenie" Entwistle gave birth to her son while her husband, Herbert, was doing his part in the Royal Navy. By early 1946, John's parents split, and Queenie took him to hole up with her parents in Chiswick, a suburb just outside Shepherd's Bush.

As a boy, John was creative and inquisitive. He loved roaming through London's war-wrecked landscape, playing junior archaeologist while sifting through the rubble for military artifacts. Uncovering a cache of Nazi helmets in a blown-out warehouse, John was in heaven, snagging some of the caps to play war: a perfectly macabre pastime for a guy who'd grow up to write so many perfectly macabre songs. Collecting the detritus of war may have also played a role in adult John's obsession with collecting tin soldiers, suits of armor, guns, taxidermied animals, and guitars, guitars, guitars. After all, what were guitars to the Who but weapons of war?

The product of musical parents, Entwistle revealed an aptitude for singing and picking up instruments at a young age (see chapter 3). From Queenie he also picked up an appreciation for partying, which would belie his reputation as the Who's representative of reserved sobriety (in truth, Daltrey better embodied this role). Entwistle loved to have a laugh and a good time, which were qualities that endeared him to his Acton County Grammar schoolmate, Pete Townshend. Townshend was also impressed by

John Entwistle bedecked in badges and buttons in '65 next to John Entwistle furnished in fur a decade later.

Author's collection

Entwistle's musical abilities, and the boys often met after school to gab about music, check out bands, and have a go at their instruments.

Although Entwistle was a rock 'n' roll devotee, a spot in a Dixieland—or "trad jazz," as the Brits called it—band was more viable for English boys in the days before the Beatles became international superstars. Besides, what would a trumpeter like Entwistle do in a rock 'n' roll band? While playing with a combo called the Confederates, he extended the banjoist position to Townshend, and for the first time, two future members of the Who performed together. Townshend would not remain in the band for long, but he'd always appreciate Entwistle for believing in him enough to give him his start onstage.

Entwistle's zeal for rock 'n' roll would not subside, though, and he soon found himself playing bass guitar with Townshend in a surfy instrumental outfit called the Scorpions. Soon another boy from Acton Grammar approached Entwistle to play bass guitar in his group, and Roger Daltrey's (false) promise of regular gigs lured him into the Detours. Their eclectic sets allowed him to crack out his trumpet and even take the mic on "Twist and Shout." Entwistle's voice would prove to be as versatile an instrument as his bass, being just as expressive at a monstrously low range ("Booooooris the Spider . . .") as it was at its almost comically high falsetto ("You are Forgiiiivuu-un!").

When the Detours metamorphosed into the Who, John Entwistle's reserved stage demeanor never hampered him. OK, so he was never a sex symbol like Roger Daltrey or a room-commandeering clown like Keith Moon. While the word genius was regularly used to describe Pete Townshend, the only folks who seemed to see Entwistle that way were bass players. But—Jesus Christ!—what a bass player! So much of the Who's musicality and indomitable excitement flowed directly from his fingers. His posture—that of a corpse stood upright—completely contrasted the artistry, intelligence, and intensity of his work. To look at him, you'd never suspect he was capable of such exhilarating wildness, not when he looked like rigor mortis had already set in.

And Entwistle was wild beyond his music. He was the only member of the band who came close to keeping up with Keith Moon's nonstop partying, and the rhythm section forged a tight friendship. As Moon's out-of-control lifestyle would be his ruination, so would Entwistle's. His philandering cost him the stabilizing influence of his first wife, Alison Wise, and he ended up in a string of increasingly unstable relationships (see chapter 29). The Who's multiple reunion tours were often scheduled just to pull Entwistle out of debt. Just as soon as his paychecks arrived, they were already spent on cars, guitars, clothes, or any of the other things on which he blew his fortune. He refused to mind his health and continued to drink with youthful gluttony throughout his life. By the twenty-first century, Daltrey, Entwistle, and Queenie, who was then pushing eighty, were all terribly concerned about him, but none could convince him to look after himself or see a doctor. Queenie feared the worst might happen when the Who plotted to go back on the road in 2002. John never got a chance to take his usual spot at stage right at the opening night gig at the Hard Rock, Las Vegas. The night before, June 27, 2002, he exacerbated a preexisting heart condition by overindulging in cocaine with self-proclaimed groupie Alycen Rowse in his hotel room. Such an exit may invite all manner of judgment, but John Entwistle lived, and possibly died, according to his own rules and having fun.

The Seeker: Pete Townshend

While the bass players continue staring at John Entwistle's fingers, everyone else in the crowd may find their eyes drifting back across the stage, back past the singer still strutting in place dead center, over by the left wing where a whole lot of commotion is going down. Is it a bird? A plane? It sure has a wide wingspan. Or is it a windmill inviting all the wannabe Don Quixotes of the audience to charge it? There is threat in his body language, but there's balletic elegance too: the propelling and soaring arms, the trampoline leaps into the ionosphere, the ritualistic abuse he rains down on his poor, lovely Les Paul guitar. He does not look like your typical rock star. He does not have the singer's rugged sexuality. He just looks like another gangly geezer with a big nose. He looks like you, and he looks like me. In a way, he is.

Pete Townshend's gifts are abundant. He is an incredibly skilled, ferocious yet subtly artful musician who changed the way guitarists play their guitars. He is an intelligent yet pop-savvy songwriter who broached more untrampled territory (pop mysticism, disabilities, the cruelty of children, sexual and physical abuse, the Internet before there was an Internet, cross-dressing, masturbation, dog racing, gourd farming, magic buses) than any other songwriter of his g-g-generation. He invented the rock opera, created work adapted to the stage and screen, and attempted to merge band and audience like some sort of rock 'n' roll Dr. Frankenstein. On a short list of artists that includes Jimi Hendrix, Brian Wilson, and Prince, he is one of the very, very, very few pop musicians truly deserving of the label "genius." Yet unlike those guys, who can come off like Martians, Pete Townshend has never seemed anything less than totally human, totally relatable. Part of his genius is his ability to create music that perfectly reflects our humanity back at us, even when he's using a deaf, dumb, and blind mystic or a kid assigned the wrong gender by futuristic lab techs as his avatars.

Peter Dennis Blandford Townshend's upbringing wasn't totally ordinary. On May 19, 1945, Betty Townshend gave birth to her son in Chiswick. Betty and her husband Clifford were professional entertainers, she a singer and he an alto sax player in the Royal Air Force dance band. Before Pete came

Townshend scowling in 1965 meets Townshend scowling in 1975.

Author's collection

along, Betty and Cliff's lifestyle had been exciting and mobile. Like Harry Daltrey, Cliff Townshend was in Germany in the spring of '45. He received word of his son's birth from a motorcycle messenger.

Cliff maintained his busy work schedule even after World War II ended, gigging with that RAF big band, now called the Squadronaires. Though she continued working in an administrative capacity for the band, Betty stopped singing. Pete's home life was rarely stable, though. He and Betty lived for a while with family friends. He was sent to live with Betty's mother, Denny, a disturbed woman completely unfit to raise a child. He'd end up on tour with Cliff, whose relationship with frustrated Betty was sometimes on, sometimes off. She missed her glamorous and creative lifestyle as an entertainer. She drank and took lovers. As Pete told *Rolling Stone* in 1968, Cliff was known to imbibe as well, and in his drunken state, he might tell his boy, "Look, son, you know, looks aren't everything," having the best intentions perhaps, but inadvertently making the boy self-conscious about the size of his nose. The kids at school gave him guff about it too, and Pete was confused and angry about all the fuss about such a meaningless thing even as he was forced to be acutely aware of it. His nose also gave him something to fight against. "It was huge," he told *Rolling Stone*. "At that time, it was the reason I did everything. It's the reason I played the guitar—because of my nose. The reason I wrote songs was because of my nose." His nose would also influence his kinetic stage act. "[W]hat I wanted to do was distract attention away from my nose to my body and make people look at my body instead of at my face—turn my body into a machine."

Pete found his most positive adult influence in his free-spirited great aunt Trilby, his paternal grandmother's sister. Trilby allowed young Pete to play her piano, encouraged his musical and artistic ambitions, and introduced him to the spiritualism that would affect so much of his adult work. But it was a gift from Denny that would most change his life when she presented Pete with his first guitar when he about twelve years old. It was a diabolically cheap instrument, but its limitations would have a profound influence on his art (see chapter 3). It would also be the first guitar he'd smash, a bit of showmanship carried out in his bedroom while Denny screamed at him and his school chum John Entwistle to keep their racket down. Entwistle thought his friend had gone mad. Little did he realize how much that madness would affect his own life.

Then came the Confederates and the Scorpions and the Detours and the Who and the High Numbers and round two of the Who. Then came superstardom, and Townshend taking his rightful place as rock's resident philosopher. His ability to spin copy was second to none. Journalists loved him because his interviews were so deep and thoughtful and long. He parlayed his tremendous songwriting gifts into sideline gigs writing articles for *Rolling Stone*, *Melody Maker*, and *New Music Express*. His honesty is uncompromising, even though his beliefs, opinions, and goals can be as shifting as a clock's second hand. Townshend also has a tendency to put his foot in his mouth and be insensitive, but his willingness to give his fans such open access to his thoughts and creative process through his writing and interviews continues to endear him to us, even when he is at his most curmudgeonly. Just days before this writing, he had to publically apologize to a seven-year-old for mouthing "fuck off" to her dad at a Who gig. So what? We get grouchy sometimes too (and for the record, anyone who obstructs the view of the stage by holding up his daughter and a poster reading "Smash your guitar, Pete!" deserves to be told to fuck off). We understand his frustration over being thought of as nothing but a nose and relate to his songs about weirdos, loners, losers, and malcontents. We understand why he can get so pessimistic over world events and why his faith in humanity endures nonetheless. We understand why he is always seeking answers and a sense of fulfillment. We understand why he might numb the pain of being alive with drink or drugs. He has shared his medical problems with us, helping to raise awareness of the tinnitus he believes began when Keith Moon set off a bomb in his bass drum on *The Smothers Brothers Comedy Hour* and continued to be exacerbated by decades of deafening rock 'n' roll. We watched him suffer the humiliation of being accused of downloading child pornography and hoped the charges were untrue. We rejoiced when he was vindicated and slapped our foreheads in astonishment when he explained the absurd circumstances of the incident in his 2012 autobiography *Who I Am*. How dumb and naïve he'd been. But we can be pretty dumb and naïve sometimes too. We understand. Who are we? Who am I? Who are you? Pete Townshend, that's Who.

The Demented Clown: Keith Moon

The guitarist bounds into the air, lands on the cushioned soles of his Doc Martens boots, and turns his back on us to throw a glance at the drummer. They suddenly stop in time together, accenting the same violent downbeat. Then the drummer nearly unhinges his jaw to release a shriek so horrendous it can be heard over the walloping roar he pounds out with his sticks. Floor and rack toms, double bass drums, crash and ride cymbals, hi-hats and snares all seem to rumble in unison. The tumult is so overpowering it's impossible to differentiate one piece of percussion from the other. The rhythm seems to be spinning out of control. How is this gonna end? It can't be good, right? But he somehow manages to wrap up this frenzy and lead it back into the next verse without missing the beat. He smiles naughtily, because he knows it could have gone in the other direction. It's a good night for Keith Moon. Not every one was.

Keith John Moon was the youngest member of the Who and the only one not born amid the mayhem of World War II, arriving on August 23, 1946, in Willesden. Keith's upbringing was more stable than John or Pete's. Mum Kathleen and dad Alfred raised their three kids (Keith had two younger sisters, Linda and Lesley) in Wembley. Kit and Alf didn't party like John's mother or live a soap opera existence like Pete's parents. They were quiet, working class, by all definitions, normal. Keith was anything but.

A fresh-faced Keith Moon in iconic target shirt in 1965 beside himself looking a bit more ragged in 1975.   *Author's collection*

The eldest Moon child was an incorrigible clown and utterly hyperactive. In his book *The Who: Maximum R&B*, Richard Barnes included a snapshot of twelve-year-old Keith's report card. His Geography, Math, Science, and Technical Drawing teachers all note his "slow progress" or poor work. His Phys Ed teacher goes into more detail: "Keen at times but 'goonery' seems to come before anything." His art teacher minces fewer words: "Retarded artistically. Idiotic in other respects." Keith's English teachers are the only ones with nothing unfortunate to report, though his Music teacher does give him a B-, stating, "Great ability, but must guard against tendency to 'show off.'" Guard against it? He'd bloody well make it his reason for existing!

While Moon's uncontrollable energy drove his teachers bonkers, his classmates found his goonery a nonstop source of entertainment. He learned early on that no matter what his shortcomings might be, he could always make people laugh. He also discovered that music was one thing on which he could almost focus. For his boundless stamina and fervor for getting attention, noisy drums were the perfect instrument. Moon developed a passion for the fun and sunny surf sounds of the Beach Boys and Jan and Dean, and at the wee age of sixteen, he was playing in a local band called Mark Twain and the Strangers (whose bassist, Mike Evans, would later join the Action). The following year he found a higher-profile position in the Beachcombers while stumbling through a succession of day jobs.

Moon's personality was too outsized for the professional yet ordinary Beachcombers. He found a better match for his unruliness in 1964 when he witnessed the Who's four-man blitzkrieg at the Oldfield Hotel in the London suburb of Greenford (Andy Neill and Matt Kent's *Anyway, Anyhow, Anywhere* gives the probable date as April 30, while Tony Fletcher cites the date less specifically as "a Thursday night in the middle of May" in his biography *Moon*). Unimpressed with the session drummer sitting in with the band that night, Moon got up onstage. How he got there depends on which story you choose to believe. His bandmates tell the tale of an impudent bugger, his hair dyed ginger in a botched attempt to bleach it Beach Boy blond, swaggering up to the stage, declaring, "I can do better'en 'im'"and pummeling the poor session man's drum kit to shrapnel. In *Moon*, Tony Fletcher revised the story a bit. In this version, Moon was propping up the bar, nervously downing ale to work up his courage, while his buddy and the Oldfield's manager, Lou Hunt, offered the drummer's services to the Who. Moon's hair was its usual brown.

Regardless of which tale is true, the outcome was the same. The Who gave Moon a shot, and his performance on Bo Diddley's "Road Runner" so wowed them that they asked him to play with them again (though never officially told him he was in the band). He did, and the Who found their final element. Moon's crazed fire counterpointed Daltrey's earthiness, Entwistle's ice water, and Townshend's mystical air perfectly. Not that it made their lives particularly easy.

Fame and the nightly physical workout that came with playing drums with the Who did nothing to curb Moon's restless energy. And now he had a worldwide audience of schoolmates cheering on his every outrageous action. His antics have been relayed so often that what is true (parading in front of neighbor Steve McQueen's house dressed as a Nazi) and isn't true (driving a car into a Holiday Inn swimming pool at his twenty-first birthday party) has almost stopped mattering. There will always be Moon acolytes happy to believe any tale that supports his comic myth. Tony Fletcher's posthumous yet convincing diagnosis that Moon suffered a borderline personality disorder that may have caused him to indulge in such bizarre and destructive behavior makes these antics problematic comedy fodder, particularly since it also may have been these health issues that caused him to be so horribly abusive to his wife, Kim.

But Moon *was* funny. Any jackass can wreck a hotel room to elicit a moronic giggle. Moon made such unacceptable behavior acceptable with genuine wit. In the 1989 television documentary *Who's Back: The Story of the Who*, Townshend recounted a less often told tale about the drummer. The Who were on tour in America and wearily on their way to an airport to take them to their next gig. Hours from the hotel they'd just left, Moon suddenly sprang up and started insisting, "We've got to go back! We've got to go back!" Thinking he may have left something "illicit" behind, the driver turned the car around and drove all the way back to the hotel. Moon jumped out of the car, dashed into the hotel, and returned several minutes later, looking as though a great weight had been lifted off him. "Ok, we can go," he told the driver. Finally, after this whole inconvenient ordeal, Townshend finally thought to ask what he'd forgotten at the hotel.

Said Keith: "I forgot to smash the television."

A witty line defuses infuriating behavior.

Not everything Keith Moon did can be so easily excused. There's nothing funny about how he treated Kim and how he neglected their daughter, Mandy, nor can we locate the laughs in how he abused himself with drink and drugs or how he left this world on September 7, 1978, when he suffered his final accidental overdose. There's also nothing funny about the guilt and pain he felt about his most abhorrent actions, but maybe we can understand that like Roger Daltrey, John Entwistle, and Pete Townshend, the seemingly indestructible Keith Moon was also human, as fallible and vulnerable as anyone.

2

There's More at the Door

The Other Band Members

We've now met the band: Roger, John, Pete, and Keith. Yeah, yeah, we all know who the greatest lineup was, but what about Roger, John, Pete, Colin, and Harry? Or Pete, Roger, Zak, and Pino? What about Kenney and Rabbit? Here are some of the other faces who've passed through the Who's ranks throughout their fifty-year history.

Colin Dawson

The Who is a raging, raving, rowdy quartet of rock 'n' rollers. They smash their equipment and their audience to pieces and don't take names. Stroll onstage during one of their sets and you're liable to get swiped with a guitar as Abbie Hoffman did at Woodstock or booted in the nuts, as a cop did at the Fillmore East. Exciting? Oh, hell yes. Dangerous? That too. But professional? That might be pushing it. So it may be shocking to learn that these madmen got started as a corny party band playing Andy Williams ballads, "Hava Nagila," and "The Hokey Cokey" (better known as "The Hokey Pokey" to us Yanks).

The band was the Detours. Their leader was a blond guitarist named Roger Daltrey. Two chaps named Peter James and Roy Ellis supported Rog on six-string, while Harry Wilson kept the rhythm and the recently acquired John Entwistle (or "John Johns" as he was then known) provided the bass. Before the mic stood the conventionally handsome and conventionally voiced Colin Dawson.

The singer provided the Detours with a bit of pop idol appeal. His tendency to turn the heads of the girls in attendance might even cause a spot of trouble. According to Pete Townshend in *Who I Am*, an engagement soirée at which the Detours provided entertainment went south after the groom realized his intended had become smitten with dashing Colin.

The Detours had always been an eclectic outfit, interspersing their party standards with country and western, surf instrumental, and trad jazz numbers (for which Daltrey would set aside his axe to pick up the trombone while Entwistle switched to trumpet). They also dabbled in popular favorites by the Beatles and Cliff Richard. As Daltrey pushed for more and more rock 'n' roll in the set,

Colin Dawson seemed more and more out of place. He was okay when crooning Richard's "Move It," but he was totally inadequate for more rousing material by Johnny Kidd and the Pirates. New Detour Peter Townshend played a pivotal role in Dawson's departure by constantly pecking at the old-fashioned singer. Dawson ultimately decided to exit the Detours for the sake of his fiancée Angela Dives, his day job as a bacon salesman, and his peace of mind. In his stead was Gabby Connolly, a singer with a thing for Johnny Cash. For a brief time, Connolly shared the mic with Roger Daltrey, who soon muscled out the new guy to take his rightful place at center stage.

Reg Bowen

When rhythm guitarist Peter James departed the Detours in early 1962, Reg Bowen stepped into the vacancy. The band was a lot more interested in his equipment and his parents' willingness to endure noisy rehearsals than his musical ability. The amp-less Entwistle took to plugging into Bowen's radiogram, a primitive sound system combining radio and phonograph into a snazzy piece of furniture. His lack of guitar prowess remained an issue. Reg Bowen had ambitions of moving into a less glamorous role as the band's road manager anyway. So Entwistle recommended a replacement from groups past, and Pete Townshend joined together with the band in mid-'62.

Roy Ellis

Reg Bowen was not the first Detour welcomed into the band for practical reasons. According to *Anyway, Anyhow, Anywhere*, Roy Ellis got the gig because of his spiffy Vox amp. Such decisions are fairly common in the cash-poor world of young rock bands. Bill Wyman became a Rolling Stone at the elderly age of twenty-six because of his pro equipment. Unlike Wyman, Ellis wouldn't hold onto his job for long, but not because of his apparently limited skills. On July 30, 1962, he made a more disastrous exit when he drowned while taking a swim in the Thames.

Harry Wilson

Harry Wilson was an amiable bloke, a drummer given to only the briefest outburst of anger when he blundered the beat. With Reg Bowen out of the Detours, Wilson's home served as their new rehearsal space. His dad roadied their equipment in his van through the first half of 1962. Like so many Detours before him, Harry Wilson did not have the chops necessary to back the increasingly ambitious group. So while Harry and his pa were planning a holiday, Roger Daltrey temporarily offered the drumming position to a chap he met in front of the rehearsal hall the band frequented when they had the scratch to venture beyond the Wilson house. Doug Sandom proved a more professional musician, and Harry Wilson got back from vacation to find himself out of a job.

Doug Sandom

It's hard to imagine any drummer but Keith Moon brutalizing the kit behind the early Who. Since no recordings of them playing with Doug Sandom exist, this is something we can only imagine.

South Acton's Sandom was an unlikely replacement for Harry Wilson. About eight years older than Daltrey, the eldest Detour, Dougie supported his pregnant wife as a bricklayer. Despite his age and obligations, his position in the band was made official in mid-'62.

While Pete Townshend speaks highly of Sandom in *Who I Am*, saying the drummer "focused us" and "acted like a proper professional musician," he was less kind to Dougie when they were bandmates. His age irked Townshend, who wanted their group recently rechristened the Who to be vital, youthful. Chris Parmeinter, an A&R man at Fontana Records, was less keen on Doug Sandom's drumming and voiced this opinion openly during the Who's audition on April 9, 1964. That was the last straw for Sandom, who was already unhappy with the band's move to maximum R&B and Townshend's bullying. That day, he quit. The split wasn't the happiest, but Doug Sandom is not bitter about his exit from the band. He remains in touch with Roger Daltrey and is even on friendly terms with former adversary Townshend. And in case there are any questions about his feelings for his former band, Sandom emphatically stated in a recent video interview posted on YouTube, "My main thing I want everybody to know: I still think the Who is the best fucking rock 'n' roll band in the world."

John "Rabbit" Bundrick

John "Rabbit" Bundrick was another unlikely inductee into the Who's stage lineup. In 1978, one of the most British of British rock bands welcomed a drawling Texan into the club. Throughout the seventies, Pete's overdubbed piano and synthesizer tracks were integral ingredients of the Who's records. On March 6, 1978, they finally auditioned a musician whose sole role would be to reproduce those lines onstage.

"Rabbit," so nicknamed because of his protuberant choppers, had an impressive résumé long before hooking up with the group that would bring his greatest fame. At the age of eleven he was playing with his dad's country band. He started working as a Houston session man at fifteen.

Rabbit broke into rock 'n' roll with a group called Blackwell, who recorded their one and only LP in 1967. In 1971, Rabbit joined forces with Paul Kossoff and Simon Kirke of the recently disbanded Free to record the one-shot album *Kossoff, Kirke, Tetsu & Rabbit*. By the time it was released in April 1972, Paul Rodgers and Andy Fraser had roamed back to Free, and that band recorded a new album with Rabbit officially on the team. However, guitarist Paul Kossoff's ongoing drug problems (which would culminate in a fatal heart attack at the age of twenty-five) meant *Heartbreaker* would be Free's last record. While backing up his buddy Johnny Nash as a member of the singer's group Sons of the Jungle, Rabbit met Bob Marley and convinced the Wailers to experiment with the clavinet during the *Catch a Fire* sessions.

Next, Rabbit Bundrick tried to go it alone with his records *Broken Arrows* (1973) and *Dark Saloon* (1974), but solo success was elusive. No matter, because he had already been getting steady session work for an eclectic variety of artists, including Donovan, Sandy Denny, Jim Capaldi, and John Martyn. He continued to do so through the seventies.

One such job was the 1977 Pete Townshend/Ronnie Lane collaboration *Rough Mix*. In *Who I Am*, Townshend remembered, "He wandered into the Rough Mix studio one day looking for session work . . . musicians of his caliber didn't come around very often." Despite Rabbit's excessive ways with drink, drugs, and fish stories, he and Townshend became buddies, and when nothing came of Rabbit's next group, Crawler, he accepted an invitation to try out for the Who in 1978. Sadly, the gig coincided with Keith Moon's death, though he and the doomed drummer did manage to enjoy one night of drunken carousing after the audition. Typical of a night on the town with Moon, Rabbit ended it with a busted wrist.

When the Who convalesced enough to mount their first post-Moon tour at London's Rainbow Theatre on May 2, 1979, Rabbit Bundrick was behind the keyboards. According to Townshend in *Who I Am*, Rabbit's work is also present on *Face Dances* even though he did not include the album in his online CV and he is credited on the sleeve with nothing more than "help and inspiration on 'Another Tricky Day'" (Townshend receives sole keyboard attribution). However, the complex keyboard lines on "You Better You Bet," "Did You Steal My Money," and "Daily Records" suggest musicianship beyond Townshend's abilities. Rabbit also loaned his hands to the guys' solo records, having worked on Daltrey's *McVicar* in 1980 and regularly contributing to Townshend's LPs from *Empty Glass* to *Psychoderelict*. The sole exception was *All the Best Cowboys Have Chinese Eyes*, recorded during a period when the self-destructive Rabbit completely skirted Townshend's radar, which also accounts for his absence from *It's Hard*. More than two decades later, Rabbit Bundrick had the opportunity to work his magic on a new Who album when he rejoined Daltrey and Townshend for 2006's *Endless Wire*.

Kenney Jones

When Keith Moon died, the rest of the Who had the miserable task of finding a replacement for the irreplaceable drummer. The problem wasn't finding someone who could play like Moon. That wasn't even on the agenda. His bandmates had been tiring of Moon's inconsistency and the limitations of his

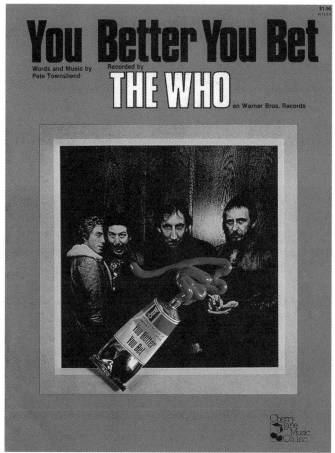

Though some fans—and some band members—don't remember his tenure with the Who fondly, Kenney Jones has the distinction of drumming on "You Better You Bet," the band's final top-ten hit in the United Kingdom and one of the mere eight singles they placed in the U.S. top twenty.

Courtesy of the Rob Abramowicz Collection, digitized by Jeffrey Uleau

very distinctive technique. Moon's flagging physique and imagination made the recent *Who Are You* sessions problematic. Complementing the tiptoe-soft 6/8 beat of "Music Must Change" was so difficult for him that a drum kit was eschewed altogether. The footsteps Townshend recorded to keep the beat on his demo were used instead. No, the problem was simply dealing with their deep, deep grief.

Filling the position with a friendly face might ease the transition, and the Who agreed on Kenney Jones. Not only was he a mate from their early days and a guest star on the 1975 *Tommy* soundtrack, but he shared the Who's mod roots as a former member of the more legitimately mod Small Faces. On one prophetic

More than two decades before he filled in for Keith Moon, Kenney Jones drummed a mighty din with Small Faces. Next to Jones at the far right is Ian McLagan, who'd one day marry Moon's ex-wife Kim.   *Author's collection*

November night in 1968, Jones and Moon even shared a drum kit during a one-off Small Faces/Who supergroup jam at the Empire Theatre in Liverpool.

More bizarrely, Roger Daltrey claimed hiring Jones was Moon's express wish, according to a *Lifestyles of the Rich and Famous* interview recounted in Tim Ewbank and Stafford Hildred's *Roger Daltrey: The Biography*. At a séance, he "heard Keith's spirit talking . . . he told me there was only one choice to make. And I made it. The group decided we had to go on and Kenney Jones was the only choice to take his place. It was what Keith wanted. We followed his decision."

Although he could certainly get wild, as he did on the first Small Faces album, Kenney Jones was generally a traditional timekeeper in the Charlie Watts mode, as was evident in his more recent work with Faces. Entwistle and Townshend would no longer have to worry about the rhythm running aground with Jones in the backline. They could also wave goodbye to the unpredictability and animal passion that made their Moon-era performances so awesome.

Jones took a lot of the heat when *Face Dances* and *It's Hard* were deemed unworthy successors to the Who's earlier albums. Some of the lashing came from the band's very own camp. Daltrey was not shy about criticizing Jones, and he did so with such regularity that he actually started receiving letters from fans demanding he zip it. Yet the Who's songs had changed in the wake of Keith Moon's death, moving closer to the more docile feel of their solo records, and though Jones's work with them isn't overwhelmingly exciting, it's not inappropriate either. His rhythms on Townshend's *Empty Glass* are just as suited to the album's mature material as his metronomic beat was on the Who's taut "Eminence Front." However, the way he tamed "My Generation," "Won't Get Fooled Again," and the other raucous classics in concert was hard to forgive. The Jones-era Who stumbled along for a few years before Townshend announced the band would be packing it in, which they did on December 16, 1983. Temporarily, of course.

Kenney Jones was still an official member of the Who when they reformed for one-off performances at the Live Aid festival in 1985 and the 1988 British Phonographic Industry awards where the band was honored for their "Outstanding Contribution to British Music." Townshend said he was done touring with the Who for good at the end of '88, but just six months later, he was back with the band on their first tour since 1982. Kenney Jones was not invited, nor would he be on any of the subsequent trips that continue to this day.

Despite a rocky experience, Kenney Jones's time with the Who was not without achievement. He is the only band member aside from the original four to be offered full partnership (despite Daltrey's protestations) and see his likeness appear on album covers. He drummed on "You Better You Bet," a top-ten hit in the UK and a top-twenty-one in the United States. Townshend and Entwistle were always most complimentary of his work. He has also dealt with the sometimes unkind treatment of Daltrey and the critics with good humor . . . though that may just make the case that he was never really right for the nasty old Who stronger.

Zak Starkey

When the Who reunited in 1989, session stalwart Simon Phillips brought the beat. Commercially, the tour was a tremendous success. Daltrey and Townshend loved how the ensemble (three backing vocalists, five-piece horn section, percussionist, supplementary guitarist, and Rabbit) made their jobs easier. Entwistle loved the money. However, calling this massive orchestra "the Who" was a stretch. Perfectly professional interpretations of Who classics were more on order than excitement. The *Quadrophenia* tours of 1996 and 1997 were also mounted with a big, big band, but the lineup was slightly different, making space for Townshend's brother Simon on guitar and another fellow from the pop bloodline on drums.

Ringo Starr didn't want his firstborn son to get lost in the mad, mad, mad world of rock 'n' roll as he had. But that funky blood kept pumping through Zak Starkey's veins nonetheless. Young Starkey received his first kit from none other than Keith Moon, one of his dad's closest drinking buddies. Indeed,

Moon seemed a bigger influence on the nascent drummer than his own father, and Starkey would fondly remember times spent with Moon away from the kit drawing or playing on the floor together like a couple of kids.

By the age of sixteen, Starkey was doing exactly what his pop didn't want him to do. Yet even Ringo couldn't deny his boy was incredibly skilled, and he invited Starkey to join him on two of his All-Starr Band tours in the nineties. On the 1995 tour, Starkey played alongside John Entwistle. A year later, he fulfilled his lifelong dream of playing with the Who when he was asked to join the *Quadrophenia* tour at Daltrey's insistence.

Starkey's new position in the Who was longer term then Kenney Jones or Simon Phillips's, but the group's sporadic schedule meant he had to consider other gigs. A stint with Oasis meant he was only available to record one track, "Black Widow's Eyes," on *Endless Wire*. His presence elsewhere on the album is missed.

Pino Palladino

Even though Zak Starkey makes a mere cameo on *Endless Wire*, he is still credited among the "principal musicians" in the CD booklet. Joining Starkey, Daltrey, and Townshend among the principals are Rabbit Bundrick, Simon Townshend, and Pino Palladino.

In the eighties, the Welsh bassist was an in-demand session man often exploited for his fretless-bass skills. Take a listen to his performance on Gary Numan's "Music for Chameleons" to hear exactly why, but it was Pino Palladino's work with David Gilmour that brought him to Pete Townshend's attention.

Townshend cowrote a couple of tracks with Gilmour for his 1984 solo album *About Face*. The following year, Gilmour returned the favor by bringing along his bassist to play on Townshend's "Give Blood" with Simon Phillips on drums. In the liner notes of *The Best of Pete Townshend*, Townshend called Gilmour, Phillips, and Palladino his "three favourite musicians of the time."

Simon Phillips would find himself onstage with the Who just a few years later, but Palladino would not get his chance until the tragic circumstances of 2002. When John Entwistle died the night before beginning their latest tour, Townshend and Daltrey had to decide whether or not their Vegas Hard Rock show would go on. The economic reality of asking thousands of fans to eat their tickets and putting the band's crew out of work forced a tough choice. The tour would continue as scheduled. Townshend immediately chose Pino Palladino to take the vacant place at stage right, and the bassist swooped in to the rescue. With a fluid style wholly distinct from Entwistle's torrents of notes, Palladino could never be accused of trying to replace The Ox, but his flawless professionalism and skill have served the Who well in the twenty-first century onstage and six tracks of *Endless Wire*.

3

Start Playing

The Who as Musicians

Before 1964, you had to visit a jazz club to hear an ensemble of virtuosos. Rock 'n' roll had its odd instrumental wizards—Danny Cedrone, Chuck Berry, Fats Domino, Sandy Nelson—but never before had there been a whole band of them. That changed in one booming instant when the Who were playing the Oldfield Hotel in 1964 and Keith Moon unseated the session man backing them that night. There was not another drummer like him, nor was there a guitarist like Pete Townshend or a bass player who even occupied the same galaxy as John Entwistle. Each musician in the Who completely changed the way his particular instrument was played. That is something that neither the Beatles nor the Rolling Stones nor the Yardbirds could claim, though in the years to come, Cream and Led Zeppelin could. But the Who were rock's first all-virtuoso group, and the mad methods of these musicians are integral to the band's collective uniqueness.

Pete

Even someone who has never put a finger on a guitar can recognize his work instantly. A sudden power chord shock. An invigorating flamenco flourish. A shuddering scrape of plectrum down strings. A flicker of pickup, on and off, transmitting nonsensical Morse code messages through the ozone. Then all of this avant-garde musicality is murdered with one final act of savagery, the crack of a wrecking ball hurling through a supercomputer. Pete Townshend stabs his instrument into his Marshall stack and finishes it off against the floorboards.

This stuff is easy to copy. The intricacies of Pete Townshend's musicianship are much harder to master.

The son of a singer and a clarinetist, Townshend was brewed in the right environment to stir his interest in music, though he had more exposure to it while touring with his parents than at home. His grandmother Denny, whose influence on her grandson was mostly harmful, did at least one momentously positive thing for the boy. One Christmas she gave young Pete a cheap Spanish guitar, its strings more likely to snap than produce music. This flaw of his trainer instrument was decisive in the development of his guitar playing. Having reduced his guitar to just its three middle strings—D, G, and B—he started figuring out three-note chords and moving them up and down the neck. Movable triads are a key element in Townshend's playing and why his voicings are so distinctive whether he's picking them out in the arpeggios of "Tattoo" and "Our Love Was" or straight strumming them in "Substitute" and "Dreaming from the Waist."

Townshend maintained his three-string guitar for about six months while learning an arsenal of new chords around them. After replacing the broken strings, he let them drone, ring out as he fingered his new vocabulary. When he got a crash course in the great blues guitarists upon inheriting his college roommate's record collection (see chapter 23), Townshend heard his droning style echoed back at him from discs by John Lee Hooker and Jimmy Reed.

Though he was enthusiastic about music, Townshend did not practice with much dedication, nor did he take proper lessons. Frustrated by his awful guitar, he transitioned to banjo for a couple of years when he played with trad jazz outfit the Confederates. On banjo he developed the kind of rapid wrist action he'd heard on Louis Armstrong and Bix Beiderbecke records. He'd perfect this technique when he resumed teaching himself the guitar after acquiring a Harmony Stratocruiser. Townshend came to realize the key to such flamenco-flecked strumming was in the plectrum. Using a standard size pick, he'd hold it as lightly as possible, so that it almost floated between his fingertips, allowing his

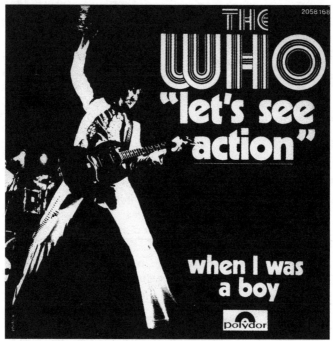

Pete Townshend gives his S.G. an action-packed thrashing on the sleeve of the Belgian edition of "Let's See Action."

Courtesy of the Rob Abramowicz Collection, digitized by Jeffrey Uleau

action a suppleness he could not achieve with a gorilla grip. Listen to the intro-duction of "Anyway, Anyhow, Anywhere" to hear this technique in full effect.

As he became more comfortable with his voicings and myriad methods, Townshend further distinguished his style by blending them together. He might broadside a delicate movable chord progression with a sudden power chord strike, or strum for a few bars only to toss in an unexpected fingerpicked passage (Townshend's Chet Atkins–inspired fingerpicking, put to finest use on "Sunrise," is one of his more underappreciated talents). Such versatility was necessary since he was in such a unique position as the counterpart of John Entwistle. Given the bass player's penchant for taking the lead, for rushing up his neck to whip off a high-end fill, Townshend often had to seesaw between lead and rhythm guitar techniques to ensure Entwistle never robbed the din of its bottom.

Another way to keep the sound from ever getting thin was to maximize resonance. Feedback, the shriek produced by creating a sound loop between an audio input and output (in this case, guitar pickup and amplifier) had long been the bane of the electric guitarist. Townshend used this annoyance to his advantage by purposely eliciting feedback from his amp by waving his guitar in front of it. The noise-filled gaps in the music was exciting in and of itself, contributing much out-of-control atmosphere to the first Who album. Raking his pick down the textured coil of his strings for a rocketing effect or flickering his pickup switch mid-chord to produce rhythmic blips (all on glorious display in "Anyway, Anyhow, Anywhere") were among his showier signatures. His insistence that Jim Marshall develop a 100-watt stack amplifier ensured he could compete with John Entwistle's excessive volume and resoundingly drown out the chatty Cathys in the front row.

Though noise is an integral ingredient of Pete Townshend's guitar work, he rarely used pedals aside from a succession of fuzz boxes: the Sola Sound Tone Bender, the Gibson Maestro FZ-1A Fuzz Tone, the Univox Super-Fuzz, the Marshall Supa Fuzz, and so on. That does not mean he was averse to manipu-lating his sound with technology. Nearly a decade before Boss invented the first chorus pedal, the CE-1, Townshend achieved a similarly watery effect on "Tattoo" by running his guitar through a revolving Leslie speaker. On "Going Mobile" and "Relay" he made a wah-wah pedal unnecessary by filtering his instrument through synthesizers (see chapter 34), adding extra percussive punch to his already punchy and precise guitar work.

John

No one had fully come to terms with the electric bass guitar since Leo Fender started mass-producing the Precision Bass in 1951. Early rock 'n' roll bass play-ers, such as Willie Dixon and Joe B. Mauldin, stuck to thumping great big double basses. Early electric rock bass players, such as Bob Moore and Shorty Horton, laid down walking lines or followed a tune's basic riff or chord progression in rumbling tones easier to feel than hear. In the sixties, a new guard led by James

Jamerson and Paul McCartney brought the electric bass to the fore, but as distinctive as their work was, they were still using their basses as basses: to hold down the rhythm and fill out the low end. John Entwistle wasn't terribly interested in being a bass guitarist. He wanted to play lead guitar like his hero Duane Eddy, who zinged twangy yet *loooooow* riffs on his bottom strings.

Entwistle was the son of a piano-banging mum and a trumpet-blowing dad. He would learn to play both instruments. He took proper piano lessons for a time before deciding he'd rather teach himself by ear. He studied trumpet more seriously, taking lessons from his dad. Since his school band had its fill of trumpeters, Entwistle was moved to French horn. After struggling with the new instrument for a bit, he got a handle on it too. His natural ability to learn new instruments was astounding.

Entwistle was also a gifted singer and reveled in entertaining his elders with an ace Al Jolson impersonation complete with jazz hands. Hopping up on his cinema seat during a Jolson movie to croon along for the audience, little John displayed an extrovert showmanship the adult Ox would prefer to keep undercover.

When rock 'n' roll hit in the fifties, Entwistle was instantly enthralled. He debated whether to teach himself the guitar or the bass. After borrowing a guitar from Pete Townshend, removing the high B and E strings, and jamming along with his Duane Eddy records, he decided four strings was the way to go. At the age of fourteen, he built his first bass guitar on his grandma's dining room table. Working off some pictures of the Fender Precision, he designed his own instrument with all the technical skill of a fourteen-year-old. It had a square neck that he later said was about nine inches too long (a probable exaggeration) and control knobs attached with glue. The cable linked directly to the pickup. Though the creation was "terrible" by Entwistle's own assessment, it was enough to keep his interest in the bass stoked.

As a member of the Detours, John Entwistle did his traditional bass player duties even as he itched to make his presence felt more dramatically. When Roger Daltrey relinquished his guitar to sing, he left Townshend as the band's sole guitarist and Entwistle with an opportunity to fill the gap. He had the chops and imagination to take the kind of low-end leads he'd heard on his Duane Eddy discs and adapt them to his instrument.

In effect, John Entwistle became something utterly new to rock 'n' roll: the first lead bass player. Between bouts of maintaining the low end, he could zoom off into improvisational nirvana while Pete Townshend's thick chords kept the sound full. Entwistle was a big guy with fingers made powerful by playing the trumpet. The role muscle played in his bass work can't be overestimated. His stamina was unflagging. He hit his strings hard both on the neck and over the pickups. Watch some footage of him playing. See how far he extends the fingers on his right hand to build momentum before striking the strings. When he makes contact, it is not McCartney's soft, humming tone. It is percussive; it *thwacks*. Entwistle fingered his frets hard too, slapping them to

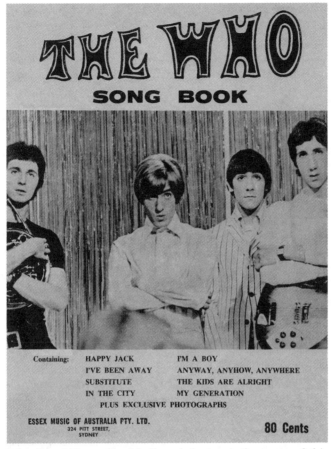

John Entwistle cradles his French horn on the cover of this Australian songbook.

Courtesy of the Rob Abramowicz Collection, digitized by Jeffrey Uleau

accentuate the note and keep his left hand limber and ready to move on to the next one. Both hands bounced.

Like Townshend, Entwistle was also a master of variety, ping-ponging from plucking the strings to slapping them to tapping them to hammering them to popping them (pulling them away from the neck for a snapping sound) to stroking chords all within the space of a single song. With his nimble right fingers he'd discharge sudden flurries of triplets or quintuplets; with his left he'd dive down the neck like Bo Diddley. Although he'd sometimes pluck the strings with all four fingers of his right hand, he did so mostly for showiness (he may not have been overly theatrical, but Entwistle's finger work is as dazzling to watch as Moon's octopus arms or Townshend's windmilling). The index and middle fingers did all the heavy lifting. When he brought his ring finger into the mix, he'd rotate his three fingers for rippling triplets, as you would while tapping your fingers on a table. The rest of his body remained stone still so he could concentrate on his hands. The days of flopping around like Al Jolson were behind him.

To keep his work from getting lost in murk, Entwistle kept his tone bright and trebly and his volume LOUD. The increased decibels allowed him to produce ringing harmonics and hit distinct notes when using a lighter touch. He was a serial string changer, new strings providing the brightest tone. Sometimes he'd change them just for a sound check! He also learned early on that he could get his brightest, punchiest sound using picks, which was his preferred method in the studio starting with "Substitute."

Unlike Townshend, Entwistle was not gun-shy about running his guitar through gadgets and doodads. In his later years, he had his bass running through a mad scientist's array of electronics: graphic equalizers, multieffects units, noise gates. He slathered his sound with overdrive and chorus effects. He didn't really need that stuff. His playing in all its raw imaginativeness, dexterity, fluidity, and power was all anyone needed to hear to know they were not listening to the typical bass player. They were listening to John Entwistle.

Keith

John Entwistle and Pete Townshend were natural improvisers and versatile musicians with seemingly bottomless trick bags. One thing they never were, though, was out of control. They couldn't afford to be when the guy who was supposed to be keeping it all together was completely uncontainable. The drummer has a very set responsibility in a band: keep the beat. Drummers get a bad rap because they don't have to play chords and don't have to find notes. They just have to beat on things like apes (oldest drummer joke in the world: "What do you call a guy who hangs around with musicians? A drummer." Hardy har). This is utter bullshit. If anything, the drummer is the most important member of a band. A bad drummer means a bad band. A drummer gets sloppy with the tempo and the whole rhythm, the unity, the professionalism of a group goes off the rails. So how did the Who manage with Keith Moon?

They managed because, in the same way that Townshend and Entwistle would swap roles as guitarist and bassist, they allowed Moon to stray from his timekeeping duties by keeping the beat firmly locked down even when at their most fanciful. Notice how metronomic Entwistle's wildest bass solos are. They are melodically unpredictable but never, ever get loosey-goosey with the rhythm. His bass lines hold everything together in a way the drummer couldn't always be relied on to.

Moon's unpredictability and his hyperactivity are the driving forces behind his drumming. He did not have the self-discipline to just stomp the bass drum on the downbeat, whack the scare on the offbeat, and ride the hi-hat like most team-playing rock 'n' roll drummers do. How would he draw attention to himself doing that? Just as John Entwistle made himself over as a lead bass player, Keith

Moon saw himself as the lead drummer, because he knew that he was the star of the band.

Moon would not just go off on his own with no regard for his bandmates (at least not on nights when he had a relative handle on his faculties). Quite the opposite. He'd lock eyes with Townshend, searching for cues and clues that might give him an idea of what was coming next because he hadn't come to class prepared. Moon never had set drum parts he'd just recreate onstage night after night. He didn't play the songs; he played with his bandmates, commenting on Daltrey's vocal inflections with a saucy fill, answering Entwistle's sudden glissando down the bass neck with an expansive roll down his toms, thrashing his cymbals in time with Townshend's power chords. Moon never practiced his drums on his own, because how could he practice interacting with his bandmates when he was alone?

The archetypal wild-man drummer started playing music as a bugler in the sea cadet corps when he was twelve. He then gave the trumpet a shot, but he never made much progress with it. His incorrigible energy was better put to use with something more physical. He vied for the bass drum spot in the cadets instead. The bass drum was big, and it made a big noise: showy and loud, right up Moon's alley.

He started getting into jazz drummers. He loved Gene Krupa and Buddy Rich as much for their rip-roaring solos as for their stick-twirling flamboyance. A rock 'n' roll drummer in that glitzy tradition was Carlo Little of Screaming Lord Sutch's band. Little was known to take deranged ten-minute solos while balancing on a motorcycle helmet. Moon accosted the drummer after a concert and demanded lessons. An untrained teacher giving an untrainable kid lessons. That must have been quite a scene.

What Keith did learn from Little was to syncopate, to kick his bass drum on *and* off the beat. Trying to actually *do* that so exasperated him that he plunged a stick through his snare skin. Syncopation and violent energy: two corner pieces fall into place in the puzzle of Keith Moon's drum style.

Another important move was to stop taking lessons and forget about trying to do everything a drummer is supposed to do. He was much too undisciplined, and much too creative, for that. If a drummer is supposed to ride the verses on the snare and hi-hat, then Keith Moon was going to roll through them on the toms and ride cymbal. If a drummer was supposed to dole out fills prudently, then Keith Moon was going to spew them forth in an unpluggable flood. If a drummer was supposed to stagger bass drum hits to establish a groove, then Keith Moon was going to keep the pulse racing by pumping his bass pedal like he was trying to inflate a flat tire. If a drummer was supposed to create drama with judicious dynamics, then Keith Moon was going to create it by always hitting as hard as he could. If the key to being a good drummer was providing predictability and consistency, Keith Moon was going to rain down chaos with impromptu rim-shots, floor tom rolls, and cymbal assaults.

Moon's drumming could have been a mess (and as we'll see in chapter 22, when he was not in control of his faculties, it was a mess). His natural stamina, his adrenaline, his inventiveness, and perhaps most importantly of all, his understanding and complimentary bandmates, made it work. He also had an innate enough sense of rhythm to not trip up the beat when he rose from the din to discharge one of his fills.

Moon kept his drum skins tuned as tightly as possible to maximize the bounce of his sticks, making for rolls so fast you'd need a radar gun to clock them. His incredible speed turned every performance into a constant adrenaline rush, though as fast and chaotic as his fills seem, one can still count out the quarter notes of the beat easily as he plays around them. His fills rarely disrupt the underlying pulse.

Because of the specificity of his style, playing with Keith Moon could be frustrating, but Pete Townshend still appreciated that he had a most original ace up his sleeve and often made room in his songs to spotlight the drummer. Townshend's sustaining chords left great spaces in the sound for Moon to fill up. "I Can See for Miles," "Pure and Easy," "Bargain," "Won't Get Fooled Again," "Bell Boy," and others set aside bars for Moon to hop out to center stage, to be what he absolutely had to be: a star.

Roger

Ask someone to name her or his favorite guitarist, bass player, and drummer, and it would be no shock if that person replied "Pete Townshend, John Entwistle, and Keith Moon" (I sure would). Roger Daltrey, however, has regularly been branded the Who's weak link. Even his bandmates were rarely complimentary of his abilities, and Daltrey himself has said that he hates his voice, and demurely offers himself as a "dramatist" of Townshend's lyrics rather than a proper singer. His voice is raspy, it's rough, and his pitch is sometimes off. A consummate singer Roger Daltrey might not be. But a great rock 'n' roll singer? Well, would you be reading this book if he wasn't?

Daltrey got his start traveling a traditional route. As a lad he sang in his church choir. In the Boy's Brigade, he played trumpet. As a teenager, he tore off his uniform and built himself a guitar. His abilities were strong enough to impress young Pete Townshend, who pinpointed him as the best guitarist at school with a style that was basic yet self-assured and fluid. Nevertheless, Daltrey's dedication to his instrument was not strong, and he basically set it aside and never looked back when the Detours found themselves in greater need of a singer than a second guitarist (Daltrey with a guitar would be a rare sight for years until he picked it up again for the Who's 1982 tour).

In his new role as lead singer, Daltrey strived to emulate his blues and soul heroes, affecting a guttural bellow in mimicry of sandblasted monsters such as Howlin' Wolf and James Brown. While he was not nearly as natural a blues singer as Steve Marriott or Mick Jagger, he certainly doesn't embarrass himself on those early covers of "I'm a Man," "Please, Please, Please," and "Daddy Rolling Stone." He had a harder time finding a voice for Townshend's poppy originals, which he found to be "peculiar" and overly sweet. Yet he ended up voicing "The Kids Are Alright," "It's Not True," and "La-La-La Lies" convincingly by traveling back to his choirboy beginnings. Perhaps without realizing it, Daltrey had located the two poles that would make him such a unique rock 'n' roll singer: posturing bluster and sweet vulnerability. Now all he had to do was blend them.

Most commentators will insist that Daltrey did not come into his own as a singer until *Tommy* gave him a part to play. The singer, too, parrots this opinion. But he had his act down earlier than that. On "I'm a Boy," he was already getting into character, trying "to sing it like a really, really young kid, like an eight-year-old," as he told *Uncut* in 2001. With the chore of making something of "Happy Jack," which sounded to Roger's ears "like a German oompah song," he located an appropriate voice by imitating Burl Ives! Daltrey's singing was not all acting and mimicry. There was great depth in his method, too, which is evident early on in the nostalgic sighing of "Pictures of Lily" and the tender "Tattoo." On 1968's "Melancholia," he forged the high drama that would be the core of his delivery for decades to follow. His singing across *Tommy* is especially sensitive, particularly in the high "See Me, Feel Me" refrain where all reservations about sweetness or peculiarity melt away.

Daltrey's increased confidence hits a peak across his ad libs on *Live at Leeds* and his commanding performances on *Who's Next*, whether getting emotional on "Behind Blue Eyes" or unleashing a terrifying primal scream at the climax of "Won't Get Fooled Again." After this, he would often be accused of mere bluster and failing to grasp Townshend's lyrics, but his heart-wrenching, nuanced performances on "Love Reign o'er Me," "Imagine a Man," "They Are All in Love," "Music Must Change," "Love Is Coming Down," "Don't Let Go the Coat," and "One Life's Enough" wipe out such charges.

Because he is such a physical singer, and because he has had serious health problems, Roger Daltrey's voice is no longer as strong as it once was. In 2009, he noticed he was having unprecedented difficulty hitting his high notes. Friends suggested he consult Dr. Steven Zeitels. The renowned surgeon detected discolored spots on the tissue lining Daltrey's throat. A biopsy revealed a precancerous dysplasia. Laser surgery fixed his cords in time for the Who's performance at the Super Bowl in 2010. As of this writing, Zeitels believes he is on the brink of perfecting a biogel he believes will make Daltrey sing like a thirty-year old again. In 2013, the very confidant doc told *The New Yorker*, "It's not 'Is it going to happen?' . . . It's *when* it's going to happen."

4

Meet the New Boss

The Management

Booking tours, pinning down recording contracts, tweaking a group's image. It's not as glamorous or fun as getting onstage, making noise, and wrecking shit. The suits have to do their thing, nonetheless, and some of pop's greatest groups have had managers that could almost match them in terms of vision. Elvis had his Colonel Tom Parker. The Beatles had their Brian Epstein. The Stones had their Andrew Loog Oldham. The Who, too, were guided along by guys in suits, some of whom, in the tradition of great rock 'n' roll management, were every bit as colorful and crazy as themselves. More than one steered the Who into doing the things that made them unlike any other band.

Helmut Gorden

Well, they weren't *all* that colorful or crazy, which is why figures such as Helmut Gorden fell by the wayside. Although he had aspirations of following in Brian Epstein's footsteps, Gorden had no background in the music world as Eppy did (before managing the Beatles, he managed the record department of his family's music shop). What he did have was a key connection. Helmut Gorden was the employer of drummer Doug Sandom's sister-in-law. He also had a background in business, not that there's anything very rock 'n' roll about being a doorknob manufacturer.

Gorden made signing a record contract for the Who his paramount goal after forming Gorden-Druce Enterprises, LTD, with Bob Druce. Druce had more practical experience as the agent of a few local groups and the booker of dances at pubs and clubs with his Commercial Entertainment Limited. Druce also made himself useful by buying the band a van. They were less enthused about his policy of taking 10 percent of everything they earned.

Despite Druce's know-how, luck played a more crucial role in the Who getting their first shot with a label. As it turned out, Helmut Gorden's barber, imaginatively known as Jack "The Barber" Marks, also trimmed the locks of Chris Parmeinter, an A&R man at Fontana (see chapter 5). The audition led to two big shake-ups for the Who: the ousting of Doug Sandom and the recording of their first single, "I'm the Face."

The Who were still put off by Gorden's farty sensibilities and wanted him to take a backseat to his new managerial partner, Pete Meaden. Playing garden party gigs for their manager's supposedly "influential" buddies—without their noisy amplifiers, no less!—was not how they pictured their rise to world domination. The problem for them was that Gorden had a contract. The problem for Gorden was that Daltrey, Entwistle, and Townshend (whose parents hadn't even countersigned on his behalf) were all underaged when they signed it. Prospective manager Chris Stamp dropped the contract on the desk of Brian Epstein's lawyer, David Jacobs, who deemed it as legally binding as a chicken sandwich. Undone by the lawyer of the very guy he aspired to be, Helmut Gorden's dreams of pulling the strings of a hot young rock 'n' roll act came to an abrupt end.

Pete Meaden

Once again, Jack the Barber shaped more than a coiffure when he altered Who history by introducing Helmut Gorden to client Pete Meaden. The twenty-two-year-old had already built up a few credentials, briefly managing Jimmy James and the Vagabonds and the Moments (starring Steve Marriott) and working as a publicist for Chuck Berry, Georgie Fame, the Crystals, and the Rolling Stones (he also claimed to have done time in the trenches as Mick and Keith's roommate). Meaden was known around town as a dedicated mod and was on the prowl for a group to remold in his own sharp image. Like the other members of his cult, he dug the usual Tamla-Motown stuff, but he also recognized the importance of having a homegrown British band for British mods to follow. The Barber suggested he pay Gorden a visit. In a rare moment of self-awareness, the Who's manager realized a bit of direction from a cat a lot younger and hipper than himself might be just what his boys needed.

Meaden really did a number on the Who, putting them in new duds, forcing John Entwistle to get a haircut (Keith Moon somehow escaped the dreaded barber's chair), encouraging them to focus their set on the Tamla-Motown numbers mods craved, penning jargon-loaded lyrics over old blues songs for the band to perform, and giving them a daft new über-mod moniker: the High Numbers. For all Meaden's tinkering, the High Numbers couldn't catch a break. The absurdly pandering "I'm the Face"/"Zoot Suit" single was a flop (see chapter 9). Pete Townshend proved to be the only band member with any affinity for modernism. Meanwhile, Meaden rolled his sunglasses-obscured eyes every time Townshend did anything as gauche as drawing squalls of feedback from his Rickenbacker or Keith Moon forwent Funk Brothers simplicity to pummel Hell out of his kit. In other words, Pete Meaden hated it whenever the High Numbers behaved like the Who. Clearly, this was not to be a long-term relationship, and Meaden ended up getting swept aside with Helmut Gorden when Kit Lambert and Chris Stamp came into the picture.

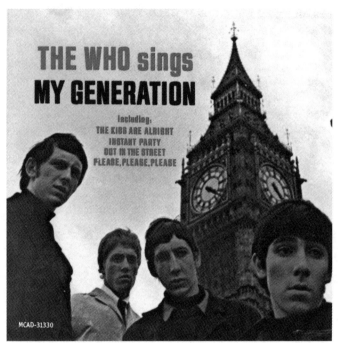

By the time *The Who Sings My Generation* came out in America in April 1966, Pete Meaden had already been out of the fold for some two years. The Modfather's influence, however, could still be felt on the cover.   *Author's collection*

Sadly, Pete Meaden never realized his fantasies of leading a group to mod stardom. As was the mod way, he was an incessant gobbler of the amphetamine Drinamyl (purple hearts) and susceptible to anxiety attacks. In the seventies, *NME* journalist Steve Turner discovered that Meaden had been institutionalized. After checking out, he tried to get back to work as the Steve Gibbons Band's comanager, but his personal problems persisted. Pete Meaden OD'ed in his parents' home on July 29, 1978.

Kit Lambert

There is no single figure in this story that had a greater outside influence on the Who than Christopher "Kit" Lambert. He realized Helmut Gorden's ambitions when he led the band to superstardom as their big-name manager. He produced many of their greatest records and helped Pete Townshend distinguish himself among a very competitive pack of young British songwriters by routing him toward rock opera. He was a business leader, a creative asset, a friend, an adversary, and ultimately, a royal pain in the band's collective ass. His life was glamorous and tragic. If the Who are the ultimate rock 'n' roll band, then Kit Lambert was the ultimate rock 'n' roll manager.

Lambert had creativity typed into his DNA. His grandfather George was a painter renowned for his portraits and depictions of war. His father, Constant, was a famed composer and conductor. Without his grandfather's artistic skills or his dad's musical ones, Lambert still had imagination to match them both and pursued a career in film. After completing his service in the British Army, he joined an expedition to Brazil to film the troupe's search for the source of an uncharted river. As his story goes (and we should always exercise our critical thinking skills when reading a Kit Lambert story), a friend was killed by a local tribe of cannibals during the trip.

So Lambert put his Indiana Jones fantasies on permanent hold and took the less harrowing position of assistant director on such films as *Of Human Bondage* and *The L-Shaped Room*. During these assignments he met fellow A.D. Chris Stamp. Both longed to make films of their own and entered into a partnership they titled New Action, LTD. The dynamic directing duo was the proverbial odd couple. Lambert: upper crust, gnomish, Oxford educated, intense, openly gay, pushing thirty. Stamp: the son of a tugboat driver, fit and handsome, in his early

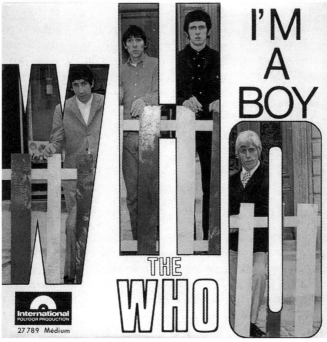

As Pete Townshend's gift for far-out storytelling came to the fore with "I'm a Boy," Kit Lambert encouraged him to expand his ambitions to operatic proportions.

Courtesy of the Rob Abramowicz Collection, digitized by Jeffrey Uleau

twenties, devil-may-care, a lad's lad. Their chemistry was on the money, and their idea for a film was ingenious and timely: they would find a band of pop hopefuls and follow its path to success.

Lambert and Stamp had been searching for the ideal group for months when Lambert's keen eye was drawn to an armada of scooters convened outside the Railway Hotel in July 1964. Kismet. He went inside and encountered a four-headed monster, "bug ugly" and "satanic" by his own assessment. Kit Lambert was galvanized by the deafening, berserk spectacle he'd witnessed and got right on the phone with his partner. Lambert and Stamp had their band, and the High Numbers were now on the path to becoming the Who again.

Already dissatisfied with Gorden and Meaden's managerial skills, and further tempted by this new team's promise of £1,000 per year—*per band member!*—the guys were easily persuaded to drop their former management. Gorden's attempts to sue for ownership fell flaccid, and Kit Lambert and Chris Stamp adopted a bouncing baby band.

Instead of trying to force his own idea of who the Who should be on the group, Lambert nurtured their oddness. That pedestrian "High Numbers" nonsense was quickly banished, and that alluring old name went back into use. All of the Who's craziest impulses, all of their onstage violence, all of their wildest pretensions were to be cultivated like rare orchids. Creatively, Lambert had a much more profound effect on the Who than Brian Epstein ever did on the Beatles.

Lambert's interests did not end with his first clients. After the Who released *A Quick One* on Robert Stigwood's Reaction label, Lambert and Stamp started their own Track Records—after months of studying the business practices of cookie and dish soap companies. Among Track's acquisitions were the Jimi Hendrix Experience, the Crazy World of Arthur Brown, John's Children (featuring Marc Bolan), and Thunderclap Newman.

Lambert led the Who through their tremendously successful *Tommy* period, but he was also developing severe personal problems that would have a detrimental effect on their working relationship. Convinced that the Who's career was to be forever linked with their first huge international hit, he pressed them to make a *Tommy* film from his own screenplay at a time when Townshend wanted to move forward with a new project called *Lifehouse*. While pretending to support the groundbreaking concept, Lambert was undermining Pete Townshend on the sly, doing whatever he could to defuse *Lifehouse*. Hard drug use was wrecking Lambert's mental and physical health. While he flounced around as the Who struggled to make *Quadrophenia*, supposedly erasing recordings in Townshend's absence, the long-simmering clash boiled over and Lambert was officially relieved of his job as producer. Roger Daltrey had his fill of Lambert and Stamp when they deemed his debut solo album unfit for release. The singer aimed to make a change in management by putting Bill Curbishley in charge of his personal wheelings and dealings. Along with the personal and creative problems were the business ones. The band came to realize they did not have the financial stake in Track Records they'd been led to believe they did, and oodles of publishing money had gone missing. As Lambert's heroin addiction deepened and his business practices grew ever more erratic, he even found himself on the outs with Chris Stamp. Early in 1974 the two received their walking papers. Two years later, Track Records crossed the finish line.

For Kit Lambert, life after the Who was a grim tangle of lawsuits, financial messes (after declaring bankruptcy he became a ward of the court, subsisting on a weekly stipend of £200), and drugs. The charming, urbane raconteur of old no longer occupied Lambert's shell. On April 6, 1981, he was at his mother's home when he took a tumble down the stairs and died of a brain hemorrhage the following day, a sad end for one of rock's great men behind the curtain.

Chris Stamp

If Kit Lambert was a more convincing and more complimentary substitute for Helmut Gorden's faux executive, then Chris Stamp filled the more youthful role that Pete Meaden tried to play. As 1964 rolled to its conclusion, and the Beatles transformed England into the globe's cultural nexus, the gritty combativeness of Meaden's mods gave way to the positivity and vibrancy of Swinging London. The male face of this new age was Terence Stamp, the East End actor who became a capital-S Movie Star when he played Melville's mythical Handsome Sailor in Peter Ustinov's 1962 adaptation of *Billy Budd*. With his chiseled bone structure, sinewy physique, and deep-set blue eyes, Terence Stamp was the man every London lad aspired to be.

Four years his brother's junior, Chris Stamp was one of Terence's five siblings. Unlike Terence, favorite son Chris got lessons in how to use his fists from his often-absent dad. He became tough and scrappy, and the movie star soon knew not to mess with his little brother. Without the sensitivity that made Terence a great actor, Chris gravitated toward the more technical side of filmmaking, and though he was a bruiser who disparaged the "poofs" (his term) dandifying themselves on Carnaby Street, he found a fruitful kinship with the older, homosexual entrepreneur Kit Lambert while toiling for Shepperton Studios.

When Lambert discovered the Who in the summer of '64, he formed an intellectual bond with Pete Townshend. Chris Stamp was electrified by their rawness, the velocity of Keith Moon's rhythms, and their on-the-surface dysfunction. The Who had found a management duo with a yin and yang as extreme as their own.

Lambert and Stamp were not complete antitheses, though. Just as Lambert made sure the breakthrough *Tommy* became a reality, Stamp nursed along *The Who Sell Out*, an album that many (including your author) now regard as the Who's finest, drawing real-life admen David King and Roger Law into the project. He shared Lambert's enthusiasm for tossing *Tommy* up onto the screen and served as executive producer of Ken Russell's film. Although he was so street-hard that he scoffed at the Who's brutal onstage destruction as "a bit airy fairy" (*Amazing Journey: The Story of the Who*), he too recognized the value of showmanship, style, and spending bails of cash. In that sense, he also shared Lambert's business naïveté and was similarly incapable of stanching the nonstop money hemorrhage. Stamp's drug intake was as excessive as his spending, and like Lambert, he'd end up with a grave addiction. After Lambert died in 1981, Stamp's addiction continued until he finally sought treatment in 1987. The use of psychodrama therapy, a rehabilitation method involving role-playing and role reversing, inspired him to pursue his own psychotherapy degree. Stamp found a new career as an addiction counselor and psychodrama therapist. In private, he was a dedicated practitioner of Buddhist meditation and a nondenominational reverend in a church called The Sanctuary of the Beloved (a sort of instant program toward priesthood). Throughout all this personal upheaval, Chris Stamp continued partnering with Pete Townshend on his Fabulous Music LTD. publication company, continued to champion the Who's music and history, and even rebuilt his relationship with Roger Daltrey after the solo album fallout of 1973. Sadly, Chris Stamp succumbed to cancer on November 24, 2012.

Mike Shaw

Kit Lambert and Chris Stamp's nuttiness could only serve the Who well if they had a more practical member on their team. Fortunately they had Mike Shaw. Chris's school chum had been a lighting tech at the Bristol Hippodrome when the managers recruited him to help out as production manager with New Action. That title meant Mike was in charge of all the drudge work Lambert and Stamp were too busy rocking and rolling to bother with the scheduling, the hotel booking, the equipment transporting, maintaining a meticulous record of which venues were worth rebooking, and contending with pain-in-the-arse promoters. More specific to his unique talents, he also choreographed the Who's lighting at a time when most bands didn't appreciate or understand the importance of this crucial facet of stagecraft.

On October 15, 1965, Mike Shaw was driving home after lighting a Merseybeats gig at Liverpool's famed Cavern Club. Fatigued from the night's work, he dozed off behind the wheel and slammed into a truck. Mike survived but was left a paraplegic. Although he could not resume his full workload, his friends in the Who family loved him too much to let him go and respected his intelligence and work ethic enough to understand they couldn't afford to. When he'd recouped enough to return to work in 1967, Mike managed Track Records, personally handling the label's *Backtrack* compilations and reissues. He continued working with the Who through the first decade of the Bill Curbishley years, only retiring when the Who claimed to be doing the same thing in 1983. One of his final tasks with the outfit was compiling that year's *Who's Greatest Hits*. For his decades of service, Curbishley and the band bought him a house in Cornwall. Mike Shaw died on November 17, 2012, just a week before his old friend Chris Stamp.

John "Wiggy" Wolff

With Swinging London in full swing in 1966, Keith Moon and John Entwistle took to spending their quid as quickly as possible around the city's groovy new nightspots. Too soused to transport themselves, they put former Walker Brothers employee John "Wiggy" Wolff on the payroll. Too much of a bright boy to chauffer the lads forever, Wiggy took on many of Mike Shaw's old duties as the band's new production manager in 1967: managing tours, moving equipment, lighting their stage shows, covering for Kit Lambert. In 1973, Wiggy masterminded the renovation of an old church in Battersea, South London, into the Who's own Ramport Studios. There the band recorded *Quadrophenia* and most of *Who Are You* and loaned it out to artists such as Supertramp, Jeff Beck, Judas Priest, Joan Jett, Thin Lizzy, Johnny Thunders and the Heartbreakers, and Bryan Ferry. He revolutionized the Who's stage act when he unveiled his 4-watt laser beam at Granby Halls, October 18, 1975. Wiggy got thinking about this new technology when he saw Led Zeppelin work lasers into their set at Earl's Court the previous May. Intrigued but unimpressed with the puny 1-watt laser Zep used, Wiggy upgraded to a 4-watter, which might not sound like much but is hot enough to light a cigarette and has the potential to blind someone if aimed directly at the eye. American lightning techs Rick Lefrak and Alope of Laughing Whitefish Productions located the argon beam and turned Wiggy on to splitting up the light with a diffraction grating, an effect that elevated the climactic organ solo of "Won't Get Fooled Again" to spectacle. Wolff was even approached by the *Star Wars* production team to bring his lasers to the screen. Although his technology was too primitive for such a use, he did dazzle Harrison "Han Solo" Ford and Mark "Luke Skywalker" Hamill by using a 60-watt laser to burn a hole through a door.

Peter Rudge

Sometimes the best way to make a good impression in the Who's calamitous camp is to make a stink. Peter Rudge had been a student booking entertainers at St. John's College when the Who backed out of a gig scheduled for June 11, 1968. Sussing that claims of Keith Moon falling ill were balderdash, Rudge tromped to Kit Lambert's London office to give the manager an earful. There he discovered his instincts were correct. Lambert had canceled the show so his boys could make a promo film for their upcoming single, "Dogs." Instead of being flabbergasted by the young fellow's gall, Lambert recognized the kind of fighter his band needed. Peter Rudge completed his college education. Then he got a job working as the Who's tour manager.

Along with such vital tasks as setting up the crucial *Tommy* tour, Rudge found himself popping on a number of hats he didn't set out to wear during his time with the Who: middleman between the band and Stamp and Lambert when their relationship soured in the early seventies; daily business handler when Stamp and Lambert were too strung out to do it; America-based manager; and jailbird when he was arrested with fifteen other tour-party members during a particularly ruthless bout of hotel destruction at the Bonaventure in Montreal, December 1973. While handling the band's affairs in the United States, Rudge also went to work for the Rolling Stones and Lynyrd Skynyrd, and stuck with those less troublesome bands not too long after Lambert and Stamp lost their jobs.

Bill Curbishley

Peter Rudge was under serious consideration when the Who started looking for a full-time replacement for Lambert and Stamp. Instead, they went with Bill Curbishley. Curbishley had been a mod. Like Mike Shaw, he'd been a friend of Chris Stamp back in their school days. When Stamp and Lambert resolved to focus their energy on partying instead of business managing, Curbishley joined Mike Shaw and Peter Rudge in picking up the slack at Track. Unlike his gallivanting bosses, Curbishley was remarkably focused, a hard fighter, and always made sure the musicians were well paid for the gigs he booked. Such qualities endeared him to the ever-pragmatic Roger Daltrey. While Peter Rudge tended to cower beneath the Who's legend, Curbishley was a fan but never a follower. Frustrated with Lambert and Stamp's flightiness, especially while negotiating the *Tommy* film and getting Ramport Studios running, he too broke ties with the wayward managers, quitting Track to begin his own management company, Five One Productions, LTD. Curbishley was also firmly in Daltrey's corner when it came to that eponymous solo album of which the managers wanted no part. This move strengthened bonds between himself and the singer, and Daltrey not only put him in charge of handling the record but gave him a cut of the profits as well.

His support through the *Daltrey* ordeal convinced Roger that Bill Curbishley would look out for the best interests of all four members of the Who, as opposed to Lambert and Stamp, whom Daltrey felt only cared about Townshend. After some reflection, Townshend agreed that Curbishley had the necessary qualities to handle the band, and in 1974, he was sworn in.

Established as the Who's official manager—a position he still holds as of this writing—Bill Curbishley eventually expanded his client list to include Judas Priest, Jimmy Page, and Robert Plant. He also worked on the production side of several Who-related films, including *The Kids Are Alright* and *Quadrophenia* and Daltrey's acting vehicles *McVicar* and *Buddy's Song*. In 2013, he coproduced his first nonrock film, the WWII drama *The Railway Man* starring Nicole Kidman, Colin Firth, and Stellan Skarsgård.

5

Sound Round

Producers and Sound Men

Harnessing the bedlam of a Who performance takes more than technical skill. Imagination is paramount, and during the days when stuffy bores in white lab coats were still trying to use their tried and true techniques to record anarchic young rock 'n' roll bands, some of the unlikeliest talents made some of the best Who records.

Barry Gray

After quitting the Confederates in the late fifties, John Entwistle and Pete Townshend went their separate ways for a while before reconvening in a Shadows-indebted group called the Scorpions. Completed with drummer Mick Brown and guitarist Pete Wilson, the group didn't accomplish much more than the Confederates had, but the Scorpions were important for two reasons. Firstly, and most obviously, the band got Entwistle and Townshend playing together again, cementing their musical relationship and prepping them to move on to better things with the Detours. Secondly, Pete Wilson provided a link to the guy who'd be the very first to record them. Wilson's dad was an associate of Barry Gray, whom TV viewers knew as the composer of music featured on such kids' shows as *The Adventures of Twizzle*, *Supercar*, and *Fireball XL5*. The bespectacled Gray could also include collaborations with such venerable stars as Vera Lynn and Hoagy Carmichael on his CV, so working with a grungy gang of young rockers must have been quite the novelty for him. The Detours convened in the basement studio of Gray's home in autumn 1963 to cut three numbers on his one-track recorder: Chuck Berry's "Come On," which the Rolling Stones put out as their inaugural single the previous summer, and two Townshend originals, "It Was You" and "Please Don't Send Me Home."

These recordings never went further than Gray's abode, and he and his young charges immediately split off in separate directions. He continued his work as a television composer on such well-loved series as *Thunderbirds*, *UFO*, and quite coincidentally, *Dr. Who*, as well as a bit of work in features, including Terence Fisher's *Island of Terror* and François Truffaut's *Fahrenheit 451*. Like Pete Townshend, he developed a fascination with electronic music, which can be heard in several of his science fiction scores.

Pete Meaden, Chris Parmeinter, and Jack Baverstock

On April 9, 1964, the Who had their very first major label audition. Unfortunately, this was not the Who with Keith Moon in the backline, but a transitional lineup with Doug Sandom on the beat. Fontana Records' A&R man, Chris Parmeinter (alternately Parmenter in *Anyway, Anyhow, Anywhere* and Parmienter in *Who I Am*. Pick your favorite, but I'm sticking with the spelling used on the *Odds & Sods* jacket), did not hide his disdain for Dougie, which helped precipitate the drummer's exit from the fold (see chapter 2).

When Keith Moon was hired and Pete Meaden gave the group their mod makeover, they were ready to give it another shot with Parmeinter the following June. The session yielded a couple of legit covers, Bo Diddley's "Here 'Tis" and Eddie Holland's "Leaving Here" (the version included on the extended edition of *Odds & Sods*, as opposed to the one Shel Talmy would later produce), and a couple of rip-offs Meaden credited to himself. These shameless steals from Slim Harpo and the Dynamics—"I'm the Face" and "Zoot Suit," respectively—would constitute the Who's first single, though one they'd release as the High Numbers after Meaden decided they needed a less interesting, more pandering name. He also decided that he deserved coproducer credit on the disc, even though it isn't likely he did more in the studio than munch French Blues and sweat.

As for Parmeinter, he has no other known production credits, which may account for the confusion over the spelling of his name. It also may be evidence that the true producer of the session was label-head Jack Baverstock (who has his own name problems: Dave Marsh rechristens him "Bavistock" in *Before I Get Old*), another A&R dude at Fontana who is fingered as the overseer of the session in several sources (and was a good friend of Pete's mum). Considering that Baverstock has a lot more production credits to his name—the Merseybeats; Wayne Fontana; Kiki Dee; and Dave Dee, Dozy, Beaky, Mick, and Tich, to name a few—he may be the likeliest culprit for recording the shuffling groove on these early discs.

Shel Talmy

The Detours worked with Barry Gray purely out of convenience. The High Numbers worked with Chris Parmeinter and Pete Meaden purely out of opportunism. The Who took up with Shel Talmy because a more ideal producer was practically unthinkable. Chicago-born, LA-raised Talmy was a precocious kid who appeared on the game show *Quiz Kids* and boasted an IQ in the upper 99.9th percentile. In the early sixties, he moved from Los Angeles to London in search of work. Talmy claimed that by passing off the Beach Boys' "Surfin' Safari" and Lou Rawls's "Music in the Air" (a record that apparently doesn't exist outside of Talmy's recollection) as his own productions, he wangled his way into a job with Decca. On the records he actually produced, his sound was thick, overdriven, dense. Technically, it left a lot to be desired. For pure excitement, pure rock 'n' roll alchemy, it was unparalleled in 1964. Talmy had also been responsible for harnessing the abounding energy of the Kinks' "You Really Got Me," so when the Who chose to make their breakout with the blatantly Kinkified "I Can't Explain," Talmy was all the more appropriate. He only had to hear a few seconds of Townshend's succinct demo to know they'd be a perfect fit.

Like so many producers before and after him, Talmy was a control freak. When he recorded "You Really Got Me," he bumped Mick Avory from the drum throne, relegating him to a bit of tambourine tapping, and brought in studio pro Bobby Graham to supply the rhythm. Even Talmy wasn't so bullish or ignorant of talent to eject Keith Moon, but he still insisted on embellishing the Who with guitarist Jimmy Page (see chapter 20), pianist Perry Ford, and singing trio the Ivy League, because in Talmy's estimation, the Who's harmonies "sucked." Although the core group had been a bit compromised, no one could argue with the exciting product of the session, which became the Who's first top-ten hit.

The downside of the Who's relationship with Shel Talmy is that he got a big stake in the profits, earning the same percentage of their returns as the band by John Entwistle's estimation. Pete Townshend also felt limited by Talmy's very "specific sound." The Who felt rushed in the studio, claiming that engineer Glyn Johns did most of the work anyway. Entwistle was offended that the producer didn't take the time to learn Who was Who, often mistakenly calling him "Keith" and vice versa. The collaboration was doomed to sour. Even though the debut LP *My Generation* is widely regarded as a prepunk classic, the Who had nothing nice to say about it amidst a release that found them struggling to dislodge Talmy's claws from their necks (see chapter 9). The Who left him to treat other artists like chattel while Townshend produced their next single, "Substitute."

Meanwhile, Shel Talmy maintained a fruitful career, continuing to work with the Kinks through the end of 1966, while also recording such worthy Who clones as Davy Jones and the Lower Third for Parlophone and the Creation for his own Planet Records (which folded after their "Painter Man" failed to hit), as well as more sedate sides for Chad and Jeremy, Roy Harper, and Pentangle. In the late seventies, Talmy returned to Los Angeles, where retro-rock groups Jon and the Nightriders and Nancy Boy, featuring the sons of sixties stars Donovan and Mike Nesmith, sought out his talents.

Glyn Johns

The Who came away from their time with Shel Talmy bitterly, but the experience yielded a good deal of good, too, and I'm not just talking about those fierce early records. They'd gotten the chance to work with Glyn Johns, who'd be integral in recording some of the best Who records and some of the best records, period.

Johns started his career in the hope that he'd be before the board rather than behind it. However, the lounge lizard croon he unveiled on "Mary Anne," one of the first singles on Andrew Oldham's Immediate label, didn't help the record zip up the charts. Neither did his efforts for the Pye, Wescot, or Decca labels. So he settled for an apprenticeship under Talmy, engineering "You Really Got Me" before fiddling the dials for *My Generation*. The Who insisted Johns performed all the real work, though Talmy continues to insist he never coproduced a record with his underling. Regardless of who was responsible for what, Johns went to bat for Talmy when he and the Who went to court, signing an affidavit confirming that his boss was their rightful producer. Though the group had been impressed with the young engineer, this move didn't endear him to them and their association came to a natural, if temporary, conclusion.

In the meantime, Glyn Johns continued to hone his engineering skills on records for such artists as the Rolling Stones, Small Faces, Traffic, Procol Harum, Eric Clapton, Led Zeppelin, and the Beatles. Not a bad client list. He'd also expand his résumé to include production for Steve Miller Band, the Move, the Band, Joe Cocker, and Johnny Halliday. By that point, the Talmy fury had essentially subsided, and Johns was ready to handle coproducer duties on *Lifehouse*. The fact that he also helped design the Rolling Stones' Mobile Studio, which the Who wanted to use to record the album, made him an even more ideal candidate for the project. Despite being just as in-the-dark about what Pete

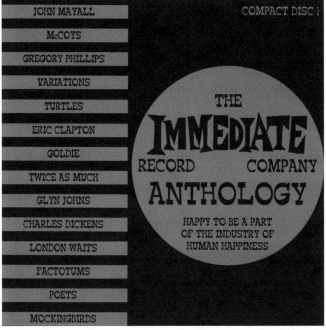

Before becoming one of the most prolific producers of the rock era, Glyn Johns had a go at a recording career of his own with Andrew Oldham's Immediate Records label. Judging from his cornball 1965 single "Mary Anne," included on the otherwise awesome *Immediate Record Company Anthology* box set, it's a good thing he found another job.   *Author's collection*

Townshend's new rock opera meant as everyone else, Johns brought a new clarity and depth to the Who's recordings. However, when he admitted he didn't understand *Lifehouse*, others started joining in on the chorus of "Huhs?," and the project was not long for this world. He still earned himself an associate producer credit on *Who's Next*, as well as the three singles leading up to *Quadrophenia*. Roger Daltrey's dissatisfaction with Johns's "airy fairy" (seriously?) work on *Who's Next* put his job as producer in jeopardy, and when Townshend resolved to bring Kit Lambert back into the creative process, Johns, who didn't get along with the unpredictable manager, stepped away. Unsurprisingly, Lambert was in no condition to do much more than cater the *Quadrophenia* sessions and waste money, so Townshend handled most of the production. Johns did receive credit for "Is It in My Head" and "Love Reign o'er Me," the two songs originally cut for the *Rock Is Dead—Long Live Rock* concept that preceded *Quadrophenia* (see chapter 15).

Glyn Johns was back full-time to receive his first solo production credit on a Who record with *The Who by Numbers*, but his work on *Who Are You* came to a violent halt. After Johns struggled to record Keith Moon fumbling with some of Townshend's more challenging material (and getting a cymbal tossed at him for his patience), Daltrey headbutted him for refusing to turn up the bass during a playback of "Sister Disco." Johns didn't need that kind of shit, so he left Daltrey's vocal sessions to assistant Jon Astley before going off to make records for Eric Clapton and Joan Armatrading, artists less likely to nut him in the face. But the Who are a strange addiction, and Glyn Johns was once more lured back into the mob for 1982's *It's Hard*. The critical thrashing the record received probably made him long for the days when he faced nothing harsher than a headbutt.

Kit Lambert

With Shel Talmy on the outs and Glyn Johns on hold, the Who needed someone else to contain their madness after *My Generation*. The job went to the one guy crazy enough to actually want the position, and the one guy who actually seemed capable of keeping the band members off each other's throats. Kit Lambert didn't have a lick of recording studio experience, but being a good producer is not just about moving levers. A producer must also keep the musicians happy, keep them on schedule, give form to their ideas, and pitch new ones when needed. Lambert had a natural knack for such things.

Pete Townshend did an exemplary job at the helm of "Substitute," but he knew that crowning himself the new producer would be a mistake, bringing the Who's ever-simmering tempers and jealousies back to a boil. His three bandmates respected Lambert as a relative voice of reason, and one of his first moves as producer was to placate their egos and give them a financial leg up by suggesting they all contribute songs to *A Quick One*. This was a potentially disastrous but brilliant move because it got all four band members working equally. Lambert also stimulated an air of creativity and fun in the studio that Shel Talmy most certainly did not. *You want to record that crazy polka Keith brought in? Sure! Why*

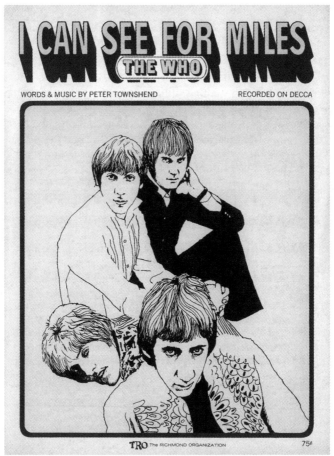

Although Kit Lambert was the ostensible producer of "I Can See for Miles," engineer Mike Ross-Trevor was really responsible for capturing its gob-smacking backing track, while Chris Huston recorded the intricate and expansive vocal harmonies.

Courtesy of the Rob Abramowicz Collection, digitized by Jeffrey Uleau

don't we parade up and down in front of the mic like a little marching band? It will be ever so much fun! On a technical level, trying to record in such a manner was idiotic, but it did wonders for morale. Lambert's toss-it-against-the-wall-and-see-if-it-sticks modus operandi could also result in genuinely revolutionary developments, as when he got Pete Townshend to complete his first rock opera by stringing together a few incomplete songs into "A Quick One While He's Away." Sure, the sound was erratic, often tinny, weak, or muddy, but the joy that went into making *A Quick One* simply floods from the speakers.

Lambert continued to serve as a valuable idea man and a smart organizer, getting Townshend back on the task of writing hit records when he started spending too much time developing "Rael" or prodding him into completing

Tommy. Meanwhile, the employment of engineers such as Chris Huston and Mike Ross-Trevor, who oversaw *Sell Out*, and Damon-Lyon Shaw, who handled *Tommy*, took care of the actual recording. Chris Huston told me that Lambert "just let Pete and the band do their thing. In fact, I do not recall one time that he went into the studio to work with them."

Sadly, Lambert's drug consumption mucked up his ideas as it had his business acumen. He and Townshend began falling out while making *Lifehouse*, and the Who started needing a producer who could offer more than corralling and wacky ideas. Although Lambert received an "executive producer" credit on *Who's Next* and a "pre-production" one on *Quadrophenia*, he was no longer making integral contributions to the Who's recordings.

Bob Pridden

The Who were frivolous enough about recording to allow the untrained Kit Lambert to produce, but their live performances were another matter. A group with the rightful reputation as the world's greatest live band needed to feel confident about who was working the soundboard. In mid-1967, this crucial job went to Bob Pridden.

Pridden started working on Team Who as road manager in December 1966. On his very first night on the job, he proved his worth by reassembling all the equipment the band smashed during their gig at London's Locarno Ballroom. Working with the Who could be a lot more harrowing than gluing together guitars. In November 1967, Pridden was cuffed by the coppers for setting off fire pots at the Hollywood Bowl after the band had been warned not to use smoke bombs . . . and didn't bother to tell the guy responsible for setting them off. During the technical-difficulty-plagued *Quadrophenia* tour, Townshend directed his anger over an out-of-sync backing tape at Pridden, dragging him over his soundboard for a most public humiliation before tearing the tapes to shreds. This is the most famous incident of Bob abuse, though not an isolated one. In *Eyewitness the Who*, Johnny Black wrote of a similar bit of Bob bashing during the Who's stop at the Coliseum in Charlotte, North Carolina, on November 20, 1971.

In happier times, Bob Pridden whacked the iconic clave rhythm of "Magic Bus" (under the pseudonym "Ben Pump") in the studio and joined forces with Townshend to develop the elephantine, 4,000-watt stereo system that gave the Who an extra boost in the seventies. Sometimes his job was nothing more taxing than clowning a bit for the boys to stave off the monotony of the road. In terms of the Who on vinyl, Pridden's greatest accomplishment was setting up the gear to tape the concert they'd release as *Live at Leeds*. With limited resources in the refractory of Leeds University where the show took place, he resolved to put an 8-track mobile recording unit in the kitchen below the auditorium, only using a few microphones to limit the degree of sound bleeding between them. Though there were some technical problems resulting from sloppily connected mics, the music Bob Pridden caught that Valentine's Night was potent magic. More recently, he received cocredit with Billy Nicholls on *Endless Wire* for producing Roger Daltrey's vocals . . . a job that never appealed to head producer Pete Townshend.

Jon Astley

When Glyn Johns decided he'd had enough of *Who Are You* and the maniacs recording it, Jon Astley took over. He had the pluses of being a knowledgeable Who fan and Pete Townshend's brother-in-law. Before screaming charges of nepotism, know that Astley was no studio novice. In 1972, he went to work at Olympic Studio after setting aside his ambition to get involved in the film industry. Though he told *Sound on Sound* magazine that he spent his first couple of years at Olympic "making tea," he eventually settled in as Glyn Johns's assistant engineer during sessions for the Eagles, Eric Clapton, Joan Armatrading, and Ronnie Lane and his sister's hubby during the *Rough Mix* sessions. Most importantly, he'd already been working on *Who Are You* when Johns extricated himself from the vocal sessions. Townshend too never hung around for Daltrey's overdubs, leaving Astley with the sage direction "Make sure he sings the right notes," before skipping off to pick up his kids at school. Following a recording hiatus, Johns just stopped showing up to work. Jon Astley found himself in charge and saw *Who Are You* to completion.

Astley went on to produce additional discs for such artists as Eric Clapton, the Pretty Things, Corey "Sunglasses at Night" Hart, and his own sister Virginia. In 1987, he gave his own music career a shot with his debut solo album *Everyone Loves the Pilot (Except the Crew)*, which featured the synth pop nugget "Jane's Getting Serious," later featured in a Heinz ketchup advert starring Friend Matt Leblanc. However, after a second LP, *The Compleat Angler*, Astley got back behind the board, distinguishing himself as a very in-demand mastering engineer, working on reissues from George Harrison, Led Zeppelin, Abba, and the Who.

Bill Szymczyk

Bill Szymczyk, oh, Bill Szymczyk. No soundman has received more guff from Who fans than this man, and it's not because his last name is so tough to decode (it's pronounced "Simzick," incidentally). It's because when Keith Moon died, he had to record a Who that was very, very different from the Who of old. No longer were they guitar-smashing, face-punching, hotel-room-annihilating freaks. They were older, wearier, saddened by the death of their friend, tempered by the soft-spoken fellow now tapping the snare. Roger Daltrey placed most of the blame for the negative reaction *Face Dances* generated on new drummer Kenney Jones. Many pointed their fingers at Bill Szymczyk.

Most of his credits contradict the anarchic brew the Who are famous for stirring. While he cut some rather Who-like records for the James Gang early in his career, most of Szymczyk's work was with B. B. King, one of the slicker bluesmen; soft-popper Elvin Bishop ("Fooled Around and Fell in Love"); and the Eagles, a group that made boring records so polished you could ice skate on them. Most definitely Bill Szymczyk would not have been the right guy to record explosive albums like *My Generation* or *Who's Next*, but the *Face Dances* material was different, more "adult." The Who should have gotten some credit for acknowledging that they'd never be the same without Keith Moon instead of pretending nothing had changed and trying to raise a ruckus as if they were still teenagers. Perhaps "Don't Let Go the Coat" wasn't the most visceral recording, but it is quite beautiful. Townshend and Entwistle's backing vocals throughout *Face Dances* are flawlessly captured.

Recording those vocals was apparently not as pleasing as listening to them. John Entwistle complained about the producer's methodical and inorganic approach, having the singers rerecord their vocals to the point of tedium, then cutting together the best bits virtually note by note. In self-defense against the criticisms lobbed his way, Kenney Jones laid the culpability on Szymczyk too. Townshend, however, has been much more complimentary. But he also likes *Hotel California*, so take that praise with a grain of salt.

6

Guitar and Pen

The Who as Songwriters

There were some great singer-songwriters in the early years of rock 'n' roll. Chuck Berry defined the sound by supercharging the blues and crafting lyrics with a poet's grasp of humor, imagination, and elegant meter. Buddy Holly expanded the form beyond the blues to craft chord figures worthy of Cole Porter that still swung and boogied like Chuck. Bo Diddley, Little Richard, Eddie Cochran, Carl Perkins, Ritchie Valens, Fats Domino, Gene Vincent, Roy Orbison, and Larry Williams all composed classics. Self-composing still wasn't a prerequisite of getting hits, and artists from Elvis Presley to Bill Haley to Jerry Lee Lewis to the Everly Brothers to the Coasters to the Drifters to the Marcels had most of their biggest hits with the songs of others. By the sixties, the pop scene had enough certified hit-making writers—Leiber and Stoller, Pomus and Shuman, Goffin and King, Barry and Greenwich—that the songwriting rocker wasn't particularly necessary.

However, the most enduring groups of the pre-British Invasion sixties, the Beach Boys and the Four Seasons, had ace in-house writers, and once Lennon and McCartney came along to show just how fine pop songwriting could be, the game was changed for good. Now, serious rock bands would always be expected to supply their own songs, and those who couldn't deliver the goods would find their careers cut short.

By the time the Who formed in 1964, the formula was just about in place. The band did not self-compose their first single, released through that little window when mega-mod Pete Meaden was calling the shots and calling them the High Numbers, but when they were back to being the Who and being shepherded by the savvier Kit Lambert, they were expected to keep the potential hits coming. Fortunately, there was a songwriter in the concern who could more than deliver his share, and Pete Townshend would soon rank among rock's greatest ones. The same could not be said of his bandmates, though John Entwistle would certainly write enough terrific numbers to further endear himself to fans and justify a solo career. Roger Daltrey and Keith Moon were less inclined to pick up the pen, though their names appear on the Who's record labels enough times to warrant a closer look.

Pete

Maybe he wasn't quite as melodically inventive as Lennon and McCartney or as harmonically brilliant as Brian Wilson, but Pete Townshend wrote lyrics as imaginative in their own way as Dylan's and was as tuned in to the sneering, swaggering essence of rock 'n' roll as Jagger and Richards. Intellectually, he had them all beat and was the first songwriter of his day to insist that pop music could—no, *should*—be art. That his art of choice was Gustav Metzger's raging auto-destruction and Peter Blake's strikingly graphic pop art made it go down very nicely as raucous, exciting rock 'n' roll. His insistence that, say, baroque composer Henry Purcell influenced his use of suspended chords (see chapter 15) did nothing to undermine the immediacy of "I'm a Boy" and "The Kids Are Alright" since suspended chords are hardly the sole property of Baroque composers. No one would accuse Keith Richards of harboring Baroque pretentions, and the suspended chord is the keystone of his work.

Roger Daltrey may have thought Pete's Townshend's "Happy Jack" sounded like "oompah" music, but it was packaged in a totally cutting-edge picture sleeve designed by Ralph Steadman (seen here in its Italian incarnation). The cartoonist would later forge a fruitful working relationship with famed gonzo journalist Hunter S. Thompson.

Courtesy of the Rob Abramowicz Collection, digitized by Jeffrey Uleau

Regardless of how loftily Pete Townshend portrays his work (Guitar smashing is auto-destructive art! Suspended chords are Baroque pop!), his songwriting tends toward simplicity. His first real Who song, "I Can't Explain," fuses two stock progressions: the main riff reverses the essential rock/blues I-IV-V progression (this song is basically "Louie Louie" backwards), while the bridge leans on doo-wop's standard I-vi-IV-V progression (found in "Earth Angel," "Stand by Me," "Duke of Earl," and well, about half the pop hits released before the Beatles' invasion).

In 1974, Townshend talked of the elevating powers of "little three chord wonders" on Melvyn Bragg's *2nd House*. He usually kept his own wonders similarly simple, even as he is too creative to subject to any sweeping definitions convincingly. "Odorono" shifts between major and minor keys and "Pictures of Lily," "Cut My Hair," and "Daily Records" run-through the whole dictionary of chords. Still Townshend's compositions rarely strayed too far from a more austere harmonic base. Even epics such as "Won't Get Fooled Again," "Love Reign o'er Me," and "Who Are You" spend most of their time skating on three or four chords. "Magic Bus" never leaves G major. Pete does love to trick the ear with the modulations of "My Generation," "La-La-La Lies," "Disguises," "So Sad About Us," "I Can See for Miles," "I Can't Reach You," "Pinball Wizard," and "Pure and Easy," but a modulation just moves the established chord progression up a whole step. It doesn't require constructing a whole new progression.

Townshend still made his simplest songs unique by employing signature touches, such as the suspenseful "Happy Jack" riff, which ascends to an unre-solved sixth before tumbling back down to the root note, allowing the listener's heart to resume beating. Reconfiguring first-position chords (the most elemen-tary chord voicings) by dropping the sixth note or adding the ninth add color to his most straightforward progressions, as do his distinctive use of movable triads (see chapter 3). Such variations from the usual major triads are responsible for the dreaminess of "Tattoo" and make "Melancholia" and "Naked Eye" brood without the easy exploitation of minor keys. They maintain the listener's inter-est without undermining the pop directness that makes Townshend's songs so universally accessible. They are what makes Pete Townshend's songs sound like Pete Townshend songs.

Roger

The member of the Who with the fewest writing credits was the first to receive one after Pete Townshend, and he did so with the second original song the band released. Malcontent Roger Daltrey always seemed satisfied with one aspect of the Who: the fact that Townshend lugged the songwriting burden. In the band's early years, Daltrey wasn't yet convinced the sensitive guitarist could create material worthy of his own machismo. Townshend invited the singer to get involved when it came time to carve their second single during a rehearsal at the Marquee Club. At the time Townshend only had a title and the first verse.

"Here for More" would be the second and last Roger Daltrey solo composition the Who released.

Courtesy of the Rob Abramowicz Collection, digitized by Jeffrey Uleau

Although his involvement has been sometimes downplayed (in 1971, Townshend wrote that Daltrey only helped with the arrangement), Daltrey apparently contributed quite a bit to "Anyway, Anyhow, Anywhere," helping to complete the second verse and writing the bridge. Though the lines he contributed to the verses don't reveal any great lyrical talent ("I can talk anyhow, and get along" particularly lacks force), he did contribute the song's most inspired line— "Nothing gets in my way, not even locked doors"—which suggests the borderline supernatural abilities that best supports Townshend's later claim that he was trying to write a "spiritual song" with "Anyway, Anyhow, Anywhere."

Though the collaboration was a success, supplying the Who with their second top-ten UK hit and their first disc to really capture the chaos of their live act, the experience didn't particularly inspire Daltrey to push for a Lennon/McCartney–style partnership. In 1977, he explained to *Melody Maker*, "I could have written songs for the Who years ago that were alright and would have been recorded just because I wrote it. That's bullshit. If I have a song on a Who album I want it there because it's as good as a song by Pete." Townshend similarly decided that collaboration was not for him, and wouldn't seriously partner up again until meeting Rachel Fuller in the next millennium.

Without his peer's encouragement, Daltrey settled back into his role as singer and shelved any songwriting ambitions. When Kit Lambert called on him to contribute two songs to *A Quick One*, he could only be bothered with one, and one apparently completed with Townshend's assistance. Although few would rank the scanty "See My Way" among the Who's finest two minutes (or 1:54) of vinyl, it is a nice Buddy Holly pastiche that reflects Daltrey's position in the band quite well. Like "Anyway, Anyhow, Anywhere," it is arrogant, almost bullying on the surface, a threat from a guy bent on forcing everyone to share his point of view. However, there is an underlying vulnerability and self-doubt ("Although at times when you kept on I thought that I was mad") that humanizes the singer. The "Peggy Sue"–inspired tune is just as sweet as Townshend's early songs that made Daltrey wary.

Despite the mixed results of loosening up Pete Townshend's writing monop-oly on *A Quick One*, each member of the group once again contributed songs when the Who went to work on their third LP. "Early Morning Cold Taxi," which Daltrey said he'd written in collaboration with Who roadie Dave "Cy" Langston, was a more sophisticated piece than "See My Way," and it was under serious consideration for the record that would become *The Who Sell Out*. However, in *Who I Am*, Townshend claimed that Langston's last-minute confession that he'd written the song all by himself is what kept the track from release in its own time (it has since appeared on *Thirty Years of Maximum R&B* and expanded editions of *Sell Out*). After that, Daltrey only had the gumption to contribute one more song to the Who, a passable country plea for persistence called "Here for More" released as the B-side of "The Seeker." The stock Townshend lick that opens the track (which would reappear in "In a Hand or a Face" and Keith Moon's "Wasp Man") suggests that he got a bit of outside help again.

John

He may not have been as adept or prolific a writer as Pete Townshend, but John Entwistle was as individual. In 1996, he articulated his agenda to *Goldmine*: "I wanted (my) songs to be like no one else was writing." Entwistle was referring to his lyrics, but that uniqueness is equally apparent in the music that accompa-nied his fractured fairy tales. Just as the limitations of his three-string guitar had a profound effect on the uniqueness of Townshend's songs, Entwistle's bass shaped his. The bass is not a very good composing tool. Chords tend to sound like mush on it, so the instrument does not lend itself to formulating a rich harmonic base for a song. It is more useful for creating single-note riffs, which is how Entwistle went about writing songs. That Townshend rarely composed single-note riffs—"Happy Jack" and "Dogs" being a couple of exceptions—helped Entwistle's songs stand out on the Who's records (he'd only ever recycle "Louie, Louie" or "Earth Angel" on his solo albums for purely parodic purposes). That he favored chromatic intervals helped them stand out from most other songwriters, too.

Two of John Entwistle's finest songs, "My Wife" and "When I Was a Boy," were packaged together on a single in Japan.

Author's collection

The chromatic scale consists of twelve pitches moving upward or downward by half steps. Unlike minor or major scales, the chromatic scale is not rooted in a particular key, which makes for an uncertain listening sensation. Since all notes are fair use in the chromatic scale, a progression can take any number of unexpected side trips uncommon in pop music, which tends to rely on major and minor keys. While a major or minor scale riff will likely resolve with the root note, a chromatic riff might just land anywhere. One can play a chromatic riff simply by moving one's fingers up and down the neck of a guitar fret by fret. It's the kind of thing someone might try to play the first time he or she picks up a guitar, or the kind of thing one might improvise if asked to deliver a new song on the spot, as John Entwistle was the day he tossed off "Boris the Spider." He had already submitted his demo for "Whiskey Man," which met with the band's approval, when Townshend asked the bass player if he'd written his second song for *A Quick One.* Entwistle told Townshend that he had and that it was about a spider. He was lying. He had not done his homework, and the creepy-crawly topic was just the first thing that popped into his head. While downing drinks at the Scotch of St. James Club the night before, he and Rolling Stones Bill Wyman and Charlie Watts were cracking each other up by making up silly names for animals. The spider he named in honor of Hollywood's creepiest star lingered in Entwistle's head because he was scared of the little buggers. When

Townshend asked to hear a bit of the song, he moved his fingers down his bass neck chromatically, then rushed home to complete the sketchy idea.

Although he would create another extended descending chromatic progression for "Cousin Kevin," Entwistle couldn't return to that well too often unless he wanted all his songs to sound like "Boris." However, he'd still use chromatic movements to create uneasy passing moments in "Silas Stingy," "Success Story," and "You," contributing as much to the songs' macabre atmospheres as their grim lyrics. In "Fiddle About," he varied the downward riff he hit upon while first improvising "Boris the Spider" by spacing the notes by whole steps instead of half steps, though the grungy tone of his bass gives it very much the same flavor. Such songs bear the stamp of a guy eschewing typical pop progressions by writing on the bass guitar.

Keith

Roger Daltrey had his dubious moments as a songwriter, but most of Keith Moon's "compositions" were outright shams. One could hardly imagine the Patent British Exploding Drummer sitting still long enough to write anything. Yet he has been credited with contributing material to all four of the Who's sixties albums and a couple of B-sides. Closer inspection of the facts reveals how little interest Moon had in songwriting (though he did like the credits). On *My Generation*, he is noted alongside Pete Townshend, John Entwistle, and session man Nicky Hopkins as cowriter of "The Ox," a straight-up rewrite of the Surfaris' "Waikiki Run." "Cobwebs and Strange," one of Moon's two contributions to *A Quick One*, was another rip-off, this one copped from "Eastern Journey," a piece of incidental music from NBC's *Man from Interpol* TV series (funnily, Entwistle would also lay claim to composer Tony Crombie's melody, both when saying he was the true author of "Cobwebs" and when he reused it for "Heinz Baked Beans"). Entwistle insisted that Moon's sole contribution to their "collaboration" on the B-side "In the City" was three words: "And they go . . ." Less suspicious drum and bass collaborations were the incidental commercials on *Sell Out* that Entwistle and Moon composed while knocking back ale at a pub, though pasting "John Mason we got the best cars 'ere" over the "Colonel Bogey March" (famously whistled in *Bridge on the River Kwai*) ain't exactly Gershwin. The admittedly inspired idea of setting Tommy Walker's spiritual retreat at an old-fashioned British holiday camp was Moon's, but he didn't write a note of "Tommy's Holiday Camp" despite Townshend giving the drummer full credit. As previously indicated, Moon's final credit with the Who, the B-side "Wasp Man," is completely built upon a Townshend guitar lick. To his credit, Moon was likely the sole author of the lyrics, which I will now reprint in their entirety:

"Wasp Man. Sting."

Strangely, no one has stepped forward to admit writing the two most sophisticated songs credited to Keith Moon. "I Need You" is an enticingly moody minor key power-popper abounding with his zeal for surf and sarcasm (even his falsetto sounds good on the track). Could he have really written something this melodically and harmonically strong, or something so complete, without the assistance of Entwistle or Townshend? Is the harpsichord tag at the track's end that teases "A Quick One While He's Away" a sly clue that Townshend really did help the drummer write "I Need You"? Townshend reportedly did help the others finish off their *Quick One* songs (which, quite understandably, irked John Entwistle, the only guy who could have written "Whiskey Man" or "Boris the Spider"), but even if Moon merely cowrote "I Need You," even if he only wrote the Fab Four–parodying lyric ("Let us come and sitar with you." Ha!), it is something of an achievement. Less impressive is "Girl's Eyes," Moon's rejected offering to *Sell Out.* It is a sub-bubblegum trifle with a silly lyric for sure, but again, it is a complete song: melodic and with all necessary verses and choruses intact. Even if this was unfit material for the Who, maybe Freddie and the Dreamers could have done something with it. With Townshend having spilled his guts in *Who I Am,* and Entwistle and Moon having exited this mortal coil, we may never know how responsible Keith Moon was for "I Need You" and "Girl's Eyes." Let's just respectfully call him a two-hit wonder and move on to take a look at Townshend and Entwistle's ways with words. . . .

7

A Little Thread

Recurring Themes

S ongwriters with strong visions tend to revisit certain themes obsessively. Brian Wilson and Mike Love were fixated on youth and California. Ray Davies and Bob Dylan regularly tackled social issues. Mick Jagger and Keith Richards had their decadence and disdain. Robert Plant had Dungeons & Dragons and his penis. A writer with an exceptionally clear vision and a tendency toward obsession, Pete Townshend had his pet topics too, and as John Entwistle developed his compositional chops, those subjects often overlapped between the two writers' work, weaving into little threads running through the Who's body of work.

Love

The love song: the go-to topic for lazy pop songwriters in search of a universally relatable topic. In the early days of rock 'n' roll, a song about anything but "boy meets girl, boy loses girl, boy and girl go to the hop" was practically unthinkable. Non–love songs were usually the kind of generic calls to rock 'n' roll that always implied grabbing a partner for dancing or sexing (though there were also a few daft novelties of the "Purple People Eater" variety). When John Lennon and Paul McCartney arrived on the scene to make self-composed songs obligatory for pop groups, they took some three years to branch beyond "I Want to Hold Your Hand"–style sentiments. Before 1966, the less romantic listener had to rely on Bob Dylan for lyrics with more than minimal imagination, and even he trafficked quite regularly in love songs (their domination of 1964's *Another Side of Bob Dylan* offended many of Dylan's most dogmatically politicized followers).

Even after John and Paul realized they could write unromantic pieces with "Nowhere Man" and "Eleanor Rigby," they regularly peddled love songs for the rest of their careers. So did Mick and Keith, Brian and Mike, Bob, and most of the other pop writers of their day. However, once Pete Townshend expanded his horizons beyond love songs, he rarely leaned back on that much-leaned-on topic.

Not that the Who's discography is lacking in love songs. Their first hit single, "I Can't Explain," is, indeed, a love song, though hardly the mushy sort, as was Pete's first song, "It Was You." Now that he'd progressed past such soppy sentiments as "It was you who set my heart a-beating," he started taking a more insightful look at new love. "I Can't Explain" conveys the frustrations of self-expression and paranoia that come with not knowing whether or not one's feelings are reciprocated ("Things you said, well *maybe* they're true") and the adolescent sexuality that would soon feature more prominently in Pete's work (those "funny dreams" probably aren't the dry kind).

With the Who's second single, the braggadocio anthem "Anyway, Anyhow, Anywhere," Townshend had already moved beyond love topics, something no other first-wave British invader could claim of his sophomore single. When he found himself having to compose an album's worth of fresh material for the Who's debut, he continued dealing with the overexploited topic in a more complex way than his peers. Not one of the love songs on *My Generation* is content to express the usual "I love you, you love me, everything's peachy keen" drivel.

Always aiming for loftier ideas, Pete Townshend contended that his love songs were terrible. This is neither accurate nor fair, and the ones he knocked off for the Who's first LP are exceptionally thoughtful and varied. "Much Too Much" expresses how overwhelming love can be for kids too emotionally underdeveloped to handle it. "The Good's Gone" takes an almost nihilistic stance on the end of a romance, while "A Legal Matter" handles that subject in the more comically businesslike way Ray Davies would later perfect in "Sunny Afternoon." "The Kids Are Alright" and "La-La-La Lies" transform the romantic song into something defiant, expressing a love strong enough to survive one's significant other having a dance with one's mate or the slander of jealous parties.

Despite the quality of Townshend's early love songs, it is understandable that an intellectual already working on such unconventional pop material as "I'm a Boy" and "Happy Jack" would have little regard for valentine clichés. His songs that deal with romance on *A Quick One*—"Run Run Run," "Don't Look Away," "A Quick One While He's Away"—are parodic. Only "So Sad About Us" takes the topic seriously, and it does so with uncommon maturity, greeting the end of an affair sadly but without a trace of the macho/juvenile bitterness that tarted up most breakup songs of the period.

Despite Townshend's ambition to extend the pop song beyond its conventions into something operatic, and the year's atmosphere of experimentation, 1967 found him churning out love songs again. *The Who Sell Out* is full of them, though "Odorono," a tale of romantic disappointment and body odor, the slightly surreal "Sunrise," the free-love-celebrating "Relax," and "I Can't Reach You," a spiritually yearning ode that Townshend implies is as much about God as it is about girls, are hardly conventional love songs. The most typical one is "Our Love Was," yet it appealed to love-song-hater John Entwistle, who named it as one of his favorite Townshend songs. Despite categorizing love songs as "repellent" in a 1974 talk with *Rolling Stone*'s Chet Flippo, Entwistle managed one of the Who's more charmingly sincere ones with 1967's "Someone's Coming," a look at young lovers having trysts behind their parents' backs.

Nineteen sixty-seven may have been the Who's year of the love song, but they rapidly shed them as Townshend became preoccupied with grander schemes.

"Rael" lost a love subplot when he whittled it down to six minutes for inclusion on *Sell Out.* "Sensation" began life as a tribute to a woman named Rosie whom Townshend met while touring Australia, but by the time he reworked it for *Tommy*, all romance was gone. The love songs "Mary" and "Greyhound Girl" are two of the few songs he wrote for *Lifehouse* that have never surfaced as Who recordings. "Athena," which he wrote while in the throes of an obsession with actress Theresa Russell, is so lyrically impenetrable that's it's hard to identify as a love song without knowing its backstory. Then when the Who were reborn as a two-piece for the *Endless Wire* comeback album, Townshend contributed one of his purest love songs. Considering that he identified the subjects of "You Stand by Me" as girlfriend Rachel Fuller *and* former foe Roger Daltrey, he apparently still hasn't figured out how to write a boring old conventional love song.

Sex

Contrasting the adultness of his early love songs, Pete Townshend's first songs about sex veered toward the adolescent. Introduced to sex prematurely by one of his grandmother's boyfriends (see chapter 30), his attitude toward sex in song remained in a sort of arrested development for some time. "A Quick One While He's Away" plays like a dirty joke about a "little girl" who has sex with a dirty old engine driver (likely inspired by the 1959 animated TV series *Ivor the Engine*) while her boyfriend is away, but years later its writer would subject the track to a darker and more personal interpretation. While the term "little girl" was rarely used to indicate an actual child in pop songs at the time (see Bo Diddley's "Little Girl," Syndicate of Sound's "Little Girl," the Monkees' "Little Girl," etc.), Townshend now says he was unconsciously writing about the molestation of an actual child in "A Quick One," and the loved one requiring forgiveness at the piece's climax was not a boyfriend but an absentee mother who should have been taking better care of her child, as he wished his own mother had when he was left in the care of his disturbed grandmother Denny.

"Pictures of Lily" takes on a more acceptable adolescent initiation into sexuality: masturbation. A boy dealing with the frustrations of his budding sexuality seeks advice from his father. Rather than blocking out the topic, preaching abstinence, or offering some other unrealistic and unhelpful advice, Dad shares his stash of nudie pics with his son. The relationship depicted in "Pictures of Lily" is highly unusual for a pop song, but child psychologists might argue that it's a healthy one. The parent does not shame his child about his sexual urges and curiosities, nor does he become inappropriately involved in relieving them either. As Dr. Laura Berman wrote in "Having the Sex Talk with Your Kids" (March 26, 2009, Oprah.com), "The secrecy can be more damaging than just telling it like it is."

Townshend says the song was inspired not by a similar encounter with his own father (had he had one, it probably would have gotten a mention in the frank *Who I Am*) but by his own normal adolescent experiences trading dirty postcards with pal John Entwistle. "Lily" was vaudeville star Lily Bayliss, whom Townshend discovered from a card pinned to his girlfriend and future wife Karen Astley's bedroom wall.

Manual stimulation is a less lonesome act in "Mary Anne with the Shaky Hand," though the song—wonderful as it is—is also one of Townshend's silliest. Nearly ten years later, he was still capable of reducing sex to a juvenile joke in "Squeeze Box," with its unsubtle references to breasts ("Mama's got a squeeze box she wears on her chest . . .") and intercourse ("she goes in and out and in and out . . ."), but on the same album, he started addressing the topic in a more adult manner, even as the anxiety-ridden "Dreaming from the Waist" found him expressing just as much frustration as he'd expressed in "Pictures of Lily." On "How Can You Do It Alone," his attitude about sex continues to darken. Surely, this piece tracking the pain of two lonely male masturbators and the liberation of a woman who finds pleasure alone in the bathtub while her mate is left locked out must be pop's most depressing ode to onanism. A few years earlier, John Entwistle composed a similarly morose and unlikely exploration of sex. "Trick of the Light" portrays a john (or is it a John?) anxious that he has failed to please a prostitute, though considering the grim humorist who wrote the song, he

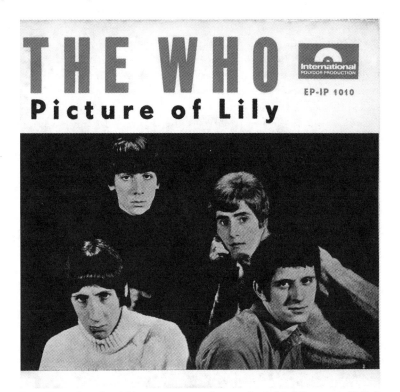

Pete Townshend paid homage to you-know-what with "Pictures of Lily."
Courtesy of the Rob Abramowicz Collection, digitized by Jeffrey Uleau

likely intended it to elicit uncomfortable giggles rather than sober reflection. So with very rare exception—"Love Ain't for Keeping" and "One Life's Enough" being two—sex generally gets a bum rap in the Who's discography. Outside the ranks of those sneering cynics, Pete Townshend has celebrated the subject more healthily in his solo songs "And I Moved" and "A Little Is Enough," which he rates as one of his best.

Youth

As any Chuck Berry fan knows, rock 'n' roll belongs to the young. Few rockers have been as consistently obsessed with the travails of adolescence as the Who, or at least, few have approached them in the same way. Brian Wilson and his multiple lyricists gave voice to the maudlin melodrama of teen romantic anguish brilliantly, though such work was an extension of earlier teen sob stories as told by Little Anthony with "Tears on My Pillow" or Dion with "A Teenager in Love." John Lennon sat at the opposite end of the pole, often writing of his youth so obscurely that "She Said She Said" and "Strawberry Fields Forever" could only be fully understood after reading his biography. Pete Townshend wrote of youth in ways both universal and highly unique, if not always utterly personal. "My Generation" is a sneering rejection of the old guard any put-upon kid could grasp, yet no other pop writer at the time had the nerve to write a line as fatalistic and nihilistic as "Hope I die before I get old"—not Lennon, not Dylan, not even Jagger or Richards. Nor did any writers have so much faith in their fellow youths, or were so comfortable in their own "masculinity," that they could write a lyric like "I don't mind other guys dancing with my girl." Certainly Lennon, the picture of violent jealousy who wrote the demented "Run for Your Life," would never have made a statement like that. The sight of his girl dancing with his buddies probably would have sent Brian Wilson running to his room to bury his face in his mattress in a fit of self-doubt and self-pity. Townshend's earliest visions of youth tossed out the self-absorption of his peers. His songs were about community: teens uniting in revolution against the older generation or romping together in egalitarian spirit.

With two such statements under his belt, Pete Townshend could peer deeper into the teenage heart and mind. While "The Kids Are Alright" scoffed at youthful macho posturing, "I'm a Boy," "Pictures of Lily," and "Tattoo" looked keenly at the desires of and expectations placed on young boys. As previously discussed, "Pictures of Lily" is a bittersweet look at the realities of the adolescent onset of sexual desire. "I'm a Boy" is more obscure, as its story line requires a bit of research to understand (see chapter 15), but this expression of a boy's primal urge to engage in such wholesome activities as playing cricket, leering at his own blood, and coming "home all covered in mud" still rings through, even as the notion that girls can't do the same things (the song relegates them to the kitchen and the beauty salon) is horribly dated. "I'm a Boy" is not just about a boy's desire to pursue his maleness; it vocalizes every child's need to be free of the limitations of adult authority and expectations (Townshend would explore the same theme in a more sexually equitable way in "Join My Gang"; see chapter 17). The freedom to make one's own decisions will always be Pete Townshend's—and rock 'n' roll's—chief political stance, though he added a self-destructive twist. Carl Perkins laid out the rock 'n' roll philosophy by warning, "Don't step on my blue suede shoes"; Pete Townshend rewrote that statement as "I'd rather destroy my own fucking shoes than let you do it." In this way, "I wanna . . . cut myself and see my blood" is as strong a statement of youthful independence as "Hope I die before I get old."

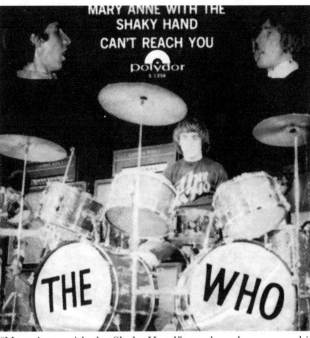

"Mary Anne with the Shaky Hand" may have been a wee bit too sexy for the Dutch; it flopped when released as a single in Holland.   *Author's collection*

"Tattoo" is more subtly declarative than "I'm a Boy." That single looked at a boy yearning to be boyish. "Tattoo" inverts that theme with a hippie teen who prefers looking girlish, much to his dad's consternation ("Only women wear long hair!"), and yearns to be a man at a time before he understands what it really takes to be an adult. Townshend discussed the song's genesis in his 1980 interview with *Oui*: "When I was eleven or twelve, street guys always had a mass of tattoos down one arm. You really felt, 'Jesus, that's gonna happen to me sometime.' It was such a relief when I finally got to be sixteen or seventeen, and you didn't have to do that anymore."

The brothers in "Tattoo" get their arms decorated before having any such similar realizations, and they must suffer beatings from a jealous father and an uptight mother. "Tattoo" is more explicit about oppressive parenting than "My Generation" or "I'm a Boy." The tone is not as defiant or angry. Rather, the narrator seems resigned to the beatings, as if he realizes he's made a rash move and deserves the punishment. Nevertheless, he not only doesn't regret his tattoo but commits to it, getting "tattooed all over" as an adult and even marrying a woman who's "tattooed too." Considering Townshend's attitude about tattoos as things to be dreaded, this is yet another self-destructive expression of personal freedom.

As he grew more distant from his own boyhood, Townshend never stopped looking back at that stage. Through the elaborate story lines of *Tommy* and *Quadrophenia*, Townshend told his own story, even though their rock-opera conceits helped mask their personal natures. It was not Pete Townshend who was being poorly minded by his parents, beaten by his peers, and sexually abused by his "uncle," it was Tommy Walker. It was not Pete Townshend struggling with his sensitivity and searching for enlightenment amidst a swarm of teen thugs, it was Jimmy the quadrophenic mod. Pete Townshend was still trying to come to terms with his own troubled youth when he passed his mid-twenties, but as he approached thirty—the age at which one can no longer be trusted by youthful rock 'n' rollers—a new obsession emerged in his songs.

Aging

Always keenly aware of rock 'n' roll's core ideology and his own relationship to it, Pete Townshend was not one to grow old without a lot of pushing and pulling. However, it was John Entwistle—a guy less clearly self-conscious about enjoying rock's immature and self-indulgent pleasures—who first railed against Father Time. His "When I Was a Boy" does not have the depth of Townshend's songs on the subject, but it does develop on the idea of aging as an enemy introduced in "My Generation" by viewing it from the point of view of a full-grown man. Notably, this is the bassist's first Who song that totally lacks his trademark jokiness, and what "When I Was a Boy" lacks in complexity or poetry, it makes up for in directness: lines such as "When I was five it was good to be alive, but now I'm a man, I wish that I was dead" require no decoding.

The songs Townshend wrote while approaching dreaded age thirty were not quite as direct, but they still left no doubt about his stance on aging. "I know it's all hot air . . . I'll get back to that rocking chair." "Goodbye all you punks, stay young and stay high / Just hand me my checkbook and I'll crawl off to die." All of these lines appear on *The Who by Numbers*, an album often described as Townshend's "suicide note." In *Who I Am*, he wrote that he was not especially suicidal at the time, though rather weary with the entire Who experience and his constant clashes with Roger Daltrey, who selected these particular songs to sing. At the same time, the weariness of a now mature man in a young man's business resonates through these songs. The Who would never embody rock 'n' roll's arrested development as comfortably as say, Mick Jagger, who's still laddish in his wrinkly seventies. Townshend would soon lament how he feels foolish wearing youthful "ripped shirts" ("Slit Skirts") and how his kids "ridicule the bunch" of aging rockers ("Daily Records"). Keith Moon would soon die from his childish excesses. John Entwistle would hide his better, but they too would catch up with him in time. Roger Daltrey had long since hung up his boyish boxing gloves for a more measured adulthood. He and Townshend were always self-aware enough to understand that one cannot remain a kid forever, even in the juvenile world of rock 'n' roll. Tragically, Moon and Entwistle never had that realization.

Excess

The indulgent lifestyles that killed Keith Moon and John Entwistle often loomed in their band's lyrics. The Who's first songs about chemical dalliances tended to be flippant or comical. Their first was "Instant Party Mixture," a doo-wopping Dion spoof in which the guys used cheeky self-edits and Cockney rhyming slang to mask its celebration of pot, pills, and "sausage and mash" (hash). That the track went unreleased in its time probably had more to do with the troubled release of the "Circles" single on which it was to serve as the B-side (see chapter 9) than its drug references. Before pop stars started really opening up about the forbidden subject, the Beatles ("Day Tripper"), Small Faces ("Here Come the Nice"), and the Stones ("19th Nervous Breakdown") all had big hits with songs cagily referencing drug use.

Ironically, it was over-indulger John Entwistle who started writing disapprovingly of indulgence, though not without his glum humor. Though he was no stranger to drunkenness, he did not pursue oblivion as alarmingly as Keith Moon did. Perhaps it was concern for his friend that inspired him to write of an alcoholic's descent into delirium in "Whiskey Man." It's certainly what drove him to write "Dr. Jekyll and Mr. Hyde," a cartoon rendering of how monstrous Moon got when he had enough to drink. The duality exacerbated by Moon's alcoholism—generous and entertaining when a bit buzzed; an abusive beast when totally crocked—moved Townshend to repeat the Robert Louis Stevenson metaphor five-years later in "Doctor Jimmy."

Like Entwistle, Townshend could be both overindulgent and highly critical of indulgence. His affair with hallucinogens ended in 1967 when he had a disturbing hallucination aboard an airplane after taking some superstrong acid cooked up by Owsley Stanley. Witnessing the drug-related deaths of such close friends as Brian Jones and Jimi Hendrix made him all the warier of excess, a sentiment expressed in the moderation-championing "Too Much of Anything." As he slid back into overindulgence in the seventies, Townshend turned his poison pen on himself in "However Much I Booze." Written to commemorate the start of one of his extended periods of abstinence, the song is beautiful yet ruthlessly self-critical. Flawed Pete Townshend may be, but you can never accuse the guy of going easy on himself or making light of his own excesses.

The Macabre

In contrast to Townshend's intellectualism and honesty, Entwistle offers a smirking counterpoint. While Townshend was seeking enlightenment and introspection, Entwistle was digging down into the "black kind of stuff" (*Goldmine*, 1996)

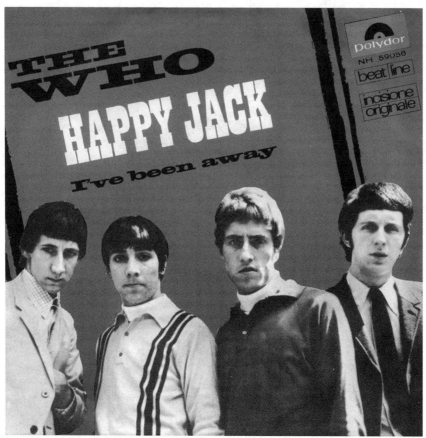

John's Entwistle's "I've Been Away," the tale of a man who plans to murder his own brother as soon as he finishes his prison time, is an underappreciated example of his macabre humor.   *Author's collection*

inspired by his love of horror movies and stemming from his macabre sense of humor. From his twisted imagination came the rubber-room-residing "Whiskey Man," the arachnophobe of "Boris the Spider," the ex-con with fratricide on his mind of "I've Been Away," the husband-hunter of "My Wife," and the all-around misanthrope of "Had Enough." Horrific themes haunted rock 'n' roll from its inception. Records such as Billy and Lillie's "The Monster" and Jackie Morningstar's "Rockin' in the Graveyard" melded the movie genre parents found most objectionable with the music they hated most. Screamin' Jay Hawkins and Screaming Lord Sutch concocted full-on horror personas for themselves, opening concerts by bounding from coffins. Entwistle didn't take the act that far, though he was known to slip into a skeleton suit before taking the stage (see chapter 12). The wackiness of his horror sideshow was at odds with Townshend, who was irked by the "punters'" preference for "Boris." Yet he was aware that

Entwistle's lyrical proclivities could be an asset too, and when he couldn't bring himself to compose the darkest subplots of *Tommy*, he assigned "Cousin Kevin" and "Fiddle About" to Entwistle.

Outsiders

If Entwistle would never write anything as introspective as "However Much I Booze" and Townshend wouldn't write anything as gross as "Boris the Spider," they did have one thing in common: their empathy with outsiders. The loners and losers of the world had not been completely shut out of rock 'n' roll before the Who. In the fifties, teen screwups got their due in the Coasters' "Charlie Brown," and in the sixties, some of pop's biggest stars were making confessions of being outsiders: Brian Wilson with "In My Room," John Lennon with "I'm a Loser," Ray Davies with "I'm on an Island." Sometimes ostracized as a boy because of his looks, the introspective Pete Townshend might have related to such sentiments. Even as "My Generation" and "The Kids Are Alright" trumpeted youthful community, there was "I'm a Boy" and "Little Billy," with its schoolboy shunned because of his weight problem and refusal to smoke, for the kids who weren't totally alright. Tommy spends three-quarters of his rock opera isolated from society by his sense-depriving disabilities and ends it rejected by his followers. *Quadrophenia*'s Jimmy longs to melt into the mod clique, yet he can't quite get the moves down, fretting over his fashionableness and his job as a trash collector, and surmises that his cohorts don't share his self-doubt and spiritual longing. Adults could suffer segregation too, as Townshend explored through the bullied beach bum of "Happy Jack," the b.o.-afflicted starlet of "Odorono," and the fragile villain of "Behind Blue Eyes," so terrified of having his sensitivities exposed. On the profoundly personal *The Who by Numbers*, he allowed himself to be his own outsider character, rejected by the younger generation in "Slip Kid," ostracized by the cool "children of the night" in "However Much I Booze," rejected by unimpressed girls in "Dreaming from the Waist," and fitting in nowhere in "They Are All in Love." But what about your success, Pete? What about your status as a world-renowned rock star? Well, he could feel disconnected from that too, not understanding why anyone would want to buy his "recycled trash" in "They Are All in Love" and plagiarisms in "New Song" from *Who Are You*. On that record, he insists "I'm not a loser" in the devastatingly isolated "Love Is Coming Down," letting it be known in no uncertain terms that he means the exact opposite.

Less of a solitary character than Townshend, Entwistle's offbeat sensibilities are what drove him to create characters isolated from society by their crimes ("I've Been Away"), their mental issues ("Whiskey Man," "Doctor, Doctor"), greed ("Silas Stingy"), lack of humanity ("905"), and anger ("Had Enough"). Unlike Townshend, he didn't have much faith in society, and his songs creep from scorn instead of compassion. In his most explicitly personal song, "The

Quiet One," Entwistle snarls that the problem isn't that he's quiet but that "everybody else is too loud."

Identity

All of the most enduring artists to emerge in the early sixties arrived with strong identities. There may have been little to distinguish, say, the Dave Clark Five or Herman's Hermits from all the other bushy popsters in matching suits, but the Beatles stood out as the wittiest, most charming, and most preternaturally talented of the bushy popsters in matching suits. Andrew Oldham marketed his Rolling Stones as their threatening, sloppily attired antithesis. The Kinks were the leering fops in hunting jackets, the Beach Boys the clean-cut California boys, Dylan the hobo town crier, etc., etc.

The Who had more distinguishing characteristics than any of these bands, with their instrument smashing, iconic poses (The wind mill! The birdman! The microphone lasso!), and four strikingly distinct personalities. That fact never restrained their restless search for an identity. The Who did not become confident of their distinctiveness until becoming "the band with the rock operas" in 1969. Before then they continually tried on and discarded personas like high school kids who'd come back from summer vacation as jocks one year and burnouts the next. The Who might return to school as mods in collegiate sweaters or pop art purveyors in outrageous Union Jack jackets and target tees.

Identity seeking was strong in Pete Townshend's lyrics too. Intellectual and introspective, he was as bent on figuring out who he is as he was on figuring out who the Who were. This theme ties in with his obsession with adolescence, a time when young people undergo the physical and emotional changes that shape the adults they will become. Townshend's lack of passivity drives this theme as it does all themes threading through his songs. "It's Not True" retaliates against the lies a young man's peers spread about him like an angrier, more defiant cousin to "La-La-La Lies." "Substitute" is an anguished confession, an admission of going through the poseur phase that so many young people do while figuring out who they are (*Quadrophenia* would later treat mod as just another youthful phase to be sampled and discarded). As previously discussed, "I'm a Boy" and "Tattoo" also fall into this category, while "Disguises" expresses the frustration of decoding the identity shifts of a significant other.

As the Who matured and stopped experimenting with contrived personas, Pete Townshend continued to confound himself and take journalists to task for using his lyrics to analyze his character in "I Don't Even Know Myself" (Guilty!). "Behind Blue Eyes," a song intended to be sung by *Lifehouse*'s villain Jumbo, is difficult to not read as a confession of the tenderness lying behind Townshend's tough-talking intellectual persona. Despite being the ostensible expressions of the fictional character Jimmy, "The Real Me" and the otherwise Moon-inspired "Doctor Jimmy" also allow Townshend's concerns about his own identity to peek through. That obsession would continue through "However

Much I Booze," "Imagine a Man," and "Who Are You," his most direct quest for self-identification. With "Eminence Front" he turned confrontational, calling out the decadent rich for hiding their true selves behind the status symbols—the speedboats, fancy clothes, ski vacations, and chichi parties—that leave them spiritually bankrupt.

Spirituality

Religion is one of Pete Townshend's main tools for self-understanding. When acid experimentation proved a dead end, he treated his out-of-body hallucination aboard an airplane as a gateway to spiritual discovery. Like George Harrison, who similarly exchanged drug-induced hallucinations for God, Townshend bypassed more conventional Western religions. His choice of leader and guide was the Indian mystic and self-proclaimed "avatar" (i.e., personification of God on Earth) Meher Baba (see chapter 32). Townshend was wise enough to never turn preachy on Who albums (he would save his most explicitly religious statements for his early solo recordings, particularly the prayer-set-to-music "Parvardigar"). "Faith in Something Bigger," his first tentatively religious song, alludes to finding comfort in the idea that God is greater than humans, but ultimately reveals the more self-empowering directive, "We've got to have . . . faith in something big inside ourselves" (however, the idea that the "something big inside ourselves" *is* God remains heavily implied). It's a pretty song, ambiguous enough to not alienate nonbelievers, but Townshend was not remotely happy with his first song to address the Man in the Clouds. "Faith in Something Bigger" lacks the complexity of "Glow Girl," a tale of reincarnation inspired by his air flight traumas, or "Christmas," which asks the practical religious question, "If a guy is deaf, dumb, and blind, and can neither pray nor even know of the God concept, how can he be saved from damnation?" Townshend does not pretend to have an answer to that one.

Townshend's best religious songs are similar to his secular ones: they ask thoughtful questions the writer refuses to resolve with clichés (which may be why he dislikes the fairly clichéd "Faith in Something Bigger"). They never reach smug plateaus; they seek. "Bargain" is about the difficult task of losing his ego to become a better follower of Baba. "Drowned" is Jimmy the Mod's quest for a tributary leading to God. "A Man in a Purple Dress" scornfully questions the peacocking of religious leaders.

"Don't Let Go the Coat" is a rare example of Townshend directing his listeners to God, though he also said it can be interpreted secularly as a suggestion for clinging to anything stable in times of trouble . . . even your "Mum and Dad!" That Pete Townshend is religious does not mean he demands his fans live their lives similarly; that would completely violate his core belief that we should all choose our own paths. In fact, he once lashed out at Ricky Gervais, not for the comedian's atheism, but because he thought Gervais was accusing Townshend of trying to convert him! Townshend even allowed "The Seeker" to be used by comedian Bill Maher in his film *Religulous*, an insightful and very funny documentary questioning religious beliefs. He also gamely played along on "Heaven and Hell," John Entwistle's mockery of religious seeking.

The Business

Pete Townshend is a religious dude, but he also finds tremendous transcendence in the below-the-belt thrills of rock 'n' roll. Celebrating rock 'n' roll has always been an integral theme in the rock 'n' roll song. Bill Haley ("R-O-C-K"), Chuck Berry ("Rock and Roll Music"), Elvis Presley ("Good Rockin' Tonight"), the Coasters ("This Is Rock & Roll"), and countless others sang completely sincere tributes to the great liberator. Townshend's love of the music was equally sincere, though he rarely expressed a sentiment as simple and unselfconscious as "It's gotta be rock 'n' roll music if you wanna dance with me." The Who's songs about rock 'n' roll are self-reflexive, addressing the band's own experiences in the unruly music business. These songs could be very funny, as exemplified by Pete's concert-out-of-bounds recollection "Long Live Rock" and "Guitar and Pen," an underappreciated Gilbert and Sullivan parody about the trials and joys of songwriting, or "Postcard," John Entwistle's wry memoir about touring life. They could also reflect the angst that informs so much of the Who's music. On "Success Story," Entwistle offers an insider's exposé of the rock business and the Who's history in it. On "They Are All in Love" and "New Song," Townshend mercilessly takes himself to task for recycling musical ideas and lashes out at his fans for accepting them. These two poles unite in the lovely "Daily Records," which celebrates and censures the music-making process, at once funny, insightful, and brutally honest. With "Join Together," Townshend managed to hang up his tendency to overanalyze and overthink, and fashioned a celebration of rock 'n' roll as pure and sincere as anything by Chuck Berry.

The Future

Pete Townshend's respect for rock 'n' roll history did not preclude him from exploring and even steering its future. He's no technophobe, as his embracing of synthesizers, laser light shows, the Internet, and digital recording proves. He has spoken of his fondness for the futuristic tales *A Clockwork Orange* and *2001: A Space Odyssey*, both realized for the screen by fellow big thinker Stanley Kubrick. From that fascination with things to come came several of Townshend's conceptual works: "I'm a Boy," "Rael," and *Lifehouse* (see chapter 15 for closer looks at these pieces). John Entwistle conceived his own science-fiction concept more in line with his darker, pulpier sensibilities. In *905*, the world would have been populated by identical beings grown in test tubes . . . because all of the women had been cannibalized by the men. Though this charming tale never saw completion, two of its tracks, the title song and "Had Enough," ended up on *Who Are You*.

8

Hiding Here

A Dozen Underrated Songs of the Sixties

For such a popular band, the Who have a surprisingly small reserve of songs so well known that even the most clueless music listener has heard them. While you'd be hard-pressed to unearth many Beatles songs that might be consider underplayed, the Who's back catalog is rich with them. Sure, the schmos all know "My Generation," "Who Are You, "Pinball Wizard," "Won't Get Fooled Again," "Baba O'Riley," and a dozen or so other "greatest hits," but how many but the most dedicated fans are familiar with such wonderful obscurities as "Melancholia," "Tattoo," and "Naked Eye?" What about the Who's greatest nonhits?

In this chapter, and another you'll cross further along in this book, I attempt to assemble the most beloved Who songs you—or your less Who-savvy associates—have never heard. Since "What does Mike Segretto think are the most underrated Who songs?" is not a frequently asked question, I've made an effort to find out what my fellow fans think are the band's best deep cuts. My criterion for "underrated" was simple: any song that did not appear on the Who's most exhaustive greatest hits compilation, *The Ultimate Collection.* This removed forty songs from the running. I conducted polls on the Who Forum and my personal site, Psychobabble, scoured the Internet for similar polls, and contacted fans directly to get as thorough an idea of the favored underrated tracks as possible. In the end, I'd compiled hundreds of votes covering 115 songs ranging from the relatively obscure (the somewhat sidelined single "Relay") to songs only a nut could love (yes, brethren, there was one vote for "Wasp Man"). Because most fans really seemed to favor the Who's seventies output, I figured it would be fairest to split the final tally by decade to ensure the band's two most prolific periods got their due. There weren't enough votes for their post-seventies tracks to warrant a third list, but I can report that the most popular latter-day underrated tracks are "Daily Records," "One at a Time," and "It's Hard" . . . though they aren't *that* popular.

While these are not necessarily the lists I would have compiled if I hadn't been seeking outside input, I am pleased with the results. This sixties-centric list and the seventies-centric one that follows in chapter 34 give fairly equal attention to all of the Who's core LPs of the sixties and seventies, as well as a nice smattering of underrated singles and outtakes. I'm happy to report that John

Entwistle is represented on each list too. So maybe this will inspire you to make a mix disc (or whatever the twenty-first century equivalent of a mix disc is) for a friend who's sick to death of "Magic Bus" and wants to know what else is worth hearing. Or maybe it will inspire you to dig out that old copy of *Odds & Sods*. However you make use of the following list of underrated favorites, I hope you enjoy the selection. After all, you may have helped choose it!

"The Good's Gone" (1965)

When Pete Townshend first started writing material for him to sing, blues aficionado Roger Daltrey was often uncomfortable with how poppy the songs were. Here's one that must have been right up Rog's alley. With its nagging minor-key riff and lunging beat, "The Good's Gone" is the song that most clearly conveys the early Who's thuggish menace. It is the snarling threat before the inevitable assaults of "My Generation" and "The Ox." It is a breakup song without a single lingering doubt ("I know when I've had enough"), and Daltrey's guttural vocal is chilling.

"Circles" (1966)

"Circles" might not have been eligible for this list had it become the single Shel Talmy intended it to be. When the Who fell out with their former producer, "Circles" fell into the hands of Southampton combo Les Fleur de Lys, who released their recording on the Immediate label in March 1966. The following month, "Circles" sneaked onto *The Who Sings My Generation* in the United States. That version is a fuzzed-out blitz elevated by John Entwistle's Wagnerian French horn. On the flip side of "Substitute," the Who issued Pete Townshend's leaner, cleaner production of "Circles," which would soon be withdrawn, then rereleased on the *Ready Steady Who* EP at the end of the year. No matter what version you prefer (hell, even the Les Fleur de Lys one is great), "Circles" is a heady, yearning love song that deserved to be the hit it was never allowed to be.

"Whiskey Man" (1966)

Who knew the Who had two great songwriters? Well, we all did after Kit Lambert commissioned two original compositions from John Entwistle for the band's second album. Ironically, a ditty he dashed off on the spot about a doomed spider would become his signature song and the most enduring track from *A Quick One*. But the first song he wrote was just as terrific, if not quite as weird. "Whiskey Man" is the eerie tale of an alcoholic and his unhealthy relationship with his imaginary drinking mate (okay, it's still pretty weird). Inspired by the recent western *Ride Beyond Vengeance*, in which Claude Akins had his own Whiskey Man, Entwistle infused the song with a slightly Spaghetti-Western-flavored

Though Pete Townshend's "Happy Jack" anchored this EP in France, the rest of it belongs to a trio of equally quirky John Entwistle compositions, including the underrated fan fave "Whiskey Man."

Courtesy of the Rob Abramowicz Collection, digitized by Jeffrey Uleau

ambience: moody, reverby, snaky. His tortured French horn solo provides the anguish his deadpan vocal never betrays.

"So Sad About Us" (1966)

While "The Good's Gone" was a sneering send-off, "So Sad About Us" is an unusually mature, bittersweet farewell for a sixties pop group. The singer is pained to see his relationship end but understands when a chapter has come to a close. Instead of chiding his soon-to-be-ex for her "rough" love, he concedes their relationship can't go on while admitting that he'll always love her. This sure isn't the kind of sentiment you'd have heard Mick Jagger expressing in 1966! But lest you fear the Who have gone all doughy, they balance Townshend's sensitive lyric with some of their most powerful power pop.

"A Quick One While He's Away" (1966)

Daffy sex song or grim tale of abuse? Majestic mini-opera or last-minute salvage effort? Label it whatever you wish, but by a long shot, "A Quick One While He's Away" is the fans' favorite underrated song of the sixties. The story has been told often (and elsewhere in this very book, as a matter of fact): The Who were short on material for their second album, so Kit Lambert goaded Pete Townshend into stringing together some of his unfinished songs to fashion a mini-opera. This would be the trampoline from which the Who would spring to make *Tommy*, the album that cemented their rock star status and their career, so "A Quick One" has great historical import. It also happens to be an exhilarating way to spend nine minutes. From the dramatic a cappella opening passage through the contrapuntal "You Are Forgiven" climax, this is the Who at their most exciting (well, maybe not the dreary "Soon Be Home" bit), and it would get even more so when they took "A Quick One" to the stage, as evidenced by the Who's jaw-dropping performance of it in *The Rolling Stones Rock and Roll Circus*. John Entwistle's falsetto is a literal highpoint in non-castrati male singing.

"Tattoo" (1967)

Pete Townshend's songwriting had been growing by tremendous bounds since he wrote "It Was You" back in 1964. "Tattoo" is a high-water mark of his flourishing ability. In the span of less than three minutes, he creates a conflicted character, gives him a complete story arc (boy wants to prove his manhood, boy gets tattoo, boy gets thumped by parents, boy grows up to be a totally tattooed dude), and does it all to a backdrop of sublime melody and a gorgeous, elliptical chord structure. Producer Kit Lambert and engineers Mike Ross-Trevor (who handled the early *Sell Out* sessions at CBS studios) and Chris Huston (who handled the later ones at Mirasound and Talentmasters) do right by Townshend's masterpiece by presenting it as an ethereal soundscape. The guys' harmonies have never been captured so magically. Townshend plays his guitar through an organ's rotating Leslie speaker for added psychedelic alchemy. The Who recognized that "Tattoo" was a special track, and it would be the only number from *Sell Out* to regularly feature in their live act throughout their career, receiving much more stage time than the hit single "I Can See for Miles." Despite that, "Tattoo" has never really received its due, failing to find a spot on any of the Who's multitudinous greatest hits collections. As far as I'm concerned, it is their greatest recording, hit or otherwise.

"Our Love Was" (1967)

Pete Townshend thought that much of the material on *The Who Sell Out* was "poor" and "lacked teeth." Fans feel differently. A particular favorite among the romantic fancies sprinkled throughout the album is "Our Love Was." Like

"So Sad About Us," it is a resigned, melancholic, but never bitter breakup song. The lyric is sparse and poetic. The sound is bright, reverby, and spacious, a wide blue sky dappled with white clouds. Then comes one mighty storm as Townshend shatters through the cosmos with a lightning-bolt guitar solo, as nasty and noisy as the rest of the track is light and lovely (this is preferable to the clean solo used in the mono mix, which is more complementary to the dreamy atmosphere but a hell of a lot less exciting). Once again, the group's harmonies are as luscious as anything on *Pet Sounds*. Perhaps its writer is not a huge fan of this particular number, but when *Goldmine* asked John Entwistle for one of his favorite Townshend songs in 1996, the bass player with a penchant for the macabre named "Our Love Was." Perhaps Entwistle really was the closet romantic Townshend painted him as in *Quadrophenia*.

"Sunrise" (1967)

Townshend breaks yet more new ground on this overwhelming fan favorite from *The Who Sell Out*. He'd written "Sunrise" years earlier in an attempt to prove his talents to his mother. Betty Townshend had little to say in response to her son's divine achievement. Bolstered with an arsenal of new chords culled from the teachings of jazz great Mickey Baker, Townshend composed a complex, fluid chord sequence that he fingerpicks with breathtaking mastery on his Harmony twelve-string acoustic. Like "I Can't Reach You" and "Rael," "Sunrise" introduced elements Pete would recycle on *Tommy* (the mid-song interlude would reappear as the intro of "Pinball Wizard"), and like those songs, "Sunrise" is a perfect composition that didn't deserve to be salvaged in such a way. Keith Moon fought to prevent "Sunrise" from being included on *Sell Out* because it bumped his vocal spotlight, "Jaguar," from the album. Who knows why they both couldn't have been included?

"Glow Girl" (1968)

While touring with Herman's Hermits in the summer of 1967, the Who traveled by a rickety charter plane that on at least one occasion had to be landed prematurely when its engines started sputtering. Normally a cool flier, Pete Townshend ended up in a tailspin of obsession, writing song after song about air disasters. Only one of these made it to vinyl and only after considerable delay. The Who recorded "Glow Girl" in January 1968 but held it back, because according to Townshend in his liner notes for the record on which it eventually appeared, "better material came along." The writer ended up recycling bits of the track on *Tommy*: an opening riff plucked for "Sensation," an "it's a girl" refrain given gender-reassignment surgery and revived as "It's a Boy." "Glow Girl" has not been made redundant by those tracks. Its shrieking mid-section—an aural plane crash—is one of the strangest and most moving noise orgies in the Who catalog; the lyric is one of Townshend's most subtle and evocative. A woman's mind strays to the random contents of her luggage, then the random moments of her life, as her plane descends. After impact, she is reincarnated, a happy ending to a harrowing scenario. The story of "Glow Girl" itself had a happy ending when John Entwistle reincarnated it as the centerpiece of *Odds & Sods* in 1974, delighting many fans who've come to appreciate its underrated charms.

"Dogs" (1968)

Long scoffed at as one of the Who's biggest blunders, "Dogs" is finally getting its due from fans. Actually, way back in 1968, Bob Dawbarn of the *NME* tipped the single for the top five and lauded its "tremendous instant appeal." He may have been right about the appeal, but he was dead wrong on the chart placing. Townshend's paean to dog racing and the comfy pleasures of marriage and child rearing only hit #25 on the UK charts . . . which was still one spot higher than the much more fondly remembered "Magic Bus" reached. Because it wasn't progressive, wasn't heavy in the mode of, say, Jimi Hendrix or Cream, "Dogs" has often been dismissed as a bit of silly nonsense released when the Who should have

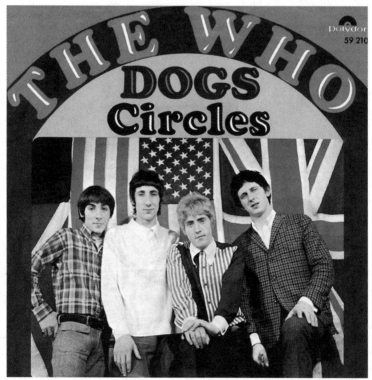

Often dismissed as an embarrassing novelty ditty, "Dogs" is actually greatly appreciated amongst the Who's hippest and most humorous followers.

Author's collection

been getting as serious as their peers. But is it really so unsophisticated? Listen to the winding structure, how its disparate elements—the clip-clopping opening riff, the verses full of thrilling momentum, the powerful sing-along chorus, the nutso spoken-word interludes—fit together. "Dogs" is actually a delightful and surprisingly complex piece of Cockney pop. Sure, *Tommy* and *Who's Next* and *Quadrophenia* were more thoughtful or ambitious or whatever, but the Who never again made music this *fun*.

"Melancholia" (1968)

Case in point there's this item recorded precisely one week after "Dogs." As downbeat as "Dogs" is joyous, "Melancholia" is the darkest song the Who had yet to record, a portent of *The Who by Numbers* seven years ahead of schedule. We got our first taste of this song in 1983 when Townshend included the demo on his *Scoop* compilation. In his liner notes, he wrote, "I'm pretty sure the Who didn't even hear this song." Eleven years later, we learned he was totally wrong. The Who not only heard "Melancholia," but they recorded their own version of it, which finally surfaced on the *Thirty Years of Maximum R&B* box set. The band transformed Townshend's spacey, super-phased demo into an absolute scorcher. More enraged than melancholic, Daltrey reaches for notes he has no business trying to hit and delivers a truly spine-tingling performance. His bandmates bring "Melancholia" to a shattering conclusion, duplicating their live ferocity more convincingly than they had since "My Generation."

"Amazing Journey/Sparks" (1969)

The same year that Pete Townshend was reveling in domestic bliss on "Dogs" and lamenting depression on "Melancholia," he was developing an ambitious project that would render such earthly concerns passé. He had already written a few songs that would wind up on *Tommy*, such as "Sensation" and "Welcome," but the first one he wrote with his revolutionary rock opera specifically in mind was "Amazing Journey." In fact, he considered it as a title track before deciding to just name the damn thing after its main character. "Amazing Journey" would have served as a fine title track, because it maps out the story line more explicitly than any other *Tommy* track. Musically, it encapsulates the record's sounds too: the gentle movable acoustic guitar figure of its opening, the light psychedelic touches of its backward tapes, then the powerful instrumental feats of "Sparks," a riff recycled from "Rael" from the previous LP. Here Entwistle completely cuts loose on disc for the first time, introducing record listeners to the dynamics the Who would continue to develop on the heavier, more improvisational recordings they'd make in the seventies.

To be continued . . .

9

We (Don't) Got a Hit

The Flop Singles

In the United States, the Who were never really a singles band. They only managed to slip a disc into the top ten once when "I Can See for Miles" crawled to *Billboard*'s ninth position in late 1967. The group fared so poorly in the world's biggest pop market that when it came time to compile their singles for the United States in 1971, Pete Townshend wanted to title the collection *The Who's Greatest Flops*.

In their home country, the story was quite different. From 1965's "I Can't Explain (#8) to 1981's "You Better You Bet" (#9), the Who were regular visitors to the upper regions of the UK singles charts. They even got as far as #2 with the unlikely quirk of "I'm a Boy" (which, even unlikelier, claimed the top spot of the *Melody Maker* chart). Not every single the Who put out performed so well. Quite a few missed the top forty altogether on both sides of the pond. Even in Europe, the following fourteen 45s truly do qualify as the Who's greatest flops.

"I'm the Face" b/w "Zoot Suit" (1964)

After Meaden the Mod modishly rechristened the Who as the High Numbers, he needed a cool couple of numbers that would really sell his boys to the In Crowd. Not a songwriter himself, he settled on the ol' five-finger discount, slipping his sticky fingers into the repertoires of other artists and writing new lyrics resplendent in mod jargon. From blues elder Slim Harpo he swiped "I Got Love If You Want It," which became "I'm the Face." From Detroit soulsters the Dynamics, he stole "Misery," rewriting it as "Zoot Suit."

Released on the Fontana label in the summer of '64, "I'm the Face" b/w "Zoot Suit" tanked. Pete Townshend chalked up its failure to self-consciousness, which the two sides have in spades. "I'm the Face," with its references to "faces" (top mods) and "tickets" (bottom mods), probably came off as poseur-ish to its intended audience and had little meaning to the unconverted. "Zoot Suit" reads like catalog copy ("zoot suit jacket with side vents five inches long"). The performances are slick, smooth R&B, confident and professional but lacking the anarchic electricity of the singles that followed when the High Numbers reclaimed their former name.

"I'm the Face" b/w "Zoot Suit" was unable to capitalize on mod's first wave in 1964. It did better when rereleased on Back Door Records amidst a mod revival in 1980. That time it managed to get as high as #49 on the UK charts—still not high enough to shake its flop status.

"The Kids Are Alright" b/w "The Ox" (1966) and "La-La-La Lies" b/w "The Good's Gone" (1966)

Kit Lambert and Chris Stamp's decision to hitch the Who to Shel Talmy's star must have seemed like a shrewd idea at the time. He'd produced "You Really Got Me," a big hit for the Kinks that Pete Townshend admired so much he attempted to rip it off and ended up with "I Can't Explain." Perhaps more importantly, at least from the business side, the producer had an ongoing relationship with Decca Records in the United States that made placing the records a breeze. In the United Kingdom, his productions would be released on the Decca-owned Brunswick label.

Lambert, Stamp, and the band soon came to regret their deal with Talmy. Their five-year contract left the producer with total control in the studio and ownership of the recordings. Artistically, he proved to be a great match for the early Who, translating the rawness of their live act to tape by maxing out the volume, resulting in a crushing, noisy, dense sound, but the contract favored his interests so completely that the band understandably wanted out and right away. That the old farts at Decca neither understood the Who nor showed any interest in presenting them with the respect they deserved (see: *Magic Bus—The Who on Tour*) made the deal all the more sour.

When Talmy proved unwilling to let the Who out of their contract and became determined to release his production of "Circles" b/w "Instant Party Mixture" as their next single, they were forced to break the agreement themselves. In a baffling scheme to coax Talmy into court, the Who released a Pete Townshend–produced remake of "Circles" on the B-side of their latest single, "Substitute," also produced by Townshend, on Robert Stigwood's Reaction label. As expected, Talmy called for an injunction against the single on the grounds of copyright infringement. Legally banned from the recording studio while the injunction was in effect, and in need of keeping new product flowing in the public bloodstream, the Who decided to rerelease "Substitute" with a new B-side, an ominous, jazzy instrumental by the Graham Bond Organisation called—quite pointedly in reference to Shel—"Waltz for a Pig." Three days later, the injunction was lifted.

Talmy got in his own licks when he started mining *My Generation* for competing singles to release on Brunswick. The first of these, released a week before the rejiggered "Substitute" single, performed reasonably well. The appropriately litigious "A Legal Matter" got as high as #32 in the United Kingdom. On the flip was Talmy's original production of "Circles" mislabeled as "Instant Party."

Keith Moon blamed the sloppy stagehands at Polydor for this particular bungle. Fortunately for our heroes, the record had no discernable effect on "Substitute," which made it to #5 on the UK charts. No surprise since it was more powerful and purposeful than "A Legal Matter," an excellent tune in its own right, though one sung in Pete Townshend's comparatively noncommercial, adenoidal croon.

Talmy kept up his little Shel game with the next two Who singles. Two weeks before they released "I'm a Boy," he released "The Kids Are Alright," his most cagily commercial choice. Yet this one fared even worse than "A Legal Matter," only reaching #41, while "I'm a Boy" soared as close to the top of the charts as the Who would ever get. When Talmy's third single, "La-La-La Lies," failed to put the slightest bump in the flight of "Happy Jack" to its destination at #3, Talmy conceded that his attempt to capitalize on increasingly old-fashioned-sounding recordings was neither lucrative nor a significant irritant to his rivals. However, he had the last laugh when his out-of-court settlement with the Who left him with a 5 percent piece of their pie for the remaining five years of their contract.

"The Last Time" b/w "Under My Thumb" (1967)

When the age of chemical experimentation exploded in mid-sixties London, Donovan was the first pop star the Blue Meanies busted. The cops found nothing more than a smidgeon of grass on Don, and the charges evaporated. No matter. The law had bigger game in mind.

At the time, no band better represented pop's disgusting decadence than the Rolling Stones, regardless of the fact that they were no deeper into drugs and orgies than the Fab Four. In fact, according to Simon Wells's *Butterfly on a Wheel: The Great Rolling Stones Drugs Bust*, Mick Jagger didn't even sample acid until well into the psychedelic era on February 12, 1967. As it turned out, he would have done well to prolong his abstinence.

A few weeks earlier, a reporter from the *News of the World* had been trolling through London's swingingest spots in search of zonked pop stars to feature in the paper's series exposing drug use in the music world. That's when they came across a Rolling Stone at Blaises in Kensington. He unabashedly snacked on a handful of Benzedrine in their presence and invited everyone over to his flat to puff some hash.

On February 5, the *News of the World* published its exposé on Mick Jagger. Only problem was, the daft reporters hadn't been chatting with Mick at Blaises; they'd been chatting with Brian Jones. Jagger pursued a libel suit. *The News of the World* resolved not to take such retaliation from the scruffy little sod lying down. When the paper received a tip-off that Jagger and Keith Richards were planning a little acid soiree at Richards's country house, Redlands, senior reporter Trevor Kempson snitched to the fuzz.

Jagger's first experience with acid had been pleasant. He spent the day romping on the beach with his girlfriend, Marianne Faithfull, Richards, art dealer Robert Fraser, Fraser's gentleman's gentleman Mohammed Jajaj, photographer Michael Cooper, and friends Christopher Gibbs and Nicky Kramer. Also in tow was Richards's driver, a Belgian named Patrick, whom Richards believes was the snitch who tipped off the *News of the World*, and drug dealer David "Acid King" Schneiderman, who was apparently in cahoots with the cops.

After playing on the West Wittering shore for a half hour or so, the party retired to Redlands, where they zoned out while Richards spun the Who's latest LP, *A Quick One*, at full blast. When the record ran its

The Who's hearts were in the right place when they covered "The Last Time" and "Under My Thumb" to help out Mick Jagger and Keith Richards, but good intentions couldn't make it a hit.

Author's collection

course, he dropped Dylan's *Blonde on Blonde* on the turntable. A short time later he heard a rapping on the door.

What the police found wasn't nearly as lurid as the *New of the World* would later report. Jagger had four pep pills in his jacket pocket. Marianne Faithfull was wrapped in a rug after taking a bath, but she was not doing anything untoward with a Mars Bar. There were a few roaches. The biggest find were the heroin tablets in Fraser's possession. What wasn't found was Schneiderman's massive drug supply stored in a case he prevented the cops from examining by claiming it was filled with unexposed film.

While the case against Fraser was legit, Jagger and Richards (charged for allowing cannabis smoking on his property) were raked over the coals because of their reputations. The *News of the World* took particular pleasure in the crucifixion. What the paper hadn't counted on was the tremendous outcry in support of the unfortunate Stones, particularly in the pop world. Mike Nesmith and Peter Tork of the Monkees, the most seemingly family friendly (and, therefore, the most subversive) of contemporary acts, appeared onstage at the Wembley

Empire Pool wearing black armbands to get the message out. The decidedly un-family-friendly Who jumped into the fray too.

The *News of the World* had already fingered Townshend in its inflammatory "Pop Stars and Drugs: Facts That Will Shock You" series. Since he was already a big Stones fan, he now had two good reasons to fight back.

The Who wasted not a second organizing their counterattack. On June 28, 1967, the day before Jagger and Richards were to learn their fates, the Who gathered at De Lane Lea Studios to record a benefit single to support their peers in rocking and drugging. John Entwistle had just embarked on his honeymoon aboard the *Queen Elizabeth*. When he was awoken at three in the morning to field a shore-to-ship call, he assumed someone back home had bit the dust. When he learned the call was to obtain permission to put out a single of the Who performing Jagger/Richards's "The Last Time" and "Under My Thumb" with Townshend on bass, he responded—understandably annoyed and groggy—"The Who could release LSD into the Nation's water supply for all I fucking care."

On June 29, Jagger and Richards were found guilty. Jagger received a three-month sentence. Even more outrageously, Keith was to be put away for a full year. The next day, Track Records published an advert in the *Evening Standard*: "The Who consider Mick Jagger and Keith Richards have been treated as scapegoats for the drug problem and as a protest against the savage sentences imposed on them at Chichester yesterday, The Who are issuing today the first of a series of Jagger/Richards songs to keep their work before the public until they are free to record again themselves."

Fortunately for the Stones, Jagger and Richards got bail a week later and were ultimately vindicated after William Rees-Mogg, the ultraconservative editor of *The Times*, put the madness in perspective by speaking out in favor of Jagger (while forgetting to mention the lower-profile Richards) in his famous "Who Breaks a Butterfly on a Wheel?" editorial on July 1. Unfortunately for the Who's charity act/publicity stunt, it instantly took the wind out of the "Last Time" b/w "Under My Thumb" single, which was, in all fairness, not up to the standards of the Who's usual stellar singles. The performances were certainly feisty with plenty of punk spirit, but the ragged, rushed recording situation was evident, and Townshend was no Entwistle on the bass. The record stalled at #44 on the UK charts, and the Who never needed to cut another Jagger/Richards composition as the Court of Appeal exonerated the Glimmer Twins on July 31, 1967.

"Love Reign o'er Me" b/w "Water" (1973) and "The Real Me" b/w "I'm One" (1974)

Frustrated with a label so disrespectful of their singles that it hacked 8:33 of "Won't Get Fooled Again" down to 3:38, the Who started losing interest in being a singles act in the seventies and were all but through with it by 1973. Over the first three years of the seventies, they put out the last of their exclusive A-sides:

"The Seeker," "Let's See Action," "Join Together," and "Relay." Only "Join Together" charted particularly well on both sides of the Atlantic (UK #9, US #17). The rest missed Britain's top ten, and "Relay" just missed the top twenty. In 1973, the Who released their last exclusive B-side on the flips of "5:15" in the United Kingdom and "Love Reign o'er Me" in the United States.

The Who's floundering state on the singles charts had nothing to do with flagging interest in the band. In fact, they were more popular than ever, particularly in the once elusive United States. None of their postsixties albums of fresh material missed the top ten in the States, and only *It's Hard* missed it in the United Kingdom, where it still rose to a respectable #11.

The times were really to blame. The release of *Sgt. Pepper's Lonely Hearts Club Band* way back in June 1967 had been the first major blow against the rock singles market. Now bands became far more invested in making great, artful records, and most ceased to release exclusive singles. Singles were largely left to the teenyboppers, and anyone who heard their tunes exclusively through the AM dial in the seventies may have had no idea how rich the decade was in great music. Serious rock fans spread open their wallets to invest in excellent LPs by the Who, the Stones, Van Morrison, and Led Zeppelin, who so disdained the singles market that they never released a single one in their home country. Everyone else had to make due with—get your airsick bag—the Carpenters, the Partridge Family, Tony Orlando, Donny Osmond, Ray Stevens, and John Denver.

I'm being flippant. There were some great singles in the seventies, and some great pop artists who thrived on the singles charts (I'm thinking of such folks as Elton John, Wings, Stevie Wonder, and yes, the Stones). But without a doubt, LPs were where it was at. So when MCA started pulling singles from the Who's #2 hit LP *Quadrophenia*, the public simply didn't need them. "5:15" managed to make it to #20 in the United Kingdom, but the US singles of "Love Reign o'er Me" (#76) and "The Real Me" (#92) performed pathetically. What's more, such serious and seriously heavy items sounded well out of place amidst the dross littering radio in '73 and '74.

"Postcard" b/w "Put the Money Down" (1974)

The same held true when MCA tried to yank a single from *Odds & Sods*, although its failure may have been down to the choice of song instead of how many people owned the compilation (which didn't do quite as well on the charts as the Who's current albums of new material). "Postcard" is, indeed, a fun travelogue of the Who's roadwork, penned with the droll wit we've come to expect from John Entwistle. Thing is, the track isn't very catchy and has no chorus to speak of. Released in November 1974 to compete with the commercial likes of Bachman-Turner Overdrive's "You Ain't Seen Nothing Yet," John Lennon's "Whatever Gets You Through the Night," and Billy Swan's "I Can Help," "Postcard" didn't stand a chance.

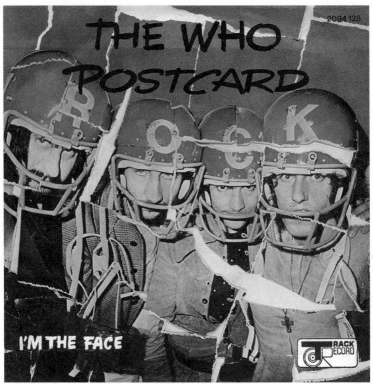

"Postcard" was the first John Entwistle composition released as an A-side in the United States and Europe. Shame it flopped.

Courtesy of the Rob Abramowicz Collection, digitized by Jeffrey Uleau

"Slip Kid" b/w "Dreaming from the Waist" (1976)

As the Who's interest in singles continued to wane, so did their labels' interest in giving them a push. When pulled from the otherwise despondent *Who by Numbers* in late 1975, the jolly, mildly smutty "Squeeze Box" easily made the top twenty in the United States and United Kingdom on its own catchy merits. The somewhat more complex "Slip Kid," released as a US single in August 1976, didn't fare nearly as well. The Who thumbed their collective nose at a single released so long after the album from which it was taken. MCA didn't bother to promote the single, even as the label released it for the sole purpose of boosting *By Numbers'* flagging sales. In the end, the "Slip Kid" single didn't make so much as a thumbprint on the charts and was passed over by Track in the UK altogether.

"Trick of the Light" b/w "905" (1978)

Yet MCA still wasn't happy to content itself with a single obligatory single per album. Once again, the first single from a new Who album did quite well on the charts, as the severely edited version of "Who Are You" made the top twenty in the two main pop markets in 1978. This slighter edit of Entwistle's "Trick of the Light" wasn't a terrible choice for a follow-up. It is one of his catchier songs, though in a year dominated by falsetto-fueled Bee Gees disco and sappy pap by Anne Murray and Neil Diamond, "Who Are You" was already pushing into uncommercially heavy territory. That song did have an unbelievably infectious chorus sung in falsetto harmony that would have made Barry, Robin, and Maurice envious. "Trick of the Light" was too uncompromisingly heavy, too mean. With the usual lack of promo for a sophomore single from a Who LP, it was bound to fail. And that's just what it did.

"Don't Let Go the Coat" b/w "You" (1981)

The farce continued after Keith Moon died and the Who reconvened with Kenney Jones to record *Face Dances*. Single number one, "You Better You Bet," muscled its way to #9 in the United Kingdom and #18 in the United States, no doubt aided and abetted by its regular rotation on the all-new MTV network. On MTV's premiere date, August 1, 1981, it was the fourth video to air right after the Buggles' "Video Killed the Radio Star," Pat Benatar's "You Better Run," and Rod Stewart's "She Won't Dance with Me." If my memory serves me well, the second single from *Face Dances* also received a good amount of play on MTV in the days when it was so desperate for clips that half of them showcased Rod Stewart's spandexed ass. Like "You Better You Bet," "Don't Let Go the Coat" was a slickly produced, radio-friendly, and rather lovely pop song, and like "You Better You Bet," the video came from the same black-and-white filming session (which also produced a promo for the album track "Another Tricky Day"). Unlike "You Better You Bet," "Don't Let Go the Coat" flopped.

"Eminence Front" b/w "One at a Time" (1982) and "It's Hard" b/w "Dangerous" (1983)

The Who's recent spate of big-hit freshman singles ended with the release of *It's Hard*. The lush, mature, and perhaps too reserved "Athena" only made it to #28 in the United States and #40 in the United Kingdom. With MTV becoming an increasingly important promotional tool, there was really no excuse for the failure to support the single with a video. Still, a video didn't help "Eminence Front" much when it was released as a single in December. With its very-eighties synthesizers and a lead vocal by Pete Townshend, who'd recently had a big solo hit with "Let My Love Open the Door" in the States, the track was a fairly commercial one, but the whole Who enterprise had wound down at that point. That same month, the band played their "farewell" concert at Toronto's Maple Leaf Garden. With that, the already flagging promo machine ground to a halt. When released as a single the following February, the middling title track of the Who's "final" album didn't have a shot in hell.

"Twist and Shout" b/w "I Can't Explain" (1984)

Ahhh, but *It's Hard* wasn't the final Who album, now was it? Two years after the band stopped functioning, MCA cashed in on its tapes of the Toronto finale, which made up the bulk of the live *Who's Last*. Dull in its own right, and downright pointless in the shadow of *Live at Leeds*, the album flunked on the charts (UK #48, US #81), and the accompanying single of the Entwistle-sung cover of the Beatles' cover of the Isley Brothers' "Twist and Shout" went only as high as #87 in the United Kingdom.

"Real Good Looking Boy" b/w "Old Red Wine" (2004) and "It's Not Enough" b/w "Tea & Theatre" (2006)

And so, with the exception of the odd reissue, the Who took a twenty-year hiatus from the singles market. In 2004, they broke it with their first original studio recordings since *It's Hard*. By that time, the band had sadly been reduced to a two-man operation by John Entwistle's death, but there was still some of the old Who spark in the pretty "Real Good Looking Boy." Yet their former troubles on the UK singles charts continued to dog them in an era when radio was increasingly dominated by hip-hop and insipid teen pop (despite the late George Harrison's "My Sweet Lord" going to number one for a *second* time in 2002). So "Real Good Looking Boy" did not chart even as the compilation on which it appeared, *Then and Now*, went top five in England. *Endless Wire*, the first LP of original studio recordings in twenty-four years, continued the new Who's success on the LP charts (UK #9, US #7), though the accompanying single, "It's Not Enough," had no real commercial impact. The Who's reign as a singles group was obviously done for good, but then the single had long since ceased to be a rock 'n' roll medium.

10

You Stand by Me

The Cronies

B ecause the four members of the Who were so often at each other's throats, they tended to look outside the group for companionship while on the road, at work on new projects, or during their time off. Their cronies helped keep them sane (well, relatively sane) and often helped direct their story and the telling of it.

Richard Barnes

For much of Pete Townshend's tumultuous life, the patience, understanding, and encouragement of Richard Barnes were a comforting constant. Since the two became roommates in early 1963, the cat Townshend affectionately calls "Barney" has been one of the Who's key photographers, chroniclers, and champions. It was Barney who shouted out "the Who" during a pivotal band-naming brainstorming session.

Townshend became tight with Richard Barnes after his first college roommate, Tom Wright, was ejected from school for pot possession. Barney, a peer at Ealing Art School, took Wright's spot in the flat on Sunnyside Road. When Townshend and Barney were kicked out of the flat, they holed up together in a van for a while before admitting defeat and moving into a five-room apartment above Townshend's parents on Woodgrange Avenue.

Despite being in such close proximity to mater and pater Townshend, Pete and Barney maintained their bohemian lifestyle: smoking dope, blasting records, entertaining mates, flapping their jaws about art and politics, and dumping rubbish all over the joint until Pete abruptly fled to new manager Kit Lambert's posh flat on Eaton Place in Belgravia.

Although Townshend and Barney were no longer sharing space, they continued to be tight for a time. As the Who's schedule became busier, and Townshend started running in more glamorous circles, Richard Barnes fell by the wayside for a couple of years. In 1967, they reconnected over a mutual appreciation for Meher Baba. Atheist Barney was more impressed by how "The Master" lightened Townshend's mood than any of the more ethereal aspects of his teachings.

From this point, Townshend often used his friend as a valuable sounding board for his ideas. Barney also became a dedicated collector of the band's memorabilia and stories, cowriting *The Story of Tommy* with Townshend in 1977. In 1982, Barney published *The Who: Maximum R&B*, the first great visual document of the band's first two decades, which received effusive praise from no less an authority than Pete Townshend, who never shied from deeming his friends' work "shit." Barney had always been similarly honest, and in 1980 Townshend actually gave his old friend a house in exchange for joining him on the road and letting him know when he was slipping out of control, which was not infrequent. Richard Barnes has since worked as the codeveloper of Townshend's *Psychoderelict* concept and compiled and authored the acclaimed photo-history *Mods! Over 150 Photographs from the Early '60's of the Original Mods!*

Irish Jack Lyons

He was just a face jiving at the Goldhawk Social Club in 1964 when Jack Lyons received his first aural punch in the face from the Detours. Though the band was not yet waving the mod flag, Lyons was hooked. The ace face led his band of mods backstage and began chatting with Pete Townshend, who wanted to know why these natty pill poppers were so impressed with his ensemble. "I can't explain" was the gist of Lyons's reply. Townshend now had the idea for his first great song, not to mention a new friend and booster. When Kit Lambert met Jack Lyons, he responded to the scrawny lad's thick Cork brogue and knighted him "Irish Jack." That name would become familiar and dear to Who fans because he was their most vocal member.

From inadvertently inspiring the Who's inaugural hit to being the alleged model for Jimmy of *Quadrophenia* and the counterfeit-ticket scalper of "Long Live Rock," Irish Jack buzzed around the Who's inner circle like a bumblebee pumped with purple hearts. While his fave band ascended to stardom, he kept himself salt of the earth as a bus driver and postman. He has also established himself as a colorful raconteur, imparting his expertise on mod life and Who history, copenning the essential *The Who: Concert File* with Joe McMichael in 1998. On his spotlight section of The Hypertext Who, he has generously shared numerous tales of the 'Oo, reminiscing about his legendary nickname, meeting Kit Lambert and Chris Stamp, and taking a bad acid trip in the company of Jimmy the Mod-portrayer Phil Daniels.

Nik Cohn

The critic is often the sworn enemy of the rock star, cowering behind the safety of his typewriter while spooling off opinions without having any clue what it's like to actually tread the boards of a stage, toil in a recording studio, or even write a song. The rock star is a doer, the critic a blatherer.

As a doer *and* a blatherer, Pete Townshend has a special place in his heart for the critics and an extra special one for Nik Cohn. At a time when rock criticism generally entailed insights like "Commercial sounding; should top the charts," Cohn took his often brutal, often clueless criticism ("The White Album" is "boring almost beyond belief"? Dylan is a "minor talent"? *The Who Sell Out* is "a failure"?) as seriously as Townshend took making the music the critics criticized. Cohn's work appeared in such periodicals as the *New York Times*, *Queen*, the *Observer*, and *New York* magazine. In 1969, he published *Awopbopaloobop Alopbamboom: Pop from the Beginning*, one of the first serious studies of rock's still nascent history. That same year he was giving Pete Townshend feedback on his first full-length rock opera. When Cohn criticized *Tommy* for lacking humor, Townshend took that fair evaluation and went to work on a key song the critic was sure to appreciate. He and Cohn loved hanging out in arcades and challenging each other to pinball duels. As an in-joke and a bit of relief from all the heavy spiritualism, Townshend made Tommy Walker gain fame for his extrasensory gaming expertise. Tommy was now a "Pinball Wizard," as Cohn dubbed the best flipper flippers. Townshend not only won himself a good review from the tough-to-please critic, he scored the Who another huge hit. Nik Cohn's efforts to script *Lifehouse* and *Rock Is Dead . . . Long Live Rock* were less fruitful. The critic easily redeemed himself after those nonstarters with his 1976 *New York* magazine article, *Tribal Rites of the New Saturday Night*, which would inspire the monster hit movie *Saturday Night Fever* the following year. That the article was basically a complete work of fiction did nothing to hurt the film's mega success, and it remains his biggest claim to fame. Who fans are free to disagree.

Chris Charlesworth

Chris Charlesworth was another journalist who managed to get sucked into the Who's inner circle. As a staff writer for *Melody Maker*, he wrote extensively about the band and became a close associate of the group after the Who's PR man, Keith Altham, proffered an introduction. When Townshend was writing his "Pete Townshend Page" for the *MM*, it was Charlesworth's job to pick up the latest column from the guitarist's abode on Eel Pie Island, where he often found himself welcomed at the family table and enjoying a cuppa tea with the Townshends. In 1982, Charlesworth published a brisk illustrated biography simply titled *The Who* with Omnibus Press. The following year he became the press's editor, and has now been overseeing high-quality music-related books for over thirty years. In the early nineties, Townshend put Charlesworth in charge of *Thirty Years of Maximum R&B*. After producing, compiling, and composing a timeline for the box set, Charlesworth went on to coproduce the major reissue campaign of the Who's back catalog that continued through the decade.

Neil Boland

After John "Wiggy" Wolff was promoted from driver to production manager in 1967 (see chapter 4), Keith Moon was back in danger of getting behind the wheel. Instead he hired kindly Cornelius Boland to pilot his Bentley around town.

Neil, as he was known to loved ones, was a Tipperary, Ireland–born cabbie whose reliable service led to permanent employment with Keith Moon. As was the case with everyone in Moon's employ, Neil's chores extended beyond anything in his previous experience. He was Moon's bodyguard, his minder, and his friend. Although Neil cared about Moon, he was unprepared for the 24-hour-a-day job his position became. Longing to spend more time with his baby daughter, Michelle, Neil gave his three weeks' notice on January 2, 1970.

Two days later, Neil was once more doing what he did, chauffeuring Moon, his wife Kim, "Legs" Larry Smith of the Bonzo Dog Doo-Dah Band, and Smith's girlfriend Jean Battye to the Carnbourne Rooms in Hatfield. Moon would be the guest of honor, opening a new discothèque.

What happened that night has been a matter of some contention, but the outcome is not. Neil Boland was run over and killed by the very car he'd been driving for the past three years.

The most common version of events, recounted in the first edition of Tony Fletcher's biography *Moon*, laid the blame at the feet of skinheads, claiming that when the entourage arrived, they discovered the place to be overrun by the bald hooligans. Skinheads were a sort of new offshoot of the mods; working-class kids who so despised hippie ideals that they shaved their heads to stand out from the longhairs. Instead of favoring the kind of electrified, jammy rock the Who played, the skins preferred Afro-Caribbean ska—ironic, considering that a sizable segment of their populace hated anyone who wasn't white.

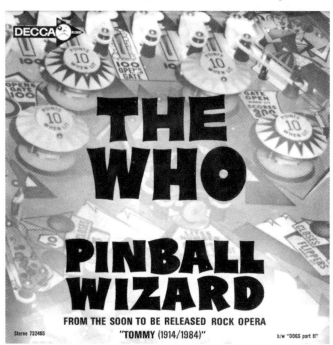

With their hatred for hippies, immigrants, and the wealthy came violence. Despite Keith Moon's own complete lack of hippie ideology and his history in former-mod poster boys the Who, the skinheads may have seen him as another rich pop star who deserved to get whacked down several rungs.

In this version of the story, the bad vibes finally boiled over when

If it wasn't for Pete Townshend's pinball-playing, record-reviewing buddy Nik Cohn, Tommy Walker probably never would have been a Pinball Wizard. *Author's collection* the discothèque shut down at 10:30 that night. After a small skirmish broke out between Moon and a skinhead, he, Kim, and Neil made a quick getaway to the Bentley (disturbed by the atmosphere, Smith and Battye were already waiting in the car). A mob descended on the car: some well-meaning fans, some skinheads. The more antagonistic element pelted it with rocks and coins. That's when Boland stepped out of the Bentley, apparently to force a path through the throng. The car suddenly lurched forward. Neil fell under the tires and died. Keith Moon was believed to be behind the steering wheel.

Although Moon pled guilty to the charges, another version of the story suggests he may not have been. Unconvinced by Fletcher's book and an account by Larry Smith in a Keith Moon documentary on Channel 4, Neil Boland's daughter started reaching out by email for an eyewitness present at her dad's death. She received one reply from one of the eight young men charged with "causing an affray" that night. Peter Thorpe responded, claiming the mood at the Carnbourne Rooms had actually been perfectly pleasant, that he and his mates were not racist skinheads at all (Thorpe wrote that he is from a multicultural family) but Who fans. A joking request for a ride home from one of the attendees prompted Kim Moon to shout "fuck off," after which the fans started tossing pennies at the car as it drove away. Neil stopped the vehicle, got out, and started tussling with someone. At that point, the car took off again. Neil ran after it, and the throng followed. When the Bentley stopped, Thorpe said he saw who was driving it: Kim Moon. As everyone surrounded the car and the melee resumed, Kim jammed it in gear again and drove over Neil Boland.

Regardless of whether Keith or Kim was driving that night, it was Keith who took the blame when he appeared before the Hatfield Magistrate on March 23, 1970. Pleading guilty to all charges of "driving with excess alcohol, without insurance, and without a driving license," he was cleared of all three charges and released. This did absolutely nothing to clear Keith's conscience, and he was wracked with anguish over the incident until the day he died.

As for Neil Boland's daughter, Michelle, she championed Peter Thorpe's story on her own web page, titled "Keith Moon Was Not Driving," to leave no doubt about her stance on the subject. The page inspired Fletcher to seek out Thorpe and include his version of events in an updated edition of *Moon*. Larry Smith and Smith's girlfriend Jean Battye, however, have stuck by their original story.

Peter "Dougal" Butler

When Neil Boland went to work for Keith Moon, John Entwistle employed one Peter Butler to drive his French Citroën. With his tousled mop of dusty blond hair, Butler reminded Pete Townshend of a certain puppet pup from the children's program *The Magic Roundabout*. Thus, Entwistle's driver won a new nickname: Dougal.

Peter "Dougal" Butler had been a mod frequenting the Marquee, the 100 Club, and all the other early sixties top spots. The band he fancied above all other was the Who, so when fellow former-mod crony Bob Pridden offered him a job chauffeuring the band's equipment around Scotland in 1967, Dougal joined the team enthusiastically. From there he was promoted to Entwistle's personal assistant. Keith Moon, however, was always in much greater need of assistance than John Entwistle, who agreed to release Dougal in 1971.

Unlike Neil Boland, Dougal Butler was a lot more aware of how life with the Moon might play out. As Entwistle's driver, he was well acquainted with Moon's manic lifestyle and mood swings, the inhuman hours he kept, and the often-inhuman way he treated anyone in his employ. Dougal agreed to the shift nevertheless.

And so, Dougal Butler would spend the next six years witnessing firsthand, and often partaking in, Moon's pranking, womanizing, drinking, and drugging. He was hardly capable of going bottle for bottle or line for line with his boss . . . after all, he's only human. In one improbable incident, he and Moon mindlessly snorted a few lines that turned out to be heroin, after which Diana Ross marched Dougal out onto a beach and belted him in the stomach until he barfed his way back from an overdose. Moon, of course, was completely unfazed by his own unintended smack consumption and eager to keep the party raging. There were times when even his mythic constitution could not handle the chemical load, and more than once, Dougal yanked him back from oblivion with a bit of on-the-fly nursing or a well-timed emergency call.

Dougal also knew when basic morality took precedence over any loyalty he had toward his boss (which was quite a lot). On occasions when Moon became unmanageably abusive toward or destructive around his own family, Dougal rushed in and escorted Kim and Mandy to a safe place. He too suffered Moon's callousness and cruelty with some regularity, and when one drug-fueled argument over Dougal's acceptance of an assistant director job on *The Kids Are Alright* escalated to fisticuffs, Dougal knew it was time to put an end to their working relationship.

Despite the insanity of his six years with Keith Moon, and Moon's considerable personality flaws, Dougal harbored no ill will toward his ex-employer. After a rocky period, they managed to resume a tentative friendship, mostly over the phone, before Moon's death.

In 1981, Peter "Dougal" Butler reminisced about his crazy days in a memoir called *Moon the Loon* (or as we Yanks received it, *Full Moon*). Often hilariously funny, often horribly sad, sometimes just plain lurid, it is a frank portrait of a truly troubled man, too lovingly conceived to be completely condemned as exploitative. Still, one could imagine why Kim Moon might have preferred to read something else. Although Tony Fletcher wrote that the book "served to estrange" Dougal from the Who and Moon's family, in 2012, Dougal told Mark Raison of *Mod Culture* that he speaks with "Roger five or six times a year," spends "a lot of time with" Alison Entwistle, and lives close enough to Keith's mother to "pop in for a cup of tea with her and Keith's sister" from time to time.

11

I'm the Face

The Who and the Mod Movement

T here they are, buzzing down Carnaby Street on their Vespas like a swarm of natty hornets, decked to the nines in their Ben Sherman drainpipes, Union Jack blazers, and furry anoraks, blasting "I Can See for Miles" from their portable turntables on their way to a big, bloody row with some greasy-haired, Cliff Richard–worshipping rockers down on Brighton Beach. They are the mods, they are the mods, they are, they are, they are the mods.

It's a popular, even romantic image of the mid-sixties mod scene. It's also dead inaccurate. So many of the things we later generations associate with mid-sixties modernism have nothing to do with the reality. It has all been twisted by reinterpretations of the movement and movies like the Who's own *Quadrophenia*. So where does true modernism end and the posing begin? And where do our boys fit into it all? As it turns out, the Who both sat on the periphery of the scene *and* led the new In Crowd.

A Brief History of Modernism

Wind back your watch before Oasis and Blur, before *Quadrophenia* the film and the record, before frilled dandies paraded down Carnaby Street, before London swung, before the Who, the Kinks, and the Beatles. It is now the late 1950s. The youth culture that began emerging scattershot throughout the Western world in conjunction with the rise of rock 'n' roll was looking for places to convene. In London, those spots were coffee bars. Unlike the pubs that made last call well before midnight, coffee bars stayed open all night. There, hip students could exercise their intellects discussing art and existentialism over a French roast while be-bop spiraled from the jukebox. They dug the unpredictable shocks of sound discharging from John Coltrane's sax or Miles Davis's trumpet, the aural equivalents of Jackson Pollock action paintings. They left stodgy trad jazz and low-brow rock 'n' roll, as well as the feuding and fisticuffs, to the yobbos. They were intellectuals fashioning their minds and garb after the French. They kept their hair carefully styled and as trim as their "bumfreezer" jackets. Their look was collegiate: skinny trousers and beautifully tailored shirts, but with key splashes of audacity. Vivid ties popped from their collars as they pranced on radically elongated winklepicker shoes. In 1959, novelist Colin MacInnes chronicled this new subculture in *Absolute Beginners*, and for one of the very first times, their team name appeared in print: modernists, so called for their adoration of modern jazz.

So how did these genteel sophisticates morph into the snarling, Who-loving thugs so often associated with mods? Appropriation and the desire to be a member of the In Crowd. The next generation of mods wasn't necessarily interested in the intellectual trappings of this new movement. They just dug the fashions and the promise of belonging. In his key study of the era, *Ready, Steady, Go! The Smashing Rise and Giddy Fall of Swinging London*, Shawn Levy describes an incident in which a young man with aspirations of modernism named Andrew Oldham barged into Burton's, pointed to the tailor's sign promising bespoke suits for just twelve pounds, and forced them to make a mod-styled mohair suit. Though Oldham didn't give a toss for the originators' politics and penchant for philosophizing, his dapper duds won him access to the clique. Similar poseurs would rapidly take over the scene as the pioneers grew up and out of mod.

In came the new guard. They had little patience for bebop. They preferred sounds you could dance and peacock to: American rhythm and blues. Amphetamines kept them doing the Shake and the Block all night long at The

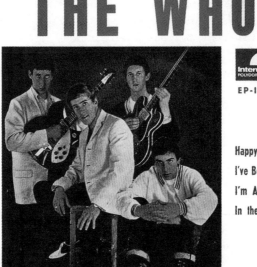

Though there's nothing terribly mod about the song selection, the Who never looked modder than they do on the sleeve of this EP from Israel.

Courtesy of the Rob Abramowicz Collection, digitized by Jeffrey Uleau

Scene Club and lowered their sex drives so the urge to "pull birds" never got in the way of their showboating. They were working-class lads looking to set themselves apart from the drab drones of the older generation. They liked the clothing because it made them stand out, whereas their dads, teachers, and bosses were intent on blending into London's gray fog. That continental sense of style extended to their preferred transport: small, Italian scooters, the top-of-the-line being the Vespa and the Lambretta. For these children of the early sixties, "mod" didn't mean modern jazz: it meant modern *everything* and death to all that was old, and that included the stale rock 'n' roll of the 1950s. Any cretin crass enough to cling to his Elvis Presley records, his filthy old motorcycle, and his leather jacket deserved a thumping. The rockers returned fire against boys they derided as uppity and possibly homosexual. And so, war was declared between the mods and rockers—at least, that's how the story goes.

Were the mods and rockers really bent on nothing more than mutual anni-hilation? Or was the conflict nothing more than media hysteria fueled by scared, aging journos harboring disgust for the young? There certainly were clashes—most notably the so-called Battle of Margate when fifty-one kids were arrested during a riot in the seaside resort community on May 17, 1964—but perhaps they carried no greater importance than any brawl between teenagers. Besides, as Richard Barnes noted in *Won't Get Fooled Again*, fighting was a good way to get your fancy trousers soiled. No mod wanted that.

Strangely, the mods paralleled one of the least savory aspects of the older generation. Instead of foreshadowing the sixties' egalitarian spirit, they created their own class system. At the top sat the Faces, the most attractive, the most fashion-forward, the ones who set the steps to which all lower-rung mods danced. The Numbers were the second generation, the youngest mods. Way down at the bottom of the system were the lowly Tickets: poseurs of the poseurs with no sense of fashion. So when these English boys finally got their own homegrown mod band, it is odd that Peter Meaden settled for designating them Numbers instead of Faces. But then again, the High Numbers weren't really mods.

The Who: Ace Faces or Third-Class Tickets?

As detailed back in chapter 4, the Who's transformation into the modder-than-mod High Numbers was mostly contrived. Mod Meaden wanted a band to call his very own, latched onto the Who, and remolded them in his own image. Keith Moon and rocker Roger Daltrey went along with it with as much enthusiasm as it takes to shrug one's shoulders. John Entwistle was another rocker, but he wasn't as easily swayed by Meaden's promises of success as Daltrey, and he rebelled in his own inimitably quiet way, combining his newly shorn hair forward in the best approximation of the mop top he lost as possible.

The High Numbers did house one mod, though one whose dedication to the movement was brief. Always one to lose his heart easily, Pete Townshend got lured into mod style by a girl: Roger Daltrey's pretty sister Carol. Roger and

Carol's older sister Gillian had been dating a mod lad, and Carol had an affinity for the fashion herself. During a make-out session with her brother's gangly schoolmate, Carol told Pete he had a "real 'modernist' look," as he wrote in *Who I Am*, and prodded him to purchase a PVC coat. With the promise of sharpening his style and sex appeal, Townshend began dabbling in mod.

Even as he gave himself over to Meaden's influence, Townshend knew that it wasn't right. As *the* mod band, the High Numbers should have been leading the pack. Instead, they were just another quartet of followers. They put out the transparently self-conscious single, "I'm the Face," and tried to acclimate to their new duds. However, the High Numbers were always several months behind the latest fashions, and even as their mod audience seemed to appreciate the effort and having a group to call their own, they were not fooled. When Meaden was out as manager and Kit Lambert and Chris Stamp were in, the High Numbers went back to being the Who, and their new buzzwords were "pop art" and "auto destruction." Union Jack jackets replaced mohair suits. Small Faces, the Action, the Eyes, the Birds, and the Manish Boys had much more legitimate mod pedigrees and were happy to fill the void.

The Who: Changing the Face of Modernism Since 1964

The Who's mod phase was over in a blink, and they weren't even called the Who for most of it. Yet they were without question the most famous band ever associated with mod, so much of what they introduced to popular culture has taken on a modish hue. Their pop art gear would have been far too garish for the pioneering modernists. Mod was essentially on its way out by the time the Who started dressing in flags and targets in late '65 anyway. However, flags and targets became enduring emblems of later-generation mods because of their Who association. The synthesizer-saturated sounds of *Quadrophenia* couldn't be more antithetical to the stomping Tamla-Motown and Blue Note ska records the sixties mods adored, yet the album is now considered a key mod artifact for attempting to tell the movement's story, as is Franc Roddam's similarly anachronistic film, which features a riot scene patterned after the so-called Battle of Margate. And so mod became an increasingly elastic term, and it has now expanded to include seventies punk, eighties acid jazz, and nineties Britpop. Pop Art, the phase that replaced the Who's mod dalliance, has come to gather mod connotations. With a surge of websites such as ModCulture.com and The Modcast, mod has arrived fit and flourishing in the twenty-first century, remaining true to its ever-evolving modernism.

12

I'm the Snappiest Dresser

Who Style

Whie the Beatles coordinated in their collarless suits, the Kinks donned foppish hunting jackets, and the Beach Boys looked squarer than chessboards in their striped shirts, the Who took a more individual and radical approach to fashion. Sure, Pete Townshend's nose was big. Sure, Roger Daltrey had a touch of acne. Sure, John Entwistle perpetually looked like he'd rather be getting skinned alive than standing onstage. But they always looked fabulous because they were decked out in top gear. Townshend's Union Jack jacket, Daltrey's fringed buckskin ensemble, Keith Moon's target turtleneck, Entwistle's skeleton suit—these outfits are as iconic as anything else in Who history. Who style could be sharp or outrageous or workmanlike, but it never failed to grab eyes.

Mod Style

Surely, the dullest shots of Entwistle, Daltrey, and Townshend are the ones snapped when they were a bunch of crew cut, suit, tie, and pocket square bedecked dorks called the Detours. These cats look like they should be taking your dinner order, not prepping to smash shit onstage. Where's the flair? Where's the razor-sharp style we associate with the early Who? Well, it wouldn't really arrive until Pete Meaden strutted into the picture. Pete Townshend had already been dabbling in mod style since Carol Daltrey prodded him into purchasing that PVC coat back in 1962 (see the previous chapter). The shiny outerwear suited Townshend, whose style had already been teetering on the mod precipice. Further impressed by Gillian Daltrey's dapper mod boyfriend, Townshend started cultivating his own mod look.

When Pete Meaden became the Who's manager, he gave the entire group a total mod makeover. The High Numbers looked tight in their skinny trousers, two-tone shoes, striped sweaters, Fred Perry shirts, and cuffed, shrink-to-fit Levis. However, half the band loathed the mod makeover. Entwistle resented having to cut his hair short. Daltrey thought his build was too stubby and boxy for high fashions that look best on a lanky frame. Happily for the two, Meaden's reign was short lived. When Kit Lambert and Chris Stamp entered the picture, they encouraged the High Numbers to revert to their old name and become the four distinct individuals that would make the Who so great to gawk at.

The Union Jack Jacket

According to Daltrey, Lambert's first and most enduring sartorial brainwave struck in 1965 when the Who draped their amps in UK flags. The banner layers England's St. George's cross and Ireland's St. Andrew's saltire over the blue backdrop of the Scottish flag, symbolizing the three countries comprising the United Kingdom. Jack is a common British synonym for flag; hence the British Admiralty's christening its flag the "Union Jack" in 1801. With its striking criss-cross of bloody red streaks, the Union Jack was a perfect icon for a band both violent and distinctly British. Seeing these graphics flanking his boys onstage inspired Lambert to rush off to a Saville Row tailor with one in tow.

Kit was shown the door by respected tailors reluctant to deface the Union Jack despite Britain's lack of flag desecration laws. So the manager rushed off to the rough and ready East End where tailors were less reluctant to snip and sew the national emblem. The finished jacket beautifully suited Pete Townshend, who'd already been sketching boldly graphic clothing concepts inspired by pop art's appropriation of mundane imagery. When he slipped on the jacket for an *Observer* cover story, he looked fabulous and completely confrontational, his schnoz jutting out at the reader like heavy artillery over the iconoclastic garment. The jacket also thrilled John Entwistle, who'd snatched it from Townshend to drape over his shoulders during the *My Generation* photo shoot. It would later take pride of place on the cover of *Who's Greatest Hits*.

The Union Jack jacket has become a mod icon because of its association with mod icons the Who. The flag has also taken on broader appeal outside the mod clique, and it can now be found slapped across any number of items, from furniture to guitars to handbags to cufflinks to mugs to jewelry to turntables to motorcycle helmets to Def Leppard's underwear to Geri Halliwell's ultramini dress to Liam Gallagher's parka custom made by his clothing company, Pretty Green (named for a song by one of the most committed Union Jack enthusiasts, Paul Weller). For his role in turning the Union Jack into such a ubiquitous commodity, Roger Daltrey believes Kit Lambert should be "posthumously knighted"!

The Target Turtleneck

Packing just as much iconographic pop art power as Pete's Union Jack jacket is Keith Moon's target turtleneck. As pop art symbol, the target has its origins in a work by Townshend's favorite pop artist. Peter Blake's 1961 painting *The First Real Target* is a parody/homage to works by Jasper Johns and Kenneth Noland that depict the standard archery target in rougher form. Blake's "first real" one

Targets, Union Jacks, and badges. The Who are at their most pop-art iconic on the sleeve of the "Substitute" single.

Author's collection

is a target fit for Robin Hood; perfect circles rendered in flat, strong shades of yellow, red, blue, black, and white, the title lettered in all caps at top.

The "target" Keith Moon would sport in a photo by David Wedgbury is actually more similar to the Royal Air Force's emblem: a roundel of red, white, and blue. It is this symbol that is plastered all over Who merchandise sold today, though Keith Moon did wear a variety of targets on a variety of garments. In the iconic Wedgbury photo, he wears a white turtleneck emblazoned with the RAF roundel. He was also photographed in a sky-blue turtleneck and white-collared shirt flashing the target. One image that you may find hard to come by is a shot of Moon wearing a short-sleeved, target tee, which is now the most common item of clothing featuring the symbol and the one most associated with the crazed drummer. In all likelihood, this garment is a conflation of his favored turtleneck and the ringed novelty T-shirts he often wore in 1966, such as the op-art one he sports on the *Observer* cover or the one depicting an outward-aimed handgun.

Buttons and Bulbs

As the psychedelic age dawned, the Who had to work extra hard to maintain their glitzy image. If Roger Daltrey never looked completely comfortable swanning about in a multicolored poncho, one must admit that no one wore a "pearly king" jacket festooned with thousands of reflective buttons or flashing light bulbs like Pete Townshend. While Townshend's then girlfriend Karen Astley made the button jacket he was often photographed wearing in 1967, he had to shell out a cool $200 (about $1,400 in today's dollars) for the one with the tiny flashing lights. Considering that he did so with the specific aim of "blowing minds" during the famed Murray the K shows at the RKO Theater (where, according to *Anyway, Anyhow, Anywhere*, he plugged the jacket into "the same circuit as his guitar"!), he surely got his money's worth. As he told Keith Altham in *Hit Parader*, "We won't let our music stand in the way of our visual act!"

Boiler Suit and DMs

When the Who became "the band with the rock opera" in 1969, Pete Townshend started buckling down. Guitar smashing was no longer obligatory, much of the humor went out of his songs, and he certainly never took the stage in a flashing lightbulb suit again. Looking back on his flamboyant period with a degree of embarrassment, he would never be seen in psychedelic suits or lacey Edwardian frills again. For a long time he'd rarely be seen in anything other than a plain white boiler suit and Doc Martens boots onstage. This was Townshend abandoning the acid, getting serious about his work. Not that he had completely lost his showbiz flair. He supplemented his plain-white outfit with a silver lamé one he wore at North London's Rainbow Theater's inaugural concert and a multicolored one custom tie-dyed by John Sebastian and his girlfriend Catherine. Despite these occasional aberrations of material and color, Townshend mostly kept it simple. "I was sick of dressing up as a Christmas tree in flowing robes that got in the way of my guitar playing, so I thought I'd move on to utility wear," he told the *Guardian* in 2010. The very garment suggests hard labor, boiler suits being the practical uniforms of coal-fired boiler maintenance workers on locomotives. But instead of sweeping soot out of fireboxes, Pete Townshend was in the business of hammering his guitar and leaping in the air.

To protect his tootsies on landing and give him some extra liftoff, he wore heavy-duty Doc Martens boots with their air-cushioned "Bouncing Soles." Also the garb of blue-collared sorts from factory laborers to postmen, DMs became essential rock gear after Pete Townshend first slipped them on. Punks, skinheads, new wavers, Goths, college rockers, grunge kids, and indie rockers could all be seen sporting the distinctive footwear. They were so pervasive in the underground music world that comedian Alexei Sayle wrote and sang a parody of their prevalence at benefit concerts on *The Young Ones* in 1982. In *Tommy*, Elton John wore a pair of four-and-a-half-foot high Doc Martens with stilt-like calipers that kept Sir Reg from toppling over. They can now be viewed from a safe distance amongst the world's biggest shoe collection at Northampton Museum.

Buckskin and Fringe

In *Who I Am*, Pete Townshend revealed that part of the reason he wore his white boiler suit was Kit Lambert's insistence that the group start wearing stage outfits to make them more visible when they played large venues, He and Keith Moon mostly went with bright white. Roger Daltrey settled on tan, both from the flesh he started baring and the flesh he used to cover it up. If Townshend's stage gear suggested his serious nature and workmanlike attitude, Daltrey's was an extension of his sex appeal. Below the belt he wore skintight buckskin pants. Above and fluttering about his belt, he wore a buckskin jacket, always unbuttoned in the front to display his tawny chest. Daltrey commissioned the iconic outfit from a buddy in the buckskin business in 1968, around the time he stopped murdering his naturally frizzy hair with Dippity Do and salon permanents. The new, raw Rog became one of the major rock 'n' roll sex symbols of the late sixties/early seventies, though not everyone cottoned to his current look. According to a possibly apocryphal incident, upon seeing Daltrey wearing his buckskin ensemble in a magazine, Keith Moon scrawled a succinct critique across the page: "Yuk."

The Skeleton Suit

For his own Lambert-appointed stage uniform, John Entwistle chose one in keeping with his famously outré taste in clothes. The Ox always liked to look his best and wildest onstage to give him some extra presence while his bandmates were convulsing. He might be seen in a yellow and black diamond-pattern jacket or in the S&M leather tee he wore at *The Rolling Stones Rock and Roll Circus* or a fringed red leather coat or the retina-searing red suit he wore on the cover of his *Too Late the Hero* album. But without question, his most memorable, most bizarre, most *John* outfit was his black-and-white skeleton suit, a leather jumpsuit painted to look like the stuff inside of him. For the guy who loved a good monster movie (and likely, a bad one too) and wrote the Halloween carols "Boris the Spider" and "Dr. Jekyll and Mr. Hyde," it all made some weird sense.

Entwistle unveiled the macabre togs alongside Townshend's boiler suit and Daltrey's buckskin at the Isle of Wight Festival on August 30, 1970. Not trying on the custom gear until shortly before taking the stage, Entwistle realized that the fit was so snug he couldn't even sit down in it! Impractical the skeleton suit may have been, but effective too, as one poor dim woman who allegedly screamed in terror upon seeing a skeleton emerging from the darkness backstage at the festival might attest.

13

Inside, Outside

The Album Covers

P erhaps no other band of their era understood the importance of the visual aspect of rock 'n' roll as well as the Who. This was clear in their striking dress sense (as discussed in the previous chapter), and it was clear in how they chose to adorn their music. You could always count on a Who album cover to be something special: vibrant, confrontational, and often, quite funny.

My Generation

The Who's mod phase was but a blip on their timeline. By the time they got around to releasing their first album, they'd already moved on to the pop art identity that would find them ditching their conservative collegiate togs for a punchier presentation. There's Keith Moon in his glowing white drainpipe trousers and matching jacket, vividly contrasted with scarlet polo neck. There's John Entwistle with the iconic Union Jack jacket draped over his shoulders. Roger Daltrey looks stylish in his pinstripes and sky-blue denim. Striking shades of red, white, and blue recall the band's key iconography: their flags and targets. Their faces glower with "get this over with already" attitude. Pete Townshend works his jaw as if he's getting ready to spit or unleash a torrent of profanity. They look tightly wound, ready for a rumble. The music inside the jacket delivers on that promise.

The cover of *My Generation* was shot in the autumn of 1965, and the guys look as though they're feeling the late season chill, which may account for why they all look so taut (it certainly explains why Townshend's bundled up in his overcoat and scarf). Decca's house pic-snapper David Wedgbury is responsible for catching this imposing shot (the following year he'd click another iconic British rock record cover: *Bluesbreakers with Eric Clapton*). At Kit Lambert's behest, he dragged the band to the Surrey Commercial Docks on the Thames in South London, which probably exacerbated the nippy atmosphere. Though the specific location may not be apparent in the photo, the implications are still detectable: don't be fooled by the hip outfits; these are four tough, working-class boys who'd be lugging cargo off ships if they weren't pounding out rock 'n' roll (but between you and me, only Daltrey might have suffered this fate). Shooting the Who from above, Wedgbury framed four propane tanks alongside the guys, one bulky container of combustible liquid per combustible musician.

In America, record buyers received a somewhat different package in April 1966. The outdated cover of Bo Diddley's "I'm a Man" was swapped out with the more recently recorded "Circles" (under the alternate title "Instant Party"); the LP was renamed *The Who Sings My Generation*, suggesting some sort of hootenanny group; and the cover image was completely replaced. Instead of using Wedgbury's more contemporary shot, American Decca reached back to a session he'd conducted on March 17, 1965, when the Who were still wearing their more modish gear: Entwistle, Townshend, and Moon playing the polo-necked tickets to Daltrey's seersucker-bedecked face. Decca chose a photo of the guys crowded in front of Big Ben beneath an overcast sky to leave no doubt among the American public that the Who hailed from the land of Beatles and Stones. The photo lacks the crispness and colorfulness of the one on the *My Generation* cover. But at least they still aren't smiling.

A Quick One

The cover of *My Generation* hints at the Who's pop art image. The cover of *A Quick One* trumpets it at top volume. Alan Aldridge's cover art has a touch of Peter Max's cartoony style, illustrating the funny and outlandish songs on the record as perfectly as David Wedgbury's photo snared the youthful rebellion of *My Generation*. In later years, Aldridge would be known for the more cluttered style shouting from the covers of Elton John's *Captain Fantastic and the Brown Dirt Cowboy* and *The Penguin Book of Comics*. *A Quick One* is colorful and bold, yet relatively clean and simple. Aldridge has a great skill for capturing likenesses, but he makes no real effort to do so with the Who. We know who's who because of Daltrey's blond hair and the instruments they're playing (although, for some reason, Entwistle is shown playing a twelve-string guitar). We also know because of the song titles billowing from them; each band member is represented by one of the numbers he composed for this first (and last, as far as Daltrey and Moon are concerned) record to democratize the songwriting chores.

A Quick One finds the Who on the ground floor of a new move away from the photographed band portraits that had dominated rock 'n' roll record covers until the Beatles (it's *always* the Beatles) broke the curse with Klaus Voormann's dark and creepy illustration for *Revolver*. The Who got in on this new vogue for more artful sleeves in the same year the Beatles released their audio-visual masterpiece (other early birds included the Kinks with *Face to Face* and the Yardbirds with their eponymous debut LP, better known as "Roger the Engineer"). The following year, illustrated covers would be de rigueur, containing new vinyl by the Jimi Hendrix Experience, Donovan, Love, the Velvet Underground, Jefferson Airplane, the Monkees, Procol Harum, the Hollies, Buffalo Springfield, the Moody Blues, and the Beach Boys, among others.

Alan Aldridge's busier style is in full effect on the cover of Elton John's 1975 concept album *Captain Fantastic and the Brown Dirt Cowboy*. Quite a contrast to the tasteful simplicity of *A Quick One*, don't you think?   *Author's collection*

Once again American Decca would insist on tinkering with the package, changing the title to *Happy Jack* to capitalize on what would be the Who's first (minor) US hit and removing the stark back-cover photo of their four faces peering from the darkness with the band name projected across them. The rear side of *Happy Jack* featured a black-and white collage of photos and zany profiles of the guys (Keith, of course, has a "passion for breeding chickens") dashed off by Nick Jones of the *Melody Maker*. However, even dopey Decca was hip enough to understand that the front cover illustration was too groovy to alter.

The Who Sell Out

While The Who had already delivered a couple of high-class record sleeves, a whole new standard was set when photographer Michael Cooper and

Townshend's favorite pop artist, Peter Blake, collaborated on the era-defining cover of *Sgt. Pepper's Lonely Hearts Club Band*. No longer would anything as straightforward as the band portrait on *My Generation* cut the mustard. The Stones, not yet known for overly creative jackets, slipped into Middle Earth drag and roped in Cooper to shoot the 3-D cover of *Their Satanic Majesties Request*. Hendrix's *Axis: Bold As Love*, Jefferson Airplane's *After Bathing at Baxter's*, the Beach Boys' *Smiley Smile*, and Cream's *Disraeli Gears* all arrived with elaborate artwork intended to be stared at for hours while tripping one's tits off.

Amidst this atmosphere of acid weirdness, the Who devised a jacket weirder, wilder, funnier, and altogether more original than any of the *Pepper* wannabes. To represent *The Who Sell Out*—that nutso conglomeration of romantic ballads, psychedelic hand grenades, and daffy radio spots—each band member would appear in his very own advert. With one brilliant stroke, the Who rendered all of 1967's lysergic posing hilariously irrelevant (not that the Who's peers had all lost their senses of humor. All of the records mentioned above have really funny moments). Townshend battling b.o. with his giant stick of Odorono. Daltrey swimming in a tub of Heinz Baked Beans. Moonie applying an oversized tube of Medac to an oversized zit. Entwistle dressed as Tarzan and snuggling a bikini-clad blonde to prove the effectiveness of the Charles Atlas bodybuilding course (with *Dynamic Tension!*).

Chris Stamp took the cover assignment to Track Records' David King and Roger Law (who'd one day cocreate the satirical comedy *Spitting Image*, which counted a horrifically big-nosed Pete Townshend amongst its grotesque puppet likenesses). The team came up with the album title and conceptualized the cover. Crack cameraman David Montgomery shot the stills (cajoling a body-shy Townshend to remove his shirt may have helped Montgomery develop the skills he needed to convince an entire room of female models to lose their kits for the cover of Hendrix's *Electric Ladyland*).

The guys are all smiles and dribbly lips of baked beans, but the photo shoot was not all so lighthearted. John Entwistle claimed that he was originally assigned to sit in the beans and Rog was supposed to get in the clinch with model Jill Langham. This makes sense considering that "Heinz Baked Beans" was Entwistle's most elaborate advert on the record and Daltrey was just starting to develop his sex symbol image at the time. However, wisely recognizing that posing with a pretty woman was the preferable gig, Entwistle said he purposely arrived late to the shoot so Daltrey would have to be on bean duty. The singer's often-repeated story goes that, straight from the refrigerator, the beans were so cold that he came down with pneumonia. Considering that temperature has little effect on the spread of pneumonia-causing bacteria, there isn't much weight to this part of the legend.

As for the rest of the legend, Jill Langham—now Jill Bussey—does not recall whether or not she was originally scheduled to pose with Daltrey, but she retained little about a photo shoot that would end up being a lot more enduring than she realized at the time. "You must remember, that in this time, the sixties, every day was exciting, so for me, to have a day's shoot with the Who wasn't that special, especially as I was a Beatles fan," Bussey told me. "I can remember there was mayhem and chaos at the shoot, but the fact that I was supposed to have posed with Roger Daltrey, I don't remember. Had I realised that the Who and this album *The Who Sell Out* would have stood the test of time, I would have taken more notice." Considering that Bussey's schedule at the time included modeling gigs, an appearance in *The Italian Job* with Michael Caine, opening her own shop, and being a new mum, it's understandable that her session with the Who got a bit lost in the shuffle. "One thing I remember vividly was that shortly after this shoot, I opened a Boutique in Woodford, and nearby was a record store, [whose] owner . . . I knew," she continued. "The album had just been released and the whole of his window had been plastered with covers of *The Who Sell Out* showing me with John Entwistle. I was inundated with Who fans coming to my Boutique (good for business)."

In 1972, Keith Moon told *Rolling Stone* that Entwistle was always supposed to be the bodybuilder because he "had a hairy chest" (it actually looks pretty bald in the photo), though his memory is never to be trusted. Moon said that he was stuck with the pimple cream because he was the youngest and Townshend had the deodorant because, and I quote, "He had trouble with his feet. Oh-Ho-Heee-Haha!"

The Who Sell Out cover continued causing problems even after David Montgomery's photo session. Scheduled to be released on November 17, Track would have to hold the record back for an entire month while waiting for clearance from the Odorono, Heinz, Charles Atlas, and Medac companies. Apparently, that final company's OK did not extend to Australia, where Moon was shown squeezing a tube of Clearasil.

In the end, all the trouble was worth it, as *Sell Out* sports one of the Who's—and, hell, rock 'n' roll's—great album covers. Not everyone got the joke, though. Joe Bogart, the program director of NYC's WMCA radio station, called it "disgusting," hid it from his children's baked-beans-sensitive eyes, and banned the record from airplay. Writing in the *Cleveland Press* in December 1967, critic Bruno Bornino called the ads "revolting" and suggested that pop fans should "buy the record and throw away the cover." Surely, very few followed his stupid advice.

For the sake of full disclosure, let's not forget that *Sell Out* made one big concession to the psychedelic times. The first printing came packaged with a poster depicting a freakedelic butterfly by graphic artist Adrian George. It's a good thing Track had the sense to hide that thing *inside* the cover.

Tommy

From the outrageous to the sublime. *Tommy* developed upon the ethereal acoustic-based music of *Sell Out*, but its emphasis on mysticism over wackiness warranted a more enigmatic sleeve. Pete Townshend commissioned Mike McInnerney, the *International Times* art editor he'd met at the UFO club while

Pink Floyd was creating their celestial racket. Their friendship deepened when McInnerney introduced Townshend to the teachings of Meher Baba (see chapter 32), whose philosophies affected *Tommy* profoundly.

The pair's rap sessions about Baba and music helped shape *Tommy*, so the artist was particularly qualified to translate its concepts into graphics. In *Who I Am*, Townshend wrote that McInnerney decided to develop on a specific Baba axiom: life is "an illusion within an illusion." McInnerney represented this with an Escher-like piece of op art, an illustration of either a blue sky full of black diamonds or a lattice of sky, depending on how you look at it. His simple yet striking art is spread over a triptych, which reveals that the front cover image swells out of darkness when unfolded completely. The left-hand panel depicts a hand reaching out toward the viewer, shattering the illusory darkness. Tiny white shards flicker about the hand like stars, morphing into the white birds soaring all over the sky, gazing out at the viewer with eyeless faces, blind creatures trying to make a connection just like Tommy Walker.

From a commercial standpoint, there was one problem with the cover. Where was the band this ambitious concept was supposed to be thrusting into stardom? Against Mike McInnerney's intentions, small pictures of the Who, also reaching from the darkness, were inserted in some of the front-cover diamonds. These portraits were finally removed when *Tommy* was reissued on CD in 1996.

Inside the cover was an additional three-part McInnerney illustration: a hand reaching toward the light emanating from a sconce on the left panel, another sconce against a darkened wall in the center, and on the third, the hand now reaching up toward what looks like a series of stained-glass windows as more of those white birds fly through the scene, the opera's religiosity made explicit. A booklet containing additional illustrative artwork and the full libretto was also included in this lush package. Strangely, all but the artwork on the left and center panels of the front cover were left out of the otherwise stellar SACD deluxe edition Polydor released in 2003.

Live at Leeds

The Who continued giving their new legion of hard-won fans great value for their dollars and pounds with their next release. The cover didn't look too promising: the band's name and the record's title and serial number seemingly stamped on plain brown paper. But open up the gatefold, and behold all the goodies tucked inside its two pockets. On one side, a dozen reproductions of various memorabilia: a receipt for smoke generators, an outtake from David Wedgbury's *Who Sings My Generation* photo shoot, a shot of Pete Townshend holding his SG aloft at Woodstock, a handwritten tour schedule with payment info for each show from the spring of 1965, a noncommittal letter from EMI regarding the signing of the High Numbers, a gig cancellation letter from Swindon's Locarno Ballroom dated March 22, 1965, the iconic Maximum R&B Marquee poster, a nasty-looking notice from the Jennings instruments manufacturer demanding the return of some AWOL equipment, concert contracts, and Townshend's annotated "My Generation" lyrics. On the other side, the greatest insert of all: the record.

The self-consciously shoddy front cover was a humorous nod to all the shoddily packaged live bootlegs currently slithering into record stores. The concept extended to the record labels, which were plain white and hand lettered. Graphreaks—the design company responsible for such discs as Led Zeppelin's untitled fourth album, T. Rex's eponymous album, and the Move's *Looking On*—put together the witty package. The front cover stamping was allegedly performed by the Who, themselves . . . and whatever lackeys were loitering around the Track offices. I wonder who did the bulk of the work.

Who's Next

Had *Lifehouse* come together as Pete Townshend envisioned, it probably would have arrived in a sleeve emphasizing its mysticism, seriousness, and conceptual gravity, something not unlike the cover of *Tommy*. But when that grand idea puffed away like a fart in the breeze, the Who's sillier instincts prevailed. As Townshend slumped off to lick his wounds, Dave King reportedly schemed to place a parody of his own nudie *Electric Ladyland* cover on the front of *Who's Next*, a collage of completely starkers obese women, one having her legs spread eagle to reveal a little picture of the Who (the one later used on the US edition of *Who's Better, Who's Best*). Townshend's assessment: "revolting." Dave King's: "I had nothing to do with that cover" (as he told *Won't Get Fooled Again* author Richie Unterberger). A milder shot of Keith Moon in lingerie was also rumored to have been considered, but saner brains prevailed, and an Ethan A. Russell shot of the band surrounding a Kubrickian monolith taken on July 4, 1971, was used instead (the heavenly cloud-streaked sky was floated in from an early photo). Lest anyone fear the Who had retreated into dull tastefulness, the monolith was not only a concrete block rising from a slag heap (slag being the byproduct of ore smelting), but Russell's composition—and some carefully placed stains—implied the band had just pissed on it. Some of the stains were produced with splashes of rainwater. Some were made the old-fashioned way. Another Russell concept was to snap the band wrecking a dressing room, but their destruction was so perfunctory that the photo was relegated to the back cover.

While Townshend was probably glad his compromised masterpiece didn't come out in a sleeve depicting naked ladies or Keith Moon in garter belts, he still hated the finished product, seeing the pee-centric cover as a sad final insult to *Lifehouse*.

Quadrophenia

As unhappy as Townshend was with the *Who's Next* cover, he still invited Ethan Russell back, at the request of Glyn Johns, to work his skills on the elaborate packaging of the Who's elaborate next album. This time Townshend's ambitious concept did not falter, and *Quadrophenia* was released in 1973 as a challengingly constructed rock opera housed in an incredibly detailed gatefold cover.

The front shot, a moody image of Jimmy the Mod on his scooter in front of a sky-painted canvas, is just a taste of the grand photo essay inside. A booklet shot in similarly grim black and white illustrates Jimmy's adventures. He rides his multimirrored scooter as smokestacks vomit pollution into the atmosphere; has some sort of minor tussle with his folks over the breakfast table; eats a rank-looking dish of eggs, beans, and chips at a luncheonette; wanders glumly through a corridor in his target tee; eyeballs some of his fellow mods from a safe arm's length on the street and back at the luncheonette; does his dirty job hauling rubbish bins to the dump; goes to see the Who rocking the Hammersmith Odeon; sleeps one off under his wall-full of pin ups; rides the 5:15; witnesses the Ace Face toiling as a lowly bellboy; tries to drown himself and survives.

Russell's photos, conceptualized by himself and Townshend, are striking, far more authentic in their depiction of early-sixties mod life than the music inside the sleeve. Georgiana Steele-Waller, secretary at the Who's Ramport Studio, organized the models, and Richard Barnes helped dress them (and select the nudie pics that appear on Jimmy's bedroom wall). Townshend made the most important find when he caught sight of Terry "Chad" Kennett at a Cecily Street pub. Kennett conveys Jimmy's ennui, physical degradation, and spiritual questing commandingly. He was a character every bit as complex and combustible as the one he portrayed. Kennett's knuckles were tattooed with "love" and "hate," à la Robert Mitchum's demonic preacher in *The Night of the Hunter*. During the photo shoot he was arrested for stealing a bus. He died in 2011.

The 1973 Who make a couple of anachronistic yet subtle appearances among the modernalia. On the cover, each of their faces is caught in Jimmy's rearview mirrors, an effect that looks doctored, but Russell says that he actually had Townshend, Entwistle, and Daltrey crouch to reflect their faces in the mirrors naturally (Keith Moon, however, failed to show up for the shoot, so his face was edited in during postproduction). More daringly, we see the two eras clash as the guys—with their seventies long hair, beards, and clothes—clown around in front of the Hammersmith Odeon as Jimmy worships them from afar (about a decade afar).

A tremendously artistic and mature package is completed with full libretto and Jimmy's autobiography ghostwritten by Townshend. All of these elements— the music, the stills, the autobiography—would be absolutely integral to Franc Roddam's 1979 *Quadrophenia* film, which even reproduces some of the photos nearly to the letter.

The Who by Numbers

Quadrophenia was a major artistic triumph for the Who, each member having done some of his finest instrumental and vocal work (even Keith Moon turns in a shockingly lovely vocal on "Bell Boy"). However, since Townshend kept such a firm hold of the project's reins, it has often been labeled more a solo endeavor than a group one. He loosened his grip a lot on the band's next record, allowing Daltrey to select the songs he most wanted to sing. The group's album-design rotation also meant Townshend had no say about the cover. He got to helm *Quadrophenia.* Then it was Daltrey's turn to conceptualize *Odds & Sods* (see chapter 19). Now it was Entwistle's chance to have at it.

The cover of *The Who by Numbers* is as misleading a representation of its music as the jokey lead-off single, "Squeeze Box." An unrelentingly grim collection of songs about aging, boozing, sex, and the soul-crushing music industry receives a funny little connect-the-dots drawing of the Who and their broken equipment. Clearly, easygoing John had little affinity for his bandmate's personal crisis, even as his own "Success Story" complements and comments on Pete's distraught songs. This cover is even less appropriate than the urine-daubed one on *Who's*

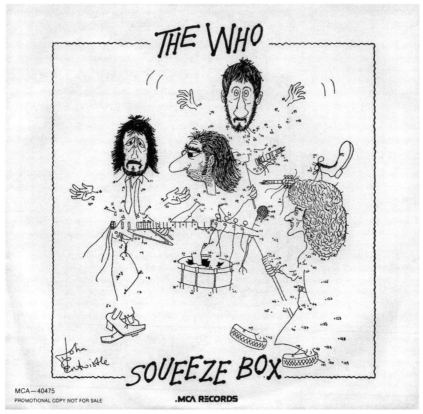

John Entwistle's connect-the-dots illustration brought a bit of humor to the grim *Who by Numbers.* Although the goofy "Squeeze Box" needed no such assistance, his illustration was used on the sleeve of that hit, too.

Courtesy of the Rob Abramowicz Collection, digitized by Jeffrey Uleau

Next. Still, it's tough to be completely immune to the charms of Entwistle's sketch, which was inspired by his three-year-old son Chris's connect-the-dots books. Entwistle completed his likeness of Townshend, Daltrey, Moon, and himself in just one hour . . . though he said the dots took another three.

Who Are You

After more than a decade of clever, artful album covers, *Who Are You* comes as a disappointment. For the first time since *My Generation*, the sleeve features a routine band portrait. Terry O'Neill's photo of the Who lined up within a mess of electrical equipment has none of the sneering attitude of their debut sleeve. Blame Keith Moon.

The *Who Are You* cover was supposed to be Moon's baby, but he just couldn't deliver an idea. An alternate shot of each band member leading his own line of followers (audience members from the Shepperton Studios performance filmed for *The Kids Are Alright*) was more interesting visually and a clearer interpretation of the album title, but it ultimately got the thumbs down. So the band settled for the weary picture with which we are all familiar.

Much has been made of the chair on which Moon is perched. Apparently, the stenciled message on the chair's back reading "NOT TO BE TAKEN AWAY" is supposed to be some sort of chilling portent of his death. More significantly, the chair was necessary to hide the gut bulging out of his eccentric foxhunter getup. The message was clear enough that no stenciled words were necessary. His zany ideas had dried up. He'd let his body go. He barely seemed able to stand. Keith Moon died less than a month after the record's release.

Face Dances

The first post-Moon Who record was greeted with a great deal of indifference and a share of hostility by a public that didn't understand how much the group had changed since Moon's death. Whether *Face Dances* is a middle-of-the-road disappointment or the work of a band that was finally allowing itself to mature is a matter of debate. Less debatable is the fact that it came packaged in a more interesting sleeve than the last one. It certainly has the most impressive artistic credentials of any Who cover. Townshend asked friend and key pop artist Peter Blake to create it. In *Who I Am*, he writes that this was Blake's first record sleeve since he coconceived *Sgt. Pepper's* in 1967, but the artist had actually designed covers for Pentangle (*Sweet Child*), Chris Jagger (*The Adventures of Valentine Vox the Ventriloquist*), and Roger McGough (*Summer with Monika*) in the interim.

For *Face Dances*, Blake imagined a checkerboard pattern, each square depicting a different band member. He supplied the illustration of new recruit Kenney Jones in the lower right-hand corner of the cover and farmed out the other sixteen panels to his artist buddies. These ranged from the photo-realistic (Blake and David Tindle's portraits of Jones, David Inshaw's portrait of Daltrey) to the fanciful (Bill Jacklin's dreamy portrait of Townshend and Richard Hamilton's comically exaggerated one) to the abstract (Colin Self's profile of Townshend, Howard Hodgkin and Patrick Caulfield's representations of Entwistle, Joe Tilson puzzle jumble of Jones's face) to the grotesque (Mike Andrews's pupil-less depiction of Daltrey and Allen Jones's skull-exposing one). Townshend was psyched to also have contributions from his art heroes David Hockney and Ron Kitaj, though Francis Bacon decided not to get involved.

It's Hard

Whatever visual inspiration that returned with *Face Dances* was long gone when the Who released their next, and reportedly final, album the following year. In a dumb attempt to make the Who look young and relevant, photographer Graham Hughes posed them in an arcade as a junior video-game wizard plays Space Duel. In their jackets and ties and with their sullen expressions, the Who look like security. "You don't got any quarters, kid?," Townshend seems to grunt. "Well, then get going!"

Endless Wire

For more than two decades, *It's Hard* had the unfortunate status of being the final Who album; unfortunate because both musically and visually it was a whimper when it should have been a bang. Then in the twenty-first century, the unimaginable happened when Roger Daltrey and Pete Townshend began work on an all-new Who album.

Because twenty-four years had passed since their last record, and because this would be their first without Keith Moon *or* John Entwistle, Townshend and Daltrey seemed to consciously create a record that would tie into the band's older work. So *Endless Wire* kicked off with a percolating synthesizer that recalled "Baba O'Riley" and concluded with a mini-opera that stirs memories of "A Quick One While He's Away" (in concept if not in sound). Consequently, *Endless Wire* sounds more like a Who album than any since *Who Are You*.

The old school Who feel of *Endless Wire* is also captured in Richard Evans's computer-generated cover design. Evans had done some time in the Who's trenches in the eighties as designer of the *Who's Missing* and *Two's Missing* sleeves. More recently, he designed the pop art cover for the *Blues to the Bush* live disc. For *Endless Wire*, Evans seemed to be channeling Mike McInnerney. There are shades of *Tommy*'s geometry and avian imagery, as well as its blue palette, on the *Endless Wire* cover. If the Who never make another LP, they've at least gone out with a cover that suits them better than the one on *It's Hard*.

14

Wish You Were Here

An International Discography

Fling a dart at a globe and you're gonna prick a Who fan. A band this good can't remain a local secret, even if it did take them a bizarrely long time to catch on outside the United Kingdom. Today, only the most head-in-the-sand earthlings are completely unfamiliar with the World's Greatest Rock 'n' Roll Band, though their understanding of Who history may vary. The Japanese Wholigan may rate "Out in the Street" as her favorite Who hit. The Spanish Who fan may have spent 1966 spinning their eponymous album over and over. So let's take a short trip around the world to take a peek at how our global neighbors came to know the Who (reissues excluded).

The Singles

The Who's international discography was diverse indeed, particularly in terms of the tracks chosen for their B-sides. Some countries released singles with no discernable equivalent in the United Kingdom or United States. Japan was home to a particularly varied singles discography, and a couple of releases there afforded John Entwistle the star status he was usually denied in the English-speaking world. A lethal case of Moon-mania in Sweden helped "Bucket T" zoom to the top of the charts, while in nearby Holland, "Baba O'Riley" hit #11 in 1971. Four years earlier, another single did not fare as well there. The exclusive "Mary Anne with the Shaky Hand" made no impression on the Dutch charts. Perhaps the release of "Pictures of Lily" just a few months earlier (a #8 hit there) filled Holland's annual quota for hit songs about jerking off.

There's less mystery regarding the variation among the Who's 1968 singles. While "Call Me Lightning" was never intended as a UK A-side, and "Dogs" was sadly never deemed fit for American consumption, most other countries recognized the charms of both tunes and released them both as local A-sides. Since "Dr. Jekyll and Mr. Hyde" had already come out on the flip of "Lightning" in most markets, the two-year-old "Circles" was usually selected to back up "Dogs." When "Magic Bus" was released around the world a few months later, there was a lot less consistency as the various markets selected an appropriate B-side.

"My Generation"/"I'm a Man" (Germany, Belgium 1965)

"My Generation"/"I Can't Explain" (Greece 1965)

"My Generation"/"The Ox" (France 1966)

"Out in the Street"/"Please, Please, Please" (Japan 1966)

"Batman"/"Bucket T" (France 1966)

"La-La-La Lies"/"Much Too Much" (Australia, New Zealand 1966)

"La-La-La Lies"/"Bald Headed Woman" (Holland 1966)

"My Generation"/"Instant Party" (Brazil 1967)

"Whiskey Man"/"Boris the Spider" (Japan 1967)

"A Quick One While He's Away" (Parts 1 and 2)/"So Sad About Us" (Sweden 1967)

"Bucket T"/"Run Run Run" (Sweden, Denmark, Norway 1967)

"Mary Anne with the Shaky Hand"/"I Can't Reach You" (Sweden, Denmark, Norway 1967)

"I Can't Reach You"/"Our Love Was" (Australia 1967)

"Armenia City in the Sky"/"Mary Anne with the Shaky Hand" (Japan 1968)

"Dogs"/"Circles" (Australia, Austria, Germany, Italy, Japan, Malaysia, South Africa, Spain, Sweden 1968)

"Dogs"/"Whiskey Man" (Argentina 1968)

"Dogs"/"Someone's Coming" (France 1968)

"Magic Bus"/"Bucket T" (Argentina, Austria, Germany, Greece, India, Italy, Japan, Spain 1968)

"Magic Bus"/"Armenia City in the Sky" (France 1968)

"Magic Bus"/"Bucket T"/"Rael" (Portugal 1968)

"Magic Bus"/"Mary Anne with the Shaky Hand" (Sweden 1968)

"Pinball Wizard"/"I Can't Reach You" (Philippines 1969)

"Go to the Mirror"/"I'm Free" (Australia 1969)

"I'm Free"/"Pinball Wizard" (Brazil 1969)

"I'm Free"/"Go to the Mirror" (Chile 1969)

"I'm Free"/"Tommy Can You Hear Me?" (France, Germany, Italy, Malaysia 1969)

"See Me, Feel Me"/"I'm Free" (Greece 1970)

"See Me, Feel Me"/"Young Man Blues" (Japan 1970)

"Summertime Blues"/"Shakin' All Over" (Japan 1970)

"Won't Get Fooled Again"/"We're Not Gonna Take It" (Chile 1971)

"Baba O'Riley"/"I Can't Explain" (Australia, Austria, Germany, India 1971)

"Baba O'Riley"/"My Wife" (Belgium, France, Holland 1971)

"Baba O'Riley"/"Behind Blue Eyes" (Portugal 1971)

"Baba O'Riley"/"I Don't Even Know Myself" (Spain 1971)

"Behind Blue Eyes"/"Going Mobile" (Belgium, France, Holland 1971)

"Behind Blue Eyes"/"Let's See Action" (Greece 1971)

"Going Mobile"/"Bargain" (Philippines 1971)

"Let's See Action"/"Behind Blue Eyes" (Japan 1971)

"When I Was a Boy"/"My Wife" (Japan 1972)

"Relay"/"Join Together" (Greece 1972)

"5:15"/"Love Reign o'er Me" (Greece 1973)
"Love Reign o'er Me"/"Is It in My Head" (Holland 1973)
"The Real Me"/"Water" (Japan 1973)
"The Real Me"/"Doctor Jimmy" (Belgium, France 1973, 1974)
"Postcard"/"I'm the Face" (Brazil 1974)
"Long Live Rock"/"Pure and Easy" (Italy 1974)
"Slip Kid"/"They Are All in Love" (Guatemala 1975)
"Slip Kid"/"Squeeze Box" (Spain 1975)

The LPs

There was less variation among the Who's original LPs than their singles, though several countries were treated to the aforementioned *The Who* album in 1966, which essentially followed the proposed lineup of the scrapped *Jigsaw Puzzle* record (see chapter 16). Their international compilations, however, are quite the assorted bunch. The following is just a small selection of international LPs released before Who compilations really started flooding the market in the seventies.

In 1968, Japanese fans were treated to this useful and "exciting" compilation that gathered up "Happy Jack," "Pictures of Lily," "Substitute," "The Last Time," and their B-sides, as well as a couple of choice cuts from *A Quick One*.   *Author's collection*

Instant Party (Holland 1965)

  Side A: "Instant Party"/"Bald Headed Woman"/"My Generation"/"Anyway, Anyhow, Anywhere"/"The Kids Are Alright"/"The Ox

  Side B: "I Can't Explain"/"A Legal Matter"/"Daddy Rolling Stone"/"Much Too Much"/"Shout and Shimmy"/"It's Not True"

The Who (Germany, Holland, Indonesia, Israel, Italy, South Africa, Spain 1966; issued as *I'm a Boy* with different cover and slightly different running order in Japan)

  Side A: "Run Run Run"/"Heatwave"/"In the City"/"Boris the Spider"/"I Need You"/"Circles"

  Side B: "Don't Look Away"/"See My Way"/"Whiskey Man"/"Cobwebs and Strange"/"Disguises"/"I'm a Boy"

Best of the Who (Australia, New Zealand 1966, same cover image as the eponymous European album)

  Side A: "Substitute"/"Pictures of Lily"/"Disguises"/"Batman"/"Barbara Ann"/"In the City"

  Side B: "Happy Jack"/"I'm a Boy"/"Doctor, Doctor"/"Circles"/"I've Been Away"/"Bucket T"

The Who (Argentina, South Africa, Uruguay 1968, same cover image as *A Quick One*)

  Side A: "Dogs"/"I Can See for Miles"/"Run Run Run"/"Don't Look Away"/"Whiskey Man"

  Side B: "I'm a Boy"/"Pictures of Lily"/"Boris the Spider"/"Call Me Lightning"/"A Quick One While He's Away"

Exciting the Who (Japan 1968)

  Side A: "Happy Jack"/"Pictures of Lily"/"Substitute"/"I've Been Away"/"Doctor, Doctor"/"Waltz for a Pig"

  Side B: "The Last Time"/"Under My Thumb"/"So Sad About Us"/"A Quick One While He's Away"

Best of the Who (France 1970)

  Side A: "Happy Jack"/"Magic Bus"/"Mary Anne with the Shaky Hand"/"Pictures of Lily"/"Call Me Lightning"/"Substitute"

  Side B: "Overture"/"I Can See for Miles"/"Armenia City in the Sky"/"Whiskey Man"/"Pinball Wizard"/"I'm a Boy"

Best of the Who Vol. 2 (France 1970)

  Side A: "Heaven and Hell"/"The Seeker"/"The Hawker (Eyesight to the Blind)"/"I'm Free"/"Go to the Mirror"/"Tommy Can You Hear Me?"

  Side B: "Run Run Run"/"I Can't Reach You"/"So Sad About Us"/"I Need You"/"Circles"/"Someone's Coming"

The EPs

While the extended play never really caught on in the United States, it was big business in Europe, even earning its own charts in several UK publications (*Disc and Music Echo, Melody Maker, NME,*). For those who didn't have quite enough scratch for an LP but wanted more than a single's two allotted tracks, EPs were the way to go. Before the format fell out of favor in the seventies, there was a wide and wild assortment of Who EPs throughout the globe.

"I Can't Explain"/"Bald Headed Woman"/"Anyway, Anyhow, Anywhere"/"Daddy Rolling Stone" (France 1965)

"My Generation"/"Out in the Street"/"Anyway, Anyhow, Anywhere"/"Anytime You Want Me" (Australia 1965)

"My Generation"/"Out in the Street" (as "You're Gonna Know Me")/"The Kids Are Alright"/"I'm a Man" (France 1965)

"My Generation"/"La-La-La Lies"/"The Ox"/"Much Too Much" (France 1965)

"My Generation"/"Out in the Street"/"I Can't Explain"/"Bald Headed Woman" (Mexico 1965)

"My Generation"/"A Legal Matter"/"I'm a Man"/"Out in the Street" (Portugal 1965)

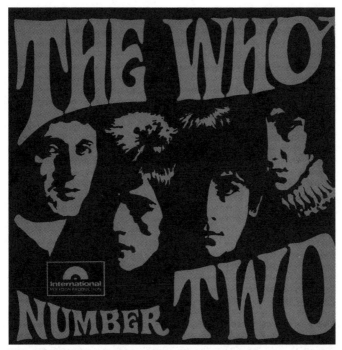

The Who appear as a brooding silk screen on the cover of this Australian EP.

Courtesy of the Rob Abramowicz Collection, digitized by Jeffrey Uleau

"My Generation"/"Out in the Street"/"It's Not True"/"La-La-La Lies" (Spain
  1965)
"A Legal Matter"/"My Generation"/"La-La-La Lies"/"Bald Headed Woman"
  (Holland 1966)
"A Legal Matter"/"Instant Party"/"The Kids Are Alright"/"Much Too Much"
  (Spain 1966)
Dance Session: "The Kids Are Alright"/"It's Not True"/"A Legal Matter"/"La-
  La-La Lies" (1966 Australia)
"The Kids Are Alright"/"It's Not True"/"I Don't Mind"/"Please, Please, Please"
  (France 1966)
"Out in the Street"/"A Legal Matter"/"Instant Party"/"I'm a Man" (France 1966)
"Substitute"/"I'm a Boy"/"In the City"/"Waltz for a Pig" (Australia, New Zealand
  1966)
"I'm a Boy"/"In the City"/"Disguises"/"Circles" (France, Portugal, Spain 1966)

Ready Steady Who: "Heatwave"/"Batman"/"Bucket T"/"Barbara Ann" (France
  1966)
"Happy Jack"/"Whiskey Man"/"Boris the Spider"/"I've Been Away" (France
  1966)

German Polydor got extra creative with the spelling of "Pinball
Wizard" for this 1975 retrospective EP.   *Author's collection*

"Happy Jack"/"I've Been Away"/"I'm a Boy"/"In the City" (Israel 1966)

"Happy Jack"/"I've Been Away"/"Don't Look Away"/"See My Way" (Portugal 1966)

"Happy Jack"/"I've Been Away"/"Substitute"/"Waltz for a Pig" (Spain 1966)

"Pictures of Lily"/"Doctor, Doctor"/"Happy Jack"/"I've Been Away" (Australia, New Zealand 1967)

"Pictures of Lily"/"I Need You"/"Doctor, Doctor"/"Run Run Run" (France, Portugal 1967)

"Pictures of Lily"/"Doctor, Doctor"/"Run Run Run"/"Whiskey Man" (Israel 1967)

"Pictures of Lily"/"Doctor, Doctor"/"Don't Look Away"/"Whiskey Man" (Spain 1967)

"The Last Time"/"Under My Thumb"/"Barbara Ann"/"Batman" (Spain 1967)

The Who Number Two: "I Can See for Miles"/"Mary Anne with the Shaky Hand"/"I Can't Reach You"/"Our Love Was, Is" (Australia 1967)

"I Can See for Miles"/"Boris the Spider"/"Whiskey Man"/"Someone's Coming" (Portugal 1967)

"I Can See for Miles"/"Someone's Coming"/"Pictures of Lily"/"Doctor, Doctor" (Yugoslavia 1967)

"Armenia City in the Sky"/"Heinz Baked Beans"/"Mary-Anne with the Shaky Hand"/"I Can't Reach You"/"Spotted Henry (Medac)"/"Odorono" (Thailand 1967)

"I Can See for Miles"/"Someone's Coming"/"Call Me Lightning"/"Dr. Jekyll and Mr. Hyde" (Mexico 1968)

"Dogs"/"Silas Stingy"/"Call Me Lightning"/"Dr. Jekyll and Mr. Hyde" (Portugal 1968)

"Pinball Wizard"/"Dogs Part Two"/"Magic Bus"/"Bucket T" (Mexico 1969)

"Pinball Wizard"/"Dogs Part Two"/"The Last Time"/"Substitute" (Portugal 1969)

"I'm Free"/"Smash the Mirror"/"Tommy Can You Hear Me?"/"Eyesight to the Blind" (Mexico 1969)

"I'm Free"/"Tommy Can You Hear Me?"/"Sally Simpson" (Portugal 1969)

"I'm Free"/"The Hawker (Eyesight to the Blind)"/"Sally Simpson"/"Tommy Can You Hear Me?" (Portugal 1970)

"I'm Free"/"Overture"/"Substitute"/"The Seeker" (Malaysia 1970)

"Overture"/"Christmas"/"I'm Free"/"See Me, Feel Me" (New Zealand 1970)

"The Seeker"/"Here for More"/"Christmas" (Mexico 1970)

Tommy/The Who Best 6: "Pinball Wizard"/"Smash the Mirror"/"The Acid Queen"/"See Me, Feel Me"/"Sensation"/"I'm Free" (Japan 1971)

"Won't Get Fooled Again"/"Behind Blue Eyes"/"Bargain" (Mexico 1971)

"Won't Get Fooled Again"/"Sensation"/"I Don't Even Know Myself"/"I'm Free" (Malaysia 1971)

"Behind Blue Eyes"/"Summertime Blues"/"Won't Get Fooled Again" (Thailand 1971)

"Won't Get Fooled Again"/"Summertime Blues"/"Love Ain't for Keeping"/"See Me, Feel Me" (Japan 1972)

"Won't Get Fooled Again"/"Behind Blue Eyes"/"Summertime Blues"/"Love Ain't for Keeping"/"See Me, Feel Me" (Japan 1972)

"Postcard"/"My Generation"/"Too Much of Anything"/"The Real Me" (Brazil 1974)

15

I Get the Story

Rock Opera from *Quads* to *Quadrophenia*

Nineteen sixty-eight was a troubled year for the Who. While they were honing the skills onstage that would earn them status as the world's greatest live band, their recorded work lacked direction. The previous year, "I Can See for Miles" failed to hit the top of the charts as Pete Townshend so firmly believed it would. The marvelous *Who Sell Out* didn't fare exceptionally well either, missing the top ten in England and barely slipping into the top fifty in America. Artistically fatigued, Townshend revived a couple of his earliest compositions, "Magic Bus" and "Call Me Lightning," so the Who could at least get a couple of singles in the shops. "Dogs" was his only recent song released in 1968, and it was generally dismissed as a novelty.

"Magic Bus" has gone on to achieve classic status, and "Call Me Lightning" and especially "Dogs" are a lot better than their dismal reputations would have you believe. Plus, the Who did record a number of superb songs in '68 that they held back, including "Glow Girl," "Melancholia," and "Little Billy." Still, there's no question that the Who were not as prolific as they'd been in the past and really needed to reclaim their former inspiration. They did so with a concept Pete Townshend and Kit Lambert had been playing with since 1966.

The scheme worked, and *Tommy* jolted the Who to the tippy top of the rock heap and slapped the term "rock opera" into the pop lexicon once and for all. Forever *Tommy* would remain the most famous and acclaimed of its operatic ilk, enduring adaptations on the stage and in the cinema and providing centerpieces for many a Who concert. However, *Tommy* was neither the first nor the last rock opera. It wasn't even the Who's first.

Assemble the musicians . . .

"I'm a Boy" (1966)

It all started as a joke. To amuse opera-loving Kit Lambert on his thirty-first birthday, Townshend and pal John "Speedy" Keen composed "Gratis Amatis" (trans: "Free Love"), a parody of composer Giuseppe Verdi that was more "mock opera" than rock opera. Lambert got the joke, but the joke got his wheels turning.

The Who's producer/manager had roots in program music. His father, Constant Lambert, was the musical director of the Royal Ballet at Covent Garden. In 1965, he helped expand Townshend's horizons and got him thinking about marrying pop and art music by lending his young charge the Prague Chamber Orchestra's *Masters of the Baroque Period*. The record featured the work of Henry Purcell, a British composer best known for his opera *Dido and Aeneas*. It was not Purcell's operatic work but his "Gordian Knot Untied," incidental music from a long-lost play, that first caught Townshend's ear (he later included this piece both in his *Lifehouse* radio play and the six-disc *Lifehouse Chronicles* CD box set). He was knocked out by Purcell's use of suspended chords in the Chaconne (a moderately paced series of variations on repeated chords) from "Gordian Knot Untied."

A suspension creates tension by shifting the third interval of a chord up to the fourth, or less commonly in pop music, the fifth. It is a movement Keith Richards would regularly exploit in his rhythm guitar work, though he'd never claim a highfalutin baroque origin. Pete Townshend, however, loved claiming high-art origins and credited Purcell as the inspiration for his use of suspended chords in "The Kids Are Alright" and later "I'm a Boy".

"I'm a Boy" has origins in a longer piece Lambert took to half-jokingly calling "Pete's rock opera," inadvertently coining the phrase that would loom so large in his boys' legend. The rock opera is distinct from the concept album (a record unified by a controlling idea, such as *The Who Sell Out*) or a song cycle (a collection of individual pieces intended to play out in a specific order, such as Van Morrison's birth-to-death sketch *Astral Weeks*) in that it should follow the basic strictures of its orchestral counterpart: specific characters, lyrical dialogue (recitative) and soliloquy (aria), and plot. Based on the one piece the Who completed from the project, *Quads* would have had all of these elements.

Although it was intended as more than a joke, *Quads* may not have been much more serious than "Gratis Amatis." Townshend envisioned *Quads* as a millennial science-fiction piece in which potential parents could choose their unborn children's genders. When a couple places an order for four females, and one mistakenly arrives with the ol' bait-'n'-tackle, mum and dad decide to raise them all as girls anyway. Much comic identity confusion ensues until Jean Marie, Felicity, Sally Joy, and Bill "the head case" grow up to form a bouffanted girl group in the tradition of the Crystals. Although "I'm a Boy" was quite likely the only *Quads* song Townshend completed, the rock opera seeds had been well planted, and before the end of 1966, they'd take root.

"A Quick One While He's Away" (1966)

One of the Who's most whimsical creations has a very practical creation story. As the story is often told, the Who were short nine minutes on their second LP. Pete Townshend claimed his compositional coffers were pretty barren after *My Generation* and the six singles that preceded and followed the LP. Ambitious Kit

Lambert encouraged a game Townshend to take six of his unfinished numbers, stitch them together, and create a "mini-opera."

Such resourcefulness! Such innovation! Groping around for a way to save the Who's sophomore statement from being a half-baked hodgepodge of original material, covers, and rerecordings of previously released tracks (see *Jigsaw Puzzle* in chapter 16), Lambert had latched onto a totally new pop subgenre. Initially, Townshend had reservations about the length of such a piece. At over nine minutes, "A Quick One While He's Away" was fairly novel in late 1966, though not without precedent. In fact, Dylan's "Desolation Row" and "Sad Eyed Lady of the Lowlands," the Stones' "Goin' Home," and the Mothers of Invention's "The Return of the Son of Monster Magnet" had already broken the ten-minute barrier. What set Townshend's song apart from those recordings is its suite-like structure and narrative. Dylan's songs are epic poems. The Stones' is a jam. The Mothers' is an avant-garde collage.

The Who take best advantage of their time with snatches of music that stand on their own quite well, and a perhaps silly but clear story line (boy leaves girl, girl succumbs to the come-on of another man, boy returns, and all is forgiven). The same is true of *Tommy*, and though it would expand its predecessor's nine minutes to double-LP length and make more complex use of recurring musical themes and dialogue, it presented few other innovations beyond those that already appeared in "A Quick One While He's Away." Even the "See Me, Feel Me" chorus that climaxes the full-length opera has roots in the rousing "You are forgiven" round that concludes "A Quick One," both in its gloriously vamping harmonies and its ambiguity (who's forgiving whom in "A Quick One?" What happens to Tommy after he climbs that mountain?). And like *Tommy* would in the coming years, the mini-opera that Townshend enjoyed calling "*Tommy*'s parents" provided the Who with a powerful centerpiece for their live act.

So, here you have it. The real rock opera pioneer, a mini one perhaps, but a complete piece composed, recorded, and released for public consumption. Despite this piece of hard evidence, questions about what is the true first rock opera persist.

Mark Wirtz: *A Teenage Opera* (1967–unfinished)

Rock opera has the whiff of revolution, but when it comes down to it, it really was just a matter of time before someone stumbled onto the idea. It was a fairly obvious untapped concept just waiting for a good tapping in the wake of the sonic and lyrical innovations the Beatles, Dylan, and the Beach Boys had already been laying down for the better part of a year. So when producer/writer/musician/comedian Mark Wirtz claims he started toying with his own rock opera as early as January 1966, we shouldn't sneer him off as some sort of bandwagon-jumping charlatan.

In actuality, Wirtz admits that the music he recorded as Mood Mosaic that month, "A Touch of Velvet—Strings for Brass," was more like incidental music from a film than opera. Backing vocalists the Ladybirds sing nothing more narrative than a series of "ooohs," "aaahs," "bops," "wows," and "whoas." However, this "musical portrayal of a love making event" (as Wirtz wrote in his Internet essay "The Story Behind *The Teenage Opera*") got him thinking conceptually, leading him to create his own rock opera in a way similar to how Lambert and Purcell and *Quads* got Townshend thinking about creating his.

The actual rock opera didn't sprout in Wirtz's brain until a full year after recording "A Touch of Velvet" . . . and a month after the release of "A Quick One While He's Away." The character called Jack the Grocer came to Mark Wirtz in a dream. Jack delivered groceries door-to-door in turn-of-the-century England. Mocked for his simple trade during his lifetime, the people of his village come to appreciate him—and the convenience his work afforded—when he suddenly dies. With bittersweet irony, Jack finally finds the love of his fellow people he'd always craved in life after his death.

Lending support to the project would be Tomorrow. Like the Who, the London outfit was made up of former mods (then called the In Crowd after Dobie Gray's modernist anthem). Wirtz passed on a blossoming psychedelic troupe called Pink Floyd to take Tomorrow under his wing. While gearing up to record a proper—and quite wonderful—psychedelic pop record for the band, Wirtz put singer Keith West and guitarist Steve Howe to work on his *Teenage Opera*. A couple of singles from the project would see release, and "Grocer Jack," released as "Excerpt from a Teenage Opera," was a huge European hit in the summer of '67. However, Wirtz was receiving resistance from EMI for including a chorus of kids on "Grocer Jack." The label dismissed his big success as a fluke novelty hit, and EMI's lack of support left the larger concept in limbo for so long that Wirtz begged to be let out of his contract as a house producer even though it meant he had to give up all future royalties to the records he'd produced. His and Keith West's careers never quite recovered (Steve Howe did quite well after rising from Tomorrow's ashes to join Yes). In the meantime, another group sidled up to lay claim to creating the first LP-length character study. But it wasn't the Who.

Nirvana: *The Story of Simon Simopath* (1967)

Nearly twenty-five years before the name became internationally associated with ripped flannel and existential angst, Nirvana was known to a much tinier audience, who linked it with baroque arrangements and twee whimsy. Irish guitarist Patrick Campbell-Lyons and Greek keyboardist Alex Spyropoulos met up in mid-sixties London, where they masterminded a chamber pop sextet that would go down in history as the pioneers of the long-playing rock opera, if only among the most hardcore psychedelic cultists.

Actually, like so many so-called rock operas, *The Story of Simon Simopath* isn't really an opera at all, and its alleged plot is a mere gimmick to tether its ten songs. The album has more in common with Ray Davies's Little Britain character sketches than the kind of complex narrative on which Pete Townshend began ruminating the previous year. There's the title character, a guy who dreams of escaping his drab office job with the woman he loves to live in outer space or something, but there is no dialogue, no real plot arc, and a dearth of characters aside from our Simon. Just as John Lennon said that *Sgt. Pepper's* worked as a concept album "because we said it worked," *The Story of Simon Simopath* is a rock opera because Nirvana dreamed up a clever title for their debut disc. Most of the tracks are love songs that lose no meaning when divorced from the ostensible concept. Still, that title and the recurring references to Simon have forever bolstered the album with its rock opera rep.

"Rael" (1967)

When *The Story of Simon Simopath* was released, Pete Townshend had already been hard at work on his next operatic endeavor for quite some time. This one was not initially intended to be a pop project for the Who. Townshend had grander designs on writing and orchestrating a "proper" opera. He spent the next half-dozen weeks studying scores and formulating a story line inspired by China's swelling population and the tense relations between Egypt and Israel. In the futuristic scenario, Communist China (the "Red Chins") wages war on Israel ("Rael") while tumbling nations and wiping out religion throughout a world so overcrowded that each citizen is consigned to a single square foot of land.

Never one to keep a good idea to himself, or to have the slightest concern that one of his ideas might not see completion, Townshend didn't waste a second telling the press about his latest brainwave. The March 1967 issue of *Beat Instrumental* devoted an entire article to what the magazine erroneously labeled his "Pop Opera." Townshend divulged this synopsis:

> It takes place in the year 1999 when China is breaking out and is about to take over the world . . . The hero, or at least, central character, loses his wife and decides to go and live in this tiny country, which is about to be over-run by the Chinese.
>
> The hero goes through hundreds of different situations and there is music for each. He goes out in a boat and gets shipwrecked; he has a bad nightmare, and so on. I have used sound effects for a lot of the situations with music over them.

As gun jumping as this article may seem, Townshend was actually being crafty in divulging his concept. He often used the press to air out his ideas, test the reaction of his interviewer and the public, and gauge how mad he sounded when describing them. This is further exemplified by the fact that he begins the article by explaining he didn't even really intend this opera for the public. He was merely composing it "as an exercise for my own satisfaction." Perhaps this was more caginess. If the reaction was "Townshend's gone off his nut," he could defend himself by saying, "Well, it's not like I was actually going to make *you* listen to it."

More practical matters prevented Townshend from completing the entire twenty-five-scene rock opera he'd envisioned. Ironically, it was his biggest rock opera instigator, Kit Lambert, who put the kibosh on *Rael*. Townshend had been studying Walter Piston's guide *Orchestrations* and composing on a Bechstein upright piano he'd rented from Harrods when, as he wrote in *The Story of Tommy*, "Kit Lambert reminded me that while I was pretending to be Wagner, the Who needed a new single." Thus, Townshend hacked his sprawling political epic down to less than seven minutes, which lost an additional minute when it appeared on *The Who Sell Out* in December.

Snatches of the extended *Rael* have slipped out in the ensuing years. The extra minute of the Who's original recording has appeared as "Rael 2" on *Thirty Years of Maximum R&B* and as "Rael Naïve" on the deluxe edition of *Sell Out*.

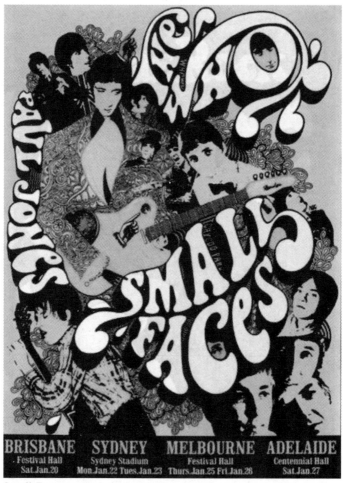

Small Faces started devising their own rock opera while touring Australia with the Who in 1968.   *Author's collection*

Less officially, Townshend's demos for the condensed "Rael," expanded to 8:26 with some baroque organ improvisation and a few lines of dialogue ("There he goes . . . what do you think?" "He's crazy . . . "), and "That Motherland Feeling" have surfaced on bootleg. By 1968, Townshend was well over his war tale of China and Israel and busy with his deaf, dumb, and blind lad, in which he'd recycle major instrumental passages of "Rael" as "Sparks" and "Undertune."

Small Faces: *Ogden's Nut Gone Flake* (1968)

As we've seen, Pete Townshend made no effort to keep his scheme to write and record a rock opera close to his chest. He continued prattling on about the project that would be *Tommy* while on tour with Small Faces in Australia in early 1968. Steve Marriott and Ronnie Lane quickly latched onto the idea in an effort to revive their latest album, which was to be filled out with covers of the soul oldies "Be My Baby" and "Every Little Bit Hurts" for lack of original material. As released in May 1968, *Ogden's Nut Gone Flake* housed a nutso string of numbers charting daft Happiness Stan's quest to make the half-moon whole again. While the released version of "Rael" reduced the LP-length rock opera concept back to the miniest of mini-operas, the saga of "Happiness Stan" managed to fill an entire side of an album, and unlike *Simon Simopath*, it worked in a genuine plot arc and dialogue between Stan and the weird characters he encounters: the hermit Mad John and a talking fly who digs shepherd's pie. To date, "Happiness Stan" was the longest and most convincing rock opera.

The Crazy World of Arthur Brown: *The Crazy World of Arthur Brown* (1968)

Pete Townshend was strolling through London's psychedelicized UFO Club in his caftan when he first encountered Arthur Brown, a madman with an alleged five-octave vocal range and a flair for the theatrical. Tasked with scouting jazz and weird pop artists for Track Records, Townshend was impressed enough with Brown's broad voice and the throng of onlookers telling him Brown was the next big thing that he signed up the singer.

The first order of business was getting some demos on tape, but recognizing that his new protégé had more convincingly operatic pipes than Roger Daltrey, Townshend was also scheming to cast Brown as the lead character in *Rael*. When that project fizzled with the release of *The Who Sell Out*, Kit Lambert dragged the Crazy World of Arthur Brown into the studio to cut the album that would make them stars. Possibly stimulated by Townshend's latest pursuits, Brown had bigger game than hit singles and pop stardom in mind. He plotted a fully conceptual debut album, a tale of gods and devils, a plunge into the deepest depths of a man's psyche. Lambert would have none of it. As Brown told Richie Unterberger in *Urban Spacemen and Wayfaring Strangers*, the producer scoffed, "Nobody's going to buy *that*." With *Tommy* in the making, Lambert may have been more concerned about Brown usurping the Who's spot in the rock opera sprint than commercial matters. The scuffle between Brown and Lambert ended in compromise. Lambert would control side B, with its Screamin' Jay Hawkins and James Brown covers, and Brown would mastermind side A, with its suite of extracts from his "Fire" concept. Reduced as it is, the tracks do not play out with a clear narrative. One might not even recognize that this was supposed to have some sort of continuity if not for the recurring images of plummeting into flames.

Although its namesake was rightfully disappointed with *The Crazy World of Arthur Brown*, Lambert was right about one thing: he was going to get Brown a hit. Ironically, the hit was "Fire," a frantic number pulled from the side A suite. The single also turned out to be Brown's sole significant chart hit, as the Crazy World soon disbanded. He was not completely through with rock opera, though. In 1975, he appeared as a priest in the *Tommy* film. Thirty years after the release of *The Crazy World of Arthur Brown*, he served as narrator during a live performance of the very first record that could claim to be a true full-length rock opera. . . .

The Pretty Things: *S.F. Sorrow* (1968)

The Pretty Things never achieved the success of the Who, the Beatles, or the band their guitarist Dick Taylor helped found, the Rolling Stones. Yet this filthy, scraggly, raunchy horde of acid-dropping blues freaks was one of the period's most exciting groups. Their debut single "Rosalyn" was as rip-snorting as any of the Stones' hard R&B, their "Defecting Grey" more demented than the Beatles' most imaginative forays into psychedelia, and their *S.F. Sorrow* as legitimate a rock opera as *Tommy*. And it was in the shops half a year before the Who's double album.

The early release of The Pretty Things' superb psychedelic opus has led to much speculation on its influence over *Tommy*. Not only is there the general rock opera concept, but there is the matter of its contents. *S.F. Sorrow* tracks a British lad from birth through tragedy through his acid-induced spiritual awakening and ultimate isolation. The only thing missing from *Sorrow* is Tom's physical disabilities. Even war looms in the tale, although unlike Tommy who is merely the son of a World War I Army Captain, Sorrow himself is a grunt in that war. Some have also pointed out the similarity between the muscular acoustic guitar intro of the Pretty Things' "Old Man Going" and that of "Pinball Wizard" as Exhibit A in the case arguing that Townshend drew significant inspiration from *S.F. Sorrow*. In his defense, that kind of aggressive strumming had been in his repertoire as far back as 1965's "Anyway, Anyhow, Anywhere."

For the Pretty Things, a phenomenal band that never came within miles and miles and miles of the Who's fame, getting credit for influencing that most ubiquitous of rock operas is a point worth pressing. In 2000, vocalist Phil May told Richie Unterberger in *Urban Spacemen and Wayfaring*

The Who may have invented the rock opera, but the Pretty Things beat them to the shops with the first LP-length one, *S.F. Sorrow*, in late 1968. Singer Phil May designed the story line and the evocative record sleeve.   *Author's collection*

Strangers, "In so many write-ups, he always said that *S.F. Sorrow* influenced *Tommy*. Just recently, Townshend's been apparently denying any knowledge. It almost sounded like a lawyer's statement—'we want to categorically deny we ever heard any copy of *S.F Sorrow*.'"

Four years later, Pete Townshend addressed the controversy in *Uncut*, saying that in '68, "We were all talking about concept and opera . . . I remember talking to [Pretty Things drummer Viv Prince] about rock opera—I don't know whether or not he took it back to the rest of the band. There may have been rivalry at the beginning. Admittedly, I got a bit self-righteous when people said *S.F. Sorrow* was the first rock opera—but it wasn't about being the first." Townshend further illustrates how *Tommy* was an also-ran of sorts by confessing, "there was a sense that what we were thinking of had already happened on *Sgt. Pepper* or *Pet Sounds* or *Ogden's Nut Gone Flake*."

Tommy (1969)

On May 23, 1969, all questions about who arrived first to the rock opera party ceased to matter. Traced back to "I'm a Boy," or at least "A Quick One While He's Away," it had been the Who all along, so all was fairly fair when everyone assumed they'd invented the form with *Tommy*. Having failed to see his *Quads* and *Rael* concepts to completion, the release of *Tommy* must have been very satisfying for Pete Townshend. And though he was unquestionably the driving force behind the project, this was a true collaborative effort of which all members of the band could be proud. Roger Daltrey credited the collective isolation the band felt while touring America in 1968 for allowing them to put their combativeness behind them and work as a more unified band. Townshend made the most of John Entwistle's macabre sensibility by assigning him the most unsavory moments in Tommy's story: his physical abuse at the hands of his Cousin Kevin and his sexual abuse at the hands of Uncle Ernie. Keith Moon contributed the zany idea of making Tommy's spiritual center a working-class holiday resort. Daltrey brought the entire concept to life by fully committing to the character of the deaf, dumb, and blind boy with nuanced sensitivity. And let's not forget the man who'd discouraged Arthur Brown from indulging in operatic folly the previous year. Kit Lambert worked hard with the band, encouraging Townshend not to give up, helping to give the story form and direction, and imploring the band to embrace the wild pretentiousness of it all.

Despite the monumental individuality the band members displayed on *Tommy*, the project became an unwieldy success that nearly consumed them. As an oft-told tidbit goes, lots of folks thought the band was called Tommy and the record was called *The Who*. While that may have been somewhat frustrating, the guys really could not complain. They'd finally hit on the ace device for which they'd been fumbling desperately over the past two years, and they did it with the unlikeliest of plots: a boy deprived of his most essential senses after witnessing his mum's lover's murder becomes a pinball-playing sensation by sniffing the ball, which naturally leads a congregation of hippies to regard him as a new-age messiah. It's a story as old as the hills.

The absurdity of *Tommy* was resoundingly consumed by the Who's completely committed presentation, both in its delicate, largely acoustic studio incarnation and its electrifying, deafening stage version. Basically, the public accepted the crazy concept because the Who sold it really, really well. Plus the individual songs were very good, and when the tenuous novelty of the concept wears off, "Pinball Wizard," "We're Not Gonna Take It," "The Acid Queen," "Sensation," "Cousin Kevin," "Amazing Journey," and so many more still hold up as great tunes in their own right.

For the Who's peers with similar ambitions, *Tommy*'s wild success could be an irritant. When *S.F. Sorrow* was finally released in America several months after *Tommy*, some critics accused the Pretty Things of leaping on the Who's wagon. The Kinks would face similar cynicism the following October.

The Kinks: *Arthur, or the Decline and Fall of the British Empire* (1969)

Ray Davies was Pete Townshend's likeliest rival for the title of British Pop's Storyteller Laureate. While Townshend's visions tended toward the grandiose—sci-fi futurism, political and religious strife, messiahs and arcade games—Davies's were intimate. With the bombast of early power-chord pounders such as "You Really Got Me" and "All Day and All of the Night" in their past, the Kinks took a sharp turn down a bucolic road. Folky acoustic guitars and baroque harpsichords took prominence in their arrangements, and Davies stopped shouting to sigh through a lop-sided grin. This was the Kinks of "A Well Respected Man" and "Sunny Afternoon" and "Waterloo Sunset" and "Autumn Almanac" and "Days," a group that valued beauty and truth over bashing skulls with the business end of a Telecaster.

With that lighter music came a more observational bent in Ray Davies's songwriting. He became a creator of characters, though like Pete Townshend, his fantasy creations—the layabout of "Sunny Afternoon," the bedraggled homemaker of "Two Sisters"—were often reflections of himself. With such a knack for creating characters, Davies gravitated toward extended story lines quite naturally. He first began toying with the concept-album concept in 1966 when he schemed to link the tracks on the Kinks' fourth album with sound effects. Pye Records was unsupportive of such a progressive idea, and *Face to Face* appeared without that unifying gimmick (though effects still flit through "Party Line," "Rainy Day in June," and "Holiday in Waikiki").

After the release and unprecedented popularity of the Beatles' ostensible concept album, *Sgt. Pepper's Lonely Hearts Club Band*, in June 1967, the kinds of ideas Ray Davies had for *Face to Face* no longer seemed so mad. Around that time, he resumed thinking conceptually about a future recording project. He set out to make *The Kinks Are the Village Green Preservation Society* his band's least commercial record and break the common (and completely ignorant) belief that the Kinks were nothing more than a singles band. Released in November 1968, the album sported fifteen utterly perfect snapshots of life in a little English village. Characters did not stroll from song to song, so *Village Green Preservation Society* couldn't be called a rock opera, but by Pete Townshend's own admission, it made a resounding impact on him. According to Dave Davies, Townshend even tried to finagle the 8-track masters of the album away from the Kinks so he might unlock its secrets.

While Ray Davies dreamed of expanding his masterpiece and making a proper musical of it, he got involved in other projects to keep the Kinks afloat during a commercial sagging point. In December 1968, he struck a deal with the BBC to compose five songs for a series called *Where Was Spring?* The following January he signed another small-screen contract, this time with Granada Television. The project would be a collaboration between Davies and novelist Julian Mitchell called "The Decline and Fall of the British Empire." Like Ray's earlier song "Rosy Won't You Please Come Home," the program was to be based on his continued pain over his sister Rose and her husband Arthur Anning emigrating to Australia in search of greater prosperity than that available in England.

Although *Where Was Spring?* came to pass, as did additional writing assignments for the films *Till Death Us Do Part* and *The Virgin Soldiers*, the film closest to Ray Davies's heart stalled right before reaching production. Nevertheless, the Kinks released their soundtrack as *Arthur, or the Decline and Fall of the British Empire*.

Like *Village Green Preservation Society, Arthur* is not a proper opera, though it bears something closer to a story arc than the earlier album did. Upon its October 1969 release, it faced the inevitable rip-off accusations even as Davies insisted he'd never even heard *Tommy*. Nevertheless, the new infatuation with rock opera and glowing notices in the United States helped resurrect the Kinks' career in the States. They would spend the rest of the seventies producing conceptual projects: *Lola vs. Powerman and the Money-Go-Round, Muswell Hillbillies, Everybody's in Show Biz*, the two-act *Preservation* project, *Soap Opera*, and *Schoolboys in Disgrace*. *Preservation*, which realized Ray's long-time desire to overproduce *Village Green*, would be the Kinks' first proper rock opera, and for the first time, a grandiose concept would take precedence over the perfectly conceived, stand-alone pop songs that are the essence of the band's brilliance. That's something the Who would never do.

Andrew Lloyd Webber and Tim Rice: *Jesus Christ Superstar* (1970)

Although the Kinks began proper work on *Arthur* during the same month *Tommy* was released, the two projects are so dissimilar and the origin of *Arthur* as a TV soundtrack is so clear that there is no reason to believe Ray Davies was trying to rip off the Who's act. Many critics thought differently.

Composer Andrew Lloyd Webber is no stranger to accusations of plagiarism either. He's gotten heat for writing melodies reminiscent of everything from Pink Floyd's "Echoes" to Barnes and Barnes's "Fish Heads." When he and lyricist Tim Rice cocomposed their own rock opera while in their very early twenties, it was hard not to trace it back to Pete Townshend, especially considering how its tale dealt with the rise and fall of a messiah. However, Webber and Rice's opera adapted a text a wee bit older than *Tommy. Jesus Christ Superstar* relates the Gospels as a double-LP worth of toe-tapping bombast voiced by the likes of Deep Purple's Ian Gillan (Jesus), Murray "One Night in Bangkok" Head (Judas), and Yvonne "If I Can't Have You" Elliman (Mary Magdalene). Like *Tommy*, the album would find its way onto the stage and screen and sells lots and lots of copies. Unlike *Tommy*, it was not written by genuine rock 'n' rollers, as should be clear to anyone who's heard it.

Lifehouse (1970–1971, unreleased)

Riding high on the success of *Tommy* and how it almost instantaneously transformed the Who from fading singles act to top-tier rock superstars, Pete Townshend devised his follow-up rock opera while still touring his first one in 1970. The public first became aware of the idea that would be *Lifehouse* in the

October 24 edition of *Disc and Music Echo*. At this point, the Who were to be the sun around which the real main character, a roadie named Bobby, was to orbit. Bobby's discovery of a mystical lost note ends in "destruction," leaving only that note remaining. As Townshend continued developing the idea, the note would still have seismic effects, but the results were to be more spiritual, less destructive.

Lifehouse was to be set in a future age when pollution has made the earth so uninhabitable that the global government has decreed all citizens must submit to an enforced period of hibernation in which they are sustained, doped, and entertained by plugging into a massive computerized grid—"a little like the modern Internet," as Townshend would observe in the liner notes of his *Lifehouse Chronicles* box set. Rock 'n' roll, that great stimulator of independence, has been banned. A girl named Mary decides to revolt from the government-imposed home detention and trek across the devastated countryside. Her destination: the Lifehouse, where a revolutionary rock concert masterminded by Bobby is rumored to be taking place. Her parents, Sally and Ray (a tribute to Townshend's hero Mr. Davies?), a pair of Scottish farmers, take to their motor caravan in their life-sustaining spacesuits in search of missing Mary. When they finally arrive, they slip out of their suits to partake in the performance by submitting themselves as "blueprints" for a magnum opus that unlocks "the one perfect note." As it plays, all attendees lose themselves in a wild dervish dance while the military convenes outside. When the army smashes into the Lifehouse to put an end to all the nasty subversion and pop music, the concert participants suddenly transcend their bodies and vanish into rock 'n' roll nirvana. Those at home listening to the concert on the grid, which Bobby has "hacked," are gone too.

With *Lifehouse*, Pete Townshend devised a far more complex, rich, and original concept than *Tommy*. Not only did he prognosticate the zombifying effects of the Internet and the ever-intensifying environmental crisis that now threatens life on Earth, but he gave the abstract liberating joys of rock music a solid shape and basically wrote *The Matrix* twenty years ahead of the Wachowski siblings. Looks like you owe Pete a couple of royalty checks, Lana and Andy!

Synopsized like this, *Lifehouse* seems pretty easy to get a grip on, but Pete Townshend had a lot of trouble getting his concept across in 1970. At first, his bandmates were game to go along with their leader even as they couldn't quite suss what he was on about. The real resistance came from his former ally in opera. Convinced that the Who's ongoing success would forever go arm in arm with *Tommy*, Kit Lambert wanted to keep the focus on all things deaf, dumb, and blind. Universal Pictures had recently bought up Decca, and Townshend wrote a script with the intent of making *Lifehouse* an ambitious record/concert/film project. Meanwhile, Lambert had written a *Tommy* script *he* wanted to get made. Feeling protective of his property, Townshend rejected the script without even reading it, thus creating a rift between himself and his manager and mentor that never healed. From that point, whenever Townshend told anyone about his futuristic rock opera, Lambert swooped in to inform them that his client was nuts and the Who were actually working on his *Tommy* film. In early 1971, the Who managed to put on their own series of *Lifehouse* concerts at London's Young Vic Theater, but the open-door policy quickly went awry when they were greeted with a bunch of skinheads uninterested in the audience participation Townshend had in mind. That the concerts didn't live up to the communal bliss in his script left him crestfallen. That Daltrey started incessantly nagging him to abandon the whole thing and get back on the road further deflated his enthusiasm. Failing to understand the project, Universal refused to provide further funding, thereby hitting the destruct button on the enterprise. *Poof*—off went *Lifehouse* to its own rock 'n' roll nirvana.

This must have been devastating to Townshend. *Lifehouse* was not the sketchy goof *Quads* was or the lofty and rather un–rock 'n' roll behemoth *Rael* had been shaping up to be. This was a genuinely innovative, quite brilliant idea, and he had the excellent songs to back it up. Fortunately, he would not toss them out with the bathwater, and the Who would recycle those songs for what many rate as the band's greatest album, *Who's Next*. Only "Baba O'Riley" did not make much sense outside of the *Lifehouse* concept. The rest worked perfectly as concept-free songs. Yet Townshend remained fixated enough on the opera to scheme to resurrect it around the time of *Who Are You*, reference it in his 1993 solo concept album *Psychoderelict* (in which rock star Ray High can't get over the abortion of his rock opera *Gridlife*), and produce it as a BBC radio play in 1999. That play would also feature in his website exclusive *The Lifehouse Chronicles* (2000), an appropriately futuristic six-disc box set featuring the radio show, a disc of orchestral incidental music from the play, a disc of Townshend's musical experiments, and two discs of his brilliant and beautifully produced demos.

David Bowie: *The Rise and Fall of Ziggy Stardust and the Spiders from Mars* (1972)

Like Arthur Brown, David Bowie was a glitzy soul with one foot in rock 'n' roll and the other in Art Theater. Not surprisingly, this grand unifier of pop and style was a dedicated mod and an ardent Who fan in his prefame days, back when he was known by his given name, David Jones. As front man of Davy Jones and the Lower Third, the future Thin White Duke drew extreme influence from the Who at their most noisily abstract. As he developed into a more unique solo artist, David Bowie combined the show-tune flair of Anthony Newley with the sharp rock 'n' roll of the Who and Stones and became one of the seventies' biggest stars.

Long after he'd left his mod gear behind, Bowie continued to draw inspiration from the Who, both in the powerful riffs that lit a glam inferno beneath his music and in his approach to record making and performing. Like Pete Townshend, he found his artistic voice by constructing extended narratives on vinyl. Like Roger Daltrey, he put his acting ability to use by personifying the characters in those narratives onstage.

Bowie's high kicks may be another thing he learned from Pete Townshend. *Author's collection*

Bowie's first and greatest such work was *The Rise and Fall of Ziggy Stardust and the Spiders from Mars*. Like Tommy (or the title guy in Webber and Rice's rock opera), Ziggy is a messianic figure. He is an alien rock star who drifts to a doomed Earth to spread a message of love and hope. His mission fails when he succumbs to the usual excesses and adulation that go with the lifestyle. Even alien messiahs can't resist a little sex, drugs, and rock 'n' roll.

As is the case with most of the non-Who albums labeled as rock operas, *Ziggy Stardust* fails to completely live up to that designation. Ziggy is the only character to whom Bowie gives voice. The story line is hazy. The concept still provided Bowie with the same things *Tommy* bestowed on the Who: it gave direction to his stage act, gave him (and his band, now christened the Spiders from Mars) iconic roles to play, and gave him his first cinematic vehicle (though as a concert film and not as a dramatic musical, as Ken Russell's *Tommy* would be). And as is the case with *Tommy*, *Ziggy*'s operatic conceit isn't nearly as important as its abundance of groovy songs.

Quadrophenia (1973)

Despite the disappointing end of *Lifehouse*, Pete Townshend refused to give up on pursuing concepts to shape his music on vinyl and stage. He also remained undeterred from his desire to make the Who the center of a multimedia project. With *Who's Next* out of the way, he started mulling a new project he titled *Rock Is Dead . . . Long Live Rock*. The subject would be the one he knew best: the Who. There would be a film and a new LP booming with songs celebrating the band's topsy-turvy career.

The idea wasn't a bad one, but it didn't have the ambitious reach of *Tommy* or *Lifehouse* despite the multimedia angle. However, like so many of Townshend's fleeting ideas, it set him on the path to a more appropriate one. Contemplating the Who's past got him thinking about their mod origins. Instead of trying to summarize the entire crazy career thus far, he'd instead focus on that one, brief period. As he planned to do with *Lifehouse*, he also sidelined the band to bring an outside character to the fore. All four members of the band were still very present in the story, as each quarter of the fellow's fractured personality reflected one of them: Roger the tough guy, Keith the lunatic, John the closet romantic, and Pete the spiritual seeker.

There once was Tommy and Bobby. Now there would be Jimmy.

The setting is England, 1965, and Jimmy is a disgruntled youth who has lost faith in family, love, and religion. Perhaps he can find a sense of belonging as a mod. This too reveals its artifice, as Jimmy becomes disillusioned with all the requisite fighting and fashion chasing. His discovery that the Ace Face, the mod all the others aspired to be, is nothing but a lowly bellboy puts the final nail in Jimmy's fealty to the clique. He ends up weeping and clinging to a rock in the English Channel after apparently trying to drown himself; another ambiguous ending for a Townshend rock opera.

The original *Rock Is Dead* plan was to musically recapture all the beats of the Who's career, from the mod row of their first discs to their recent synthesizer experiments. Townshend even composed a couple of songs in the quirky, poppy vein of *A Quick One* and *Sell Out*: "Get Inside" and "Four Faces" ("Joker James" was a genuine product of those days). After realizing that he can look back but he can't go back, Townshend decided to keep the sound in step with the currently heavy Who, while also pushing into territory bordering on prog rock. There would still be a few references to the Who oldies "I'm the Face," "Zoot Suit," "My Generation," and "The Kids Are Alright," but *Quadrophenia* ended up pretty far removed from the period of its setting. How many mods spent as much time chewing over social injustice or karma as Jimmy? Probably somewhere in the range of none. Once again, Pete Townshend's character was basically Pete Townshend, and even the toughness, lunacy, and romance that were supposed to represent his cohorts were aspects of his own complex persona.

Some have questioned *Quadrophenia*'s rep as a rock opera. Townshend certainly didn't create it as self-consciously in that vein as he did *Tommy*. There isn't much dialogue between characters. With the exception of "The Punk and the Godfather," "Bell Boy," and possibly "I've Had Enough," Jimmy voices the songs exclusively. Thus, one may argue *Quadrophenia* is as much a song cycle as it is a rock opera, even as it employs such operatic elements as aria, recurring musical themes, and leitmotifs, albeit each one refers to a different facet of Jimmy rather than a distinct individual. But can't those four different facets be viewed as four different characters?

Today, *Quadrophenia* is rated as one of the Who's very best records, many folks giving it the edge over *Tommy*. In its own day, it was a troubled project. Daltrey loved the songs but hated the mix, which half-buried his bluster. *Quadrophenia* failed to give the Who a viable new stage act as *Tommy* did. The prerecorded tapes of voices and synthesizers necessary to bring the album to life onstage were hell to play along with. Townshend grew irritated with Daltrey's need to explain each song for a confused and impatient audience.

With that, Townshend relented on his pursuit of concepts, no longer feeling he had the "arrogance" or "balls" to devise one for his band's next record. *The Who by Numbers* would be a return to ostensibly unconnected numbers, even as its unrelenting self-examination, which even extended to John Entwistle's "Success Story," made it just as thematically unified as *Tommy* or *Quadrophenia*. The Who would make movies, but none were created in conjunction with new music as he dreamed *Lifehouse* and *Rock Is Dead . . . Long Live Rock!* would be. The stage act would go back to being an assortment of hits new and old. Little did Pete realize that the Who would triumphantly resurrect *Quadrophenia* onstage decades later and as recently as 2013. But for the time being, he and the Who were done with rock opera. The Who's progeny were not.

Beyond *Quadrophenia*

Just a year after *Quadrophenia*, Genesis released their own rather impenetrable double-LP narrative called *The Lamb Lies Down on Broadway*. What's the young man at the center of this journey through a phantasmagoric NYC named? Rael!

Aside from ample use of synthesizers, *Lamb Lies Down* doesn't sound much like the Who. The same cannot be said of *2112*. Released in 1976, this sci-fi tale of outlawed rock 'n' roll and officious governments by Canadian proggers Rush shared some suspicious similarities with *Lifehouse*. Less suspicious was the band's instrumental work, as bassist Geddy Lee, drummer Neil Peart, and guitarist Alex Lifeson are all diehard Who fans. Lifeson's droning movable triads on the "Discovery" movement of "2112" are unmistakably Townshend-like. Daltrey, however, would have to run over his balls with a steamroller to sound like Geddy.

Nineteen seventy-nine saw two major rock operas, one a smarmy three-act parody by Frank Zappa called *Joe's Garage*, the other a deathly serious exploration of self-indulgence and madness by Pink Floyd called *The Wall*. On the latter, Roger Waters mined the same war-related traumas, messianic complexes, and psychological breakdowns as Pete Townshend did on *Tommy*.

In the eighties, Townshend was wading back into conceptual waters with his "novel" *White City* and taking the full plunge with *The Iron Man* and *Psychoderelict*. Before and after came such rockingly operatic items as Hüsker Dü's *Zen Arcade* and Queensrÿche's *Operation Mindcrime*, as well as records by such umlaut-free groups as Afghan Whigs (*Black Love*, a blaxploitation tale knowingly set in 1973, the same year *Quadrophenia* was released), Green Day (*American Idiot*), and the Decemberists (*The Hazards of Love*).

Then in 2006, Pete Townshend and Roger Daltrey finally returned to the long-player with *Endless Wire*, paying an extended homage to their past with an all-new mini-opera. "Wire and Glass" shook Psychoderelict Ray High out of mothballs and gave the faded rock star a new gig as manager of a young singing group. Sweet-natured and quite moving, "Wire and Glass" brought the Who's relationship with the rock opera full circle, leaving them as the first and last words on the subgenre they pioneered.

16

The Good's Gone

Abandoned Projects

Progress doesn't happen accidentally. The most ambitious artists are constantly searching for new ideas to shake up their mediums. Take *Sgt. Pepper's Lonely Hearts Club Band*, which came about because Paul McCartney consciously thrust himself into a mid-sixties art scene that extended beyond Chuck Berry and Little Richard (John Lennon, however, chose to stay home and subsist on a daily diet of acid).

Pete Townshend and Kit Lambert were always on the hunt for ways to distinguish the Who from their peers, to hit on new sounds, concepts, and ways of delivering their art. A lot of ideas came and went along the way, leaving a large crop of projects that never came to fruition. In the previous chapter, we looked at a few rock operas that never fully developed. Here are some of the other abandoned projects peppering Who lore.

The Scrapped Debut (1965)

John Lennon and Paul McCartney set a new standard for pop songwriting from the very start of their fab career. Not every rock 'n' roller was as naturally inclined toward the compositional arts as the two Beatles. Even as the promise of songwriting royalties flickered on the dollar and pound signs in many a pop singer's eyeballs, they couldn't all deliver the goods. Only the Beach Boys and the Kinks were capable of matching the Beatles' prolificacy (if we allow that folks like Dylan and Donovan had yet to become rock 'n' rollers). Other writers who would come to create some of rock 'n' roll's most enduring works required a longer running start. In contrast to the roughly 50 percent of original material the Beatles, Beach Boys, and Kinks included on their debut albums, Mick Jagger and Keith Richards could only manage a single original on the Stones' (while a couple of group jams based on existing songs offset the standards). They wouldn't earnestly commit to writing their own songs until their fourth album, *Aftermath*, released in 1966. The Hollies, the Yardbirds, and the Zombies would also have to work on their skills for several years before they were able to craft songs capable of competing with those of their peers. Some groups, such as the Animals, never really got the hang of it.

As hardworking and prolific as he was, Pete Townshend too would have to buckle down to develop his craft. "I Can't Explain" was a smashingly successful early effort, but other tunes he had in his reservoir—such as the piffling pop "It Was You"—were not going to cut it. So when the Who got into IBC Studios with Shel Talmy in April 1965, they arrived armed with all the R&B covers they'd been maximizing onstage for the past year. All of that live work resulted in punchy performances of the James Brown and Motown standards they favored, but when music journalist John Emery heard what the Who had planned for their debut LP, he scoffed. Plenty of bands would have said, "Tough shit, journo. This is all we got." The Who took Emery's criticisms under consideration, because he had a point. Only one original—"Out in the Street" (under its initial title, "You're Going to Know Me")—sat among the eight covers on the acetate. Even though the Beatles, Stones, Beach Boys, Kinks, and the rest were still putting out samplers of originals and covers, none of their recent releases had such a lame ratio. Pete Townshend commenced completing new songs furiously. The fruits of his labor can be heard in the eight impressive originals comprising the bulk of *My Generation*.

Songs recorded for possible inclusion: "You're Going to Know Me," "Leaving Here," "Please, Please, Please," "I Don't Mind," "Heat Wave," "Shout and Shimmy," "Motoring," "Lubie (Come Back Home)," "I'm a Man."

"Anyway, Anyhow, Anywhere" and "Daddy Rolling Stone" were also recorded during these sessions, but considering the contemporary practice of omitting singles from LPs, it's possible they would have been left off the album.

Jigsaw Puzzle (1966)

Pete Townshend did an impressive job of bringing his songwriting up to speed in the few months that passed between John Emery's critique and the release of *My Generation*, but the effort left his songbook pretty well drained. When the time came for the Who to start work on their second album, he had very little in reserve. One way around this was to see if the other guys had latent skills worth cultivating. Kit Lambert assigned Daltrey, Entwistle, and Moon two original songs each for the sophomore platter. Only Entwistle displayed the natural talent Lambert was seeking. Daltrey managed just one song, and Moon managed two, all three apparently completed with a good deal of assistance from Townshend and Entwistle. There still wasn't enough fresh original material, so once again, the guys returned to other artists' repertoires. They had go's at the Regents' (by way of the Beach Boys) "Barbara Ann," the Everly Brothers' "Man with Money," and the theme song to *Batman*. Still desperate, they took another crack at "Heat Wave," rerecorded their most recent single, "I'm a Boy," and revived Pete Townshend's previously released production of "Circles" (see chapter 9).

According to John Atkins in *The Who on Record*, the Who's November/December 1966 fan club newsletter announced the release of the second Who album, *Jigsaw Puzzle*. The track listing included in the letter ditched all covers but "Barbara Ann" and "Heat Wave," though "Circles" and the remake of "I'm a Boy" remained in the running. Also included was "In the City," which had appeared on the B-side of "I'm a Boy" back in August.

So *Jigsaw Puzzle* was to consist of two covers, a remake, two recycled B-sides, and seven fresh originals, only two of which ("Run Run Run" and "Don't Look Away") had been written by the band's most seasoned songwriter. Such a disc may have helped tread water in 1965, but this was late '66. The record-buying public had been spoiled by a year of spectacular statements that included *Blonde on Blonde, Pet Sounds, Aftermath, Revolver,* and *Face to Face.* The Who could surely do better, and just as fans were setting their eyes on that newsletter, *Jigsaw Puzzle* was already being disassembled for the *Ready Steady Who* EP released in early November. The remakes and B-side were flung aside, leaving "Heat Wave" as the sketchiest leftover from the *Jigsaw Puzzle* concept. In place of the scrapped tracks were a powerful rendition of "So Sad About Us," a song Pete previously handed off to the Merseys, and the effectively time-consuming mini-opera "A Quick One While He's Away." Thus, the Who had *A Quick One,* a sufficiently strong follow-up to a strong debut album.

Announced track listing as repeated in *The Who on Record*: "I'm a Boy," "Run Run Run," "Don't Look Away," "Circles," "I Need You," "Showbiz Sonato" (original title of "Cobwebs and Strange"), "In the City," "Boris the Spider," "Whiskey Man," "See My Way," "Heat Wave," "Barbara Ann."

The Instrumental EP (1967)

The Who's scrapped debut album and *Jigsaw Puzzle* were abandoned because both projects lacked imagination. The idea of putting out an EP of noisy, improvised instrumentals in a year when bands were essentially erasing their core sounds with excessive experimentation in the recording studio was actually fairly inspired. In footage filmmaker Timo Aarniala shot during a stop in Helsinki on April 30, 1967, Pete Townshend actually discussed the project from the opposite viewpoint, saying that most artists were currently making records that attempted to translate their stage act with high fidelity. This declaration was a bit dubious, as was Townshend's use of Jimi Hendrix as an example (he apparently hadn't been listening to such experimental studio creations as "I Don't Live Today," "Third Stone from the Sun," or "Are You Experienced?" very closely).

Despite a slightly misguided inspiration, the instrumental EP was an interesting idea, and Townshend, Entwistle, and Moon certainly had the musical chops and inventiveness to pull off such a concept. But in those days, the Who's ideas came easier than their commitment, and after recording just two pieces—the jam "Sodding About" (which Entwistle referred to as "Instrumental-No Title" in an *NME* interview nine years later) and a shambling yet powerful arrangement of "In the Hall of the Mountain King" from Edvard Grieg's *Peer Gynt*—they were on to other things.

Who's Lily? (1967)

Like the two albums that preceded it, *The Who Sell Out* was almost a desperate assemblage of whatever songs the band could throw together on short notice. Before hitting on the inspired pirate radio gimmick, the Who's third album was to be another hodgepodge of songs written by all four band members (eight by Townshend, six by the rest). At least they weren't counting on including any covers this time (though a punky version of the stage staple "Summertime Blues" was recorded as a possible single). On July 1, *Disc* magazine revealed that *Who's Lily?* was in the works.

Despite a good number of strong songs, the initial selection in the running for *Who's Lily?* wasn't going to amount to serious competition for Hendrix's debut or the recently released *Sgt. Pepper's.* "Pictures of Lily" and "Doctor, Doctor" had their day as a successful single; they didn't need to be recycled on LP. Moon's contribution, a pop confection called "Girl's Eyes," wasn't fit for anyone older than three. Authorship issues stifled Daltrey's offering, "Early Morning Cold Taxi" (see chapter 6), which wasn't up to the level of Townshend and Entwistle's songs, anyway. Wisely, the Who once again vetoed rush releasing their latest album. Songs were rerecorded and scrapped (the loss of "Glittering Girl," Townshend's protofeminist power-popper, was a shame, though). Others were freshly written. An ingenious pirate radio concept was envisaged. Abracadabra! Yet another potentially subpar album was transformed into something wonderful: *The Who Sell Out.*

Songs under consideration: "Armenia City in the Sky," "Early Morning Cold Taxi," "Pictures of Lily," "Doctor, Doctor," "Girl's Eyes," "I Can See For Miles," "I Can't Reach You," "Glittering Girl," "Someone's Coming," "Relax," "Mary Anne with the Shaky Hand" (electric single version), "Rael."

Sound and Picture City (1967/1968)

Imagine tuning in your TV every week to watch Pete, Rog, John, and Keith falling into various zany situations or romping along to "Odorono" or "Dogs." Imagine them slamming away on a catchy theme song or introducing celebrity guests ranging from Bob Dylan to TV's other favorite popsters the Monkees. Crazy? Perhaps, but a weekly series starring the Who was not just one of the band's longest-running projects on the table; it came surprisingly close to reality.

As early as February 1967, the Who were teasing the press with their proposed TV show. At the time, Beatles manager Brian Epstein was handling the Who's bookings, and he was really pushing for the charismatic foursome to star in their own program. Forever on the lookout for a good gimmick, the Who were game. The Michael Lindsay-Hogg–directed film they'd recently shot to promote "Happy Jack" revealed four photogenic lads capable of capering as well as the Monkees. Clearly, Townshend and Moon were natural comedians. Even

Entwistle looked comfortable in the promo! Plus their colorful, funny brand of pop would lend itself well to comedic antics. The idea could work.

In the negative column, the Who were notoriously negative, combative menaces who spoke openly about their drug use and sang songs about transgender children and masturbation. Was this group really ready for prime time? And what would a TV show do to their career? The Monkees were the most popular band in the world in 1967, but their star fell fast and hard, leaving them pariahs and punch lines for decades (though recent reevaluation of their work has been kinder to the guys, who actually recorded a good deal of their music, much of which was superb and surprisingly experimental). The Who didn't have to fret over embarrassing revelations about studio musicians playing on their records, which gave them a leg up on the Monkees, but still, the project smacked of desperation.

Regardless, a TV series remained a possibility into 1968, and in the spring, a newsletter announcing its upcoming debut on the BBC materialized. As described, *Sound and Picture City* would diverge from *The Monkees* quite a bit. Instead of a thirty-minute sitcom, it would be a sixty-minute variety show bubbling with sketches and musical guests. The Who would perform a new tune each week. Three guests had apparently already been booked: the Monkees, Lulu, and Bob Dylan. Now *that's* variety!

Just as *Sound and Picture City* seemed most likely to become an actual TV show, it pooped out. Roger Daltrey said the BBC actually wasn't all that keen on the idea, nor was the band. He said *The Monkees* series wasn't really all that profitable for NBC (their mega-selling records, however, were a different story), and that show would peter out after just two seasons. In the end, *Sound and Picture City* metamorphosed into the BBC variety series *How It Is*, on which Keith Moon would make an appearance in September 1968. The show's provisional title divulged its origins as a Who project: *My Generation*.

So it's possible the Who sidestepped a real career killer when *Sound and Picture City* faltered. Would anyone have taken *Tommy* seriously had it been made by a bunch of TV stars? Maybe; maybe not. Still, a weekly variety show starring the Who could have been a lot of fun.

John Entwistle's Children's Album (1967/1968)

Kit Lambert was one hell of an idea man, most significantly encouraging Pete Townshend to follow his rock opera muse. He was an Entwistle-booster too, and recognizing John's talent for writing tunes fit for kiddie consumption, Lambert came up with a witty idea. Entwistle would make a record exclusively aimed at the young ones. Unlike Donovan's recent kid-centric *A Gift from a Flower to a Garden*, Entwistle's LP was not to be full of fanciful fairy tales and nursery rhymes. That wouldn't be very John. His record would be aimed at those kids who wait for Halloween all year with songs in step with the macabre whimsy of "Boris the

Spider." Entwistle liked the idea, and by his own estimate, he completed some fifteen new tunes for the project. They were typical Ox fare: odes to snakes and bogeymen and witches ("Horrid Olive"). But like so many Who-related projects from this period, the children's album died in utero. Tragic, considering the quality of the songs he composed for the project that ultimately went to the Who: "Silas Stingy" and "Dr. Jekyll and Mr. Hyde." Two decades later, he would fulfill his nightmare in a way when he wrote and recorded music for a part-animated/part-live-action children's television series called *Van-Pires*, which spawned his soundtrack album *Music from Van-Pires*.

Who's for Tennis? (1968)/Covers EP (1968/1969)

Conceiving—and hastily announcing—inadequate albums was apparently an essential component of forcing the Who to make records worth hearing. This process did not always result in revision and release. A proposed album for 1968 did not go the way of *Jigsaw Puzzle* or *Who's Lily?* It merely died. This is just deserts for a project in which Kit Lambert had such little faith that he considered calling it *Who's for Tennis?* as a pathetic attempt to associate the album with the Wimbledon tennis championship. Ugh.

The songs the Who recorded for possible inclusion on *Who's for Tennis?* weren't bad, but there was little rhyme or reason to the assortment. Diversity could be a concept in itself, as Hendrix proved with *Electric Ladyland* and the Beatles did with their "White Album," but those records' immense sprawl gave them weight and helped bury the weaknesses of certain songs. More in keeping with the times was a clear and unified vision: the Kinks' lovely and nostalgic *Village Green Preservation Society*, the Stones' rough and rustic *Beggars Banquet*, Dylan's down-home *John Wesley Harding*. Not sufficiently weighty or cohesive, *Who's for Tennis?* probably wouldn't have been the masterpiece the Who needed to compete during a year of masterpieces. As evidenced by their jokey recent singles, they were not positioning themselves to go toe-to-toe with their serious peers with their serious statements about revolutions and street fighting men anyway. The Who even committed the most outdated of crimes by continuing to record a wealth of covers, though in 1976, John Entwistle told the *NME* that this was done with an all-covers EP in mind (and, amazingly, the concept did not die in '67. In fact an LP's worth of covers was considered again in 1970 and 2008).

So, for the first year since they became an LP-making outfit, the Who had no new album for 1968. That doesn't mean the year was a wash. Their months of hard roadwork—and quiet contemplation—were integral in creating the rock opera that would put them over as one of rock's top bands once and for all in 1969.

Songs that may have been included on *Who's for Tennis?*: "Little Billy," "Fortune Teller," "Faith in Something Bigger," "Melancholia," "Glow Girl," "Shakin' All Over," "Now I'm a Farmer," "Joys," "Do You Want Kids, Kids" (possible aka "Facts of Life"). (The Who's sporadic 1968 sessions also produced the singles "Dogs," "Dr. Jekyll and Mr. Hyde," "Call Me Lightning," and "Magic Bus," which could have been included on the album).

Songs that may have been recorded for the covers EP as reported by John Entwistle in the *NME*: "Road Runner," "Young Man Blues," "Summertime Blues," "Fortune Teller" (there's no evidence the Who recorded Bo Diddley's "Road Runner" in the studio, but it's possible John misremembered the songs and should have mentioned "Shakin' All Over" in the list instead).

Live at the Fillmore East (1968)

Pursuit of a studio album wasn't leading anywhere meaningful in 1968. The Who still had an ace up their Union Jack–emblazoned sleeves. They were the best goddamn live group in rock 'n' roll. So what about catching some of that alchemy on vinyl? Prior to 1968, live recording had a lot of evolving to do. Stage equipment was insufficient for pitching volume over the monstrous wail of the audience, let alone making a decent sound onstage. Early live records by the Rolling Stones and the Kinks and the Beach Boys did a good job of conveying the excitement of a rock show, but they sounded muddy and tinny.

The Who's employment of big Marshall stack amps and a 1,000-watt PA helped to change that. With such equipment and their own astounding stage ability, they had the tools to make the first truly great live album. Those who'd only heard about their set at the Monterey Pop Festival would be champing at the bit for it.

On April 5, 1968, the Who recorded their set at New York's Fillmore East for this purpose. The recording quality was incredible compared to the Stones' *Got Live If You Want It* or the Kinks' *Live at Kelvin Hall*. It was powerful, well balanced, and clear. The band too were in great humor and full vigor, and the set was rich in oddities such as "Little Billy" and a searing, extended

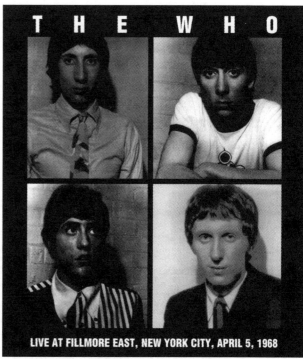

LIVE AT FILLMORE EAST, NEW YORK CITY, APRIL 5, 1968

Though its myriad "technical difficulties" kept it from official release in 1968, *Live at the Fillmore East* has since enjoyed a healthy life on bootleg.   *Author's collection*

rendition of "Relax." Serious flaws are evident and abundant too. Townshend slashes the wrong chord toward the beginning of "Summertime Blues." Entwistle and Daltrey's harmonies go horribly awry early in "Fortune Teller." Daltrey's voice cracks as he sings "Tattoo." Moon's drums vanish in patches throughout "My Way." Townshend's fingers get tangled in the strings while playing "Shakin' All Over." Daltrey mucks up "Boris the Spider" by singing the wrong words over Entwistle. *Live at the Fillmore East* was not fit for official release . . . though Track Records' loss has been the bootleggers' gain.

Songs recorded for possible inclusion: "Summertime Blues," "Fortune Teller," "Tattoo," "Little Billy," "I Can't Explain," "Happy Jack," "Relax," "A Quick One While He's Away," "My Way," "Shakin' All Over," "Boris the Spider," "My Generation."

"Christmas" b/w "Overture," "Go to the Mirror" b/w "Sally Simpson" (1969)

All of the straw grasping and fears of irrelevancy that plagued the Who throughout 1968 were washed away with the release of *Tommy* in 1969. However, with that sprawling double album came a new issue, an economic one.

Although John Entwistle always thought little of singles (even though he surely made his share of bread by scoring so many B-sides), Pete Townshend praised them as short, sharp, shocks of pop power and as economical alternatives to pricier LPs. Townshend felt the Who's new double album was particularly overpriced in England, so he and the Who's management team conspired to make *Tommy* more affordable to the public in one of their dopier schemes. If the record is too expensive to purchase as a whole, why not chop it up and put it out on a series of singles? It's not like the album had some sort of story line that might suffer by dicing it up.

In July 1969, Polydor went so far as to print up three singles for the potential series: "Christmas" b/w "Overture," "Go to the Mirror" b/w "Sally Simpson," and "I'm Free" b/w "1921." The disinterested label didn't even ship them to the shops. Yet Townshend and Lambert still hadn't let go of the idea, and Polydor placated them with a six-shilling EP consisting of "See Me, Feel Me," "Christmas," "Overture," and "I'm Free" in November 1970. Quite conscientiously, the label made arrangements for fans who bought the "See Me, Feel Me" single released the previous month to exchange it for the new EP.

American Decca pulled a similar singles stunt in 1969, although the *Excerpts from Tommy* box set (consisting of "Amazing Journey" b/w "The Acid Queen," "Sally Simpson" b/w "I'm Free," "Smash the Mirror" b/w "Sensation," and "Go to the Mirror Boy" b/w "Tommy Can You Hear Me?") was only released to radio stations for promotional purposes. As for "I'm Free," it finally got a chance to enter the charts when Decca released it as a single (b/w all seven minutes of "We're Not Gonna Take It") that July.

The Maxi Single (1970)

The Who spent a great deal of 1970 touring *Tommy*, leaving their studio output pretty sparse that year. The only new Who recordings to make it to vinyl sat on either side of a single single: "The Seeker" b/w "Here for More." Yet they did have another project in mind, and it was once again conceived to take a stand against escalating record prices. To give their fans more bang for their bucks, the Who's latest single would be a "maxi single" housing four songs instead of the usual two but selling for the same price as a conventional single.

Why the maxi single was never released depends on who you ask. Daltrey said the tracks were too long for a 45. Entwistle claimed that Polydor balked about selling a maxi single at mini-single prices. Townshend, ever the grump, said the songs simply weren't any good. Most Who fans, I'm sure, would disagree.

Songs recorded for possible inclusion: "Postcard," "Now I'm a Farmer," "Naked Eye," "Water," "I Don't Even Know Myself."

Guitar Farm (1970)

In 1970, Pete Townshend struck up a relationship with Tattooist International, a filmmaking collective led by Dick Fontaine, Mike Myers, Denis Postle, and Richard Stanley. He'd already recorded music for Stanley's 1968 comedic short *Lone Ranger*, and went on to do additional work for Fontaine's film *Double Pisces* and Postle's *Oh Dear, What Can the Matter Be?* When Tattooist started discussing developing Myers's short story "Guitar Farm" into a film, Townshend was intrigued. The tale is exactly what it sounds like: a fantasy set on a farm where guitars, woodwinds, and percussion flourish from the earth like potatoes. According to Richie Unterberger in *Won't Get Fooled Again*, "Baba O'Riley" began life as part of this project, and Townshend may have intended to build a Who album around the soundtrack. *Guitar Farm* was then sidelined as Townshend went to work on *Lifehouse*, but even after the release of *Who's Next*, there was still talk of the Who's involvement with the film. However, Myers became suspicious of Townshend and Denis Postle's plot to take his simple fairy tale into a more spiritual/metaphorical direction, and the project seems to have rotted with his interest. In August 1971, *Rolling Stone* reported that the adaptation of *Guitar Farm* was now called *Joad* and the plotline had mutated into "Adolph Hitler and Glenn Miller wheeling around in a Lincoln," which sounds more like a Keith Moon biopic. Needless to say, that movie didn't get made.

Live at the Civic Auditorium (1971)

After a few false starts, the Who finally recorded and released the ultimate live album in 1970. *Live at Leeds* was such a smashing commercial and artistic success that another live album was considered. Two performances at San Francisco's Civic Auditorium on December 12 and 13, 1971, were recorded with it in mind.

In *Anyway, Anyhow, Anywhere*, Andy Neill and Matt Kent suggest the follow-up live album was scrapped because the Civic Auditorium sets only featured one song otherwise unavailable on record: an earthquaking rendition of Marvin Gaye's "Baby Don't You Do It." After *Live at Leeds*, which housed three covers unavailable elsewhere and three classic singles so radically altered they may as well have been new songs, this might have been inadequate. However, two other numbers performed at the auditorium actually hadn't seen release yet either: "Naked Eye" and a jam on Freddie King's "Going Down." Perhaps it was just too soon to release another live album, considering that *Leeds* hadn't even been in the shop for two years. Perhaps another factor was the shaky first night on which Keith Moon had overdosed on pills and booze and needed to be dosed up with even more chemicals just to make it through the show.

Songs recorded for possible inclusion: "I Can't Explain," "Substitute," "Summertime Blues," "My Wife," "Baba O'Riley," "Behind Blue Eyes," "Bargain," "Won't Get Fooled Again," "Baby Don't You Do It," "Overture," "Pinball Wizard," "See Me, Feel Me," "My Generation," "Naked Eye," "Going Down," "Magic Bus."

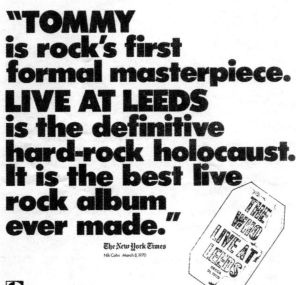

The Who finally achieved their goal of making the ultimate live rock album with *Live at Leeds* in 1970. Whether or not their goal also entailed making "the definitive hard-rock holocaust" is a mystery best left unsolved.   *Author's collection*

Rock Is Dead . . . Long Live Rock/Rock Is Dead (Rock Lives) (1972)

The collapse of *Lifehouse* (see chapter 15) and the subsequent compromise that was *Who's Next* did not kill Pete Townshend's ambition, nor did it stifle the management's desire to feature the band in a movie. Chris Stamp brought in critic Nik Cohn to spitball ideas with Townshend. Initially, he felt alienated by the brainstorming sessions in which Cohn and Stamp would get coked up and sketch malformed ideas on a chalkboard. But then the inspiration started flowing. Townshend had a title, *Rock Is Dead . . . Long Live Rock*, and a rough concept about how the crazed rock 'n' roll lifestyle can undermine the artist's idealism. In *Who I Am*, he wrote that the record would have been the Who's most collaborative since *A Quick One*, with each member of the band writing his own side-worth of songs. The idea that Daltrey or Moon could have performed their parts of that assignment is far-fetched.

In any event, Townshend went to work on his allotment of songs, while Cohn and Stamp developed a film treatment Cohn retitled *Rock Is Dead (Rock Lives)*. Its specifics are vague, though we know that it would have basically been a brief history of the Who—and rock 'n' roll—with the band appearing in a series of "cameos." In his treatment, Cohn included excerpts from interviews he'd conducted with each member of the group, but the things they had to say about each other put Townshend off. To spare his bandmates' feelings, and because he felt the treatment was more appropriate for a documentary than a plot-driven film, he decided to shelve the treatment. However, once again an unfinished project gave way to great and complete art. Inspired by the strong personalities that came through in Cohn's interviews, and still curious to explore his band's history, Townshend started meditating on the Who's quartered identity and their mod background. *Quadrophenia* would not be far behind.

Songs under consideration: "Long Live Rock," "Join Together," "Relay," "Is It in My Head," "Love Reign o'er Me," "Get Inside," "Riot in the Female Jail," "Why Can't You See I'm Easy," "Ambition."

Twenty-Fifth Anniversary Reunion Album (1989)

One of the great running jokes of the Who's career is their complete inability to stay broken up. The "never again" stance Townshend took after the band's 1982 "farewell" tour saw him through a couple of years, but an invitation to perform at Live Aid in 1985 was too irresistible, and the band re-formed for a brief set at the charity event. On February 8, 1988, they got pulled back in for a quickie reunion at the Brit Awards Ceremony, where they were being honored for their Outstanding Contribution to British Music. With the band's twenty-fifth anniversary beckoning from the near future, desire for a more committed reunion was on the rise. Pete Townshend remained firmly against it—at least in words, if not action.

He and Bill Curbishley had been meeting in secret to discuss the upcoming milestone, and on December 5, 1988, Daltrey and Entwistle were brought in to hash out the details. A tour was a given, what with the millions of sponsorship bucks already on the table. A new studio album was also under consideration.

According to Townshend, Daltrey was making his first sincere bid to place songs on a Who record, having written a few jolly tunes with a chap named Nigel (possibly novelist Nigel Hinton, who'd adapted his own *Buddy's Song* for a BBC TV series and feature film both starring Daltrey). However, the facts and figures discussed during the meeting were a bit too real for Townshend. He got cold feet, and the next day, announced that there would be no reunion.

He changed his mind when he realized how much cash was in store. A £14,000 payday *every day*? Who could pass that up? So the tour was back on. The album, however, was not. Who fans had to sustain themselves with the two new band recordings—"Dig" and a cover of Arthur Brown's "Fire"—included on Townshend's *Iron Man* album.

17

Who's Missing

Unrecorded Songs and Lost Tapes

T hough the Who only released eleven studio albums (plus an EP and a healthy selection of exclusive singles), they recorded quite prolifically, as the numerous outtakes that have surfaced on compilations and deluxe editions of their proper albums demonstrate. Pete Townshend composed an additional glut of songs the Who never recorded. Some of these were intended for other artists, but Townshend wrote many for his band. Considering that the Who recorded a number of his songs other artists had already tackled ("So Sad About Us," "Run Run Run," "Magic Bus"), the fact that he handed out some of the following songs does not rule out the possibility the Who could have recorded their own versions.

"It Was You" and "Please Don't Send Me Home" (1963, 1964)

In autumn 1963, the Detours convened in the front room of Barry Gray's house to record two of Pete Townshend's earliest compositions, "It Was You" and "Please Don't Send Me Home," a pair of frothy sub-Beatle pop songs. The following year, the Naturals would record "It Was You," complete with mop-top-wagging "ooohs," for the B-side of their "Look at Me Now" single (it flopped). Little is known about "Please Don't Send Me Home," though Neill and Kent indicate in *Anyway, Anyhow, Anywhere* that Entwistle sang it. This is tough to confirm since the tapes are lost. The guys tried "It Was You" again during a High Numbers demo session in May 1964. The session also produced an early take of "I'm the Face." Those tapes have never been released.

"You Don't Have to Jerk" (1965)

In 1964, songs about a new dance craze called the Jerk served as adequate fodder for records by the Larks, the Dukays, and the Miracles. Pete Townshend schemed to jerk onto the bandwagon with "You Don't Have to Jerk," demoed at his flat at the same time he cut "Call Me Lightning." Townshend intended to record the song with the Who, but there is no evidence that actually happened.

"Do the Strip" (1965)

Ever the forward thinker, Townshend decided to create his own dance craze with a song written for possible inclusion on *My Generation*. A jaunty and funny R&B morsel in the "Good Lovin'" mode, "Do the Strip" is an incitement to hustle onto the dance floor and disrobe. Shocking! It's a good thing the Who never actually recorded this song, which would probably have sparked the naked revolution that would have finally brought society to its knees.

"Kill My Appetite" (1965)

Pete Townshend spearheads "vore," a sexual fetish in which one fantasizes about eating someone alive. He imagines having his lady friend on a platter with a dash of salt and pepper and a dollop of gravy. "Kill My Appetite" may have been even more damaging to humankind than "Do the Strip." More likely, this weird but slight speck of soul-pop would have just gotten tossed on the "out" pile had the Who recorded it. Townshend was really reaching with this one.

"Things Have Changed" (1965)

A sweet, folkish number that never got beyond the demo stage. In his liner notes for his *Scoop* demo compilation, Townshend posited that Kit Lambert may have even prevented him from playing such a "lightweight" song for the hard and horrible Who. Surely, this would have turned Roger's stomach. Pretty tune, though.

"You Rang?" (1966)

On March 15, the Who performed an ultrarare original for the *Saturday Club* radio show. Townshend, Entwistle, and Moon's "You Rang?" sounds a lot like their other instrumental jams, "The Ox" and "Sodding About." Its most distinctive feature is Entwistle's climactic growl of the title phrase, a tribute to the butler on the ooky, kooky *Addams Family* . . . and possibly the Who's own roadie Gordon "Lurch" Molland.

"King Rabbit" (1966)

After scoring hits with their relatively straightforward early singles, the Who had their biggest yet with the weird "I'm a Boy." The next batch of songs Townshend submitted for possible Who records was even more bizarre, and one of them somehow became their first US top-forty hit when "Happy Jack" hit #24 in early 1967. There's no evidence the Who recorded the similarly childlike "King Rabbit," a charming little fairy tale about a self-appointed monarch who sets an example for his constituents by doing a lot of standing. Townshend's intention was to both expose the ridiculousness of leaders and acknowledge that some of

PETE TOWNSHEND SCOOP3

Pete Townshend's *Scoop* series of demo compilations is a key source for songs the Who might have recorded.   *Author's collection*

them actually manage to do a good job . . . even if they happen to enjoy dressing in bunny costumes. Based on his demo, it's hard to imagine how the Who would have recorded this, but considering that they managed to put their stamp on "Happy Jack," they probably would have figured out something.

"Join My Gang" (1966)

Another song that could have found a place on *A Quick One* was "Join My Gang." Alas, the nine-minute mini-opera rendered the composition surplus, so Townshend donated it to a new Reaction artist called Oscar (aka Paul "Cousin Kevin" Nicholas). This is one of Townshend's most thoughtful songs about childhood. A little boy invites a girl into his all-male circle of friends despite the sexist outcry he knows will ensue. "Join My Gang" is an innocent and refreshing feminist-leaning song written at a time when it was much more common for rock stars to denigrate women as stupid girls who belong under their thumbs. Oscar's baroque-tinged recording wasn't a hit, but Townshend was happy to learn that David Bowie was a fan of his demo (no surprise there, since the song has a definite early-Bowie sensibility). Unfortunately, that demo has never surfaced on any of the *Scoop* compilations, although Townshend did give "Join My Gang" a rare performance during his very first solo concert at the Roundhouse in 1974.

"Lazy Fat People" (1966/1967)

Managerial juggernaut Allen Klein managed to add the Beatles and the Rolling Stones to his talent roster. The bands would live to regret their associations with the unscrupulous wheeler-dealer. Knowing Klein's reputation for seizing his bands' publishing rights, the Who would not be fooled so easily. When he met with Townshend and attorney Edward Oldham to broker the Who's settlement with Shel Talmy, Oldham grew suspicious that Klein had designs on the band. According to Dave Marsh, Townshend expressed his own feelings about the corpulent businessman in a nasty jig called "Lazy Fat People." Demoed in late '66/early '67, the song was another odd novelty that probably would have been wrong for the Who. It was wrong for Episode Six (which spawned future Deep Purple-ites Roger Glover and Ian Gillan), who passed on it, but the jokey Barron Knights bit, releasing "Lazy Fat People" as a single in March 1967.

"Politician" (1967)

A powerful nod to Martha and the Vandellas, "Politician" is not a criticism of the fat cats in power but a celebration of developing one's own ethical code, of being one's own politician. The Who had moved beyond Maximum R&B by 1967, but this still could have been turned into a strong recording.

"Blue Caravan" (1967)

Roger Daltrey had a minor triumph when the Who recorded "Early Morning Cold Taxi," a song he cowrote with Who roadie Dave "Cy" Langston. When it seemed likely the song would end up on the group's third album, Cy made the claim that Daltrey was cowriter in name only (according to Townshend in *Who I Am*). Thus, the song was relegated to the outtakes heap. The alleged songwriting team of Langston and Daltrey did manage to cut one other demo for a number called "Blue Caravan." That title is all that's known about the song.

"Bob Sings Soul" (1967)

Another mysterious song from the *Sell Out* sessions. The Who supposedly managed to get the jokey "Bob Sings Soul" on tape. The fact that Bob Pridden supplied the lead vocals (such truth in advertising!) accounts for why it didn't end up on the album, though there is no account for why it apparently hasn't been heard since 1967.

"That Motherland Feeling" and "Party Piece from Rael" (1967)

Two years before he gave birth to *Tommy*, Pete Townshend was hard at work on an opera called *Rael*. He never completed the full-length piece (see chapter 15), but he did write more than the six minutes that made it onto *The Who Sell Out*. Townshend recorded a 1:30 demo for "That Motherland Feeling," a country and western number in which the singer chews over his friend Zach's decision to fight on the side of the "Red Chins." Lyrics for the love song "Party Piece from Rael" appeared in the September 1968 issue of *Eye* magazine. A couple of years later, Pete would rework the opening line of "Party Piece"—"She was the first song I ever sang"—into "The Song Is Over," the climactic track of another doomed rock opera, *Lifehouse*.

"I Always Say" (circa 1968)

This groovy, riffy tune has often been misdated as a product of 1965, and though the straight blues feel might cause one to place it in the *My Generation* era, the polish Townshend gave his demo indicates he recorded it at a later date. That it received its one and only official release as a bonus track on the 2006 reissue of his 1972 album *Who Came First* confuses the calendar further. In *The Who on Record*, John Atkins estimates the recording date around '67 or '68, which is probably closer to the mark. Though its lack of originality may explain why the Who decided not to record "I Always Say," it's still a nice little number.

"Cookin'" (circa 1968)

In *Who I Am*, Townshend writes that he was going through his domestic period in 1968. Having just wed Karen Astley, he was enjoying kicking around the house, being a good hubby, and writing ditties about the simple pleasures. This period produced the single "Dogs" and "Welcome," which would soon find a home on *Tommy*. "Cookin'" is also likely to be a product of Townshend's early '68 domestic phase. It has the country and western flavor that spices up much of the Who's early seventies work ("I Don't Even Know Myself," "Here for More," "Going Mobile," etc.), so in that way, it may be ahead of its time. Lyrically, it's a step backward to the sex and food correlations of "Kill My Appetite," though without the cannibalism angle. In his *Scoop* liner notes, Townshend calls "Cookin'" "chauvinistic" because it praises a woman's culinary aptitude. Compared to the collective works of the Rolling Stones or Led Zeppelin or, well, pretty much any other classic rock band, it's a feminist manifesto.

"Goin' Fishin'" (1968)

"Goin' Fishin'" has an experimental feel that may indicate it was intended more for Pete's personal use than the Who's. Of course, his demo for "Magic Bus" is similarly freaky, and the Who managed to work their magic on that one. This time the topic is Townshend's aversion to fishing, a pastime that makes him "wince." The sound was his attempt to recreate the eerie, echoey sound of the Beach Boys' *Smiley Smile* album in his home studio. He does a bang-up job of giving this evocative tune the Brian Wilson treatment.

"Joys" and "Facts of Life" (1968)

The Who's 1968 output may be their most criticized of the Keith Moon era, but they still produced a lot of great music that year. Few of us can make any such value judgment regarding "Joys" and "Facts of Life." According to *Anyway, Anyhow, Anywhere*, these two mysteries are listed on the Who's May 29, 1968, recording log. On that same date, the band recorded several other oddities at Advision Studio: "Melancholia," and covers of "Fortune Teller" and "Shakin' All Over." Studio and live versions of those three songs are now readily available, but "Joys" and "Facts of Life" are apparently lost. Were they jams? Were they proper Townshend or Entwistle compositions? Were they under consideration for the scrapped album *Who's for Tennis?* The answers to those questions may be just as lost as the recordings themselves.

"Do You Want Kids, Kids?" (1968)

There has been some Internet speculation that "Facts of Life" is actually an alternate title for a Townshend song called "Do You Want Kids, Kids?" That the latter title is not mentioned at all in the otherwise incredibly thorough *Anyway, Anyhow, Anywhere* may support that theory. Plus there are the similar sentiments of their titles, both of which suggest parents sitting down with their kids to have the "No sex for you!" talk. In *Before I Get Old*, Dave Marsh gives a different background for "Do You Want Kids, Kids?," lumping it in with "Little Billy" as another antismoking ad for the American Cancer Society. Does the song refer to the time-honored practice of enjoying a smoke after a bout of sweaty shagging? We may never know.

"Beat Up," "Success!" and "Girl from Lincoln County" (1968)

While shaping *Tommy*, Townshend tried and discarded several ideas. He considered working covers of Mose Allison's "Young Man Blues" and, according to John Atkin's *The Who on Record*, Mercy Dee's "One Room Country Shack" (also covered by Allison) into his operatic character study (not a totally far-out idea considering that a cover of Sonny Boy Williamson's "Eyesight to the Blind" found a place on the record). A number of originals didn't make the cut either. In *The Who on Record*, John Atkins describes "Beat Up" as "short" and "purely expository." Based on its title, it sounds like it would have been an interlude leading into "Cousin Kevin" as "Do You Think It's Alright?" sets up "Fiddle About." On his website, The Hypertext Who, Brian Cady places it after "Sparks." "Success!" is a ten-second ascending chord sequence with the lyric "Success, I think we have success" linking "Go to the Mirror" and "Tommy Can You Hear Me?" on Townshend's *Tommy* demo. Atkins also refers to a song called "Girl from Lincoln County," though nothing else is known about it.

"A Normal Day for Brian, a Man Who Died Everyday" and "There's a Fortune in Those Hills" (1970)

Jonathan Cott refers to these two songs in his lengthy 1970 interview with Townshend for *Rolling Stone*. Townshend played Cott the demos, "A Normal Day for Brian, A Man Who Died Everyday" being a tribute to his recently deceased friend Brian Jones, and "There's A Fortune in Those Hills" being "a slow wailing country song." While Townshend's intentions for his Brian Jones elegy are unknown, John Atkins suggests that "Fortune" was intended for a post–*Live at Leeds* studio album shunted aside for *Lifehouse*. It is unlikely the Who recorded it.

"Teenage Wasteland" (1971)

All those clowns who think "Baba O'Riley" is called "Teenage Wasteland" got one thing right (-ish): there *is* a song with that title. The Who never recorded "Teenage Wasteland," but Townshend gave its demo the same elaborate polish as his other *Lifehouse* home recordings. The track is a dramatic, panoramic introduction to the story, incorporating a good deal of the lyrics and some of the melodic passages that wound up in "Baba."

"Mary" and "Greyhound Girl" (1971)

"Mary" is one of the most frustrating items in this chapter, because unlike most of these songs, a Who version is generally known to have existed. Pete's demo, released in edited form on *Scoop* and uncut on *Lifehouse Chronicles*, is one of his loveliest and most powerful, and the likelihood that the Who's take will never be released is a rock 'n' roll tragedy. In his liner notes for the 1995 edition of *Who's Next*, John Atkins indicates that the recording was either "lost" or has "deteriorated beyond repair," but he says the same thing about "Time Is Passing," which surfaced a few years later on the expanded edition of *Odds & Sods*. But don't let that get your hopes up, because Jon Astley told me, "I have scoured (the archives) for missing stuff—the saddest thing for me is that two or three tracks from *Who's Next* are still missing multitrack tapes as they were thrown out by

Although we may never hear vintage recordings of the Who playing "Mary" and "Greyhound Girl," Pete Townshend's excellent demos of them can be heard on *Lifehouse Chronicles*. Available only through Townshend's website, the box set is a lavish reconstruction of his doomed rock opera comprised of demos, classical pieces, a radio drama, odds, and sods. The booklet contained in the corrugated box is pictured here.   *Author's collection*

Virgin, the new owners of Olympic Studios, years ago." This same fate may have befallen "Greyhound Girl," another romantic *Lifehouse* ballad, though it is not known whether or not the Who recorded it. Townshend eventually released his demo on the B-side of "Let My Love Open the Door" and on *Lifehouse Chronicles*.

"Riot in the Female Jail" (aka "Ladies in the Female Jail"), "Why Can't You See I'm Easy?," and "Ambition" (1972)

This is a triad of songs Townshend wrote for possible inclusion on the aborted *Rock Is Dead . . . Long Live Rock* album. None of them have ever been released in official capacity, though Townshend's vintage demos for "Riot in the Female Jail"—a very-seventies slow funk with jokey lurid lyrics worthy of *Caged Heat*—and "Why Can't You See I'm Easy"—a moody, minor-key rhumba—have been bootlegged. There is no evidence the Who ever recorded these two songs. "Ambition" remained virtually unknown until 2005 when Townshend performed it on *In the Attic*, his and Rachel Fuller's web series. He prefaced his performance by saying the Who actually recorded "Ambition," though once again, no trace of it has ever emerged from the archives. It certainly is the most Who-like of these three songs.

"Get Inside," "You Came Back," and "Anymore" (1973)

Like *Tommy*, *Quadrophenia* had its share of casualties. Several songs were trimmed when Townshend decided to take the music in a heavier direction less reminiscent of the Who's actual mod days (or more accurately, their quirky, poppy postmod phase) and more in line with the brooding hard rock of *Who's Next*. The Who actually recorded a few of these songs: "Four Faces" and "We Close Tonight" during the 1973 sessions and "Joker James" during the 1979 sessions for the *Quadrophenia* soundtrack. Several never got that far, such as the sweet "Get Inside," a tale of familial harmony quite out of step with the dysfunctional clan portrayed on the finished album. In his liner notes of the *Quadrophenia* "Director's Cut" box set, Townshend wrote that the song was originally intended for *Rock Is Dead*. The lilting waltz "You Came Back" is another nice one, though the idea of Jimmy the Mod contemplating reincarnation might have been just as hard to swallow as his karmic contemplations in "The Dirty Jobs." The airy, rippling "Anymore" sounds like it belongs on *Tommy*, Townshend's piano phrases on his demo calling to mind his acoustic guitar work in "It's a Boy." Its revelations of despair are pure *Quadrophenia*.

"Wizardry," "Unused Piano," "Recorders," and "Fill No. 2" (1973)

Townshend also demoed several instrumental experiments for *Quadrophenia*. The most substantial of these is the synth-burbling "Wizardry," which would have served a similar transitional function as "Quadrophenia" or "The Rock." Townshend wrote it to indicate Jimmy's journey from London to Brighton, though I think we can all agree that "5:15" accomplishes that better and is a much stronger piece of music. These other pieces are slighter, intended for use as link tracks, though each is more evocative than "Wizardry." "Unused Piano" is a beautiful piano melody based on "The Dirty Jobs," and "Recorders" is a simple, eerie piece on which Townshend "plays" his daughter's Whirling Tube, a corrugated plastic tube that produces a whistling sound when spun. He included both of these on *Scoop*, while the equally pretty piano solo "Fill No. 2" had to wait for the *Quadrophenia* "Directors Cut" box to see official release.

"Fight Until You're Mine" (aka "Gonna Fight to Make You Mine") and "Girl in a Suitcase" (circa 1975)

Pete Townshend wrote some thirty songs for possible inclusion on *The Who by Numbers*. Townshend left it up to Roger Daltrey to select the ones he wanted to sing. "Gonna Fight to Make You Mine" and "Girl in a Suitcase" were two of the rejects. Had Daltrey liked what he'd heard, the Who would have been wise to only record one of these songs since they are very melodically and lyrically similar. Both songs address sex, "Gonna Fight to Make You Mine" sharing the middle-aged horniness of "Dreaming from the Waist" and "Girl in a Suitcase" being a subtler ode to on-tour flings. Townshend included his demo for "Girl in a Suitcase" on *Another Scoop*. "Fight Until You're Mine" has yet to see nonbootleg release.

"Bogey Man" (1978)

John Entwistle was not nearly as prolific as Pete Townshend, but even he composed more songs than the Who could use. Most of these songs ended up on his solo records. This is true of "Bogey Man," though this typically terrifying Ox number would have to wait twenty-two years to appear on *Music from Van-Pires*. That recording was begun way back in 1978 as a demo submitted for *Who Are You*. Entwistle claimed the Who said "nah" to his paranormal song because it was "too humorous." For years, he believed his demo was lost, but discovered it in the nineties, so he could complete the recording for inclusion on the soundtrack. If that percussive storm toward the end of the song sounds familiar to you, there's a good reason for that: the drummer is none other than Keith Moon.

"Zelda" (1981)

The sight of Pete Townshend's niece waving to him through a car window inspired this windy whirl of viols. Townshend cut this stirring demo while recording *Face Dances*, though he may not have submitted it for inclusion. This recording, made with the help of *Face Dances* assistant engineer Allan Blazek, is so odd that it's hard to imagine what the Who would have done with "Zelda." Townshend name checks Rabbit Bundrick, Roger Daltrey, and the late Keith Moon and drops an unmistakable reference to himself (the "genius" with a taste for "brandy"). Poor John Entwistle gets left out.

"Certified Rose" (2002)

In 2002, Townshend, Daltrey, and Entwistle entered the recording studio together for the first time in more than a decade to rehearse new material. Townshend brought along "Real Good Looking Boy," which would ultimately end up on the *Then and Now* hits compilation. Entwistle had some songs, but was allegedly gun-shy about suffering Daltrey's assessment of their quality (possibly contradicting Daltrey's claim that he loved everything the bass player wrote). As for the singer, he gave his bandmates a rare treat: he presented his very own composition for possible recording. In *Who I Am*, Townshend wrote that he really liked Daltrey's "Certified Rose," comparing it to Ronnie Lane's earthy brand of country and western. Sadly, the Who didn't actually record it.

"Uncertain Girl" (2006)

On April 11, 2006, the new Who were busy as bees on *Endless Wire* when Townshend took a break from the work to film an episode of *In the Attic*. He prefaced his performance of a tune called "Uncertain Girl" by saying the Who had recorded it earlier in the day with Zak Starkey on drums. He then played a pretty little number that sounds like it could have fit well in the "Wire and Glass" mini-opera. When *Endless Wire* hit the shops six months later, "Uncertain Girl" was nowhere to be heard, left to languish among the rest of the Who's missing.

18

All Mixed Up

Variations in Mixes and Edits

E ven before reggae and disco artists brought them into vogue in the seventies, varied mixes and remixes were staples of pop recording. They were natural by-products of the gradual move from mono to stereo in the sixties. Variations in mixes from continent to continent were not uncommon either.

Because labels throughout the world have fiddled with the Who's recordings to an extreme degree, and because those records have been reissued so many times, their back catalog is riddled with more variations than most other artists in their league. Neither Beatles fans nor Stones fans nor Dylan fans nor Beach Boys fans nor Zeppelin fans have had to sort through so many remixes and reedits. For the sake of space and sanity, we will focus on the most radical variations in the Who's ample discography in this chapter.

Vintage Variations

This first section deals with the remixes and reedits present in the days when the compact disc was barely a glimmer in inventor/audiophile James T. Russell's eye. While the majority of mix variations in the vinyl age were due to the mono/stereo divide, other factors sometimes affected how listeners heard music.

"Substitute" (US Edit)

In the United Kingdom, the Who envisioned their fourth single as 3:49 of raw confrontation and self-laceration. UK listeners were most appreciative, and "Substitute" zipped assuredly into the top five. In the United States, executives at staid Decca Records weren't so sure about the Who's latest. The label already had several flops on their hands from the group. Clean-scrubbed American teens (and more realistically, skittish DJs) were not ready for the eardrum-raping rackets of "Anyway, Anyhow, Anywhere" and "My Generation."

With its chiming acoustic guitar and sweet harmonies, "Substitute" had more viable commercial prospects than the Who's last two singles. So why oh why did the band have to muck it up with an epic running time and—*gasp! shudder!*—a dash of biraciality: "I look all white but my dad was black." That length would have to be clipped, and that controversial line would surely have to go.

A month after Reaction released the unadulterated "Substitute" in England, Decca put out a seriously altered disc in the colonies. The entire second verse and chorus were excised (reducing the track to 2:59), so we'd have to wait until after the bass solo to learn that our narrator was born with a plastic spoon in his mouth. Changes are afoot even before the edit, as Daltrey's vocal on the first chorus has been replaced with newly recorded lines (with detectably different timbre and attitude from the rest of the record). Now the substitute's dad has been hip-checked aside by an innocuous new bit about his own clumsy gait: "I try walking forward but my feet walk back." Another newly recorded chorus is swapped for the controversial original at the end of the track too.

Americans would have to wait until the 1971 release of *Meaty, Beaty, Big, and Bouncy* to hear the unadulterated "Substitute" without investing in an import. Since the single tanked in the United States, most didn't know what they were missing anyway.

"A Quick One While He's Away"

In 1966, stereo was regarded as an audiophile fad, while the mass of record buyers continued clinging to their mono hi-fis. The Beatles were so disinterested in their stereo mixes that they didn't even stick around to hear how the sessions went as George Martin got them over with as quickly as possible. As recently as his 2010 autobiography, *Life*, Keith Richards continued to rail against stereo, and many audiophiles have now reversed the stereo-is-better stance to embrace mono for its power and unity.

As the Who continued to release singles in mono in accordance with the accepted format, they too began experimenting with stereo when Kit Lambert took over production duties in 1966. Their first such effort, *A Quick One*, was a tentative jumble in which true stereo mixes mingled with fake stereo blunders of "Whiskey Man," "Heat Wave," "Don't Look Away," and "See My Way" ("fake stereo" refers to a mono recording in which the treble sounds have been hard panned to one channel and the bass sounds are hard panned to the other to simulate the sound of stereo. Fake stereo sounds like shit).

One instance in which the stereo *A Quick One* trumps its mono counterpart is the title track. The mini-opera "A Quick One While He's Away" was stitched together from six miniatures recorded at three different studios. This Frankenstein job is most noticeable in the mono mix. The mighty two-note bang that kicks off the third section ("We Have a Remedy") fades in on the mono mix. In stereo, it begins at full volume, resulting in a seamless and rather awesome transition from the previous section ("Crying Town").

"Our Love Was"

The mixes on *The Who Sell Out* display greater consideration than the mishmash that comprised the stereo *A Quick One*. The stereo mix of *The Who Sell Out* also displays clearer thinking than its own mono counterpart. There are certainly pluses to the mono mix. The shaky effect that finishes off "Mary Anne with the Shaky Hand" is more severe in mono, Pete Townshend's vocal is treated to a bit of psychedelic echo on the bridge of "Relax," and John Entwistle's bass is more prominent throughout. However, in direct contradiction of mono's main selling point, several of *Sell Out*'s mono mixes sound vacant compared to the stereo versions. The instrumental backing fades further into the background on "Tattoo," and "Odorono" is missing its integral lead guitar. The biggest changes are apparent in "Our Love Was." The stereo version of this ethereal fancy is grounded with a searing, distorted guitar solo that skids in just when the track seems poised to float off to the heavens. The mono mix emphasizes the track's psychedelic undertones with phasing effects that rise and fall throughout randomly and a tamer guitar solo in which Townshend bends strings rudimentarily in unison overdubs. This take may be more complementary to the song's romantic air, but it never takes off the way the screeching solo in the stereo mix does.

"Dr. Jekyll and Mr. Hyde"

Even in a year in which the Who released a mere four fresh songs, variations continued to abound. In the United States, they began 1968 with a new recording of one of Townshend's earliest songs, "Call Me Lightning." On the flip was Entwistle's monsterrific "Dr. Jekyll and Mr. Hyde." Desperate to keep new product on the AM dial on the top-ten-breaking heels of "I Can See for Miles," the Who rushed the single into existence. "Dr. Jekyll and Mr. Hyde" was recorded and mixed on the very same day (January 5, 1968). Such hastiness is apparent in the grooves, and the track was wisely remixed for its UK debut on the B-side of "Magic Bus" the following September.

The differences between the mixes are glaring from the very opening. On the US mix, Entwistle doubles his initial cry of "Hyyyyyde" with a variation on his patented "Boris the Spider" growl. It's a neat flourish that establishes the monster movie atmosphere instantly, but the mix otherwise suffers from a lack of finish. The UK mix sports a deeper, more resonant sound with upfront bass and French horn triplets in the bridge. While the "Boris" voice is missed in the intro, the track climaxes with horror flick madness as Moon goes wild on his kit behind his own mad cackling and a bit more of Entwistle's "Boris" groaning. Volume-pedal-controlled guitar swells from the debris and into the fade, adding thirteen additional seconds to this superior remix.

"Magic Bus"/"The Magic Bus"

No Who recording is available in a wider variety of mixes than the goofy classic and fan favorite "Magic Bus." Take a listen to one of the many CDs in your collection containing the Who's quest for a psychedelic conveyance. If you selected *Meaty, Beaty, Big and Bouncy* or *The Ultimate Collection*, you will hear a true stereo version that begins with a couple of seconds of maracas and rhythmic breathing.

Pop in *Magic Bus—The Who on Tour,* and this stereo mix gets started with Bob Pridden's clattering claves. The UK mono single mix found on the bonus disc of *The Ultimate Collection* moves the acoustic guitar nearly to the track's start. So does John Entwistle's mono remix on *The Kids Are Alright,* but the fade is a couple of seconds longer, and the whole thing plays in the key of G instead of the twilight zone between G and G# like the more common sped-up mix. Confused yet?

Dig out your old vinyl copy of *Meaty, Beaty* to find the most radical alternate of "Magic Bus." The major difference will be obvious to anyone who looks at the title and running time on the label. Listed as "The Magic Bus," the name isn't the only thing that's long. This version runs a full 4:35—more than a minute longer than the usual 3:22 length. This is not a different take but an unedited mix, though, like the UK mono single mix, most of the percussion has been chopped off the intro. Otherwise, the track plays out naturally.

On the more readily available mixes, there are several significant edits. The jam that follows the second verse leading into the "You can't have it/I want it" breakdown loses thirty seconds. The breakdown loses fifteen. After Townshend puts the boot in with his electric guitar, the noise fest fades after fifty-six seconds. On the long mix, it lasts 1:22 and ends naturally.

The other major difference in "The Magic Bus" is apparent in the vocals, which are completely different from any of the shorter mixes. This is probably an earlier vocal take than the one on the single, because the abundant edits on the single mix likely made it necessary to rerecord the vocal tracks completely. Daltrey is more reserved in the long mix, not reaching for the higher notes he hits on "I don't care how much I pay, gonna drive my bus to my baby each day." The backing vocals are sweeter, wilder, sung in a higher register, more country and western flavored. There is more of a natural back and forth between Rog and the Greek chorus in the breakdown. On the shorter mix, his "I want it" and the chorus's "You can't have it" overlap. In the longer mix, there is a dialogue: (The Chorus: "You can't have it." Daltrey: "Think how much I'll save!" etc.). The backing vocals also proceed through the "Thruppence, sixpence . . ." bit on the long mix, while Daltrey sings his lead unanswered on the short one.

Compared to the long mix, the short version of "Magic Bus" sounds rushed and trivial, though it's easy to understand why it had to be cut down. The long mix is a hypnotic groove, more psychedelic in the spirit of the lyric, but it definitely takes its time, lacking the immediacy necessary to catch one's attention when booming from the radio. It's a seductive slow burn that sounds great on an album, but it's not exactly the stuff hits are made of.

The vinyl *Meaty, Beaty* mix's main problem is that it's in fake stereo. So it doesn't have the sonic thrust of the shorter mixes, whether they be mono or stereo. That it's hard to come by is also an issue. In the three decades since that original vinyl release of *Meaty, Beaty, Big, and Bouncy,* "The Magic Bus" has only resurfaced on the now-deleted British compilation *The Who Collection* (1985) and a bonus disc included with the *Then and Now* compilation in Japan. In 2011, it finally appeared in proper mono with the full maracas-and-breathing intro courtesy of Jon Astley. Unfortunately, this appearance was on the pricey SHM-CD edition of *The Singles* only released in Japan (see chapter 19). That's a terrible shame because this is by far the best mix of "Magic Bus" available.

"Postcard"

John Entwistle's wry travelogue was originally cut for a 1970 EP, or "maxi single," that never made it past the recording studio (see chapter 16). Four years later, he selected "Postcard" to commence the outtakes assemblage *Odds & Sods*. For that release, Entwistle completely remixed the track and supplied a fresh bass line in his newfound busier style. The EP mix also shakes with a very upfront maraca track. This rare mix can only be found on Japanese imports. It first appeared on the bonus disc of the *Then and Now* compilation, which also included such oddities as "The Magic Bus," a mix of "Eyesight to the Blind" with a tamer alternate vocal track (now available domestically on the deluxe edition of *Tommy*), an advert for Great Shakes (likewise the deluxe *Sell Out*), and an early version of "I Don't Even Know Myself" also recorded for the scrapped EP. More recently, it appeared as a bonus track on the Japanese SHM-CD edition of *Who's Missing* in 2012.

The SHM-CD twofer of *Who's Missing* and *Two's Missing* is a treasure trove of alternate mixes, including "Eyesight to the Blind," "Postcard," "Fortune Teller," and "Melancholia."   *Author's collection*

"Who Are You"

When *Who Are You* was expanded and rereleased in 1996, it included a "lost verse" mix of the title track with completely different lyrics in the second verse that Pete Townshend decided to rewrite (a good call on his part, as the first half of the verse was a clichéd look at dreams of superstardom, and the second was a peek into the boardroom that strayed from the on-the-street narrative introduced in the first verse). In its original state, "Who Are You" was even more drastically different from the released version, lasting some twenty minutes by Jon Astley's estimation. In *Sound on Sound* magazine, the producer recalled the missing fifteen-or-so minutes mostly consisting of "Pete fiddling on piano and more acoustic guitar parts" in the meandering midsection. Although he has yet to dig up the scraps of tape as of this writing, he believes they still exist somewhere, perhaps "down the road" from Eel Pie Studios.

"Who Are You" was among the more drastic single edits.   *Author's collection*

Single Edits and More

The Who's lengthier classics were often sliced and diced to comply with the rigid singles market. "Won't Get Fooled Again's" 8:33 was reduced to a scant and jarring 3:38. "I hated it when they chopped it down," Roger Daltrey told *Uncut* in 2001. "I used to say 'Fuck it, put it out as eight minutes,' but there'd always be some excuse about not fitting it on or some technical thing at the pressing plant. After that we started to lose interest in singles because they'd cut them to bits."

While the album version was clearly too long for a single and the track's tremendous quality made it ripe for radio, there's little logic to the extremity of its reduction. The Beatles were allowed all seven minutes of "Hey Jude." Crosby,

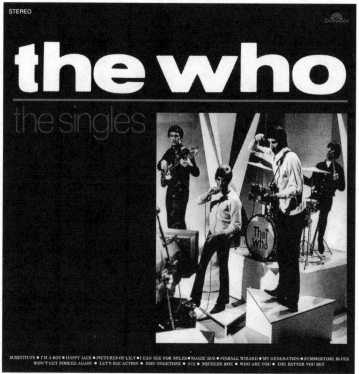

Released in the United Kingdom in 1984, *The Singles* was a sampler of A-sides from "Substitute" to "You Better You Bet." The SHM-CD edition released exclusively in Japan in 2011 expanded the compilation to a double-disc (the second of which is pictured here) set featuring every British A-side with a notable difference: instead of the single version of "Magic Bus," it features the rare long mix originally released on *Meaty, Beaty, Big, and Bouncy.*   *Author's collection*

Stills, and Nash received the same courtesy when they released "Suite: Judy Blue Eyes." Couldn't the Who at least get a little more time than 3:38?

Later, the less epic "5:15" (5:00) was more judiciously cut to 4:16 on 45, but "Love Reign o'er Me" was nearly halved (3:07). "Slip Kid" lost a minute, and "Trick of the Light" shed half a minute when released as flop singles (see chapter 9). "You Better You Bet" was chopped down to 3:58, although "Eminence Front" only suffered a modest seven-second edit (the more DJ-friendly promo edit, however, is only 4:05). "Who Are You" shed 1:23 in the United Kingdom; in the United States, it was snipped down by nearly three minutes to 3:22, and Roger's offending "fucks" were replaced with impotent "hells." Only on one occasion was a Who single actually longer than its LP equivalent: "The Real Me" jammed on for a few extra seconds and faded out, while the version on *Quadrophenia* is cut short with a shock of delay effects.

Shel Talmy's decision to edit "The Kids Are Alright" probably had more to do with cynicism than time constraints, as he took the most overtly commercial track on *My Generation* and made it even more palatable to sensitive American ears by cutting some of the midsong ruckus. When "The Kids Are Alright" appeared in the United States on *The Who Sings My Generation* and as a single in the summer of 1966, twenty seconds were hacked from the exhilarating instrumental break. All for nothing, since the single flopped. Mind-bogglingly, the full-length version of "The Kids Are Alright" would not be released in the States until 1994's *Thirty Years of Maximum R&B*. Meanwhile, an oddity became odder when the mono mix of the *Jigsaw Puzzle* remake of "I'm a Boy" finally surfaced on the *Ultimate Collection* bonus disc in 2002. The track lacked the opening twenty-three seconds of the stereo mix from *Meaty, Beaty, Big, and Bouncy*.

Recent Remixes

In the mid-nineties, Jon Astley and Andy Macpherson started poring over tapes and tapes, seeking out rarities and remixing more familiar items for MCA's major Who reissue campaign. Although Astley told me that he and Macpherson remixed the tracks for no more nefarious reason than "we thought at the time they would be nice alternatives," some fans were not pleased to hear revisions of their favorite Who recordings. Astley and Macpherson took the greatest liberties with *Who Are You*, of which Astley can claim partial artistic ownership, and *Odds & Sods*, an eccentric collection perhaps not considered "canon" enough to warrant extreme reverence. Once again, noting every volume adjustment or instrument that has been placed differently in a mix is a task beyond the scope of this chapter, but here's a rundown of the biggest changes.

"The Ox" (*My Generation* Deluxe Edition)

Stereo remix with complete ending instead of fade.

"Rael" (*Thirty Years of Maximum R&B*, *The Who Sell Out* Expanded and Deluxe Editions)

Extended mono edit including the second half of the first verse missing from the original mix.

The story goes that engineer Chris Huston had left the tape of "Rael" sitting unboxed on a shelf in Talentmasters Studio. Naturally, the studio's janitor assumed the tape was garbage, because it wasn't in a box. So he tossed it in the trash behind the building. After some frenzied dumpster diving, Huston managed to retrieve almost every piece of the shredded tape. "The damage to the ½-inch four track tape was quite extensive, requiring five sections being edited together," he told me. "Recording tape was made quite a bit differently in the early days and it didn't stretch, it broke!"

Chris Huston either doesn't know or doesn't remember why that half verse ("The country of my father . . . like a goldfish being swallowed by a whale") didn't make the cut on the original stereo *or* mono mix of *The Who Sell Out*, but he does clarify that it was not part of the damage. "It was the intro and first couple of lines of the song that were missing, not the second half of the verse. The parts of the song I could fix, but the intro and first couple of lines were not found in the dumpster. No doubt they were there, but I couldn't find them."

How Jon Astley recovered the half verse for its debut on *Thirty Years of Maximum R&B* is less mysterious. "I found it in a separate piece of tape in the archives and thought it would be of interest, so I added it to the box set," Astley told me. "It must have been considered too long a version to go on the original album so was edited down. I did a lot of this sort of thing myself in the seventies when the mix was finished, however I imagine most of my edits went in the bin, so we have Chris to thank for putting it on a separate spool!" Thanks, Chris! And thanks Jon, because this complete edit is the best way to hear "Rael."

"Glow Girl" (*Odds & Sods* Expanded Edition)

Presented in the key of B (on the original *Odds & Sods* mix, it was sped up to the space between B and C) and includes a complete ending instead of a fade.

"Postcard" (*Odds & Sods* Expanded Edition)

Includes alternate (and inferior) bass line.

"Now I'm a Farmer" (*Odds & Sods* Expanded Edition)

Includes complete ending.

"Put the Money Down" (*Odds & Sods* Expanded Edition)

Remix with fade extended by twenty-nine seconds and overlaid with Daltrey's vocal ad-libs.

"Music Must Change" (*Who Are You* Expanded Edition)

Includes alternate lead guitar track.

"Guitar and Pen" (*Who Are You* Expanded Edition)

Missing final line ("Never spend your guitar or your pen" at 5:40) and features bass drum stomped in unison with the keyboard at the end of the track. The "Olympic '78" mix included as a bonus track is more similar to the original mix, yet it still has bass drum on the last two keyboard hits, and both mixes of "Guitar and Pen" on the expanded *Who Are You* are slower than the original. The original mix was sped up to the space between G and G#. The remixes are squarely in the key of G.

"Eminence Front" (*It's Hard* Expanded Edition)

Remix fixes an out-of-sync vocal overdub on the first line of the first chorus.

"Cry If You Want" (*It's Hard* Expanded Edition)

The ending is extended by forty-four seconds.

Absentee Tracks

Some of the remixes are missing tracks not because Astley and Macpherson deemed them unnecessary but because they simply were not available for remixing. In the days when mere four-track machines limited overdubbing options, it was common practice to record overdubs during the mixing process. Such tracks only appear on final masters and not on remixable tapes. Since remixing was the name of the game of the reissue campaign, certain audio parts had to be sacrificed. Here are some of the missing touches.

"I Can't Explain" (*My Generation* Deluxe Edition)

Tambourine.

"My Generation" (*My Generation* Deluxe Edition)

Lead guitar.

"A Legal Matter" (*My Generation* Deluxe Edition)

Lead guitar.

"Circles" (*My Generation* Deluxe Edition)

French horn.

"Under My Thumb" (*Odds & Sods* Expanded Edition)

Lead guitar.

"5:15" and "The Dirty Jobs" (*Quadrophenia* 1996 and 2011 remixes)

Apparently sixteen tracks still weren't enough to capture all the details Pete Townshend envisioned for *Quadrophenia*. Many of the double LP's scenic sound effects were added during the mixing process. Townshend and engineer Ron Nevison played the effects live on the kinds of cartridge tapes radio stations once used for advertisements and station identifications. Among the field recordings Townshend and Nevison made to bring the period piece to life were a train whistle near the start of "5:15" and a more mysterious noise in "The Dirty Jobs." As Nevison explained in a Q&A with The Who Forum in 2007, he'd recorded one tape "at Hyde Park corner (Speaker's Corner) of people shouting at each other. Supposed to be strikers rioting. Since most of the sound effects never were recorded on the master tape it doesn't surprise me that some things were misplaced or lost." This lost bit of squawking has sometimes been compared to a seal's bark and can be heard on the 1973 mix of "The Dirty Jobs" immediately following the line "You men should remember how you used to fight." On all subsequent remixes, it is missing.

19

Ultimate Collections

The Essential Compilations

he Who came to the swinging sixties ball later than any other original British Invader. By the time they dropped their first LP in December '65, the Rolling Stones already had enough big hits to release their first compilation four months later. The Beatles had theirs out by the end of 1966. In the interim, peers such as the Kinks, the Beach Boys, Peter and Gordon, and the Dave Clark Five had been anthologized (in Clark's case, twice—not that *More Greatest Hits* had many actual hits). More hits collections would be in store from Dylan, the Byrds, and the Turtles in 1967. It was as if rock 'n' roll was eulogizing itself while still in adolescence. More accurately, it was as if record companies realized they could milk more dollars from fans by tossing together proven hits at a time when certain groups were taking their art into less commercial directions.

Despite the capitalism behind their conceptions, compilations were still neat ways to own the hits without having to tax one's bank account with multiple LP purchases. In the United Kingdom, where LPs were generally released unsullied by singles, compilations had even greater value. And as compilers grew more creative and record companies opened their vaults to dust off previously unheard material (sometimes against the artist's wishes), comps became more essential than ever.

With their share of hits, outtakes, and oddities, the Who have been well compiled throughout the years. One might even say "over-compiled." As of this writing, there have been more than twenty-five compilations released in the United States and the United Kingdom alone. So let's just focus on the most essential compilations, the ones you should own if you are determined to possess every studio recording and significantly unique mix the Who officially released.

Magic Bus—The Who on Tour (1968)

The first rumblings of a Who compilation appeared on the pages of *Hit Parader* in February 1968. At that point, the group had accumulated a dozen singles and three LPs: not a bad track record considering their late start. Though most of those discs hit big in their homeland, the Who had only recently begun to etch out a spot in America. They created an air of awe and terror with their smash-up gig at the Monterey Pop Festival in June 1967, first cracked the top thirty that same month with the unlikely "Happy Jack," and broke the top ten in November with "I Can See for Miles." The following year was just the right time to show off all they'd accomplished in the United Kingdom with a smart selection of hits, finally introducing America to "I Can't Explain," "My Generation," "Substitute," and the rest. Sprinkle in a bit of self-effacing Who humor and you've got *The Who's Greatest Flops*, the title Townshend announced in that issue of *Hit Parader*. Decca Records had something else in mind.

That landmark gig at Monterey clued Americans to something the Brits had known for years: the Who are one terrifying live act. As fine as their singles are, most of them present a very different band from the one that pummeled the flower children at Monterey. The best way to capitalize on the gig would be a live recording that transferred all the thunder of a Who show to your very own hi-fi. As explained in chapter 16, a gig at the Fillmore East was captured on tape for this very purpose, but the band nixed the disc, leaving Decca without a live album for 1968. That didn't mean the label couldn't create the illusion of one. Take a few recent singles, a couple of EP tracks, a handful of numbers that had already appeared on LP, and a deviously selected title, and *voilà!*—it's *Magic Bus—The Who on Tour!*

Recently converted American fans must have felt hoodwinked when they dropped their needles on a very un-live album most certainly not recorded on tour. Those who owned *Happy Jack* and *Sell Out* were further incensed to discover that three of the eleven tracks were already in their collections. The calculation that went into its title did not go into compiling the album. What were the Decca execs thinking when they passed on the marvelous assortment of sides at their disposal? Since the label had legal access to Shel Talmy's productions, "I Can't Explain," "Anyway, Anyhow, Anywhere," and "My Generation" were fair game. Even if this wasn't the case, "Substitute," "I'm a Boy," "Dogs," and their respective B-sides were still up for grabs. Instead, *Magic Bus* utilized just six single sides: "Pictures of Lily," "Doctor, Doctor," "Someone's Coming," "Call Me Lightning," "Dr. Jekyll and Mr. Hyde," and the title track. These were all good numbers, though the prevalence of Entwistle compositions created a deceptive picture of what the Who were really about. Including the vaguely psychedelic "Disguises" wasn't a bad idea, but that cover of Jan and Dean's "Bucket T" already sounded laughably old-fashioned when it first appeared on the *Ready Steady Who* EP way back in late 1966. The inclusion of several poor masters and mixes—the US single mix of "Dr. Jekyll and Mr. Hyde," the fake stereo presentations of "Disguises," "Call Me Lightning," and "Bucket T"—shows the compiler wasn't thinking at all.

The biggest blunder was handing over slots to previously issued LP tracks—"Run Run Run" from *Happy Jack* and "I Can't Reach You" and "Our Love Was, Is" from *Sell Out*—instead of any of the eighteen uncollected single and EP tracks. Perhaps this crime would have been diminished if the album was more upfront about being a compilation. By masquerading as an original LP (and a live one, no less) makes such redundancy unforgivable. While groups as respected as the Rolling Stones had been subjected to this kind of shabby treatment, even the most unscrupulous labels recognized that *Sgt. Pepper's* had changed the game for good, and LPs should now be regarded as art rather than mere product. It's a shame that sixteen months into the LP revolution, a group as revolutionary as the Who was being treated like it was still 1966. American Decca had little rapport with the newest crop of rock 'n' roll bands, so as far as the label was concerned, it might as well have been. In *Before I Get Old*, Shel Talmy recalled hawking the Who to American Decca to discover that "[t]he youngest guy there was sixty-three" and not too keen on the noisy lads. Despite such lack of empathy, Talmy's position with British Decca gave him an in with the label's American cousin.

As if the contents of *Magic Bus* weren't enough to humiliate the Who in the market they'd been desperately trying to crack for years, the album cover offered more opportunities to scoff. Just a couple of months before the Beatles and Stones would display minimalistic taste with "The White Album" and *Beggars Banquet* (the white invitation cover, not the rejected toilet graffiti one), here was the world's greatest rock 'n' roll band "farting around with [an] absurd bus," as Townshend told Chris Van Ness of *Free Press*. It made Paul Revere and the Raiders' record sleeves look like conceptual art.

Fortunately for the Who, this shoddy piece of merchandise was not enough to knock them back in the States. Peaking at #39, *Magic Bus* was the Who's first album to cross the top-forty threshold. It was also the Americans' only source for "Disguises" and "Bucket T," and in the CD age, the only place to get the US mix of "Dr. Jekyll and Mr. Hyde." To this day this unique version of Entwistle's ghoulish B-side has never been otherwise issued on compact disc outside of Japan, where it appeared on the pricey SHM-CD edition of *Two's Missing* in 2011 (more on that series later). For that alone, *Magic Bus* might be worth holding onto.

Meaty, Beaty, Big, and Bouncy (1971)

Back home, Track Records put together a disc closer in spirit to Townshend's vision of *The Who's Greatest Flops*. In a market where the group had been quite successful on the singles charts, that title would be the first thing to go. Instead, British record buyers were treated to *Direct Hits*. Not as confounding as *Magic Bus—The Who on Tour*, *Direct Hits* still suffered from its share of issues. Most glaring was the lack of Talmy productions for the legal reasons already discussed. So the earliest thing here is "Substitute." Without "My Generation" or "I Can't Explain," *Direct Hits* could only present a partial portrait of the Who. That image was further sullied by mastering that made *Magic Bus* sound like the future of hi-fidelity. All twelve tracks were slathered with booming echo that turned the already dense productions into muck. The selection of Track Records tracks wasn't quite ideal either. The eight single A-sides were givens, but the decision to represent *Ready Steady Who* with "Bucket T" was dumb. Even dumber was the decision to open the entire compilation with that piddly number! That it was a number one single in Sweden is no excuse for its place on this UK comp. "In the City," the weakest of the Who's uncollected B-sides, was another questionable selection. A better choice would have been "Dr. Jekyll and Mr. Hyde" or "Someone's Coming." Since all of its tracks had been previously released in the United Kingdom, *Direct Hits* didn't have any of *Magic Bus*'s rarity value. This could have been remedied by swapping the LP version of "Mary Anne with the Shaky Hand" with the electrified version issued as the flip of "I Can See for Miles" in the United States. And even with the Brits' known aversion to including singles on contemporary albums, the lack of "Magic Bus" (released in the United Kingdom just a month before *Direct Hits*) feels like an oversight. Let's not even get into that awful cover, which looks like a shadow box in a stalker's bathroom.

While it was never intended to be great art, *Direct Hits* didn't even serve its commercial purposes. The compilation made no significant dent on the charts, failing as a pre-Christmas stopgap while the group were busy making *Tommy*. And because it was deleted in the early seventies, it didn't have any long-term purpose as a way to obtain obscurities like "Dogs" or "In the City." Nice job, *Direct Hits*!

But fear not, fans looking for the ultimate compilation. In 1971, the five-year legal mess between the Who and Shel Talmy ended, which meant Track Records

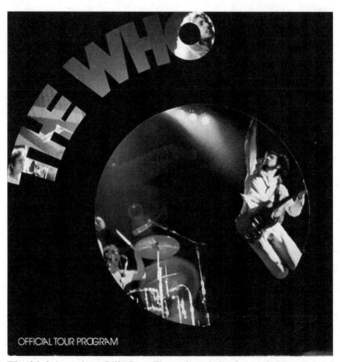

The high-jumping skills Pete Townshend displays on the cover of this 1975 tour program may account for the "bouncy" in *Meaty, Beaty, Big, and Bouncy*.   *Author's collection*

could now mix and mingle its catalog with the litigious American's productions. At long last, the great collection that could have been *The Who's Greatest Flops* could now become a reality on both sides of the Atlantic. Since the Who had another two years of record making since Townshend first announced that ill-fated collection, there was enough new product to eliminate the need for the lesser-loved titles "Call Me Lightning" and "Dogs." Connoisseurs of the odd and fabulous may have lamented those songs' absence, but who could really complain about what was included? Every major single from "I Can't Explain" through the very recent "The Seeker" was accounted for among the fourteen tracks collected as *Meaty, Beaty, Big, and Bouncy* (by this point, another band had beaten the Who to the self-deprecatingly titled singles compilation with 1970's *The Worst of Jefferson Airplane*). At Townshend's behest, "Boris the Spider" was included both to represent John Entwistle and to apologize for not having released it as a single. In his delightful essay on the compilation published in *Rolling Stone*, Townshend said it had only been relegated to LP-track status because of his "own shaky vanity." Perhaps, Pete, but our beloved "Boris" may still have been too weird for the hit parade.

Meaty, Beaty, Big, and Bouncy was universally praised upon its release (when Peter Nickol of *Gramophone* already declared it a "classic") and continues to hold status as an unsurpassed compilation (Stephen Thomas Erlewine called it the Who's "best" in his AllMusic review). There are still a couple of opportunities to nitpick, so let's nitpick. The most glaring mistake was the decision to include the neutered US edit of "The Kids Are Alright" (see the previous chapter). Though good, "The Seeker" was recorded after the Who's metamorphosis into a heavier, harder, more "seventies"-sounding band, and it feels a little out of place alongside the lighter, poppier sixties singles. Some listeners have taken issue with the decision to include extended versions of "I'm a Boy" and "Magic Bus" that differ significantly from the familiar singles, though others have cherished them for their rarity and, by some tastes (including my own), superiority. That the original vinyl version of *Meaty* is the only US release to contain that lengthy mix of "Magic Bus" has been a source of irritation in the CD age.

Among the album's detractors was Kit Lambert, who hated the sequencing and choice of tracks. He even managed to get Polydor to halt distribution for a couple of days, but by that point, too many *Meaty, Beatys* had made it to the shops to stop it.

But enough griping about what is a magnificent snapshot of the Who at their freshest and most exhilarating, the days when Pete Townshend wasn't ashamed of his sense of humor and his band effortlessly rolled out a series of ditties too scrumptious to bury on LPs. Hearing them gathered together, one can only marvel at how the Who didn't really break through in the United States until the sixties had nearly run its course.

These delightful selections were packaged in a witty jacket photographed by Graham Hughes (also known as Roger Daltrey's cousin). To illustrate a discarded album title, *The Who Looks Back*, Hughes and Bill Curbishley scoured the East

End of London for kids to pose as little Pete, Roger, John, and Keith. One of the little models was Curbishley's brother Paul. Hughes then combined sepia shots of the boys in fifties-style outfits with color pics of the band to suggest the Who looking back on themselves through a window on the front cover and vice versa on the back.

While Kit Lambert had his issues with the album, he did get his way on one point: he lobbied against calling it *The Who Looks Back*, because according to Townshend (as quoted in Andy Neill and Matt Kent's *Anyway, Anyhow, Anywhere*), "Kit thought it made it sound as if we were all dead!" So Track issued the record with its iconic, vaguely obscene title, which Hughes had heard was "a line from a dog food commercial," according to Neill and Kent. Typically unsupported speculation on Wikipedia proffers this more plausible claim: "The album title is referential of traits of the members of the band, Meaty: Daltrey, who was quite fit at the time, Beaty: Moon, for his drumming, Big: Entwistle, who was a large person, often referred to as 'The Ox', and Bouncy: Townshend, who jumped about quite acrobatically during performances." After all, who wants their dog food to be "bouncy," or for that matter, "beaty." What the hell could "beaty" dog food be, anyway?

Backtrack 14: The Ox (1970)

With the end of the sixties, the time had come to take a look back at Track's hits and misses of the decade with a series of compilations grounded by the label's two brightest stars: Jimi Hendrix and the Who. The Backtrack series produced fourteen volumes, numbers eight and nine being reissues of *A Quick One* and *Sell Out*, respectively. These were budget releases, most in a generic jacket sporting a shot of a small Vietnamese boy smoking a ciggie.

Volume one was the lightest on Who cuts, only collecting "Pictures of Lily," "I Can See for Miles," and "Call Me Lightning." This left space for Hendrix, Townshend's protégés the Crazy World of Arthur Brown, Mick Jagger's girlfriend Marsha Hunt, Eire Apparent (featuring Henry McCullough later of Spooky Tooth, Joe Cocker's Grease Band, and Wings), Marc Bolan's pre-T. Rex outfit John's Children, and that group's Andy Ellison as a solo artist. Those particular Who songs would be trotted out again on *Backtrack 4*, which allotted an entire side to our boys. So did volumes three and five.

For serious fans, the *Backtrack* records have value as collectibles but aren't great ways to build a Who collection. However, *The House That Track Built*, a sort of precursor to the series, was something special, not only including choices cuts from Hendrix, the Sandpebbles, the Precisions, Thunderclap Newman, John's Children, the Parliaments, and Fairport Convention, but featuring the Who's very exclusive studio version of "Young Man Blues," which would not see wide release until it scored a spot on the super deluxe edition of *Tommy* in 2013 (a different take was used in 1998's expanded *Odds & Sods* and a different mix on 2003's deluxe edition of *Tommy*).

Backtrack 14: The Ox has more lasting worth. The final volume in the series is a handy-dandy collection of every Who song John Entwistle wrote from 1966 to 1970. Here was a compilation with more purpose than *Magic Bus* or *Direct Hits*, a treat for Ox-heads desiring nothing more than a full plunge into the bassist's darkly comic and comically dark waters, from LP tracks such as "Boris the Spider" and "Cousin Kevin" to B-sides such as "Doctor, Doctor" and "Dr. Jekyll and Mr. Hyde" in its superior UK mix. It's even well programmed, opening with the jokey "Heinz Baked Beans," which seamlessly segues into the devastating "Heaven and Hell" with a big, bad *bang*.

These days, there's not much on *The Ox* that can't be found elsewhere, although that version of "Dr. Jekyll and Mr. Hyde" is tough to obtain without springing for the Japanese SHM-CD edition of *Who's Missing*. But as a sustained tribute to the Who's most underrated member, it's a must have—definitely worth a trip to ebay or Discogs.com, where copies sometimes show up at reasonable prices.

Odds & Sods (1974)

Meaty, Beaty, Big, and Bouncy is the ultimate way to collect most of the Who's great A-sides in one spot. *Magic Bus* and *Backtrack 14* are necessary for "Dr. Jekyll and Mr. Hyde" completists. But for sheer rarity, for utter necessity, none of them touch *Odds & Sods*. Of the original LP's eleven tracks, only "I'm a Face" had been previously released, and tracking down a copy of that Fontana single was no easy task in the sixties. In 1974, it was basically impossible.

At that time, vault-raid records were coming into vogue among record labels looking to beat the bootleggers and keep the dollars flowing in. The previous year, Reprise records issued *The Great Lost Kinks Album* to capitalize on that band's back catalog after they'd jumped ship to RCA. Ray Davies was angered by the release of tracks he considered rejects and by John Mendelssohn's mean-spirited liner notes and enacted litigation that resulted in the record's withdrawal a couple of years later. Less controversial was Jefferson Airplane's *Early Flight*, released on their own Grunt label in early 1974.

Odds & Sods was officially sanctioned too, even though Townshend would later deem it substandard in his infamously bitchy 1975 interview with *Creem*'s Roy Carr. As the mastermind behind the project, John Entwistle was more enthused, though as was often the case, you wouldn't know it from his attitude.

"Sod is a swear word [in the United Kingdom]," Entwistle mumbled to *Circus* magazine's Steven Gaines. "When the word's used in the respect of *Odds & Sods*, it means bits and pieces. You know, rubbish, stuff that's been gathered from everywhere and stuck together."

Entwistle selected eleven choice pieces of rubbish representing each phase of the Who's career thus far, from their days as the High Numbers to 1972. Several tracks were tied to grander aborted projects. The delightful and slightly gruesome "Little Billy" was recorded as an advert for the American Cancer

This funky minifolder is one of the neat extras included with the Japanese SHM-CD edition of *Odds & Sods*.   *Author's collection*

Society. "Pure and Easy," "Too Much of Anything," and "Put the Money Down" (the latter two featuring newly recorded vocals by Roger Daltrey) were *Lifehouse* rejects, and "Long Live Rock" was to be the centerpiece of the ill-fated autobiographical *Rock Is Dead . . . Long Live Rock*. "Now I'm a Farmer" and "Naked Eye" were to be included on the scrapped maxi single. Entwistle mixed two other rogue EP tracks, "Water" and "I Don't Even Know Myself," for possible inclusion, but the former was tacked onto the B-side of "5:15" instead, while a remake of the latter had already seen release on the flip of "Won't Get Fooled Again," making it less of an odd than the other sods.

What really distinguishes *Odds & Sods* from similar projects such as *The Great Lost Kinks Album*, *Early Flight*, the Byrds' *Preflyte*, and the Stones' *Metamorphosis*—all worthwhile collections in their own rights—is the absolute consistency of quality. Not one of these tracks deserved to be left on the shelf, and some are so brilliantly conceived—"Little Billy," "Glow Girl," and "Pure and Easy" being three obvious examples—that it's criminal they had to linger in the dust at all. And don't listen to anyone who tells you that "Faith in Something Bigger" is subpar. It's lovely.

Conceptualized by Roger Daltrey, the packaging radiated the same quirky charm as the music. The cover flaunts an absurd Graham Hughes photo of the guys wearing American football helmets spelling out "R. O. C. K." Each of their names is etched onto the helmets too, though sizing problems forced Townshend and Daltrey to swap. Townshend was no more a fan of the album's exterior than its interior. When he expressed this to Hughes, the irritated photographer tore up the cover, which pleased the curmudgeonly guitarist, who then gave the shredded version his stamp of approval. Die cutting approximated the shredded look, while allowing a photo of the band onstage at Chicago's International Amphitheater to peek through beneath. The LP also included a supplemental lyric sheet with humorous track-by-track notes by Townshend and a poster depicting the band onstage at Maryland's Capital Center. The British edition took an extra step by printing the song titles in Braille . . . yet another good deed from the group who so desperately wanted to protect you from cancer with "Little Billy."

Odds & Sods was a grand success, so it's unfortunate that Entwistle's plan to follow it up with a second volume never came to be. In 1976, he revealed his plans in the *NME*: "There's an unedited version of 'Join Together,' three minutes longer than the single. We've got The High Numbers' 'Zoot Suit,' 'Early Morning, Cold Taxi', those two instrumentals, a couple of out-takes from *Quadrophenia*, and things that aren't finished like 'Glittering Girl' which only has a guide vocal." Although *Odds & Sods: The Sequel* didn't materialize, most of these tracks eventually did on expanded editions of the Who's albums in the nineties (that enticing extended version of "Join Together" remains in the shadows). *Odds & Sods* got the expanded treatment in 1998, more than doubling in size with the MIA singles "Under My Thumb" and "Water," a studio version of the concert fave "Summertime Blues," and plenty more outtakes, such as the *Lifehouse* leftover "Time Is Passing" and the excised *Quadrophenia* cut "We Close Tonight," featuring a rare duet between John Entwistle and Keith Moon. Unfortunately, the disc made the mistake of smoothing out the original track sequence with a less interesting chronological presentation and remixes that would give anyone familiar with "Glow Girl," "Postcard," or "Put the Money Down" a start. However, with eight recordings unavailable elsewhere, you still wouldn't want to be without it.

The Kids Are Alright (1979)

In 1976, Bill Curbishley assembled the Who's first double-LP compilation and the first to span the band's entire career. Well, almost. Since bitterness with Talmy persisted, and the producer was still entitled to a cut of his productions despite the end of his stranglehold over his former charges, Curbishley only included the absolutely essential "My Generation" from the Talmy era. So, as the compiler admitted, *The Story of the Who* didn't quite live up to its name. The decision to include the trivial tracks "Heat Wave" and "Tommy's Holiday Camp" while passing on such recent singles as "Let's See Action" and "Join Together" and ignoring the existence of *Quadrophenia* completely further devalued the collection.

Leave it to John Entwistle to oversee a quirkier history. He had his thunderfingers in *The Kids Are Alright*, the double-LP soundtrack of Jeff Stein's attention-deficit-disordered and utterly exhilarating documentary on the Who. Like the film, the soundtrack is all over the place. The jaw-dropping, heart-stopping version of "A Quick One While He's Away" from *The Rolling Stones Rock and Roll Circus* and the *Smothers Brothers Comedy Hour* version of "My Generation" are delectable rarities that sit alongside weak remixes of the studio cuts "Magic Bus," "Long Live Rock," and "I Can See for Miles" (the sleeve erroneously credits this as a performance from *The Smothers Brothers Comedy Hour*, where the group mimed to the original mix). The latter track isn't even in the film! Neither is the version of "My Wife" captured at Gaumont State Theatre in 1977, or the *Live at Leeds* version of "Happy Jack," which received its first official release here. The performances of "I Can't Explain" from *Shindig!* (August 3, 1965) and "Anyway, Anyhow, Anywhere" from *Ready Steady Go!* (July 1, 1965) have historical significance, but the scratchy, audience-scream-slathered recordings aren't terribly listenable. The fine version of "Young Man Blues" from London's Coliseum Theatre (December 14, 1969) isn't that essential since we already had a perfectly great one on *Live at Leeds*. Though it's nice to finally get a live rendition of "My Wife," Entwistle's off-key vocal sours the moment.

Still, there is a lot here for live-music aficionados to cherish. The versions of "Baba O'Riley" and "Won't Get Fooled Again" (which is a different take from the one in the film), recorded at a special private performance at Shepperton film studios, are mighty and exciting. These recordings are also important for being the final ones Keith Moon would ever make. We're also treated to a nice run of numbers representing both Woodstock and *Tommy* (only "See Me, Feel Me" being previously available on the *Woodstock* soundtrack) and an interesting medley of "Join Together," Bo Diddley's "Road Runner," and "My Generation" performed as a chugging blues (cut from the soundtrack's original release on CD).

The most vital pieces on *The Kids Are Alright* are those TV versions of "A Quick One While He's Away" and "My Generation." Here's where the album sort of qualifies as an essential collection for anyone who wants all of the Who's studio work. Though "A Quick One" is 100 percent live, "My Generation" only features live vocals. The instrumental and vocal backing is canned. It's also a really exciting alternative to the Shel Talmy version. While it has nothing on that first version's density and sheer power (transposing the key up a whole step lightens the feel too), Entwistle's bass solo is springier, more effortlessly fleet-fingered than the one on the single. Townshend also tears off a killer riff leading into the first modulation. We lose the final verse, but the overall effect is distinct enough that you'll want a copy of this recording no matter its flaws. The interview with Tommy Smothers that precedes it is hilarious too.

Music from the Soundtrack of the Who Film Quadrophenia (1979)

The Who continued to buy time in the year following Keith Moon's death with another film and another soundtrack. This time John Entwistle's remixes presented radical enough changes to warrant purchase among those (such as Roger Daltrey) who took issue with the original mix, which tended to bury certain elements (such as Roger Daltrey). John gave Rog a boost, and the tracks generally breathe more than they did on the original album. More controversially, Entwistle redid his bass tracks with brighter sound and more elaborate lines perfectly fine for the stage but perhaps too audacious for recordings many Who fans already knew by heart. Had "The Punk and the Godfather" always contained such ornate bass work, Entwistle's revisions might not be so distracting, but in light of his original part, the new one treads all over the rest of the track. The addition of an opening rumble from Moon also detracts from the shock of Townshend's opening riff.

Some additions were less offensive: a few moments of barely detectable flute on "Love Reign o'er Me" and some pretty piano improvisation in "I'm One." Yet there are thoughtless edits ranging from the unnecessary (the early fade of "Love Reign o'er Me") to the confounding. "Helpless Dancer's" 2:34 is reduced to 22 seconds. *Twenty-two seconds.* No fooling. Granted, this is the only portion of the song heard in the film (right before the closing credits), but including the title on the sleeve without any indication that the song barely makes a cameo on the vinyl is an unforgiveable con.

Collectors should still note that there is more purpose to the soundtrack than a clutch of questionable remixes and reedits. The album boasts three tracks unavailable anywhere else. "Get Out and Stay Out" illustrates Jimmy getting the boot from his mother in the film. "Four Faces" is a sprightly, piano-driven jingle. "Joker James," which Townshend actually composed around the time of "I'm a Boy," reports Jimmy's proclivity for playing practical jokes (it was under consideration for Keith Moon's theme until "Bell Boy" came along). "Get Out and Stay Out" and "Joker James" are also notable for featuring the debut of Kenney Jones behind the drum kit, though his playing is a bit awkward.

While these tracks do recall the Who's earlier days, they're hardly the kind of stuff real mods would have ever given the time of day. So the soundtrack is filled out with additional material more authentically representative of the era, if not exactly mod tastes. Without access to the Motown-Tamla sides that were the mods' main meat, James Brown's "Night Train" and Booker T. & the M.G.'s "Green Onions" are the only true mod anthems on the record. Otherwise, classics from the Ronettes, the Kingsmen, the Cascades, the Crystals, and the Chiffons had to suffice. Representing the seventies' new guard of mods was a pub group called Cross Section, who offered a competent version of Tommy Tucker's "Hi-Heeled Sneakers" in their only released performance. The soundtrack's sole artifact of the days when the Who—or the High Numbers—were actually playing the mod game themselves is "Zoot Suit." Its inclusion would also make

Music from the Soundtrack of the Who Film Quadrophenia important to collectors over the next fifteen years before it found a second home on the *Thirty Years of Maximum R&B* box set.

Who's Missing (1985); Two's Missing (1987)

An era had assuredly come to an end when Keith Moon died on September 7, 1978. Surprisingly, a flood of compilations eulogizing that era did not immediately follow. A full three years passed before MCA released the first major US retrospective. Though *Hooligans* has since been made redundant by more comprehensive compilations, it was the only one to collect such stray singles as "Let's See Action," "The Relay," and "Join Together" in the United States at the time. Wisely, it overlapped little with the still essential *Meaty, Beaty, Big, and Bouncy*, only repeating three tracks, though the lack of the career-defining "Won't Get Fooled Again" was a major flaw. MCA remedied that issue two years later with *Who's Greatest Hits*, but this was a problematic package because several tracks—"Won't Get Fooled Again," "5:15," "Love Reign o'er Me," "Who Are You"—were presented in their ruthlessly condensed single edits.

Between *Hooligans* and *Who's Greatest Hits*, Polydor released a more worthwhile collection in Australia called *Join Together: Rarities*. Polydor would release that same comp in the United Kingdom as *Rarities Vol. 2: 1970–1972* in 1983. Together with its companion first volume, *Rarities* mostly featured previously uncollected singles (the US single version of "Mary Anne with the Shaky Hand," "Under My Thumb," "I Don't Even Know Myself," "When I Was a Boy," "Waspman," "Here for More," "Water," "Baby Don't You Do It") and cuts that had only appeared on the out-of-print platters *Direct Hits* ("Dogs," "Call Me Lightning") and *Backtrack 14: The Ox* ("Dr. Jekyll and Mr. Hyde," "Heaven and Hell"). *Rarities Vol. 1: 1966–1968* also featured the *Ready Steady Who* EP in its entirety.

The *Rarities* collections were certainly important pieces of the puzzle even as certain sides still remained unaccounted for. While issues with Shel Talmy persisted, all of the B-sides he produced in 1965 were missing. The wild instrumental "Dogs Part Two," which had been released as the B-side of "Pinball Wizard," fell in the 1969 crack between *Rarities Vol. 1: 1966–1968* and *Rarities Vol. 2: 1970–1972*. There was also a wealth of unreleased tracks waiting for their coming-out party.

Part one of that party was finally scheduled in late 1985 when MCA released *Who's Missing*. There is much overlap here with the *Rarities* albums, and though the album is programmed chronologically, there isn't much rhyme or reason to what has been included and what has been left out. Even when a second volume with a more random running order called *Two's Missing* followed in 1987, there were still some obvious holes that required filling. Neither compilation made room for such US-deprived B-sides as "I've Been Away" or the British mix of "Dr.

Jekyll and Mr. Hyde" or the still uncompiled "In the City" or "Batman" from *Ready Steady Who*.

Yet there was much for US fans to rejoice over. *Who's Missing* marked the first time—believe it or not—that the original single version of "I'm a Boy" had been released in the United States since it appeared on a flop single nearly twenty years earlier. The Yanks also got their very first taste of the non-US single sides "Daddy Rolling Stone," "Shout and Shimmy," "Circles," "The Last Time," "Under My Thumb," and "Dogs." But best of all, *Who's Missing* and *Two's Missing* dug deeper into the vaults to give a number of tracks legal release for the first time ever. There were four tracks recorded for the debut album that would have largely consisted of covers (see chapter 16): a scalding take on Eddie Holland's "Leaving Here," a more polished version of "Heat Wave" than the one that would appear on *A Quick One*, renditions of the Vandellas' "Motoring" and Paul Revere and the Raiders' "Louie—Go Home" (complete with fumbled lyric and title: "Lubie [Come Back Home]"). There were also three ferocious performances recorded at San Francisco's Civic Auditorium in 1971 for the proposed live album also discussed in chapter 16 ("Bargain," Freddie King's "Going Down," and "My Wife," which was mistakenly credited as having been recorded in 1972 on the *Two's Missing* cover).

In 2011, Universal Music reissued the Who's catalog, including several choice compilations, in Japan. Because they are imports, and because they were issued in the Super-High Material Compact Disc, or SHM-CD, format (which supposedly delivers superior audio quality on a longer-lasting polycarbonate plastic disc), these reissues are expensive, a single disc going for about $35 as of this writing. However, collectors with money to burn may find reason to spring for *My Generation* in its superior mono mix, a spectacular double-disc edition of *A Quick One*, *The Singles* with fresh remasters of "Relay" and the *Meaty, Beaty* version of "Magic Bus," and *Odds & Sods* presented in its original sequence and mix not available on the 1998 US reissue (but be warned that the SHM-CD issued in 2013 is a jewel case edition of the 1998 mix).

Tastiest of all are expanded versions of *Who's Missing* and *Two's Missing*. Jon Astley told me, "I went to great lengths to try and find original mixes for these—unlike the original releases!"

Along with the original twenty-five oddities are:

On *Who's Missing*:
"Doctor, Doctor"
"Someone's Coming" (US single mix)
"Dr. Jekyll and Mr. Hyde" (UK mix)
"Fortune Teller" (original 1968 mix)
"Postcard" (maxi-single mix)
"Baby Don't You Do It" (unedited version of the B-side of "Join Together")

On *Two's Missing*:
"Dr. Jekyll and Mr. Hyde" (US mix)
"Call Me Lightning"
"Melancholia" (original 1968 mix)
"Eyesight to the Blind" (alternate vocal version)
"I Don't Even Know Myself" (early maxi-single version)

Again, these SHM-CDs are costly, but considering that the expanded *Who's Missing/Two's Missing* double-disc set (in spiffy mini-LP cover packaging) negates the need to supplement your collection with *Magic Bus—The Who on Tour* and *Backtrack 14: The Ox*, not to mention the domestic versions of *Who's Missing* and *Two's Missing* (both out of print), it isn't a horrible deal (as of this writing, copies can be found online for around $50). And if Universal Music ever decides to release these discs in the United States, they will probably be both essential and more affordable.

Thirty Years of Maximum R&B (1994)

After years of lopsided compilations, MCA finally released a fairly comprehensive collection in 1988. Capitalizing on the name of the Who's most recent hit, *Who's Better, Who's Best* is notable as the first US comp to include "You Better You Bet" (it had appeared on the UK compilation *The Singles* in 1984). Because of the breadth of the Who's catalog of hits and classic-rock radio staples, a single CD compilation was doomed to be lacking. The US edition of *Who's Better, Who's Best* once again trots out the single edits of "The Kids Are Alright," "Won't Get Fooled Again" (mistakenly listed as "Extended Version), and "Who Are You" and offers no representative from *Quadrophenia*. The British edition is preferable, appending "5:15" to the running order and including the full-length versions of "The Kids Are Alright" and "Won't Get Fooled Again." An infinitely more comprehensive overview of Who history was six years away.

Discussed by Pete Townshend as early as 1989 (when he told New York *Newsday*, "we found some wonderful little bits and pieces, including a great version of 'Fortune Teller,' and a really good version of an awful song I wrote called 'Melancholia'), *Thirty Years of Maximum R&B* finally arrived in the summer of 1994. With four discs packed with fresh remasters, all of the essential singles and album cuts, and a wealth of previously unreleased live and studio tracks, how could it fail?

Well, some may say it still did. *Thirty Years of Maximum R&B* offers much pleasure for collectors and nitpickers alike. The latter will note that studio versions of the essential singles "Substitute" and "The Real Me" are absent, while "5:15" and "Who Are You" are unforgivably presented in their single edits. Producers Jon Astley and Andy Macpherson also get too creative with their remixes at times. Editing together studio and live versions of "A Quick One While He's Away" and "See Me, Feel Me" was a bad idea. Several other tracks are carelessly pruned ("Jaguar," "Slip Kid," "Love Reign o'er Me," "Eminence Front," live versions of "Bargain" and "Naked Eye") to make room for maximum tracks. But couldn't some of the lesser pieces have been left aside to make room for full-length versions of these treasures? As magnificent as *The Who Sell Out* is, and as nice as it is that this formerly underrated record was finally getting its due, was it truly necessary to include a total of eight tracks from it? Losing just a couple of them would have allowed space for the edited tracks to run their courses without interruption.

So *Thirty Years of Maximum R&B* should not inspire anyone to trade in their proper Who albums (nothing should). John Entwistle was critical of the set in a 1996 interview with *Goldmine* (he particularly disliked the remixes of the *Live at Leeds* tracks), and the best Townshend can say about it in his vitriolic liner notes is it's "an OK job." Definitive *Thirty Years of Maximum R&B* is not, but essential it most certainly is. Nowhere else are nuggets such as "Here 'Tis" (a Bo Diddley cover from the High Numbers sessions), the aforementioned "Fortune Teller," and a version of "Dreaming from the Waist" from the celebrated Swansea Football Ground gig of 1976 available in the United States and United Kingdom. Less fun to hear, but still worth noting for their rarity, are a version of "Twist and Shout" from one of the Who's final shows with Kenney Jones, a version of "I'm a Man" from the 1989 reunion tour, and a version of "The Real Me" recorded during Jones's audition for the band (hard to believe he made the cut after this plodding performance). A version of Larry Williams's "Bony Moronie" from the Young Vic *Lifehouse* gig was only otherwise available on an obscure 1988 EP called *This Is My Generation*. The addition of some very funny Townshend stage rants and Moon's BBC skits further fill out this unwieldy look at three decades of Wholiganism.

Thirty Years of Maximum R&B is also important for its many firsts. The box set marked the first time US fans could get their hands on the unedited "The Kids Are Alright" and "Mary Anne with the Shaky Hand" with full ending previously only available (with unseemly echo) on *Direct Hits*. The '67 outtakes "Girl's Eyes," "Early Morning Cold Taxi," "Jaguar" (foolishly edited), and Pete's "awful" (wonderful) "Melancholia" also make their debut.

MCA's reissue campaign that began in the nineties has unearthed a mass of additional rarities. For the most complete collection, the compilations in this chapter must sit side by side with the most recent editions of these reissues. Though these releases are controversial among purists because of Astley and Macpherson's remixes, they are vital for such rarities as "Instant Party Mixture" (on the deluxe edition of *My Generation*), "Man with Money" and "Happy Jack (acoustic version)" (on the expanded *A Quick One*), "Glittering Girl" and "Sodding About" (the deluxe edition of *The Who Sell Out*), a lighter early version of "Pure and Easy" (the deluxe edition of *Who's Next*), the Who's version of "Empty Glass" (the expanded *Who Are You*), and "I Like Nightmares" (the expanded version of *Face Dances*). Once again, the best way to own these expanded and deluxe editions are the 2011 Japanese versions.

BBC Sessions (2000)

At the outset of the 1960s, the British Broadcasting Company was slow to adapt to the new era of shaggy rock 'n' rollers. The Musicians Union stipulated that the Beeb could showcase no more than eighty-two hours of prerecorded music per week. So in-studio performances were the only way pop groups could peddle their wares to the public on a more regular basis . . . well, at least outside of the overseas Radio Luxembourg and illegal—and therefore very, very naughty— offshore pirate stations Radio Caroline and Radio London. As *Sell Out* attests, the Who were great supporters of the pirates and vice versa, but they knew well enough to play the BBC's game too.

The guys first auditioned for Auntie on April 9, 1964, when they were still the Detours and Doug Sandom still occupied the drum throne. Failing to pass muster, they tried again with their more familiar name and their more familiar drummer on February 12, 1965. Not surprisingly, three of the BBC's stodgy old judges were highly unimpressed ("Ponderous!" "Unentertaining!" "Below standard!" they shouted), but the Who still managed to wrangle a majority vote, thus beginning five years of kowtowing to the BBC through nine separate sessions.

The Who's first sessions were recorded for the relatively pop-friendly programs *Top Gear* and *Saturday Club* (at Delaware Road studios) on May 24, 1965. They quickly laid down "Daddy Rolling Stone," "Anyway, Anyhow, Anywhere," "I Don't Mind," and an exclusive version of the Olympics' "Good Lovin'" recorded during the *Top Gear* session at Studio Two on New Bond Street, before motoring over to Delaware Road studios to cut "Leaving Here," "Please, Please, Please," and "Just You and Me, Darling," another James Brown groove, for *Saturday Club.*

Without much control over how the BBC's session men recorded them, the Who lost the overdriven heft of their recent recordings with Shel Talmy, so radio listeners heard a very different band than the one that roiled a maelstrom on both sides of the "Anyway, Anyhow, Anywhere" single. However, the otherwise unrecorded numbers "Good Lovin'" and "Just You and Me, Darling" were treats. So would be renditions of Martha and the Vandellas' "Dancing in the Street," the Everly Brothers' "Man with Money," and the Lovin' Spoonful's "On the Road Again" recorded during future BBC sessions.

While the Who's BBC recordings collected dust, the ever forward-thinking Beatles scooped together more than two years of their sessions onto a double-disc set in 1994. Like everything the Beatles released, *Live at the BBC* was a massive hit, reaching #3 in the United States and the top spot in the United Kingdom. Throughout the nineties, Fleetwood Mac, Dire Straits, the Damned, Led Zeppelin, ELO, and the Pixies all cottoned to the commercial prospects and bootlegger-frustrating potential of releasing their own BBC discs.

After some delays, the Who released their own *BBC Sessions* collection in the twenty-first century. Along with those raw takes of "Good Lovin'," "Just You and Me, Darling," and "Dancing in the Street" were alternative versions of some twenty Who classics: "Disguises" with Daltrey's cheekily whined vocal and

Townshend's barely-there guitar work; a wilder, noisier "Run Run Run"; "Pictures of Lily" overlaid with ethereal organ; "Happy Jack" with acoustic lead guitar and Entwistle supplying the "I saw ya!" in his "Boris" grunt; a veritable studio version of "Shakin' All Over" complete with sci-fi echo effects, etc. The latest sessions on the disc—"Long Live Rock" and "Relay," recorded for *The Old Grey Whistle Test* in 1973—were merely the familiar studio versions with new vocal tracks. Yet even these were of some interest, particularly when Daltrey sings a verse of "Long Live Rock" that Townshend would handle on the version that climaxed *Odds & Sods*.

In the United Kingdom, *BBC Sessions* was further adorned with "Man with Money" and an unedited version of "Shakin' All Over" featuring a few lines from Willie Dixon's "Spoonful." According to The Who.com, these moments were trimmed due to copyright restrictions, which is odd considering that the Kit Lambert–produced version of the Everly Brothers cover had already appeared on the extended edition of *A Quick One* five years earlier. Americans who frequented the Best Buy record store chain received an even bigger boon via a bonus disc of seven additional tracks ("Pinball Wizard," "See Me, Feel Me," "I Don't Even Know Myself," "I Can See for Miles," "Heaven and Hell," "The Seeker," and "Summertime Blues") and an interview of Townshend discussing *Tommy*.

Then and Now: 1964–2004 (2004)

Thirty Years of Maximum R&B kicked off a massive remastering, remixing, rejiggering campaign that saw all of the Who's core albums released with bonus tracks throughout the nineties and into the twenty-first century. The onslaught began on February 28, 1995, when *Live at Leeds* celebrated its twenty-fifth anniversary with eight bonus tracks, a whole new running order, and the band's banter reinserted between tracks. After the booze peddlers at the Seagram Company and Matsushita Electrical Industrial Company paid $5.7 billion in cash for 80 percent of MCA on April 9, 1995, the campaign shifted into high gear with expanded editions of *A Quick One* and *The Who Sell Out* following on June 20, and the rest dribbling out over the ensuing seven years.

The less dedicated follower could help him or herself to a number of compilation choices. First up was 1996's *My Generation: The Very Best of the Who*, essentially a chronologically arranged expansion of *Who's Better, Who's Best* that deleted "The Kids Are Alright" and "See Me, Feel Me" but allotted space for "Boris the Spider," "The Seeker," "Let's See Action," "5:15," and "Won't Get Fooled Again" in its lengthy natural state. The merely Who curious, and those on a tight budget, might have selected the scanty, ten-track *The Best of the Who: 20th Century Masters* upon its 1999 release.

Those looking for a comp of more serious heft got what they were seeking in 2002 with the excellent *Ultimate Collection*. All of the major singles and several key album tracks were present, sounding good and unedited. Even "Who Are You" makes its first full-length compilation appearance since *Hooligans* two decades earlier. The discerning collector had several variations on offer as different markets had their own ideas of what constituted the ultimate collection. In the United States, the set was released with thirty-five tracks while the first 150,000 pressings included a "collector's bonus disc" EP featuring the bowdlerized US single edit of "Substitute," the inferior mono mix of the *Jigsaw Puzzle* version of "I'm a Boy" (mistakenly listed as "early version"), the acoustic take of "Happy Jack" previously available on the 1995 reissue of *A Quick One* (mistakenly credited as "previously unreleased"), and the UK single mix of "Magic Bus." Pop the disc into a computer and watch footage of "Baba O'Riley" and "Substitute" from the Who's gig at the Charlton Athletic Football Club on May 18, 1974. In the United Kingdom, "Don't Let Go the Coat" and "Another Tricky Day" were added to the running order, while a limited-edition issue further loaded the lineup with "Had Enough," "The Quiet One," and "Athena." The decision to include so many latter-day tracks as bonuses was odd, but since there are no egregious absences, *The Ultimate Collection* does a pretty good job of earning its name.

The following year, MCA was gone for good, having been fully consumed by Geffen Records. In 2004, the first Who compilation under the new regime emerged, and those who already figured they had all they needed on *The Ultimate Collection* may have been forced to think again with *Then and Now: 1964–2004*. The familiar tracks weren't too distinct from the other recent hits collections, and "Love Reign o'er Me" and "Who Are You" were back to their sad single-edit states. But wait . . . what about that odd title? 1964 to *2004*? *Then and Now* included the Who's first two studio recordings of original material in twenty-two years. Though one might argue that a two-man Who isn't really the Who, "Real Good Looking Boy" and "Old Red Wine," a tribute to the recently deceased John Entwistle, are pretty good songs and the sole arguments for *Then and Now*'s essentialness. More important than these tracks' intrinsic qualities are the revitalizing effect they had on Pete Townshend's creativity and his relationship with Roger Daltrey. The duo would soon get to work on the first studio Who album since *It's Hard*: *Endless Wire*.

The year 2009 saw the release of the generically titled *Greatest Hits*, which has the distinction of being the first compilation to include *Endless Wire* material, but it's useless otherwise. The same could be said of the equally redundant *Icon* and *Icon 2* collections released in 2011. The Who's ultimate collections were behind them at this point, and the eleven ones profiled here are all the completist really needs.

20

Come to This House

Special Guest Stars

E ven a band that was home to musicians as versatile as John Entwistle and Pete Townshend had to look outside the team for assistance from time to time. Sometimes producers hired these guest musicians against the band's will, but more often than not they were welcomed into a rock 'n' roll family far more communal than is often believed.

Jimmy Page and the Ivy League

In the early sixties, it was common practice for a producer to bring in studio pros to ensure recording sessions proceeded smoothly with a minimum of wasted time (trans: wasted money). That is Andy White drumming on "P.S. I Love You" and the LP/US single version of "Love Me Do," not Ringo Starr. Roger McGuinn was the only Byrd to pick up an instrument while recording "Mr. Tambourine Man." Like George Martin and Terry Melcher, Shel Talmy had little faith in his acts' professionalism, relying on a dependable troupe of session men. When he recorded "You Really Got Me," he had Jimmy Page on hand in the event Dave Davies couldn't cut it. He could, though Talmy claims Page ended up playing a bit of rhythm guitar so Ray Davies didn't have to worry about singing and riffing at the same time. Page was also in tow when the Who recorded their first single under their proper name. Contrary to popular myth, he did not play a lick on "I Can't Explain," supposedly because Pete Townshend refused to lend out his twelve-string Rickenbacker. Two could play at that game, and when Pagey with-held his new fuzz box from Pete, the future Led Zeppelinite ended up playing the sludgey licks on the B-side, "Bald Headed Woman." Page's presence at the session has long roiled rumors that he played on "I Can't Explain," and it's been repeated so often that even Daltrey has started remembering it this way, telling Howard Stern in 2013 that Page handled the guitar solo to spare Townshend from overdubbing. Talmy's dissatisfaction with the Who's falsetto harmonies also moved him to use slick singing trio the Ivy League on both sides, while the League's Perry Ford supplied piano.

Nicky Hopkins

Perry Ford did a fine enough job on the Who's first session with Shel Talmy, but he was no match for the fleet-fingered Nicky Hopkins. One of the most in-demand session men of the sixties, Hopkins's rippling tinkles can be heard on choice discs by the Kinks, the Beatles, the Rolling Stones, the Yardbirds, the Move, P. P. Arnold, the Jeff Beck Group, the Creation, Donovan, Jefferson Airplane . . . well, you get the picture. He was very popular. Hopkins was particularly popular with Shel Talmy, who recruited him to jangle the keys on "Anyway, Anyhow, Anywhere" and *My Generation*. Hopkins's hyper piano runs contribute much amphetamine fuel to "A Legal Matter," "La-La-La Lies," "Much Too Much," and especially, "The Ox," for which he received cocomposer credit with Townshend, Entwistle, and Moon. The Who had their fill of Talmy after making that album, but they invited Hopkins back to play on "Dogs," "Pure and Easy," "The Song Is Over," "Getting in Tune," "Let's See Action," and *By Numbers*. Although he didn't love all the musicians he jammed with (he had a particularly tough time with the Kinks), Nicky Hopkins had a great deal of affection for the Who, and even claimed Pete Townshend asked him to join the band around *Who's Next*. Townshend did not share that particular memory.

John "Speedy" Keen

Pete Townshend had a keen eye for talent and generously took many a protégé under his birdman wing. One of the first was his chauffeur, John "Speedy" Keen, who displayed a knack for songwriting that his boss and buddy encouraged. When Speedy composed a sci-fi tune about a fantasy city with glass skies and brown seas for the Who, the group agreed it was worth recording, even inviting him to sing along with Roger Daltrey during the session. "Armenia City in the Sky" would be Speedy Keen's last compositional coup for the Who. No matter, because he'd soon write a genuine hit called "Something in the Air" for his short-lived band Thunderclap Newman.

Chris Morphet

According to John Entwistle, Pete Townshend's brief fascination with greyhound racing began when he and band photographer Chris Morphet took Townshend to White City Stadium in London to watch the puppies prance. Entwistle claimed the spectacle so overexcited the guitarist that Townshend started hopping up and down as if he was onstage and betting money as if the Who weren't in perpetual debt. Our most vivid evidence of Townshend's dog-racing delirium is the wonderfully daft single "Dogs," on which fellow enthusiast Morphet honked the harmonica.

Jess Roden

In 1968, Jess Roden was singing lead with The Alan Bown! (formerly the Alan Bown Set) when he loaned his golden throat to the Who as they recorded "Magic Bus" at IBC Studios. Before the end of the year, Roden would resume his role as backup singer on the song when the Who performed it at the London College of Printing on June 15 and the University of Reading on December 12. He would later perform similar duties on the *Tommy* soundtrack and would return to center stage with such groups as Bronco, his own Jess Roden Band, and the charmingly christened Butts Band, featuring former Doors John Densmore and Robby Krieger.

Simon and Paul Townshend

The Who only employed two outsiders to support them while making their key album, and they weren't very outside at that. As the name implies, Paul and Simon Townshend were Pete's little brothers. Paul was just eleven years old, and Simon was a wee thing of eight when they contributed backing vocals to "Smash the Mirror" on *Tommy*. Paul's center-stage ambitions apparently ended with an abortive attempt to make a record with his brothers in 1992 (though he would later play his older brother on an episode of *The Simpsons*). Little Simon was up for a long career in rock 'n' roll, and that is precisely what he has had, both as a solo artist (brother Paul mixed his *Among Us* album in 1997) and a regular supporter of the Who onstage and in the studio. His vocals can be heard on "Sound Round," "Pick Up the Peace," and the title track of *Endless Wire*.

Leslie West, Kenny Ascher, and Al Kooper

In March 1971, the Who began preliminary recordings for *Lifehouse* at the Record Plant in New York City. Backing up the band were guitarist Leslie West of Mountain and pianist Kenny Ascher, a valuable session man who'd go on to cowrite songs for *The Muppet Movie* with Paul Williams (Bob Dylan/Blood, Sweat, and Tears organist Al Kooper has also been associated with these sessions, though he denied it. He did play organ a few years earlier on "Armenia City in the Sky," though). The sessions were promising but lacked the Who's usual heft, and none of the recordings ended up on *Who's Next*. During the reissue campaign of decades later, these recordings of "Baby Don't You Do It," "Behind Blue Eyes," "Pure and Easy," "Won't Get Fooled Again," and an electrified "Love Ain't for Keeping" would get second lives on expanded editions of *Who's Next* and *Odds & Sods*.

Dave Arbus

One of the oddest elements of the odd "Baba O'Riley" came from an odd mind indeed. *What if,* Keith Moon posited, *there was a whirling-dervish fiddle solo over the climactic jam?* A good idea is a good idea, and Townshend gave Moon the go-ahead to hire his friend Dave Arbus of prog rockers East of Eden to rake his violin. Thus, Arbus received his most famous credit, and the cover of *Who's Next* arrived with the bizarre credit "Violin on 'Baba O'Riley' produced by Keith Moon."

Mylon Le Fevre

An even weirder credit can be read on the back cover of the *Two's Missing* compilation, where annotator John Entwistle mentions a guest artist "sniffing in time to" Moon's loony B-side "Wasp Man." The sniffer is Mylon Le Fevre, the southern Christian gospel singer who wrote Elvis Presley's "Without Him."

Chris Stainton

When Nicky Hopkins's busy schedule prevented him from lending his services during the *Quadrophenia* sessions, Pete Townshend gave the job to Chris Stainton of Joe Cocker's band. This was just and fair, considering that Townshend had straight-up stolen Stainton's piano line on Cocker's "Hitchcock Railway." Stainton bore no hard feelings for the thievery and replicated his work when laying down "Drowned," while also furnishing keys on "The Dirty Jobs" and "5:15."

Andy Fairweather-Low

British pop mainstay Andy Fairweather-Low began his career with the bubble-gummy Amen Corner before becoming a hardworking session man in the seventies. He got to work with the Who during their final sessions with Keith Moon, contributing backing vocals to "New Song," "Had Enough," "Guitar and Pen," "Love Is Coming Down," and "Who Are You." While Pete Townshend was sorting himself out in rehab in 1982, Fairweather-Low stepped in to get the *It's Hard* sessions started on schedule, and his rhythm guitar work can be heard on John Entwistle's "It's Your Turn." Two decades later he was back in strong voice on *Endless Wire.*

Rod Argent

The *Who Are You* sessions were assisted by a cavalcade of guest musicians, and another key component of British pop, Rod Argent of the Zombies and his own hard-rocking outfit Argent, played synth on "Had Enough" and piano on "Love Is Coming Down" and "Who Are You."

Billy Nicholls

Townshend also put his friend and fellow Meher Baba follower to work during the *Who Are You* Sessions. Nicholls previously did some recording for Immediate Records in the sixties and contributed the weedy yet infectious "Forever's No Time at All" to Townshend's *Who Came First*. He also loaned his backups to Townshend and Ronnie Lane's *Rough Mix*. On *Who Are You*, he did the same for "New Song" and "Had Enough," and would return to lead the vocal ensembles during their *Kids Are Alright* tour of 1989 and *Quadrophenia* tour of the mid-nineties. In the twenty-first century, he was back to crooning in the studio during the *Endless Wire* sessions.

Tim Gorman

While Rabbit Bundrick was AWOL during the *It's Hard* sessions (see chapter 2), Glyn Johns handed the keyboard seat to his regular collaborator Tim Gorman. His synths blend with John Entwistle's on "Dangerous." On the subsequent "farewell" tour, Gorman got himself another job with the Who.

Greg Lake

Like Tim Gorman, Greg Lake filled in for a more regular Who sideman when Pino Palladino was too tied up touring with a reformed Simon and Garfunkel to play on the reunion single, "Real Good Looking Boy." Though John Entwistle rehearsed the song, he died before the final version was recorded. So the former King Crimson/Emerson, Lake, and Palmer bassist stepped in to plunk the four strings.

The Endless Wire Crew

Because Townshend and Daltrey were just half-a-Who, they relied on a lot of outside help to complete *Endless Wire*. In addition to the musicians and singers already indicated, Townshend's lady friend Rachel Fuller played keyboards on the track she coauthored, "It's Not Enough." Her drummer Peter Huntington filled in for Zak Starkey while he was busy touring with Oasis, and her bassist, Stuart Ross, and guitarist, Jolyon Dixon, joined in on "It's Not Enough." Computer science whiz Lawrence Ball contributed his electronic burble to "Fragments" and "Fragments of Fragments." The "Trilby's Piano" string section consists of Vicky Matthews on cello and Gill Morley, Brian Wright, and Ellen Blair on violins.

21

Join Together with the Band

The Who on Loan

The Who were a tight little group, almost Mafia-like. They were also a bunch of combative, foul-mouthed sods, and the drummer was trouble on every imaginable level. Yet, somehow, they weren't completely ostracized in the rock world. On the contrary, they had comrades of all stripes and could be quite generous with their talents. Townshend, Daltrey, Entwistle, and Moon have appeared on a multitude of sessions through the years, collaborating with legends and more obscure artists alike.

The Merseybeats

After Lambert and Stamp began managing the Merseybeats in 1965, the Liverpudlians desperately needed someone to wang away on a gong during the final verse of their classic single "I Stand Accused." Clearly, there was no better man for that job than Keith Moon.

The Merseys

In 1966, the Merseybeats shed their backing and were reduced to the singing duo of Tony Crane and Billy Kinsley. Their involvement with Lambert, Stamp, and the Who, however, survived the Merseybeats' transformation into the Merseys. That July, they became the first group to release a rendition of Pete Townshend's "So Sad About Us." On the self-penned flipside, "Love Will Continue," John Entwistle chipped in with French horn. Townshend produced both sides despite Kit Lambert getting the credit.

Jeff Beck

The Who were going through their usual turmoil when Keith Moon agreed to play on a session for Jeff Beck in May 1966. According to the guitarist, they both had motives beyond making a good noise together: Moon was trying to

John Entwistle not only laid claim to naming Led Zeppelin; he suggested he also masterminded the design of their debut album!

Author's collection

make his bandmates jealous, and Beck was trying to lure Moon away from the Who. Nothing came of either scheme, but at least they had "Beck's Bolero," a fierce instrumental that also featured the talents of Jimmy Page, John Paul Jones, and Nicky Hopkins. Several sources maintain that when this one-off ensemble discussed a more permanent alliance with Steve Marriott on vocals and John Entwistle in Jones's place, Moon announced the band "would go over like a lead zeppelin." Entwistle said the band was originally going to consist of himself, Moon, and their former driver, Richard Cole, who was managing Jimmy Page's New Yardbirds at the time. Page and Steve Winwood were also being batted around as potential members of Lead Zeppelin, and John said he'd even conceived a nifty cover depicting a zeppelin in mid-crash for their first record. Allegedly, Cole promptly relayed the band name and cover concept to Jimmy Page, a guy who never had any reservations about swiping someone else's good ideas.

Originally released as the flipside of Beck's solo single "Hi-Ho Silver Lining," "Beck's Bolero" appeared on the classic LP *Truth* the following year, which included the cheeky credit "Timpani by 'You Know Who.'" Moon may have deserved a vocal credit too, since he can be heard screaming bloody murder just as the track jolts into high gear.

The Beatles

Keith Moon's vocal performance on the Beatles' hippie anthem "All You Need Is Love" is less distinct and a lot less screamy than his one on "Beck's Bolero." When the Lonely Hearts Club Band invited some of their celebrity buddies to chirp the ad nauseam "love, love, love" chorus, Moon was among the choir.

The Crazy World of Arthur Brown

"Fire" was the smash hit, but if you wanted to hear Pete Townshend jam with the Crazy World of Arthur Brown in 1968, you would have had to flip the single over to hear the jazzy "Rest Cure" on which he plays subtle rhythm guitar.

Thunderclap Newman

Thunderclap Newman had a lot going for it: a good writer in John "Speedy" Keen, a great guitarist in young Jimmy McCulloch, a pianist with the supercool nickname "Thunderclap," and the guiding involvement of Pete Townshend. One thing they did not have was a bass player, so Townshend stepped into that role when he produced their one and only album, *Hollywood Dream*, in 1970. Oops . . . did I say "Pete Townshend"? I meant "Bijou Drains," of course.

Vivian Stanshall's Gargantuan Chums

When the Bonzo Dog Doo-Dah Band was put to sleep in 1970, the resilient Viv Stanshall forged ahead with support from his Gargantuan Chums. Two of the gargantuanest were John Entwistle and Keith Moon, who played bass and drums on Stanshall's cover of Doc Pomus and Mort Shuman's "Suspicion," a hit for Terry Stafford in 1964. Moon is also credited as producer, which probably means he supplied the brandy.

Mike Heron

A less plausible collaboration than Keith Moon and twee folkie Mike Heron of the Incredible String Band is tough to picture, but it happened in 1971 when Heron decided it was time to rock out on a number called "Warm Heart Pastry." On guitar was Pete Townshend, though you wouldn't know of any Who involvement if you looked at the jacket of the *Smiling Men with Bad Reputations* LP, where our boys are credited as "Tommy and the Bijoux."

The Rolling Stones

The jacket of the Rolling Stones' *Sticky Fingers* doesn't even bother with aliases, yet Pete Townshend's on the record, yowling along on the chorus of "Sway." Ten years later, he'd scoot under the radar again when his uncredited backups (and according to some sources, guitar) could be heard on "Slave" from *Tattoo You*.

Marsha Hunt

Marsha Hunt was an associate of the Stones too. Specifically, she was Mick Jagger's girlfriend and the mother of one of the kids he sired (and by her own claim, the inspiration for "Brown Sugar"). When she recorded her album *Woman Child* in 1971, Pete Townshend put his guitar on her versions of "Long Black Veil," a country standard popularized by the Band, and the Troggs' "Wild Thing." Two years later she sang the role of the Nurse in Lou Reizner's concert production of *Tommy* (see chapter 33).

The Scaffold

The Scaffold was a comedy-musical trio comprised of Roger McGough, John Gorman, and Mike McGear (aka "Paul McCartney's brother changing his name in an effort to not ride on his brother's coattails"). On the group's 1971 A-side "Do the Albert," Keith Moon brings the beat.

Gallagher and Lyle

The Scottish duo of Benny Gallagher and Graham Lyle started their careers as McGuinness Flint before going by their names and recording the "Give a Boy a Break" single, featuring Pete Townshend on bass harmonica, in 1972.

Dave Carlsen

Dave Carlsen (real name: Dave Clarke, but not the Dave Clark you've heard of) was a drinking crony of Keith Moon's at the Speakeasy with rock 'n' roll ambitions of his own. He rang up Moon and bassist Noel Redding of the Jimi Hendrix Experience to assist him on "Death on a Pale Horse" for his 1973 charity album *Pale Horse*. Proceeds went to the National Society for Mentally Handicapped Children.

John Otway and Wild Willy Barrett

When Pete Townshend took notice of the folkish duo John Otway and Wild Willy Barrett, he welcomed them into Eel Pie Studio, where he produced and played bass on their debut single, "Murder Man" b/w "If I Did," for Track Records in 1973. He was even more gracious in 1976 when he not only resumed his role as bass player and producer but allowed Otway and Barrett to rip off his "Substitute" riff for their "Louisa on a Horse" single.

Yvonne Elliman

Hawaiian chanteuse Yvonne Elliman is most famous for such light entertainments as her role as Mary Magdalene in *Jesus Christ Superstar* and her massive hit "If I Can't Have You" from the *Saturday Night Fever* soundtrack. In more rocking mode, she recorded a version of "I Can't Explain" in 1973 on which its composer slashed out the iconic guitar lick.

Harry Nilsson

During the most excessive days of the 1970s, Keith Moon fell in with a drinking/drugging crew that antichristened themselves the Hollywood Vampires. Flapping about the inner circle were such hedonists as Alice Cooper, John Lennon, Ringo Starr, Micky Dolenz, Bernie Taupin, and Harry Nilsson, who was apparently hell-bent on destroying his acclaimed multioctave voice with smoke, coke, and booze. In 1974, Lennon blearily dragged Nilsson into the studio to record the ragged rock 'n' roll record *Pussycats*. With steadfast session drummer Jim Keltner on hand, Keith Moon's kit skills were not highly required, but he did manage to chip in on drums for "Loop De Loop" and Bill Haley's "Rock Around the Clock." He also banged percussion on "All My Life" and "Mucho Mungo/Mt. Elga."

Roy Harper

In 1974, one of rock's most thoughtful and socially conscious singer-songwriters sought accompaniment from a guy who spent his free time blowing up toilets when Roy Harper invited Keith Moon to play drums at his star-speckled "Valentine's Day Massacre" show at London's Rainbow Theatre. Joining Harper and Moon were all members of Led Zeppelin except for John Paul Jones, who wasn't required since Ronnie Lane was sitting in on bass. That this performance was eventually released on Harper's double disc *Flashes from the Archives of Oblivion* would not quite earn Roy Harper a place in this chapter devoted to studio albums. Pete Townshend's guitar work on "Cloud Cuckooland" from Harper's 2013 record *Man and Myth* does.

Ronnie Wood and Ronnie Lane

In the year before their momentous collaboration on *Rough Mix*, Ronnie Lane and Pete Townshend rocked together on *Mahoney's Last Stand*, a duo disc by Lane and his Faces crony and fellow Ronnie, Ronnie Wood. Townshend played guitar on the opening instrumental "Tonight's Number" and percussion on "Car Radio."

Fabulous Poodles

The Fabulous Poodles had just the right combo of old-timey rock 'n' roll reverence and campy humor to appeal to He Who Took Nothing Seriously. In a rare stroke of mentoring (usually Townshend's gig), John Entwistle helped the Poodles get a leg up by producing and playing bass on their eponymous debut album in 1977. His efforts did not help make it a hit.

Angie

Surely one of the weirdest signees on the eclectic Stiff Records label was child singer Angela Porter. On her one and only single for Stiff, Angie received a great deal of guidance from Pete Townshend, who produced and contributed guitar and vocals to the bubblegum-chewing "Peppermint Lump." Townshend's voice is unmistakable as he chants the Baba-inspired chorus "Don't you worry, be happy, Peppermint Lump." Although Radio One selected "Peppermint Lump" as a single of the week in 1979, it went nowhere on the charts. Angie's chipmunk pipes would be heard by a much wider audience when she "ow ow'ed" her way through the Buggles' "Video Killed the Radio Star" a month later.

Pete Townshend's collaboration with little Angie Porter on "Peppermint Lump" was one of the oddest and catchiest side projects of his career.   *Author's collection*

Paul McCartney

One of the most distinguishing features of Paul McCartney and Wings' under-rated *Back to the Egg* was the presence of the Rockestra, an ensemble of top-tier musicians including Ronnie Lane, John Paul Jones, John Bonham, Gary Brooker, Dave Gilmour, Bruce Thomas, Kenney Jones, and Pete Townshend. McCartney intended to invite Keith Moon too, but he did not live to see the 1979 sessions that produced the thunderous "Rockestra Theme" and "So Glad to See You." On Paulie's less mighty 1986 disc *Press to Play*, Townshend played guitar on the not-nearly-angry-enough "Angry."

David Bowie

At the dawn of the 1980s, Pete Townshend assisted another superstar buddy when he added some signature string scraping on David Bowie's "Because You're Young" from *Scary Monsters (and Super Creeps)*. Twenty-two years later, Townshend did some more exemplary fretting for Mr. Stardust on "Slow Burn" from *Heathen*.

T-Bone Burnett

T-Bone Burnett belongs to that very exclusive club of superstar producers. He worked his wizardry on records for Elvis Costello, Los Lobos, Roy Orbison, B. B. King, Marshall Crenshaw, Sam Philipps, John Mellencamp, Kris Kristofferson, Natalie Merchant, Willie Nelson, Spinal Tap (!), and on and on and on. Before he made a major name for himself as a producer, Burnett had a more modest career as a recording artist. For his third LP, 1983's *Proof Through the Night*, he recruited Pete Townshend on guitar. In 2008, Townshend considered recruiting Burnett to produce an all-covers album for the Who but decided to put the project on hold, which is where it remains as of this writing.

Simon Townshend

These days Simon Townshend is deeply associated with the Who, as an integral member of both their and Roger Daltrey's touring bands. When at work on his solo career, Simon collaborated less with his brother. Pete produced and sang on Simon's first disc, 1984's *Sweet Sound*, but Simon assembled his own group, Moving Target, for their eponymous 1985 album and gave the production job to Neil Kernon (Kansas, Hall and Oates, Queensrÿche, etc.). After a twelve-year recording hiatus, Simon recorded his third album, *Among Us*, with his new Simon Townshend Band (featuring current Who skinsman Zak Starkey). Again, nepotism was not an issue . . . well, aside from the involvement of son Ben on drums, brother Paul on the mixing board, and Pete's then brother-in-law Jon Astley on the mastering side. But that's really the extent of family involvement on *Among Us*.

Mick Jagger

Mick Jagger's first solo album, *She's the Boss*, is a prime example of why the guy needs Keith Richards's rock 'n' roll fealty. Jagger sought out the next-best collaborators in Jeff Beck and Pete Townshend. Beck does his damnedest to fight through the overbearing keyboards and processed drums of "Lonely at the Top" and the synthesized schmaltz of "Hard Woman," but on supporting rhythm, Townshend wisely lays low. He had a bit more to work with on Jagger's 2001 *Goddess in the Doorway*, making his presence felt most assuredly with his totally recognizable power chords on "Joy" (a duet with Bono) and the dancey "Gun."

Elton John

Pete Townshend's acoustic guitar juts out in an unfamiliar setting on Elton John's countrified "Ball and Chain," a flop single from his *Jump Up!* album from 1982. Townshend's electric rhythm is buried deeper under banks of synths on "Town of Plenty" from 1988's *Reg Strikes Back*. If this was as hard as Reg could strike, he probably didn't even leave a bruise.

Ringo Starr

Pete Townshend's been dominating the guest spots here, so let's set him aside for a bit to spend some time with John Entwistle. Yes, Entwistle had his own superstar buddies, and though he didn't record with McCartney or Elton John or Mick Jagger, he did jam a lot with Ringo Starr, and that's not too shabby. On "Everybody's in a Hurry but Me" from Starr's 1983 disc *Old Wave*, he also played with Eric Clapton, Joe Walsh, and former "Drowned" collaborator Chris Stainton. Entwistle would resume work with Ringo Starr a dozen years later for one of his All-Starr Band tours.

Barry Gibb

And now we finally check in with a guy who up until this moment had steered clear of making guest appearances. That's about to change, though, but why Daltrey chose to break his abstinence by harmonizing with Olivia Newton-John on Barry Gibb's cheesy synth-pop peanut "Fine Line" is anyone's guess. Hey, it was the eighties.

Meatloaf

Daltrey trades in his cheese for chopped meat. In 1984, the same year he hammed it up on "Fine Line," he got involved in one of Meatloaf's typically histrionic slabs of bung called "Bad Attitude." This time Daltrey's voice gets a brighter spotlight. Not a good thing.

Prefab Sprout

Roger Daltrey did not corner the market on suspect collaborations. Perhaps hearing his old singer blab along with mediocrities such as Olivia Newton-John and Meatloaf made Pete Townshend declare, "Hey, I want a piece of that action too!" So Townshend put some guitar on the dooby-dooing "Hey Manhattan!" by limp synth-poppers Prefab Sprout in 1988. You'd never realize this by listening to the song.

Susanna Hoffs

John Entwistle's collaboration with Susanna Hoffs in 1991 should have been more promising than Daltrey and Townshend's recent extracurricular activities. She's a member of the Bangles, a pretty good pop group with genuine reverence for sixties rock. The song is a good one—David Bowie's "Boys Keep Swinging," which has a terrific bass line. However, the production is so inundated with synthesized baubles and bangles that Entwistle's usually up-front bass work is way, way in the back. A real waste.

Ramones

Now this is more like it. OK, so the covers on the Ramones' all-covers *Acid Eaters* album from 1993 don't have the fire and amplitude of the ones on their first few records. That's a tall order. Their version of "Substitute," featuring the composer on backing vocals, is still a hell of a lot better than those recent unholy unions with Gibb, Meat, Sprout, and Hoffs.

Glenn Tipton

John Entwistle is a guy who prefers to keep his fingers busy, so he said "yes" when manager Bill Curbishley asked if he'd like to play on a disc by another client, former Judas Priest guitarist Glenn Tipton. Atlantic records liked the heavy-metal mishmash more in theory than execution, and the original sessions with Entwistle and drummer Cozy Powell (Jeff Beck Group, Whitesnake, Rainbow, etc.) were shelved so that Tipton could record new tracks with a younger ensemble. Sadly, Entwistle and Powell had both passed by the time the sessions were finally released under the banner of Tipton, Entwistle, and Powell as *Edge of the World* in 2006.

Joe Strummer

In 2001, Roger Daltrey hooked up with a collaborator worthy of his talents when Joe Strummer called on him to sing on the epic dark groove "Global a Go-Go," the title track of Strummer and the Mescaleros' second album. The track is a

Joe Strummer promised there'd be no Beatles, Elvis, or Rolling Stones in 1977 on the Clash's classic B-side. The Who were OK, though.   *Author's collection*

classic "calling all DJs" Strummer broadcast, shouting the praises of international music legends the Stray Cats, Rocksteady Freddie, Nina Simone, Bo Diddley, Sun Ra, Baaba Maal, the Skatalites, the Stooges, the Bhundi Boys, and the Who. Receiving special mention are *Quadrophenia* and "Armenia City in the Sky" (the latter by the song's original singer).

Gov't Mule

When their bass player Allen Woody died in 2000, jam band Gov't Mule paid tribute to him with an album called *The Deep End, Volume 1*. Standing in for Woody was an astounding all-star lineup of guest bass players including Bootsy Collins, Jack Bruce, Flea, Mike Watt, Larry Graham Jr., and John Entwistle, who played on the somewhat Who-like "Same Price." Released in 2001, this would coincidentally be Entwistle's last released studio performance.

Anthrax

In 2003, Anthrax were as much of an institution in the metal world as the Who were in the slightly less metal one. So it is somewhat fitting that Roger Daltrey loaned his voice to the anti–music industry "Taking the Music Back," complete with "Won't Get Fooled Again"-style scream, on their *We've Come for You All* album.

Rachel Fuller

Even more fitting is Pete Townshend's collaborations with girlfriend Rachel Fuller. In fact, her 2004 disc, *Cigarettes and Housework*, is a veritable way station for Who-related musicians on their way to recording *Endless Wire*. Jon Astley, Pino Palladino, Simon Townshend, and Pete all pitched in.

B. B. King

Blues hero B. B. King celebrated his eightieth year on Earth with one of those celebrity duets records. Titled, not coincidentally, *80*, the album found B. B. swapping lines with artists such as Van Morrison, Eric Clapton, Mark Knopfler, Elton John, and Roger Daltrey, who digs in his heels on "Never Make Your Move Too Soon."

Martha Wainwright

Like the Townshends, the Wainwright family is rich in talent, producing a quartet of acclaimed singer-songwriters: dad Loudon Wainwright III, mom Kate McGarrigle, brother Rufus, and sister Martha. Martha Wainwright promoted her first album on Townshend and Rachel Fuller's *In the Attic* web series in 2006. Two years later, Townshend was strumming away on "You Cheated Me" and "Comin' Tonight" from her second record, *I Know You're Married but I've Got Feelings Too.*

Steve Ellis

Steve Ellis is best known as the singer of Love Affair, which scored a huge hit in 1968 with the pop valentine "Everlasting Love." His career was still going in 2008, when he released his *Best of Days* album, which showcased Roger Daltrey's harmonica talents.

Laurent Voulzy

In 2011, Daltrey was back to doing that stuff he's most famous for doing, but he was doing it in a most unexpected way. That thing: singing. That guy he was doing it with: French singer/composer Laurent Voulzy. That song they were doing it together on: "Ma Seule Amour," an adaptation of a medieval poem by medieval poet Charles d'Orléans. With a bare minimum of instrumentation and a maximum of choral backing, this might be the strangest and most un-Who-like collaboration in a list of strange and un-Who-like collaborations.

22

Hit the Stage

A Dozen Milestone Concerts

We didn't make as good of records as the Beatles, but we could have blown them off the stage." So said John Entwistle in the *Thirty Years of Maximum R&B* documentary. Who fans might find a bit to nitpick in the first part of his statement (certainly *Sell Out* and *Who's Next* were stronger than, say, *Help!* or *Let It Be*), but the second part can be filed under "most obvious observations of the century." Really, there are few bands that could ever contend with the Who onstage. Led Zeppelin on a good night might be in the running, assuming you're capable of staying awake through all fourteen hours of Bonham's "Moby Dick" drum solo. The Stones could put on a great show, though they lacked the Who's instrumental flash and—Mick excluded—showmanship. Jimi Hendrix came close, but partly because he copped the Who's act. KISS were very good at spitting up fake blood and wearing clown makeup, but there was no contest when it came to the music.

No, the Who are pretty much unchallenged when it comes to explosive stagecraft and rock 'n' roll musicianship. Everyone has their favorite shows, the ones at which the band was particularly on fire or the ones that hold some sort of personal significance. Remember that night at the Rosenblatt Stadium when you caught that Kleenex Keith Moon flung into the crowd? Pure magic.

It is not the purpose of this chapter to qualify the Who's best shows. Rather, we will set our sights on the more reasonable task of distinguishing their most historically important, the concerts that loom largest in their legend, honing decades of pugnacious performances down to a dozen major milestones.

The Railway Tavern (June 30, 1964)

It began as just another night for the Who, shaking and shimmying out their Bo Diddley and Howlin' Wolf covers for the mods at the Railway Tavern in West London. Pete Townshend was subjecting his Rickenbacker to the usual abuse, giving it a good rub against his mic stand, whacking the pickup on and off and bouncing it before his amp to produce his trademark flutters and wows. Then in one big gesture to really get the hipsters frothed up, Townshend thrust his instrument skyward and . . . *whoops!* As the headstock cracked against the tavern's low ceiling, he had to make an instantaneous decision: either fall to his knees and weep over an expensive mistake or pull an "I meant to do that" of Pee Wee Herman proportions. Pivotally, he opted for the latter, stabbing his guitar into the ceiling again and again until he'd completely demolished the poor thing. He tossed the guitar aside, picked up a spare Rick, and resumed strumming as if nothing had happened.

In that moment, the who became THE WHO (ironically doing so at their last gig before becoming the High Numbers). Townshend had accidentally stumbled upon his band's key gimmick, the thing that drew many a punter to a Who show expecting nothing more than a bit of brute smashing. Those who know nothing else about the band know that the Who are those blokes who smash up their equipment. It was a masterstroke of publicity, though one that would get the guys in a fair amount of debt, especially since Keith Moon and Roger Daltrey were quick to get in on the act. Never one to allow himself to be upstaged, Moon took to demolishing his kit, while Daltrey put undue strain on his share of leads by whirling his microphone like it was Will Rogers's lasso . . . despite his initial horror about Townshend treating valuable equipment so frivolously.

In *Who I Am*, Townshend revealed that he'd actually been planning to give his guitar the what-for before that fateful Railway gig. At the time he was fascinated with the autodestructive art of Gustav Metzger, who was known to melt canvases with hydrochloric acid, a technique he began as a protest against nuclear arms. Metzger's lecture about autodestruction at Ealing College made a strong impression on Townshend. In private, he had already smashed an amp when he was a teenager as an angry reaction against his grandmother's demands that he turn it down.

Townshend also contradicted the common notion that this particular Railway gig took place in September (*Eyewitness the Who* gets specific enough to place the date as the 8th of the month). The guy who was actually there bumped the gig back a few months to June, and according to *Anyway, Anyhow, Anywhere*, the band did play at the Railway—their very first gig at the venue, as Townshend's book acknowledges—on the final day of the month.

Music in the Fifth Dimension Series at the RKO 58th Street Theater (March 25–April 2, 1967)

The Railway Tavern gig was a mere hors d'oeuvre of destruction, a teensy taste of the damage the Who would do three years later during a punishing marathon of shows in Manhattan for bigwig DJ Murray the K. As the first jockey to regularly spin the Beatles in the states, Murray Kaufman admittedly played an instrumental part in breaking them stateside. Christening himself the fifth Beatle, however, was a little much. He barely had any hair.

Nevertheless, the K parlayed his Beatles connection into an influential role few of his fellow DJs ever enjoyed. This included curating a series of concerts at Manhattan's RKO Theater in the spring of 1967. The schedule was ridiculous:

ten daily acts (plus special headliner spots for Phil Ochs, the Young Rascals, Simon and Garfunkel, and the Blues Magoos), five shows a day starting at the ungodly time of 10:15 a.m. for nine days.

According to Roger Daltrey, Murray the K invited the Who to join the daily revelers on the recommendation of Paul Simon. For the Who, the invite was a boon. They would be playing their first shows in America and saturating one of its most important and artist-friendly metropolises for more than a week. The shows weren't great opportunities for the band to flex their artistry, mind you. As Keith Moon pithily recalled in *The Kids Are Alright*, "One and a half minutes of 'I Can't Explain' and one and a half minutes of 'My Generation,' smash your guitar and run off." While the other band members similarly recall playing two-song sets, attendee Nicholas Shaffner recalled a lengthier performance consisting of "Substitute," "So Sad About Us," "Happy Jack," and "My Generation" in his book *The British Invasion*. To maximize the impact of the latter two numbers, the Who performed "Happy Jack" in front of a screen depicting Michael Lindsay-Hogg's bumbling-burglars promo film and wrecked their equipment at the climax of "My Generation" five times a day. Pete Townshend's most vivid memory of the event was all the time he spent gluing his guitar back together.

Music in the Fifth Dimension may have been a crazy undertaking, but the gig apparently paid off. By all accounts, the Who consistently upstaged a formidable selection of coperformers that included Cream, Mitch Ryder, Wilson Pickett, and the Blues Project. The good press and that flashy presentation of "Happy Jack" helped the single—a uniquely British bit of eccentricity that almost wasn't released in the States at all—crack the US top forty. It would peak at #24 just two weeks before the next gig on this list.

The Monterey Pop Festival at the Monterey County Fairgrounds (June 18, 1967)

So the Murray the K shows and "Happy Jack" had introduced the Who to America, but only adequately. The Who's foothold in the States was no overnight deal, and the next step in their world domination occurred on the precipice of the "Summer of Love." Vietnam gave young people something to rail against, acid and pot caused them to rail gently, and the pill made them all the more loving. Our brutal boys from Britain were unlikely intruders on this lovefest, even if they arrived in multicolored ponchos and Edwardian ruffles.

The Who's rotten attitude was key in setting them apart from placid acts such as the Mamas and the Papas, Simon and Garfunkel, and the Association, but they were not without competition. John Phillips's festival would enter the history texts as not only the making of the Who's career in America, but also those of Otis Redding (sadly, just a few months before his death), Janis Joplin, and Jimi Hendrix. Ah, Jimi Hendrix. Like the Who, the guy was an uncontainable star, and flying in from his adopted UK home, he too was determined to leave

THE CRITERION COLLECTION

MONTEREY POP

DIRECTED BY D.A. PENNEBAKER

The Criterion Collection's ultra-deluxe edition of D. A. Pennebaker's *Monterey Pop* also includes bonus performances of the Who demolishing "Substitute," "Summertime Blues," and "A Quick One While He's Away." *Author's collection*

a welt on the face of America. Hendrix probably could have accomplished this with nothing more than his supernatural talent, but he wanted to make a much bigger splash. He wanted to be the star of the festival. And how would he accomplish this? By stealing the Who's act.

When Pete Townshend caught wind of the Voodoo Chile's unethical plan, he confronted Hendrix, and a debate over who'd go on first ensued. As Hendrix leapt on a chair and started playing his guitar *at* Townshend, as if it was a weapon that could mow down his rival, Phillips suggested a coin toss to put the rumble to rest.

Hendrix did not come up the victor in the toss, so when he'd come out in his garish pink garb, coaxing feedback from his Marshall stack and smashing the knobs off his Stratocaster, he'd look like an also-ran poseur, right? However, the fact that the Who were playing on borrowed equipment rather than their own Marshalls made for a less devastating performance than usual, and Hendrix's inborn panache meant he could repeat the same destruction immediately after the Who and still make it seem totally unique. After all, the Who did not set their gear on fire or mime sexy sex with it like Hendrix did.

Who won the pissing match? Many have named Hendrix the champ, Pete Townshend being among those voices, insisting that Hendrix was not "stealing" but "doing" his act. Entwistle was less forgiving, saying that Hendrix was just being an "asshole." Regardless of who came out on top and who was the asshole, the effect the Who had on those West Coast hippies was profound. Their next single, "I Can See for Miles," would be their first—and last—to punch into the US top ten.

Woodstock Music Festival at Max Yasgur's Farm (August 17, 1969)

And now, the gig that solidified the Who's reputation in America once and for all. Ironically, this would be another performance they did not rate among their finest. The conditions were actually worse than those of the Murray the K shows. Forty-five minishows over nine days was cake compared to the scene waiting in Bethel, New York, forty-three miles from Woodstock.

Traffic so severe that a two-mile drive to the festival grounds took an hour and a half. Gloppy expanses of mud everywhere. Another mile-long trek through the muck on foot. A complete absence of dressing rooms. A young hippie getting electrocuted on a power line while trying to touch a photo of Meher Baba—a sight seemingly designed to disturb Pete Townshend. It all reminded him of a war zone. Not the best atmosphere in which to get dosed with acid after taking an innocent sip of water or coffee, or in John Entwistle's case, dropping a spiked ice cube into your bourbon and Coke. The Who would have some time to ride out their trips after learning that their performance had been delayed. By fifteen hours.

By the time the Who took the stage, it was 5:00 a.m. on the final day of the festival. Imagine yanking yourself out of bed at 5:00 a.m. to blearily shower, have a cup of coffee, and trudge out the door to your job. Now imagine doing that without the shower and your job is entertaining approximately 400,000 people with deafening rock 'n' roll on the downside of an acid trip. Who's masochistic enough to enjoy that?

Enjoy the show the Who did not, but the documents reveal a typically powerful performance. The glorious sight of the sun rising as Pete Townshend holds his S.G. over his head as if in the midst of some remarkable pagan rite says everything that needs to be said about the religiosity of rock 'n' roll. So what if a few minutes earlier he was using that same guitar to thump Abbie Hoffman (see chapter 31)? Once again, the Who emerged among a handful of stars in a formidable lineup of acts. Even Hendrix could not follow the Who this time, half the crowd having deserted before his performance. That sunrise set would prove the most transcendent moment in Michael Wadleigh's unwieldy documentary about the event. *Tommy*, the album showcased during the set, went gold in the United States the very next day. The Who were now and for all posterity international rock stars.

Leeds University (February 14, 1970)

All of their roadwork transformed the Who into a very different band from the one that power-popped their way through "I'm a Boy" and "Happy Jack" or even the ethereal *Tommy*. They had been wanting to represent their newfound heaviosity on vinyl for some time, but recording the intensity of a Who concert without the flubs and flaws that sometimes intervened was hard to accomplish.

After a few abortive attempts to seize the definitive live document (see chapter 16), the stars finally aligned over the refectory of Leeds University on Valentine's Day 1970. The crowd was respectful and responsive. Intent on making the recording a good one, Pete Townshend played with concerted care. Even Keith Moon's wisecracks from the peanut gallery were not enough to discombobulate him. Rather, everyone seemed in unusually good humor. Maybe if Abbie Hoffman had chosen to hop up onstage during this gig he would have gotten a peck on the cheek.

Despite a few technical difficulties affecting John's bass track, Bob Pridden's recording went smoothly, and the Who—and rock 'n' roll itself—were left with a definitive artifact of live music at its most exciting, raw, and spontaneous (the latter is only an illusion, as evidenced by the nearly identical set the group played at Hull's City Hall the following day). The band played enough unreleased material and altered the warhorses "Substitute," "My Generation," and "Magic Bus" enough so that *Live at Leeds* was immune to accusations of redundancy and is that rare live album unanimously considered 100 percent essential to a band's discography.

The bootleg concept of the *Live at Leeds* album cover carried over to this rare promo single of "Young Man Blues" b/w "Substitute."
Courtesy of the Rob Abramowicz Collection, digitized by Jeffrey Uleau

Tommy at the Metropolitan Opera House at Lincoln Center (June 7, 1970)

Now that the Who had entered wanton destruction into the rock 'n' roll rule book and recorded the genre's definitive live album, they were ready to do the unthinkable: make rock 'n' roll respectable. By marrying it to opera, they at least made it respectable enough to get the attention of Sir Rudolph Bing, general manager of the Metropolitan Opera House in Manhattan. After giving *Tommy* a spin, he agreed it was time to inject the Met with its first dose of rock 'n' roll.

Bing was taking a gamble. The Met was still pristine, not even four years old. Revered artist Marc Chagall contributed the two murals in the lobby where fine sculptures by Aristide Maillol and Wilhelm Lehmbruck stood. Crystal chandeliers from Vienna dangled from every inch of ceiling space. Plush red carpeting swathed the floors. For all Bing knew, the rock 'n' roll crowd would end up dangling from the chandeliers and barfing on the Chagalls. Instead, the initially wary Met ushers informed the press that the kids were more respectful than the usual opera crowd. Pete Townshend, however, lived up to rock 'n' roll's disrespectful rep. When some audience members booed at the band's refusal to play an encore, the guitarist responded with a curt "Fuck you," tossed his mic into the crowd, and clomped off the stage in his Doc Martens. As she reported in the *NME*, attendee Vicki Wickham heard Townshend grumble to Kit Lambert from off mic, "You really book us on some bum gigs, man!" Townshend 1; High Culture 0.

The Who didn't exactly usher in a new rock 'n' roll era at the Met. In fact, no other rock band was ever invited back to the venue. For that alone, the two shows the Who performed on June 7, 1970, would be historic. The series was also historic for being their very first farewell, as they announced it would be their final *Tommy* concerts. Of course, the Who is notoriously poor at saying "farewell" and meaning it.

Isle of Wight Festival at East Afton Farm (August 30, 1970)

The Who didn't waste a moment breaking their first farewell promise, and at their second appearance at the Isle of Wight Festival, they were bulldozing through *Tommy* again. The crowd-pleasing performance helped relieve a somewhat tense atmosphere. Expectations for the festival were grand. A world record–breaking audience of 600,000 would be in attendance. Finding a venue to accommodate such an audience was highly problematic, and authorization to stage the show at East Afton Farm only went down at the very last minute. Bill, Ray, and Ron Foulk, the team of brothers behind the event, refused to allow the show to turn into a Woodstock-style free-for-all in which gate jumpers might storm the field without having paid their three quid at the box office. When a barrier fence was constructed around the field, some viewed the move as violating the spirit of peace, love, and music. The Desolation Row commune on the perimeter of the farm made their feelings known to the Foulk brothers, but the talks were tense and the fence remained. When the Foulks attempted to put a hippie-ish spin on the barrier by supplying the opposition with paint and allowing them to turn it into a mural, the kids painted swastikas and messages of scorn. The Foulks' misguided collusion with the cops to get everyone under the age of seventeen to relinquish their drugs didn't sit well with the counterculture either.

The clash continued into the show. A representative of Desolation Row leapt onto the stage during Joni Mitchell's set to shout his displeasure. One young American got on the stage to famously declare "the festival business is becoming a psychedelic concentration camp where people are being exploited." Kris Kristofferson put an early stop to his set when he misinterpreted the audience's calls to fix his sound problems as heckling. Master of ceremonies Rikki Farr shot back at the crowd, unceremoniously addressing them as "bastards" and "pigs" and inviting them to "go to Hell" for trying to bring down the barrier.

Into this air of unpleasantness tromped the Who. What would the nastiest, most violent quartet of thugs in rock 'n' roll do but escalate the tension to the boiling point? Instead, Townshend commanded the sullen "buggers" to "smile." That's just what a good share of them did as the band brought down the house with a three-hour set stretching toward 5:00 a.m. Emerging as the stars of the festival despite the presence of such staunch competition as Sly and the Family Stone and Jimi Hendrix (in his final major live appearance), the Who had played the biggest show of their career.

Lifehouse at the Young Vic (February 15 and 22, March 1 and April 26, 1971)

With *Tommy* now put to rest—at least for the time being—the Who were free to move on to other projects. *Lifehouse* was to be their most ambitious. An ongoing live performance was to be an integral element of Pete Townshend's science-fiction fancy. He symbolically selected the Young Vic, a brand-new theater constructed as a gathering place for young crowds, as opposed to the century-and-a-half-old Old Vic, also located in London's Lambeth borough. The Young Vic would be the perfect spot to stage a futuristic concert in the spirit of youthful optimism and revolution. The doors would remain open to any kid interested in wandering in and, hopefully, getting in on the music making as the Who spontaneously created new material. Townshend would feed the audience members' personal and astrological information into some sort of supercomputer/synthesizer, which would then spew out the music of the spheres. As it all came together, a film crew would come in to catch key footage for the movie. In essence, the Young Vic would *be* the Lifehouse.

As was the case with most aspects of this project, the Young Vic stint did not go as planned. Six weeks were reduced to four days as the band failed to lure more than thirty or fifty people (by Townshend's varying estimates) into the theater. Perhaps there would have been more if it had actually been advertised as a series of Who concerts. The management failed to supply any musical equipment for the few passersby who stumbled over the Vic's threshold, though one over-amped hippie took it upon himself to leap behind Keith Moon's drum kit and give it a bash—just moments after receiving a pounding from Townshend for calling the band "Capitalist pigs." This was not what he had in mind for his real-life Lifehouse commune. Plans for developing new music in concert with their fans gave way to sets of precomposed songs and greatest hits to placate the skinheads who'd stormed in. The lack of support from Townshend's confused bandmates, the technical difficulties with the synthesizers recently incorporated into the act, the volume complaints from the Young Vic's neighbors, and the theater's schedule, which only gave the band access on Mondays, further derailed the project. *Lifehouse* was to be the Who's greatest and grandest artistic failure, though they did manage to wrangle a belated live album out of their April 26th return performance when it was finally released on the deluxe edition of *Who's Next* in 2003.

Cow Palace (November 20, 1973)

The infamous performance at Daly City, California's Cow Palace managed to accomplish something the Young Vic Lifehouse shows were supposed to. That night, the Who allowed a young man to come out of the audience and make music with them. The situation, however, didn't have much to do with communal ideals.

The show kicked off one of the Who's more troubled tours. Supporting the freshly released *Quadrophenia*, they would be performing along with an elaborate rig of prerecorded tapes to best replicate the album's soundscapes. That this new element threatened to put a severe clamp on Keith Moon's abandoned drumming may have accounted for a severe case of backstage jitters that night. So it is possible that he consciously took the tranquilizers that would be his undoing, though some have speculated Moon was a victim of a monster-sized mickey slipped into his preshow tipple. The lady friend who joined him in the alleged indulgence was no Keith Moon and had to be taken to the local hospital immediately. With his legendary fortitude, Moon remained determined to take the stage.

The Who prefaced the *Quadrophenia* set with a few oldies. In *Thirty Years of Maximum R&B*, Roger Daltrey described this intro, explaining that "I Can't Explain" was "erratic" and "'Substitute' went from very fast to nonexistent" (footage of the concert, in which they didn't even perform "Substitute," doesn't really support Daltrey's account). The band soldiered through the *Quadrophenia* portion despite Moon's continued inconsistency. After launching into "Won't Get Fooled Again," the beat disappeared again. Moon was out cold. A roadie dragged the drummer backstage where efforts were taken to revive him with a cortisone shot. After twenty or thirty minutes, he returned triumphantly, if briefly, conking out before the Who could complete "Magic Bus." Townshend and Daltrey pulled him from behind the kit, at which point he came to long enough to thrash around a bit. His bandmates restrained him, and Townshend tried to put a humorous spin on the dire situation by giving the crowd the thumbs up. Offstage, no more patchworks were attempted. Moon was taken to the hospital to have his stomach pumped of PCP, according to biographer Tony Fletcher and contrary to Townshend's assumption it was some sort of elephant tranquilizer.

Despite Townshend's earlier nervous declaration from the stage that the Who were not a group without Keith Moon, the band remained intent on seeing this disastrous tour-starter to completion. After a drum-less run-through of "See Me, Feel Me," Townshend apologized for Moon, who'd come down with "A slight touch of . . . errr . . ." That's when he asked every young musician's dream question: "Can anybody play the drums? I mean somebody good." At the same time, a young concertgoer named Mike Denese was pushing his friend, nineteen-year-old Thomas Scot Halpin, to the front of the stage. When Halpin entered the Palace with a scalper's ticket, he could not have imagined it would end with him onstage. Promoter Bill Graham listened to Denese's impassioned plea for his beat-keeping buddy and gave Halpin the green light.

Bizarrely, the Who decided to stick to the set list instead of going easy on the sudden recruit by playing familiar favorites. They resumed with a jam medley of "Smokestack Lightning" and "Spoonful" and then ended the show with the biggest curve ball they could toss at the poor guy: the stopping-and-starting, tempo-and-time-signature shifting "Naked Eye," an eight-and-a-half minute version, no less. Halpin didn't even have the luxury of hearing the as-yet unreleased song on *Odds & Sods*, so he can be forgiven for failing to find the groove.

After joining the remaining band members for a quick jig at center stage, the thoroughly exhausted yet elated T. Scot Halpin retired backstage, where he was paid with a tour jacket (later to be stolen by some jerk). *Rolling Stone* magazine later crowned him "Pick-Up Player of the Year." Halpin remained in the music world, comanaging a San-Fran-based punk club called The Roosevelt with his wife Robin, composing, and putting his multi-instrumental skills to work with various bands. Sadly, in 2008, T. Scot Halpin died of an inoperable brain tumor at the age of fifty-four. He will forever be remembered, at least by those who did not know him personally, as the kid who fulfilled a million fan fantasies by getting onstage and jamming with the Who.

The Who Put the Boot In at Charlton Athletic Football Ground (May 31, 1976)

The Who had settled well into their Greatest Band in the World status by 1976, and rarely was their well-seasoned expertise on finer display than when they put the boot in at Charlton Athletic Football Ground in London. The Who saved a day sullied by frosty temperatures, torrential downpours, and audience rumbles more befitting the usual football stadium entertainment than a rock concert. Their lateness to the show did nothing to tamp down tempers, but once they came springing onstage, all was forgiven. Or at least, the hooligans in the crowd were beaten into submission by the band's skull-crushing sound system. At a distance of 164 feet from the speakers, the noise pinned the meter at 120 decibels. Try pressing your ear up against the engine of a Harley Davidson and you'll get a sense of the volume the Who were putting out. While the set list was safe as houses—the usual greatest hits interrupted by a brief tribute to *Tommy*, "Squeeze Box" and "Dreaming from the Waist Down" being the only post-*Who's Next* numbers—the amplification was enough to make Charlton special for it was at this show that the *Guinness Book of Records* logged the Who as the "World's Loudest Pop Band." Pete Townshend, who later described the concert as "a nightmare," is still suffering the ill effects of that dubious honor today.

Shepperton Studios (May 25, 1978)

The Who continued gigging through 1976, but shunned the stage the following year to recoup and reconsider, to work on the *Who Are You* album and film material for Jeff Stein's documentary *The Kids Are Alright*. As Stein assembled his footage, he became aware of a flagrant oversight. *Who's Next*, perhaps the band's most popular album, was completely unrepresented. This left the filmmaker with the unenviable task of wrangling the Who back onstage so he could shoot them performing the essential favorites "My Wife," "Baba O'Riley," and "Won't Get Fooled Again."

Pete Townshend was reluctant, partly out of concern for the physically failing Keith Moon. Eventually, he relented and a performance was scheduled at Gaumont State Cinema in Kilburn for December 15, 1977. With a venue of just two thousand seats, an audience of just eight hundred bodies (despite producer Tony Klinger's promise that there'd only be five hundred), and a set of just fifteen songs, this was not to be the Who's typical mega-concert. Townshend was in exceptionally poor humor. Paranoid that the punks in the crowd were having a go at the dinosaurs onstage, he challenged the heckling gits to get up onstage and take his guitar. A nine-second clip of the tirade was the most substantial Kilburn footage used in *The Kids Are Alright*.

So a new show had to be scheduled. On May 25, 1978, the Who performed for an invited audience of five hundred at Shepperton Studios in Surrey. They'd intended to get in, run-through those three select *Who's Next* numbers, and get out, but the spirit in the room was so pleasing that the band put a bit more effort into the show. The audience was plied into a good mood with wine from the canteen. Most likely in an effort to preempt the need for any further performances, Pete Townshend made a very conscious effort to put on a good show, wagging his ass for the camera, flailing like a soused dervish, performing an incredible kneeling slide across the stage. Roger Daltrey wore a tiny shirt from the woman's department to show off his still impressive physique. John Entwistle played with his usual brilliance. Keith Moon looked a little bloated in his spangly purple getup, but he seemed to be in a good mood, his earphones lashed to his bobbing head with gaffer tape. Stein got his footage of "Baba O'Riley" and "Won't Get Fooled Again." The audience got bonus performances of the chestnuts "Substitute," "My Generation," and that very first hit, "I Can't Explain." And the Who got the most precious thing of all: one final show with Keith Moon.

Riverfront Coliseum (December 3, 1979)

Keith Moon was gone, but the Who did not miss a beat. Kenney Jones was expeditiously recruited, and the band was back on the road in 1979 as if nothing had happened. Of course, something seismic had happened, and the surviving members were all torn up over their comrade's death regardless of the callous statements they sometimes gave to the press. But on December 3, they'd experience something much worse than having to pick up the posthumous pieces.

There'd been the bum performances and the unruly audiences, the shitty weather and the cocked-up schedules, the preshow acid spikings and the onstage overdoses. All of these problems paled next to what happened at Cincinnati, Ohio's, Riverfront Coliseum, one of the most tragic concerts in rock 'n' roll history. The Coliseum featured festival seating, what is more commonly called general admission today, and the throng gathering outside was eager to rush to the front of the venue for the optimal position to see their idols. Standing in the bitter cold for hours waiting for the doors to open, the ticket holders were agitated, pushing and shoving each other. When a single door flung aside around 7:00 a.m., there was a mad rush forward, thousands of fans intent on squeezing through the small opening and on to the edge of the stage. People started slipping underfoot. Twenty-six were injured; eleven died: Karen Morrison, Jacqueline Eckerle, Walter Adams Jr., Bryan Wagner, Peter Bowes, David J. Heck, Stephan Preston, Phillip K. Snyder, Connie Burns, James Warmoth, and Teva Ladd.

Most attendees did not know what had happened. The Who didn't either. They played their set as usual. When it was all over, Bill Curbishley broke the

Many concertgoers enjoyed the Who's performance at the Riverfront Coliseum on December 3, 1979, as usual, unaware of the tragedy that took place before the show.
Courtesy of the Rob Abramowicz Collection, digitized by Jeffrey Uleau

news. The guys fell numb. They retired to their hotel to drink and cry while watching the victims being carried away on stretchers on the late-night news.

If the Who were at all accountable for the tragedy, it was because of their ignorance of the horrid planning of the Riverfront Coliseum staff. The press painted festival seating as a cash-grasping way to pile in more flesh and sell more tickets. The problem had less to do with festival seating, in and of itself, and more to do with the staff's disregard for its patrons, leaving them clumped and trembling in the cold all day before giving them a pinhole to squeeze through toward warmth and the reviving joys of rock 'n' roll.

The press wanted a bigger villain to bring down than festival seating. The Who were often demonized for insensitively plowing ahead with the show despite the preceding tragedy (of which they were unaware) and proceeding with the tour as scheduled (the Who would always deal with tragedy by getting right back to work). They also did a pretty good job of bringing themselves down. Roger Daltrey described the victims broadly as "kids," even though four were in their twenties and one was a mother of two. Commentators interpreted this as insensitivity, proof that he didn't know who these people were and didn't care much either. In his 1980 interview with *Rolling Stone*, Pete Townshend made a more serious gaffe, telling Greil Marcus that the show "was a very, very positive event for the Who" before angrily refusing to shed "a fucking theatrical tear" for the sake of the press. He finished shoving his foot in his mouth by declaring "when people are dead, they're dead;" true words for sure, but not the most sensitive comment so close to the tragedy.

Typically, the press and public chose to fixate on these most incendiary statements, not Townshend's clarification that the concert was "positive" because it deepened his affection for his fans and served as a much-needed reminder "that they are human beings—and not just people in rows," or his admission that Daltrey cried "his eyes out after that show."

If there is a right thing to say after such a terrible event, the Who—ever honest, ever brutal—were not the ones to express it. According to Townshend, the families of the victims were largely forgiving. Their opinions matter a lot more than any third-person commentator's.

23

I Used to Follow You

The Who's Influences

T hough they didn't flaunt their influences as blatantly as, say, the Rolling Stones, the Who's favorite music was vital in the development of their sound despite all the self-contradictory statements so rampant in Who lore. Catch Pete Townshend on a bad day and the Beatles are "flippin' lousy" and Mick Jagger is "banal." Catch him on a good one and every Beatles album is "perfect" and he's inducting the Stones into the Rock and Roll Hall of Fame. Regardless of what he asserted at any given time, the effects of certain influences resound clearly in his band's music.

Jazz

Long a musical isolationist state, England enjoyed a sudden influx of American jazz in 1956 after the Musicians Union lifted a twenty-year ban on musicians from the States. Allegedly, the ban had racist roots: a way to prevent African-Americans from taking jobs from British musicians. Ironically, or perhaps typically, it was a British musician who most benefited from his country's burgeoning fascination with jazz. Mr. Acker Bilk blew New Orleans jazz by way of Somerset, spearheading the Dixieland revival of the late fifties/early sixties. Bilk even managed to become the first British artist to top the US singles chart, though the Muzak snoozer "Stranger on the Shore" wasn't likely to stir much excitement among young trad jazz enthusiasts such as Pete Townshend.

For Townshend, trad jazz held an allure that rock 'n' roll hadn't quite hit on yet. He dug Bill Haley, but didn't appreciate Elvis on first listen. He didn't hear the raw early records, so his first taste of the King was tamer stuff like "Hound Dog" and "Love Me Tender," which in his words, "made me want to vomit." He deemed Elvis's band from this period "shitty," though when he eventually heard "Heartbreak Hotel," he was awestruck. British rockers such as Cliff Richard and producer Joe Meek's stable of pretty boy toys were anemic imitations of performers the guitarist didn't care for in the first place. Townshend found trad jazz rhythmically exciting. It also served as a mild form of rebellion, as it differed from the big band dance music of his father's ensemble, the Squadronaires. Cliff Townshend loathed trad jazz and shuddered whenever his son practiced his new favorite style of music.

The image of the Rickenbacker-smashing hellion donning a straw boater to jive along with ragtime rhythms seems ludicrous, yet trad jazz does reveal notable similarities to the music Townshend would later make with the Who. The essence of trad jazz is polyphony, the simultaneous weaving of two or more distinct melodies. Polyphonic music bears the surface aura of chaos but holds together as a unified performance. That just as easily describes any number of Who performances ("Anyway, Anyhow, Anywhere," "Young Man Blues," "Heaven and Hell," "Dreaming from the Waist," etc.) in which Townshend's improvisations work independent of, yet complimentary to, Keith Moon's cascading fills and John Entwistle's manic bass runs—heavy-metal Dixieland.

Entwistle started playing trad jazz too, but more out of necessity than a genuine love for the music. As a trumpeter, he didn't have many options in the rock 'n' roll world. He met amateur banjo-twanger Townshend while playing in a local trad outfit called the Confederates. The group only played a single gig at the Congo Club, a teen social center in Acton that, according to Daltrey, was also a hotbed of sex and fisticuffs.

The Confederates didn't last long, Entwistle leaving for a group more worthy of his skills and Townshend putting the final nail in the band after bonking drummer Chris Sherwin over the head with his book bag.

A typo on this Italian picture sleeve pays accidental tribute to one of the Who's biggest influences.

Courtesy of the Rob Abramowicz Collection, digitized by Jeffrey Uleau

Their dalliance with the subgenre was not over yet, however, as they worked a few trad jazz numbers among the rock 'n' roll, surf instrumentals, and moldy oldies in their early sets with the Detours. Period photos capture a boyish Entwistle lost in his trumpet as Daltrey blurts along on trombone. On *A Quick One*, the two would pick up their unlikely instruments again to toot the instrumental "Cobwebs and Strange," a zany boggle of trad jazz, polka, and "Indian flavour," as Keith Moon described "his" song to *Beat Instrumental* in 1967.

As important as trad jazz was in the early days of the Who, it would not hold an abiding interest for any of the guys. In 1967, the Who's biggest trad champion would muse to *Melody Maker* about how "dreadful" it would be if audiences abandoned pop for "traditional jazz." The adult Pete Townshend held a greater affinity for the subtler, more sophisticated work of jazz/blues pianist Mose Allison, bebop guitarist Kenny Burrell, and fingerpicker Wes Montgomery. Allison's influence seems the most significant as he is the composer of "Young Man Blues" and a great observer of the trials of youth in the mode of so many Townshend tunes (the Detours were also known to cover his convict-lament "Parchment Farm"). However, Burrell's nimble, bluesy bends can be detected in work as early as "Zoot Suit" and as late as "Music Must Change," while Burrell's sweet fingerpicking held sway over "Sunrise" and "To Barney Kessel."

One thing Townshend always disdained was the flash player—light-speed soloists like Ritchie Blackmore and Alvin Lee (and, strangely enough, the great Les Paul)—though he made exceptions for players whose bursts of showiness were considered, sensitively placed. Townshend deemed them "clear thinkers." One such clear thinker was country-jazz legend Chet Atkins, who would deftly veer from sparse melodiousness to a sudden blizzard of notes to invigorate a single passage. Keith Moon had no such reservations when it came to flash. Though he was rarely quick to praise another rock drummer, he admitted a love of big band drummers Buddy Rich, Jo Jones, and Gene Krupa. The latter's influence was particularly detectable, both in his neck-breaking rhythms and his flamboyant showmanship. Moon was transfixed when he saw Sal Mineo impersonating his idol in the 1959 biopic *The Gene Krupa Story* (UK title: *Drum Crazy*). Even by proxy, the "film was the only time I saw the way Krupa worked—all that juggling," Moon marveled in 1970 (as quoted by Tony Fletcher). Moon's friend and fellow drummer Roy Carr astutely observed how "If anyone sees those old forties movies of Gene Krupa, when Moon used to hunch over those drums and grab hold of a cymbal and hit it, it's identical" in Fletcher's *Moon*.

Keith Moon certainly did not have the discipline or technique of Gene Krupa, but the essential similarities between their styles is unmistakable: the syncopated snare attacks and typhoons of cymbal washes; the violent, sudden rim shots and incessantly stomped hi-hat; the instantly recognizable sound. That approach is completely in keeping with the freewheeling rhythms of jazz. In the far more rhythmically regimented rock 'n' roll, it's less typical. Moon's appropriation of Krupa's style revolutionized rock 'n' roll, broke it out of its rhythmic shackles, and laid the path for the future improvisatory combos the Jimi Hendrix Experience and Cream.

Perhaps even more profound was Krupa's determination to power the drum kit to the front of the stage, to transform the drummer into something he or she had never really been before: the star of the show. No rock 'n' roll drummer before or since Keith Moon came so close to doing that. With star-power competition in the frontline like Roger Daltrey and Pete Townshend, that is quite an accomplishment.

Blues

A closer cousin to rock 'n' roll than jazz is the blues. Robert Johnson bartered his soul to the devil and made the blues evil, menacing. Muddy Waters electrified it, gave it heft. Chuck Berry married it to country and western and made it speed. Elvis Presley made it fit for white folks, and the Stones anglicized it and dirtied it up again. When the Who got their mitts on the blues, it became all of these things simultaneously, and the effect that would have on Cream, Led Zeppelin, Black Sabbath, and other heavy British blues boomers is incalculable.

The 2007 documentary *Amazing Journey: The Story of the Who* makes a point of explaining how working-class English kids related to the nitty-gritty growling of poor, black Americans, but Pete Townshend's initial exposure to the blues couldn't have been less nitty-gritty. While attending art school in 1961, he hooked up with an American photography student named Tom Wright, who'd lugged his vast collection of blues and jazz records from Alabama all the way to Ealing. When Wright was deported for possessing a bit of pot, Townshend adopted the abandoned discs for a while. He was already well versed in jazz, but Wright's blues records were revelatory. He got his first doses of Ray Charles, John Lee Hooker, and Jimmy Reed, as well as jazz-blues hybridizer Mose Allison. Jazz continued to creep into his playing, but when it came to cases, he preferred grooving to Hooker over meditating with Montgomery.

Although he calls out Jimmy Reed and John Lee Hooker (who'd one day voice the title role of his "musical" *The Iron Man*) as his biggest blues heroes, Townshend's music bears little trace of their repetitive slow stomp. In *Before I Get Old: The Story of the Who*, Dave Marsh hypothesizes that their influence is more evident in "the sheer power" of these two "most primitive urban bluesmen." The simplicity made the blues seem "available" to the budding guitarist, while the power made it exciting.

The ghosts of Reed and Hooker most obviously haunt Townshend's original "My Generation" demo. The chugging riff and deliberate beat recall Reed's "Shame, Shame, Shame" (which the Stones would more explicitly heist for their early track "Little by Little") and Townshend's slight stammer (which Roger Daltrey would exaggerate greatly, against his desire according to John Entwistle) is allegedly an homage to Hooker's "Stuttering Blues." The Who's recording pile-drives away much of the overt bluesiness of Townshend's demo, though the singers' call and response and the tangy blue notes the guitarists slip into their improvisational flourishes reveal the track's origins.

Thievery was more rampant when the guys cut their first single under the calculating control of Pete Meaden. For the Who's doomed debut as the High Numbers, Meaden merely ripped off Slim Harpo's "I Got Love if You Want It" and grafted on his own boastful, lingo-laden lyric about being a face who puts all the tickets to shame. With Moon's up-tempo shuffle and Entwistle's color-streaking zooms, "I'm the Face" inches that much closer to R&B and that much further from Harpo's swampy, eerie blues.

The Who are at their most legitimately bluesy on their first album, though it is often blues by way of affectation. Daltrey grits up his delivery by forcing a gruff Howlin' Wolf growl on "Out in the Street," "The Good's Gone," and a heavy cover of Bo Diddley's "I'm a Man" (itself a rewrite of a legit blues item: Muddy Waters's "Hoochie Coochie Man").

Because the Who got such a late start compared to the Stones or the Yardbirds, they did not get as much time to wallow in the blues before making the requisite shift to pop in '66. When the return-to-the-roots blues boom hit in 1968, the Who were largely stage and studio bound, devoting their time to honing their craft, writing *Tommy*, and biding time with the superficially bluesy novelty singles "Call Me Lightning" and "Magic Bus." When they got back around to real blues, cutting their versions of "Young Man Blues" and Sonny Boy Williamson's "Eyesight to the Blind" during the *Tommy* sessions, the metallic former recording and the mystical latter sounded as much like the blues as a Brandenburg Concerto.

Rock 'n' Roll Pioneers

As noted previously, the man who wrote "Long Live Rock" took some time to become a true believer. Pete Townshend was first exposed to that rock 'n' roll fever when his parents took him and his buddy Graham "Jimpy" Beard to see the film *Rock Around the Clock* while holidaying on the Isle of Man in the summer of '56. Bill Haley and His Comets' hepped-up performances of classics such as "Rock-A-Beatin' Boogie," "R-O-C-K," and the monumental title tune flicked a switch in eleven-year-old Pete's head.

"I remember a chill ran up my spine as I heard them native rhythms," Townshend explained on *2nd House* in 1974. "I looked round at my father and I said: 'What is this amazing music?' He said, 'Hmm, not bad, not bad, is it?' And that was really all."

Odd that Cliff Townshend so hated a music as outdated as trad jazz but cottoned to rock 'n' roll at a time when older folks still believed it had the power to turn their kids into randy, poop-flinging clods. Yet, according to Dave Marsh, Papa Townshend appreciated rock 'n' roll, because like the Squadronaires' own brand of jazz, rock 'n' roll was rooted in black music and "[i]t recognized the economic realities that forced the music back into small combos and also got people dancing again." That Haley's approach to rock 'n' roll was not entirely different from the Squadronaires' big band dance music probably didn't hurt either.

Rock 'n' roll did not hold sway over Pete Townshend for very long, and he started drifting to trad jazz when Elvis Presley began his reign. The white rock 'n' roll of which Townshend was aware did not thrill his intellect the way the complex polyphonies of jazz did (though, ironically, he did like the whitest of white American rockers, Ricky Nelson, and particularly appreciated Nelson's guitarist James Burton). Roger Daltrey, however, had no such intellectual apprehensions. Elvis became an idol to emulate, while Scottish skiffle missionary Lonnie Donegan made music seem doable. Skiffle is the bopping style of folk that famously inspired John Lennon to form his first group, the Quarrymen. With a DIY lineup of guitar, homemade tea-chest bass, and washboard percussion, anyone could put together a skiffle group, even the son of a toilet factory employee. So Daltrey put his homemade guitar and rudimentary musical skills to work with the Detours.

Daltrey's tenure as a guitarist didn't last long. The influence of Elvis Presley was far more sustaining, and even Townshend recognized that Daltrey possessed some of the charisma and power of the world's biggest rock 'n' roll star. In his early days as a performer, Daltrey didn't do much to exploit that charisma or power, tending to hunch over his mic indifferently while Townshend and Moon worked overtime drawing attention to themselves. After a brief period in which Daltrey thought he might finally grab the spotlight by perming his hair into a fluffy bouffant and draping himself in a psychedelic poncho, he truly did find his place as a performer to rival his bandmates when *Tommy* gave him an imposing role to play. Now he could be seen lofting his fists in the air, flashing his bare chest, closing his eyes, curling his lip, and testifying to the crowd in a manner truly reminiscent of the King of Rock 'n' Roll. By the songwriter's own suggestion, Townshend's "Real Good Looking Boy" is as much a statement of awe and envy directed at Presley as it is one directed at his own singer.

As for Townshend, he was still destined to gravitate toward rock 'n' roll, and his inheritance of Tom Wright's record collection was enough to do the job. Between spins of John Lee Hooker and Jimmy Reed, he received his first sustained blast of Chuck Berry records. Like everyone who ever touched an electric guitar, Pete Townshend was knocked back several strides by Berry, though it wasn't his nimble licks—nor his music at all—that got Townshend's wheels turning. "I don't think it was until I heard Chuck Berry that I realized what you could do with words—how unimportant the music was, 'cause Chuck Berry always used the same song!" he told the *NME* in 1982.

No early rock 'n' roller composed words quite like Chuck Berry did. Rock lyrics generally mimicked the blues, with its no-good and super-sweet women, and old-fashioned simpering love standards. The most sweeping innovations early rock records made to the art of lyric composition was the overdue acknowledgment that teenagers exist ("I'm Not a Juvenile Delinquent," "At the Hop," "Seventeen"), the funky assimilation of B-movie themes ("Purple People Eater,"

"Flyin' Saucers Rock & Roll," "Rockin' in the Graveyard"), and making the word "rock" ubiquitous in the lyrical lexicon. Chuck Berry introduced storytelling with the attention to detail of classic folk songs. "Memphis, Tennessee," "Jo Jo Gunne," "No Particular Place to Go," "Johnny B. Goode," and so many others packed a level of imagination and wordplay absent from the mass of rock 'n' roll records. The future storyteller behind "Pictures of Lily," "A Quick One While He's Away," *Tommy*, and "Long Live Rock"—that rare Townshend tune to pay homage to Berry in both words *and* sound—couldn't help but be inspired.

John Entwistle drew more musical inspiration from rock 'n' roll than his fellow string picker. He was a more voracious rock 'n' roll consumer, digging everything from Buddy Holly (whose "Peggy Sue" would provide the blueprint for Roger Daltrey's first solo composition) to Eddie Cochran to the surfy British instrumental combo the Shadows. But for our bass player, the revelatory moment struck when he heard the guttural twang of Duane Eddy. Eddy's axe of choice was not the four-string Entwistle favored but a standard six-string. Yet Eddy so favored the low strings on the raunch-o-la classics "Rebel Rouser" and "Peter Gunn" that he almost could have been plucking a bass. As Entwistle noted in *Before I Get Old*, "Much of his stuff was very bass-influenced, and you could play most of it on bass." Eddy got the bass player thinking like a guitarist, setting him on a path that would lead him to completely revolutionize an instrument barely out of its infancy.

As already mentioned, Keith Moon's list of kit influences was a short one. In 1972, when Jerry Hopkins of *Rolling Stone* asked him to name his favorite drummers, Moon unenthusiastically dropped the names of jazz players Eric Delaney and Joe Morello (who received the highest praise for being "Technically . . . perfect"), as well as Bob Henrit of Argent, and later, the Kinks (Moon's most obvious forerunner, Krupa, failed to get a nod). The first name he dropped was D. J. Fontana of Elvis's band—the group Townshend thought was so "shitty." One would certainly be hard-pressed to recognize any similarities between the energetic yet disciplined Fontana and Moon's riotous bashing, but the question was about "favorites," not "influences."

One drummer Moon probably wouldn't have called an influence was Clifton James, the cat who laid down those hypnotic Afro-Cuban rhythms behind Bo Diddley. It is telling that the two Diddley numbers the Who recorded—"Here 'Tis" and "I'm a Man"—lacked Diddley's signature "shave-and-a-haircut" beat. In 1996, Roger Daltrey told the BBC, "When 'My Generation' started out it was more like a Bo Diddley song, but Keith couldn't play that rhythm very well, so we slammed it on the on-beat." The one time the Who attempted the classic Diddley beat on "Magic Bus," Moon sat out the majority of the song, only getting behind his kit to bash out his usual din for the Diddley-eschewing climax. Townshend, however, easily and often appropriated a signature Diddley move: scraping his guitar pick down the strings.

The Who's primal rock 'n' roll influences are further apparent in the songs they chose to cover—Eddie Cochran's "Summertime Blues" and "My Way," the

Everly Brothers' (one of the few groups loved equally by each member of the Who) "Man with Money," Johnny Kidd and the Pirates' "Shakin' All Over." Such artists would further form the Who's sound, Cochran being the punchiest of the old guard, the Everlys being the sweetest and most harmonious, and Johnny Kidd proving that English boys could make an authentic rock 'n' roll racket too.

R&B and Soul

In the earliest days of the Who, it was not jazz nor straight blues nor even rock 'n' roll with which the band was most firmly aligned. "Maximum R & B" screamed Brian Pike's brilliantly designed, iconic Marquee Club advert, Pete Townshend captured in mid-windmill, etched in impenetrable blackness. Kit Lambert coined the term and commissioned the poster, but the Who was already ahead of him, slipping popular R&B numbers like the Miracles' "I Gotta Dance to Keep from Crying" and Marvin Gaye's "Baby Don't You Do It" into their sets. R&B—and its smoother, tighter first cousin, soul—was the mods' poison of choice, and the Who's appropriation of it was decisive in that youth cult's acceptance of the green band.

It is significant that Lambert affixed a modifier to his motto because the Who could never be mistaken for playing R&B straight or traditionally—not with Keith Moon and John Entwistle in the back line. "Maximum" suggests a power, a level of volume, and an extremeness that no R&B artist could claim. The word doesn't even fit a huge personality and soul exemplar like James Brown. He was too disciplined, too much of a traditional showman, too impeccably professional, famously fining members of his band for arriving late to a gig or duffing the beat. Imagine the fines Keith Moon would have incurred!

Because Brian Pike's poster design was so iconic, its "Maximum R&B" label has dogged the Who for fifty years (even working its way into the title of this book). The Who's actual stint as an R&B group lasted about five minutes. *Author's collection*

No, the Who played R&B and soul with a rhythmic abandon that would have gotten any of the genres' true artists kicked out of the club. Just listen to their two James Brown interpretations on *My Generation*. Moon flops all over the beat on "I Don't Mind" and Brown's big showstopper "Please, Please, Please." He sounds almost frustrated to be playing such material, and indeed, he was. The Who recorded this kind of stuff to placate R&B freak and iron-fisted ruler Roger Daltrey, but the rest of the group would all but disown their debut for not accurately reflecting the group's complete creativity and originality. Still, they made out better than they would have if they'd gone through with plans to release a debut mostly consisting of R&B nuggets like Otis Blackwell's "Daddy Rolling Stone," Eddie Holland's "Leaving Here," Garnet Mimms's "Anytime You Want Me," and an out-of-control reading of Brown's "Shout and Shimmy" (most of these recordings crept out on B-sides through '65).

Yet by so radically interpreting a form of music largely defined by the precision of ace house bands—Motown's Funk Brothers, Stax's Booker T. & the M.G.s—the Who *were* exercising their creativity and originality, much as they would when transforming rock 'n' roll warhorses such as "Summertime Blues" into fire-breathing dragons onstage. The R&B covers on *My Generation* are not the album's most memorable tracks, but they are bone-crushers compared to the High Numbers' tame, borderline slick performance of "Zoot Suit"—Pete Meaden's rewrite of the Dynamics' "Misery."

And despite much griping from Townshend and Moon, the Who were not done with R&B or soul after their long-playing debut. They'd keep the mods happy by bashing hell out of Martha and the Vandellas' "Dancing in the Street" and "Heat Wave," the latter even making it to their second album. An earlier recording of "Heat Wave" was scrapped along with those other covers that would have constituted the first Who LP, but Townshend still managed to recycle its shuffling rhythm for his own "La-La-La Lies." Gaye's "Baby Don't You Do It" remained a Who staple for ages, bridging their mod past and their progressive present when a wild live version was smacked on the B-side of "Join Together" in 1972.

UK Pop Peers

In his book on *Meaty, Beaty, Big, and Bouncy*, John Perry describes the Who as "forerunners of a more self-referential form" of music than pop: "rock." He observes that because the Who were a little younger than the Beatles or the Rolling Stones, they had a different relationship with the pop artists of their time, noting that Townshend "was a major Stones fan."

The implication is that the Who were more consciously influenced by their contemporaries than the slightly older artists of the British Invasion's first wave, that while the Beatles, the Stones, and the Kinks were deliberately paying homage to the older blues and rock 'n' roll artists that inspired them, the Who were paying homage to the Beatles, the Stones, and the Kinks.

This is not completely off base. While Mick Jagger and Keith Richards never explicitly admitted that—for example—*Their Satanic Majesties Request* would never have existed if not for *Sgt. Pepper's Lonely Hearts Club Band*, the Who freely confessed that they borrowed liberally from their British pop peers. In 1971, Pete Townshend wrote in *Rolling Stone* that "I Can't Explain" "can't be beat for straightforward Kink copying." Thirty-three years later he less lightheartedly told *Uncut*'s Simon Goddard that the record was "a *desperate* copy of The Kinks." As quoted in Johnny Black's *Eyewitness the Who*, John Entwistle corroborated such statements in greater detail: "We were at Keith's house one night and we were playing 'You Really Got Me' by The Kinks, and Pete went home and tried to remember it but couldn't, he had such a bad memory, and so he came up with 'I Can't Explain.'"

And so it has gone down in history that the Who's first big record is—though beloved and wonderful in its own right—an unequivocal rip-off; in Townshend's words (as quoted in Grantley and Parker's *The Who by Numbers*), "'You Really Got Me' but with a different rhythm." This has been repeated so many times, it is virtually unchallenged. But is it true?

Certainly anyone with even the most rudimentary music education can identify that Pete's cyclical chord progression of E/D/A/E has nothing in

The Who have always been quick to admit the Kinks' heavy impact on their music; however, they arguably overstated the influence of "You Really Got Me" on "I Can't Explain."

Author's collection

common with the Kinks' stuck-in-gear stutter between F and G. These chords that Townshend strikes on his twelve-string Rickenbacker are curt yet full-bodied, clean, colorful. The chords Dave Davies pummels on his Harmony Meteor are compressed, glowering, rendered in dirty shades of gray. Ray Davies never alleviates his song's tension with a bridge, as Townshend does. Townshend never brings his song to the precipice of frenzy with incessant modulations, as Ray does (though he would on many of his future songs). Even Townshend's relatively simple solo displays a level of consideration that strikingly contrasts Dave's manic, two-note discharge. The only qualities the songs really share are their employments of power chords and brief drum breaks to transition between sections, their frustrated romanticism/eroticism, and the fact that they're both fucking great.

Not that this means the Kinks didn't have a profound influence on "I Can't Explain," but Townshend and Entwistle may have been misremembering the inspirational song. A more likely culprit is "All Day and All of the Night," released right around the time the Who auditioned for the EMI A&R man who told them they'd better start writing their own material. Townshend completed that assignment with "I Can't Explain," which used a four-chord cycle more similar to that of "All Day and All of the Night" than the Kinks' first hit. The differences in tone, style, and song structure still apply.

Despite possible lapses in memory, the Who have pointed out the Kinks' influence more emphatically than that of any other UK peer. When Goldmine's Ken Sharp asked John Entwistle about the "sixties rock bass players" he rated highest, the first that came to mind was Pete Quaife, who John said, "literally drove The Kinks along" (he was also mightily impressed by Paul McCartney, particularly his ability to "sing and play bass at the same time"). Townshend went so far as to declare that Ray Davies should be "Poet Laureate" in an interview for the History of Rock 'n' Roll television program, going on to say, "He invented a new kind of poetry and a new kind of language for pop writing that influenced me from the very, very, very beginning," while also rating Dave Davies as "very underestimated." The Who can even claim that they have a couple of genuine "You Really Got Me" lifts in their catalog: the mid-section of "Pictures of Lily" basically plays the Kinks' riff in reverse, while "My Generation" mimics its two-chord (again in reverse), whole-step riffing and tension-ratcheting modulations. Roger Daltrey copped to the former incident of petty theft in a 1994 interview with Goldmine; Townshend copped to the latter in his 1971 Rolling Stone essay.

Stones-fan Townshend played a similar confession game with "Substitute," saying he'd written it as "a spoof of 'Nineteenth [sic] Nervous Breakdown.'" However, aside from the droning quality of both songs, they are even more dissimilar than "I Can't Explain" and "You Really Got Me." Even the "Jagger-like accent" Townshend claimed to use on his demo sounds schoolboy sweet compared to the leering spite Jagger spews on "19th Nervous Breakdown."

"Substitute" has more identifiable roots in "Where Is My Girl?," an obscure record by an obscure group called Robb Storme and the Whispers that

Townshend reviewed favorably in the "Blind Date" feature of *Melody Maker*. From this rather repetitive, rather banal disc, Townshend pinched the central bass riff that provides so much of his record's power. In *Eyewitness the Who*, Entwistle equally convincingly described the bass line as "an attempt to play the introduction from 'I Can't Help Myself' by The Four Tops." Pete further developed the soul angle by explaining in the liner notes of *Another Scoop* that "Smokey Robinson sang the word 'substitute' so perfectly in 'Tracks of My Tears'—my favourite song at the time—that I decided to celebrate the word itself with a song all its own."

A more convincing Stones spoof is "A Legal Matter," which flaunts a nagging, droning riff that may share DNA with "The Last Time"—a number for which the Who certainly had affection, as they selected it for the A-side of their "free Mick and Keith" tribute single (see chapter 9). Townshend's vocal delivers the "Jagger-like accent" not entirely evident in his "Substitute" demo. Listen to his affected drawl, the way he draws out the word "rail" into "*raayy-ulll*"; very Jagger-like indeed. "A Legal Matter" is also a rare instance of the equitable-minded Townshend slipping into misogyny, though the song's playful tone and cute lines like "Just wanna keep on doing all the dirty little things I do" divulges a self-aware silliness Jagger didn't flash in nasty assaults such as "The Last Time" and its devastating flip "Play with Fire," hence the "spoof" aspect.

The Who's absorption of the Beatles could be spoofy too, as evidenced by one of their very, very rare excursions into pure psychedelia. "Armenia City in the Sky" streaks the manic tape loops and backwards noises of "Tomorrow Never Knows" over a pseudo-cosmic comedy number by Townshend's protégé, John "Speedy" Keen. If the robotic squawk of "Freak out! Freak out!" isn't enough to hip you to the Who's attitude about flower power and acid fancies, then Townshend's dismissal of the "post-psychedelic wetness" (of which he cited the Stones' "We Love You" as a prime example) that drove him to try and "rescue the pop song" should.

Pete Townshend has said that the Beatles did not influence him, but some of his mid-sixties pop songs seem to contradict that statement. "The Kids Are Alright" is resplendent in Beatlesque jangle, harmony, and classic pop structure. The track even adapts one of the Beatles' most recognizable signatures: the clanging chord that heralds the arrival of "A Hard Day's Night." Yet the Who's effect is quite different. The Beatles' chord (a complex mélange in which the guitarists strike Fadd9 while Paul hits a high D on the bass) establishes suspense for the euphoria to follow. The Who's chord (straight D major—lonesome Pete on his twelve-string Rickenbacker, the same instrument George Harrison used on his recording) is authoritative, not elliptical like the Beatles' but punctuated with a period. It is the sound of a surly gang barreling into the room, even as the song that follows drips with Beatle sweetness.

Keith Moon was an even bigger Beatlemaniac, and the Who's Loud One seemingly drew inspiration from the Beatles' Quiet One for his most musical composition. Like George Harrison's "Don't Bother Me," Moon's "I Need You" is a big-beat number brooding in a minor key—something Townshend rarely used (it also nicks its title from a Harrisong). Unlike "Don't Bother Me," "I Need You" is parodic rather than self-pitying. The scene is the Scotch of St. James, the club where Swinging London's biggest and brightest convened for drinks and carousing until the wee hours throughout 1966. The biggest and brightest of them all were the Fab Four, and Keith Moon sings his song from the perspective of an outsider desperate to crack into their exclusive inner circle to find the secret of their magical skills ("We want to learn, let us come and sitar with you!") or at least, be acknowledged ("Please talk to me again!"). The Who's Liverpool-bred road manager Gordon "Lurch" Molland (brother of Badfinger's Joey Molland) provides the response to the outsider's fawning: the pseudo-Beatle ignores him, drawling, "Reorge and Gingo are coming down later with the wives, you know" (which must mean we should call this song's Bizarro-World John and Paul "Pohn and Jaul"). In the January 1967 issue of *Beat Instrumental*, Moon unconvincingly claimed that Molland's cameo was not meant to be a Lennon impersonation, though John Entwistle said otherwise. Nicky Hopkins's harpsichord adds a baroque, Beatley touch reminiscent of George Martin's harpsichord-mimicking piano on "In My Life," a song Moon would later mutilate on his solo album *Two Sides of the Moon*.

The good-natured jabbing of "I Need You" indicates how the Who never followed the Beatles as doggedly as did most other groups of the period—the Stones included. They never crooned an acoustic ballad to string quartet accompaniment à la "Yesterday," never touched a Mellotron or sitar, never made their long-playing psychedelic opus. This does not mean they were not susceptible to their trippy times, as absolutely every artist was in the late sixties. For all their verbal rejection of "psychedelic wetness" (presumably by "wetness" Townshend meant "naïveté," as in "wet behind the ears"), some of the leading Dr. Feelgoods of their era made a profound impression on the Who. Townshend listened to such trippy fare as Traffic's *Mr. Fantasy* and the Beatles' *Sgt. Pepper's Lonely Hearts Club Band* incessantly. *The Who Sell Out* appropriates several of *Pepper's* gimmicks, including its segues, nonmusical sounds, epic finale, and run-out groove joke. The Beatles' disc ends with a two-second loop of sliced and spliced tapes of Liverpudlian conversation that will play infinitely on your nonautomatic phonograph if you forget to lift the needle at the end of Side B. *Sell Out* ends similarly with its "Track Records" loop. Pink Floyd's unique fusion of the ethereal and the chaotic is detectable in "Relax," a track recorded around the time Townshend could be spotted at the UFO Club zonked on acid, draped in beads, and hypnotized by Syd Barrett's otherworldly squeals. According to Henry Scott-Irvine, who wrote the liner notes for the album's 2009 reissue, Townshend cited Procol Harum's *Shine On Brightly* (1968) as "a real heavy influence" on *Tommy* during an interview Barry Miles recorded for the *International Times* in 1969. Oddly, *Uncut* magazine chose that record's compact title track for its *The Roots of Tommy*, a compilation of songs that supposedly inspired the rock opera. A more obvious link to *Tommy* is the psychedelic suite "In Held Twas in I," which almost occupies an entire side of *Shine On Brightly* and ends with a chorale not dissimilar to the "Listening to You" chorus that climaxes *Tommy*. But then again, that piece is seventeen minutes long, which wouldn't have left much time for many of *Tommy*'s other "roots."

While Small Faces' *Ogden's Nut Gone Flake* is often cited as another inspiration for *Tommy*, the inspiration may have actually gone the other way around, as explained in chapter 15. Townshend didn't escape the group's influence completely. His "Dogs" (recorded May 22) is unmistakably similar to the nonoperatic *Ogden's* track "Lazy Sunday," released as a single six weeks before "Dogs," leaving Townshend plenty of time to cop it. The two cockney knees-up romps certainly sound like they were cut from the same comic-book cloth. John Entwistle agreed that the tune "[s]ounds a bit like The Small Faces" in his liner notes for *Two's Missing*, and Roger Daltrey later went so far as to suggest Townshend actually wrote the song for Ronnie Lane.

US Pop Peers

The early-to-mid sixties pop scene unquestionably belonged to the British. As the Mersey rocked and the Thames swung, the Beatles, Stones, Kinks, and their second-tier brethren (Dave Clark Five, Billy J. Kramer and the Dakotas, Freddie and the Dreamers, Gerry and the Pacemakers, etc.) set the beat to which everyone across the world danced. That includes the leaders of rock 'n' roll's birthplace. In the United States, Dylan ditched his acoustic guitar to reinvent rock with maximum electricity and a big Stonesy beat. Galvanized by *A Hard Day's Night*, guitarists Jim McGuinn, David Crosby, and Gene Clark of the Jet Set resolved to hire a rhythm section and become the Byrds. A pair of foxy LA producers schemed to transform the Beatles' flick into a weekly series called *The Monkees*, catching the zeitgeist like Dennis Wilson catching a wave. As for Wilson, his brother Brian decided his Beach Boys were in direct competition with the Beatles, spurring him to make some of the most innovative and beautiful music of his—or any—generation. Even the soulsters got caught up in British-mania, with the Four Tops interpreting "Michelle," Otis Redding having his way with "Day Tripper" and "Satisfaction," and the Supremes cutting an entire disc of Beatles, Peter and Gordon, Gerry and the Pacemakers, Dave Clark, and Animals covers called *A Bit of Liverpool*. No matter that the Beatles and Pacemakers were the only bona fide Liverpudlians represented—in 1964, every lad with an English accent hailed from the home of John, Paul, George, and Ringo. And with a mop of hair and a Rickenbacker strapped high around your chest, you could too!

The inspiration sailed both ways across the Atlantic, and the Who being such enthusiastic pop consumers had their fair share of US favorites. The leaders among them were the Beach Boys. "What?," you ask. "Such nice, clean-cut boys had a profound impact on the meanest, surliest, most violentest group of thugs to ever barrel out of Shepherd's Bush? Absurd!"

Not half as absurd as the huge heap of surf numbers the Who hid on their LPs, B-sides, and EPs in 1966. Just as the band recorded a bunch of James Brown numbers on their first album to keep Roger Daltrey happy, the surf fixation that followed was meant to keep Keith Moon passive (or as passive as he was capable of getting). Although everyone in the Who appreciated the Beach Boys to varying degrees, Moon was absolutely obsessed with the band and their sunny Cal-I-Forn-I-A ethos. Let's not forget that the band he quit to join the Who were called the Beachcombers. Though they weren't really the surf group Moon wanted his interviewers to believe, he did manage to convince the group to play such Brian Wilson–penned favorites as "Surfin' USA" and "Surf City." The Who similarly mollified their drummer by performing the Beach Boys' remake of the Regents' "Barbara Ann." Moon was even allowed the rare opportunity to sing lead in his wee falsetto, forcing his bandmates to work extra hard on their harmonies to disguise his dodgy pitch.

Considering Moon's hyperactivity, it may be even more surprising that the Beach Boys song he most adored was the pacific "Don't Worry Baby," Brian Wilson's sensual homage to "Be My Baby." "There wasn't a day when the Beach Boys wasn't in the eight-track playing 'Don't Worry Baby,'" Turtle Mark Volman told Tony Fletcher of his time filming *200 Motels* with Moon in 1971. Fletcher hypothesizes that Moon became most possessed by the radiant, romantic song during his frequent separations from wife Kim, who didn't recall him playing it much in her presence. He certainly liked "Don't Worry Baby" enough to "sing" it on *Two Sides of the Moon.*

Still, being a fan of a group, or even covering its songs, is not the same thing as being influenced by them, and there is not a trace of Dennis Wilson's primitive restraint in Keith Moon's drumming. There certainly isn't a shred of the flawless professionalism of Hal Blaine, the great studio musician Brian employed to stomp the beat on many Beach Boys recordings. Their profoundest influence on Moon's music can be heard in the strained, mock Brian Wilson falsetto he uses on "Barbara Ann," "Pictures of Lily," "In the City," and "I Need You."

The Beach Boys also affected the singing of the Who members who could actually sing. A considerably more accomplished falsetto than Moon is John Entwistle, whose vocal range cannot be overestimated. The same guy who hit low notes that could rattle floor tiles on "Boris the Spider" and "Dr. Jekyll and Mr. Hyde" could also reach high ones that could shatter wine glasses on "Doctor, Doctor" and "A Quick One While He's Away." The latter song is a particularly magnificent example of what the Who learned from the Beach Boys, from the near-barbershop harmonies of the opening passage to the overlapping, swirling, contrapuntal voices of the final passage, which sounds like a wild interpretation of the grand finales of "California Girls" or "God Only Knows."

While the most sophisticated aspects of the Beach Boys seem to have had the strongest impact on the Who, they had a very uneasy relationship with Brian Wilson's more experimental side. Keith Moon famously heard *Pet Sounds* for the first time at a listening party attended by Paul McCartney, John Lennon, and Beach Boy Bruce Johnston. When the two Beatles started gushing over the album, Moon dutifully joined in . . . secretly hating its lush production and strange sounds. In the September 17, 1966, issue of *Disc and Music*, Pete Townshend sneered that the album was "written for an audience sympathetic to Brian Wilson's personal problems" and that "The Beach Boys' new material on the LPs is too remote and way-out. It's written for a feminine audience." Ironically, the Who's staunchest purveyor of masculinity came out in favor of the record precisely one week later. Roger Daltrey told *Melody Maker* that the Beach Boys were "fantastic" and "I had no idea that they'd ever turn out like this when I first heard them. They've helped pop music to progress so much it's not true."

So does this mean that Daltrey was behind the bold progressive Beach Boys influence that ran through the Who's music in 1967? Perhaps not, because as Townshend admitted to *Disc and Music Echo* toward the end of '66, after hearing "Good Vibrations" "80 times" he'd "begun to like it." A more recent quote from the 2003 documentary *Brian Wilson: On Tour* is a lot stronger than that. Said Townshend, "I love Brian. There's not many people I would say that about. I think he's a truly, truly, truly great genius. I love him so much it's just terrible—I find it hard to live with . . . 'God Only Knows' is simple and elegant and was stunning when it first appeared; it still sounds perfect." That love must have taken root by the time Townshend started writing songs for *The Who Sell Out* in the spring of '67.

Perhaps no other British pop album of the sixties so thoroughly captures the sweeping romanticism, the dense, echoing sound, the glorious, Technicolor harmonies of *Pet Sounds* as *Sell Out* does. The Beatles' professed *Pet Sounds* homage, *Sgt. Pepper's*, sure doesn't sound much like their American rivals' record. One could never imagine the Beach Boys doing anything as heavy as the title track or as un-American as "Within You Without You." They wouldn't have done anything like "I Can See For Miles" either, but the pretty pieces "Our Love Was," "Tattoo," and "I Can't Reach You" were well within Wilson's milieu. The whacked-out humor and weird editing of musical and nonmusical sounds also seemed like the kind of thing he reportedly had planned for his highly anticipated, never completed masterpiece *Smile*.

As for "I Can See For Miles," it seemed more a tribute to a musician who'd recently ignited the rock world when he arrived in London in late '66. With its slow, simmering menace; mesh of searing guitars; and panoramic vision, the Who's record had much in common with Jimi Hendrix's first recordings with the Experience.

Not that it started that way. Townshend had actually written "I Can See For Miles" a while before Hendrix's arrival, around the time he wrote "I'm a Boy." His demo is layered with acoustic guitars, though the addition of a fuzzy lead guitar indicates he had something grungier in mind for the Who's recording. And though "I Can See For Miles" bears some sonic similarities to Hendrix—a fusion of the expansiveness of "Hey Joe" and the heaviness of "Purple Haze"—it differs in execution. Like his favorite guitar players, Townshend did not set out to dazzle when he picked up his instrument, and this particular record contains a single-note solo so simplistic it can almost be interpreted as an act of defiance against Hendrix's pyrotechnics. So, in this instance, Hendrix may have influenced Townshend more in terms of what he *didn't* do than what he did. Believing he could never compete with Hendrix, he "decided it was worth trying to express myself through single note work," he told *Sound International* in 1980. He also suggested that Hendrix influenced his showier soloing on *Live at Leeds*, but he would never try anything so "mad" as to put himself forth as some sort of pseudo-Hendrix along the lines of Robin Trower.

Townshend found a smoother kinship with Joe Walsh of James Gang. Walsh both absorbed Townshend's seamless blend of rhythm and lead playing and passed along inspiration in less guitar-centric ways, as when Townshend nicked the organ part of "Take a Look Around" for his "Pure and Easy." While Townshend tended to speak of Hendrix with envy and something approaching awestruck fear, he was more comfortable showering Walsh with sunny praise, telling *Cleveland After Dark*, "I don't want to sound ridiculous, but he really is one of those guys I kind of go nuts—rapturous—about. I like the group, too."

Townshend has also acknowledged the influence of other critically lauded Yanks, admitting that Todd Rundgren partially influenced "Sister Disco." The Byrds' "I'll Feel a Whole Lot Better" apparently had a strong impact on the central guitar lick of "So Sad About Us" ("Needles and Pins" is usually cited as its origin, but the Searchers' soft approach is less similar to the Who's than the Byrds' muscular twelve-string attack). Townshend rates Dylan as one of his favorite artists, though his influence isn't very strong in the Who's music. Dylan's influence was more theoretical, putting the idea that rock could "say bigger and better things" in young Pete's head, as he told *Penthouse* in 1974.

24

I'm Waiting for You to Follow Me

Heirs of the Who

A band's greatness can be measured from sounds onstage and in the grooves. This is not limited to the artist's own work. The true greats, the ones that manage to survive beyond the brief window of infatuation, can be felt and heard in the work of other artists. They have long-lasting influence, and there aren't a ton of rock 'n' roll artists who've had longer-lasting influence than the Who. Chuck Berry, Little Richard, Buddy Holly, and Elvis Presley, for sure. The Who are just inched out by the Beach Boys, the Beatles, the Stones, the Kinks, and depending on when you begin counting him among the rock 'n' rollers, Dylan. Otherwise, the Who were shaking up the scene before Hendrix, before the Velvet Underground, before Led Zeppelin, before most other artists that would profoundly reshape rock 'n' roll. Some of these would arguably have a greater overall impact than the Who, but let's refrain from splitting hairs. Let's focus on the almost instantaneous and still ongoing way the Who changed how their peers approached music and inspired generations of heirs to slash a guitar, abuse a drum kit, batter a bass, and scream the walls down.

The Sixties

The 1960s was a heady time for rock's evolution. Lennon and McCartney developed a distinctively British concept of the pop song early in the decade. Folk-rock, psychedelia, funk, progressive rock, and even punk's first seedlings all sprouted before the seventies too. With so many exciting developments popping up from so many sources, there was an incredible degree of influence crossing from one artist to the next. The Beatles influenced the Kinks, the Kinks influenced the Rolling Stones, the Rolling Stones influenced David Bowie, and the Who . . . well . . . the Who influenced them all.

The Beatles

We begin with the most influential group of the sixties, the most influential group of all time. Shreds (often massive chunks) of recognizably Beatlesque melody, harmony, instrumental interplay, and production can be heard in countless peers and followers, but the Beatles were great assimilators too. Holly, Berry, and Motown were decisive in their early sound, though as they progressed, their contemporaries impacted their music more and more. In 1966, the Beatles stood in awe as the Who turned rock into a more explosive force, both sonically unified and displaying an unprecedented differentiation between instruments. That year, Paul McCartney called the Who "the most exciting thing around," and declared that the Who and Dylan were the Beatles' "two greatest influences of 1966" in *Melody Maker*. Listen to "Rain" to hear the Beatles' most Who-like performance: ringing yet grimy washes of twelve-string guitar holding down the rhythm as uncommonly busy bass and drums weave in and out of each other. McCartney doesn't strike his bass with the aggression of John Entwistle, nor does Ringo Starr achieve the complete abandon of Keith Moon, but the essential dynamic is pure Who, as is the noisy, mid-tempo drone. Just as Beatle-derived melody and jangle are clear in "The Kids Are Alright," the darker shading and rumbling undertone of that track is detectable in "Rain." Flip that disc over, and hear another dose of unfettered bass work, dirtier guitars, and smirking falsetto harmonies highly redolent of "Substitute" or "Anyway, Anyhow, Anywhere" on "Paperback Writer."

The Who's influence is not quite as obvious in the Beatles song of which McCartney most directly acknowledged their influence. That's because "Helter Skelter" was not affected by actual Who music but by a review of their music that caught McCartney's attention. After reading a write-up of "I Can See for Miles" that lauded the track as the loudest, nastiest hunk of rock 'n' roll any band had yet to produce, McCartney was disappointed when he finally heard it and it failed to live up to his expectations. The music he'd heard in his head when reading the review was more like "Helter Skelter," which is more heavy-metal progenitor than Who pastiche. Interestingly, Pete Townshend would, most likely unconsciously, receive clearer inspiration from the Beatles when he appropriated the descending riff of "Helter Skelter" for "Who Are You" ten years later.

The Rolling Stones

The Rolling Stones are among rock's greatest thieves in the night, gleefully pilfering signatures from Muddy Waters, Chuck Berry, the Beatles, and Bob Dylan and sliding the spoils along on a slick of signature Stonesy rhythms. The Who's rhythm-shoving chaos couldn't be more different from the Stones' behind-the-beat propulsion, so it isn't surprising that there are few obvious nods to the Who among the Rolling Stones' plunder. Yet the Stones were Who fans (Keith Richards was particularly fond of their early singles), and in their own way, they paid homage, most notably on the noise fests: their version of Larry Williams's "She Said Yeah" and "Have You Seen Your Mother, Baby, Standing in the Shadow?," which sounds like the final minute of "My Generation" stretched to two and a half. Among the Beatles, Dylan, and Kinks rips on *Between the*

Buttons, the Stones break from the beat as much as they ever would with "Please Go Home," a track that filters the classic Bo Diddley beat through an electrified sieve of Townshend-type turbulence and Moony arm-flailing mania.

The Kinks

The Kinks seemed wary of the Who after hearing their own sound crackling back at them the first time they caught "I Can't Explain" on the radio. But they weren't above creative borrowing either, and quite a bit of the Who's unique influence is obvious on their records. The 1968 B-side "Polly"—with its joyous crescendos and choir-boy falsettos—is more redolent of "Happy Jack" than "I Can't Explain" is of "You Really Got Me." Ray Davies would also reverse that particular theft with his "The Hard Way," which sports a riff that sounds a hell of a lot more like the one that drives "I Can't Explain" than "I Can't Explain" sounds like any Kinks song before it. The instrumental "Whip Lady" packs as many Who clichés (string scrapes, crazed Keith Moon fills, emphatic power chords) as can fit into forty-five seconds. With *Arthur, Lola Versus Powerman, Preservation Acts I* and *II, Soap Opera,* and *Schoolboys in Disgrace,* the Kinks also dived into extended character-driven rock narratives more enthusiastically than any other band . . . and that includes the one that invented the rock opera.

Small Faces

Small Faces also had their go at the rock opera, but unlike the Kinks' LPs, the saga of "Happiness Stan" only took up one side of *Ogden's Nut Gone Flake,* making it a mini-opera in the mode of "A Quick One." That Small Faces created their suite after coming off an Australian tour with the Who in which Pete Townshend supposedly talked quite a bit about his rock opera plans is significant. So is the fact Small Faces had been cribbing bits of the Who's sound from the very beginning of their career as mod upstarts, from the Maximum R&B attitude to Steve Marriott's squalling power chords to Kenney Jones's shocking rhythmic outbursts. It's hard to believe that the drummer who played the Keith Moon–like cascades of "Come On Children" played so sedately after he joined the Who.

David Bowie

Years away from superstardom and constant chameleon reinvention, David Bowie began his career in veritable uniform as a dedicated mod named Davy Jones. Because he was a genuine face—no third-class ticket—Davy was hip enough to recognize that the Who were little more than trend-hoppers, but he and his compatriots embraced the group at a time when few bands consciously aligned themselves with the mod movement nevertheless. Real mods the Who may not have been, but with their early discs "I Can't Explain" and "Anyway, Anyhow, Anywhere," they provided British mods with their own original sound, something they didn't get from the American blues and soul artists they loved. So when ace face Davy Jones fronted his own quartet of snazzily dressed, bouffanted mods called Davy Jones and the Lower Third, he completely appropriated the Who sound, right down to getting Shel Talmy to produce. On one of the most blatantly Who-like songs ever recorded, "You've Got a Habit of Leaving," the Lower Third basically reproduced the mid-song freak-out of "Anyway, Anyhow, Anywhere" to the letter. This sound would not remain in Davy Jones's repertoire for long, as he'd soon reinvent himself under his more famous moniker to avoid confusion with a certain Monkee and create music with a more theatrical flair, but he'd forever remain a Who fan, not only putting that theatricality into effect on his own rock opera (see chapter 15) but also recording both "I Can't Explain" and "Anyway, Anyhow, Anywhere" for his 1973 mod-tribute record *Pin Ups* and covering "Pictures of Lily" for the 2001 various artist comp *Substitute: The Songs of the Who.*

Hard Mod, Freakbeat, and Psych

If any bands should owe royalties to the Who for cribbing their thing, they're the Creation and the Move. Both groups chewed up the Who's violent stage act, their whimsical power rock, their sneering attitude, their self-conscious pop-artiness, their falsetto harmonies, and their colorfulness and noisiness and spat them back at an audience screeching for more. Neither band was content to merely whack a guitar against the stage. Eddie Phillips of the Creation would rake a violin bow across his guitar strings as singer Kenny Pickett blasted a canvas with spray paint, then stepped aside to allow a roadie to set the fucking thing on fire. The Move would crack out sledgehammers to bash televisions and cars—*cars!*—before their agog audience. If that's not enough, East London's less celebrated Flies were known to blow up bags of flour. John's Children detonated sacks of feathers to upstage headliners the Who—anything for a bit of *ka-boom* publicity. Decades later, John Entwistle confessed to Marc Bolan biographer Lesley-Ann Jones that John's Children had effectively "Out-Who'd the Who."

On disc, the Creation (produced by Shel Talmy for additional sonic similarity) and the Move could sound so much like the Who it was beyond uncanny and bordering on copyright infringement. The same could be said of the Birds (who'd record their own versions of "Leaving Here" and "Run Run Run"), Tintern Abbey (whose "Vacuum Cleaner," one of just two songs they released, is built on an incessant Keith Moon–style squall), the Rocking Vickers (whose Talmy-produced "It's Alright" so clearly ripped off "The Kids Are Alright" that ostensible songwriter Lemmy Kilmister credited it to Townshend), the Eyes (who recorded a song called "My Degeneration" and "I'm Rowed Out," a dead ringer for "I Can't Explain"), and in America, Powder (who covered "So Sad About Us") and Todd Rundgren's Nazz (their "Open Your Eyes" was another blatant "Can't Explain" lift). In other words, they all made some unbelievably wonderful records.

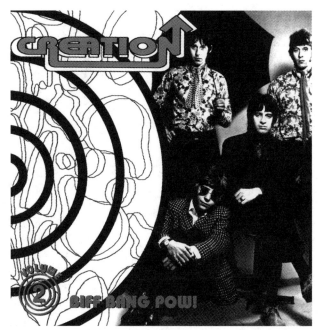

The Creation's musical debt to the Who is made more explicit with the arrow and target graphics on the cover of their 1998 compilation *Biff Bang Pow!*   *Author's collection*

The Power Trios

The Who were not the first band stripped down to bass, drums, and a single guitar. There was Johnny Kidd and the Pirates, and Buddy Holly and the Crickets often appeared as a trio. Nonetheless, the Who were the first band to compensate for lack of a second guitar or keyboard by cranking up the volume, placing greater melodic demands on the bass player, and requiring the drummer to bridge the gaps with lyrical fills ("babbling" might actually be a more appropriate adjective to describe Keith's fills). The Who never made you miss a fourth instrument because each of the three instrumentalists onstage was always working so hard, always coaxing something interesting out of his tool. With all due apologies and acknowledgments to Roger Daltrey, this is the power-trio dynamic so essential in the sounds of such bands as the Jimi Hendrix Experience, Cream, James Gang, and Blue Cheer, as well as the vocalist-appended foursomes Black Sabbath and Led Zeppelin. These groups would develop their own innovations (Cream's wider incorporation of jazz-based improvisation; Blue Cheer, Zeppelin, and Sabbath's refinement of heavy metal; Hendrix's gob-smacking reinvention of the electric guitar), but the roots of their basic sounds grew from the Who.

The Seventies

During the sixties, the Beatles and Dylan largely dictated the moves. When the Fabs proved the viability of electric combos, the solo performers that had dominated rock 'n' roll thus far largely fell by the wayside. Dylan's lyricism, more sophisticated than "She Loves You," inspired others to reach for themes beyond boy meets girl with a poeticism and surrealism new to pop music. When the Beatles adapted that surrealism to the sound of their music, everyone else followed suit, and when Dylan jammed the breaks on psychedelic progression with his down-home *John Wesley Harding*, groups lost their Mellotrons and sitars en masse and went running back to blues, folk, and rootsy R&R.

Stripped down four-piece rock. Country and folk. Heavy blues. Progressive rock. Intellectual singer-songwriter statements. All of this is the detritus of the sixties, and it would all continue glittering in the rock scene during the seventies, but that scene would splinter. Instead of one or two artists setting the pace and every other one following dutifully, a variety of subscenes popped up, each often affecting the other, but not necessarily influencing each other. Would there have been punk if prog rock hadn't given the young upstarts something to rebel against? Maybe, maybe not, but each of these subgenres often bore the stamp of the Who.

Prog

With its fantasy and sci-fi obsessions, self-seriousness, goofy Roger Dean record sleeves, arbitrarily shifting time signatures, and endless feats of instrumental wankery, prog is probably rock's biggest punch line (rivaled only by hair metal). But let's not forget that through much of the seventies, Yes, Genesis, and Emerson, Lake, and Palmer were some of the hottest tickets in town. And before we join in on the snickering, we should acknowledge the role the Who played in the development of progressive rock. *Sgt. Pepper's* often receives much of the blame because of its supposed "concept" (it actually doesn't have one) and its alleged intellectualism (with the exception of "A Day in the Life" it doesn't have much of this either, what with its songs about children's drawings, retirement, spiritualism, teen runaways, getting stoned with buddies, sexy meter maids, and the circus). The album's lack of showy musicianship and emphasis on oompah beats doesn't have much to do with prog's virtuosity or jarring rhythmic shifts either.

You want to hear some real proto-prog? Well, maybe you should check out the nine minutes of wildly shifting moods and tempos that is "A Quick One While He's Away," a suite of songs that actually share an actual unified concept. But maybe that piece is too down to earth with its sex and silly humor. OK, then. So take a taste of "Rael," with its futuristic wars, or maybe "I'm a Boy," with its sci-fi hero. Or how about two great big discs worth of *Tommy*, which has all sorts of shifty numbers ("Overture," "Christmas"), instrumental razzle-dazzle

(Entwistle's solo on "Sparks" . . . *yowza*!), lengthy bits ("Underture," "We're Not Gonna Take It"), and big ideas (ROCK OPERA!). This is not to completely undermine the very real part the Beatles—or Procol Harum or the Moody Blues or Zappa or even the Stones ("Sing This All Together [See What Happens]," anyone?)—played in progressive rock, but the ever-virtuosic Who certainly was one of its key forerunners.

As the Who shed their power-pop purity and Pete Townshend discovered synthesizers in the seventies, their sound became more purely linked to progressive rock. One could reasonably categorize *Quadrophenia* as a straight-up prog record, though it would be one of the most emotionally charged, realistic, and, well, *rocking* prog records. Prog musicians continued listening to the Who's new developments. Behold Keith Emerson's keyboard work on ELP's "Karn Evil 9," which is a direct descendant of *Who's Next*. Genesis would appropriate some very Who-like synth sounds on their *Lamb Lies Down on Broadway*, an (albeit impossible to understand) rock opera with a main character named Rael. Sixties psychedelicists turned seventies art rockers Pink Floyd would also create a double-LP opera with clear links to the Who at the decade's end with *The Wall* (see chapter 15).

The essential Who sound was also a key ingredient in prog. John Entwistle's trebly, loud, and distorted sound, as well as his astounding dynamism, is unmistakable in the bass work of Yes's Chris Squire, King Crimson's Greg Lake (who'd soon move on to ELP and later fill in for The Ox on "Real Good Looking Boy") and John Wetton, and Rush's Geddy Lee. Rush also produced Alex Lifeson, a guitarist who proudly appropriated Pete Townshend's shimmering first-position chords and arpeggios on the utterly Who-like "Fly By Night" and his even more distinctive movable triads on the "Discovery" section of Rush's mini-opera "2112." Keith Moon inspired Neil Peart to pick up the sticks, though Peart's approach to drumming was a wee bit more technical.

Glam Rock, Hard Rock, and Power Pop

Prog may be a big joke today, but in the early seventies, all contempt was pitched at glam. Dolled up in spangles, elevator shoes, and oversized glasses, playing music without enough intellectual depth for kindergarteners, the glam-bammers may have seemed laughable at the time, but they were closer tuned to the essence of rock 'n' roll than prog's po-faced intellectuals. They were also tuned to the Who, though drawing a bit less inspiration from *Tommy* or *Who's Next* and more from the jolly japes "Pictures of Lily," "Happy Jack," and "I'm a Boy." T. Rex, Slade, and the Sweet put heavy spins on playground ditties just as the Who—and dedicated Who followers such as the Move—did before them. Vincent Furnier was another young Who fan turned glam rocker, though the discs he made as Alice Cooper sucked from the darker side of the Who's early work: the nasty aggression of "My Generation" and "Out in the Street" and John Entwistle's snide horror rock. Elton John, a singer-songwriter disguised in the most outrageous glam gear, was a veritable rock 'n' roll historian masterful at creating knowing yet fresh pastiches of all the greats. The shock chords that propel some of his more legitimately rocking numbers—"Saturday Night's Alright for Fighting," "The Bitch Is Back"—don't sound like Townshend by accident. The same thing goes for Brian May's massive, sustained chords. In 1991, the Queen guitarist told *Guitar World* that he and drummer Roger Taylor "were big Who fans," which is clear in their own band's mid-seventies fling with operatic rock.

An appreciation for early Who didn't mean you had to dress up in goofy getups in the seventies. Groups who took their inspiration from the same period of the Who as the glam rockers, but preferred simple sharp suits or even a pair of jeans could sell themselves beneath the banner of power pop. The Raspberries, Big Star, the Knack, and Cheap Trick all owe a serious debt to the Who. AC/DC, one of the most refreshingly straightforward hard-rock bands of the decade, declared fealty to the Who. Schoolboy-attired Angus Young reportedly rated Townshend as the only guitarist who ever influenced him. This seems highly reductive coming from a player who clearly absorbed a fair share of Chuck Berry and Keith Richards's work, but Townshend's way with a suspended chord is readily detectable in many an AC/DC headbanger.

Some of the Who's seventies heirs are a bit harder to categorize. Elvis Costello and the Police were both lumped in with the punks initially, but no one really bought that, least of all the artists, themselves. Showcasing them with the power-pop groups mentioned above is less of a stretch, and when they've been clearest in their Who fandom—say, Elvis's "Hand in Hand" or the Police's "Born in the 50's"—they were channeling power-pop prototypes "So Sad About Us," "Pictures of Lily," and "Substitute," which Elvis called "a perfect song" in his landmark *NME* interview of August 1977. He was not a fan of the Who's later work, griping that Townshend became "too bright for his own good, too analytical." The Police, however, were more open to bright boy-era Townshend, and his seventies synth work informs such eighties Police classics as "Every Little Thing She Does Is Magic" and "Synchronicity I."

Punk

Nowhere in the seventies was the Who's impact felt more than in the fist of the decade's most exciting musical revolution. Punk was like an entire genre devoted to "My Generation," both its pilled-up sonic attack and its utter disgust for adulthood and affluence. Even as they were unmistakably indebted to the music of the fifties and sixties, many punks professed to loathe any record that wasn't made last week. However, one dinosaur act that almost never took a hit in the gobbing war was the Who, even as their synth-laden seventies records couldn't have sounded less like the punk's revved-up, two-chord filth and fury. Their first few records, however, were veritable punk Rosetta Stones. So profound was the Who's influence on punk that it gets its own chapter in this book. It's the next one, but there are still a few more decades to get through, so be a little patient, buddy.

The Eighties

At the dawn of the MTV decade, image was king. All one needed was an art-deco haircut and a Casio keyboard to get regular rotation on the decade's newest and most influential pop conveyance. The one-finger synthesizer line of Flock of Seagulls' "I Ran" was a long way down the ladder from the complexity of "Baba O'Riley." Yes, the Who's organic brand of rock and pop was less prevalent in the eighties, but as would always be the case, their influence remained.

U2

Bombastic, spiritual, revolutionary, and goaded on by insistent rhythm guitar, U2 was the early eighties' most convincing Who successors even if their essential sounds were very, very different. Drummer Larry Mullen Jr. and bassist Adam Clayton locked together to hammer forth a metronomic beat, something the Who's rhythm section rarely did. Bono's concerns were global, and his tendency toward preachiness diverged from Pete Townshend's "make up your own mind" approach to political subject matter. But the effects were very similar. Too grand to be called punks, U2 made music for arenas, rock 'n' roll to send fists and lighters aloft. They recaptured—and not unconsciously—the spirit of *Who's Next* and *Quadrophenia*, and particularly the triad of singles released between those two albums that found Townshend in a rare state of revolutionary urgency: "Let's See Action," "Join Together," and "Relay." U2 took these rallying cries, gave them greater specificity and topicality, and produced "Sunday Bloody Sunday," "New Year's Day," and "Pride (In the Name of Love)." When the Who were inducted into the Rock and Roll Hall of Fame in 1990, U2 were selected to give the induction speech, in which Bono declared, "More than any other group that ever was, the Who were our role models."

Retro Pop

Pop music and pop culture are forces of the here and now; "pop," of course, being a truncation of "popular." Yet these forms of music also bear deep strains of nostalgia, particularly for that which happened twenty-or-so-years prior when the artists of the current generation were children. In the sixties, this was evident in the "music hall" revival that gave us such items as the Kinks' "Sunny Afternoon," the Beatles' "When I'm 64," and the Rolling Stones' "Something Happened to Me Yesterday," all of which harkened back to Rudy Vallée, Noël Coward, and other stars of the thirties and forties. The seventies saw the fifties revival that resulted in the tremendous popularity of Sha Na Na, *American Graffiti*, *Grease*, and *Happy Days*. In the eighties, renewed interest in the sixties dominated

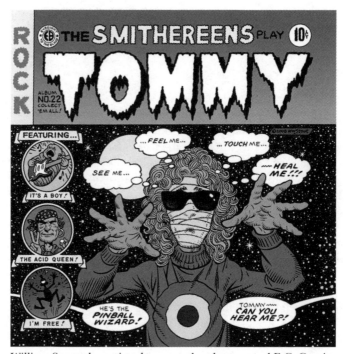

William Stout, the artist who created a phenomenal E.C. Comics parody for the *Tales from the Who* bootleg, created a similar cover for *The Smithereens Play Tommy*.   *Author's collection*

the culture (with a particular focus on the Vietnam War: *China Beach* and *Tour of Duty* on TV; *Full Metal Jacket, Platoon,* and *Casualties of War* in the cinema) and spawned numerous new artists with a decidedly retro sensibility. Because they were so integral to the sixties sound, the Who were a natural influence on Nine Below Zero's sharp mod rock, Television Personalities' lo-fi psychedelia, and R.E.M.'s Rickenbacker jangle (during the 1989 tour, Townshend guessed that if the Who had decided to yank "A Quick One While He's Away" out of mothballs, the younger audience members would mistake it for R.E.M.). New Jersey's Smithereens were one of the decade's most sixties-reverent bands, and in 2009 they paid extended homage to the Who across thirteen tracks of *The Smithereens Play Tommy* (they'd previously bestowed similar honor on the Fab Four when they recorded *Meet the Smithereens!* and *B-Sides The Beatles*).

Guided by Voices

U2 carried the Who's torch into the eighties and became the decade's biggest rock 'n' roll band. Sometime in the middle of the decade, that torch fell into the hands of the unlikeliest successors, a rotating collection of part-time musicians from Dayton, Ohio, masterminded by a fourth-grade teacher named Robert

Pollard (who was in attendance at the tragic Riverfront Coliseum concert of 1979). Driven by a desire to be as prolifically creative as Pete Townshend and as commanding at center stage as Roger Daltrey, Bob led Guided by Voices into the nineties as one of the greatest bands ever to bow down to the Who.

High-jumping, microphone-swinging Robert Pollard has incorporated a tremendous and thrilling array of influences into his music, though Guided by Voices' first release, the *Forever Since Breakfast* EP, is atypically fixated on a single band: R.E.M. However, even on this disc, the Who's influence is fully present, battering out of the tension-ridden "Fountain of Youth." From here, GBV broke from all limitations on influence, composition, and recording, shunning slick studios to make music on four-track cassette recorders (the sound will be comfortingly familiar to those who've enjoyed the homemade ambience of Pete Townshend's *Scoop* demo compilations). With a library of heroes ranging from the Beatles to Sparks to King Crimson, Robert Pollard would sing the praises of no group more often than the Who. "Captain's Dead," "Common Rebels," "Navigating Flood Regions," "Pendulum," "Over the Neptune," "Tractor Rape Chain," "Glow Boy Butlers," and "Closer You Are" are just a small, small sampling of Guided by Voices' most Who-indebted songs. When they finally stepped back into professional recording studios at the turn of the century, they did so in the hopes of making their own *Who's Next*, and yet another crop of Whotastic nuggets came tumbling from the grooves ("Fair Touching," "Christian Animation Torch Carriers," and "Closets of Henry" being some of the most delectable). Pollard also took to littering his career with weird jokey references to his favorite group, naming a gnarly EP track "The Who vs. Porky Pig" and one of his many labels Happy Jock Rock Records in a nod to an early Who hit and his love of sports. Although they released an EP and their first three LPs in the eighties, Guided by Voices would not become more than an eccentric local band until the nineties and the release of their career-making critical favorite *Bee Thousand*. By that time, a new assortment of rock bands had already arrived to adapt the Who's grungy growl for the latest generation.

The Nineties

Because of their aggression and attitude, the Who were revered as punk godfathers in the seventies, but a closer approximation of their actual sound arrived in a flannel-bedecked package throughout the late eighties and dominated the early nineties. Grunge is more mid-paced than high-speed punk. Its guitar chords are thick and resonant, unlike punk's clipped down strokes. Bass and drums roil and singers shout and rail. The production quality is as murky as a Shel Talmy record, and the lyrics are as introspective and self-loathing as *The Who by Numbers*. The movement's biggest and best stars were Nirvana, though that band's clearest link to the Who came through in their acts of onstage carnage, Kurt Cobain upping the ante by actually flinging his body into Dave Grohl's drum kit. Other nineties groups would encode their Who influences onto their CDs more explicitly.

Robert Pollard's passions include the Who and dressing like Merlin.
Author's collection

Pearl Jam

Grunge's most vocal spokesmen for the Who were Pearl Jam, led by the Pete Townshend–worshipping Eddie Vedder. In his profile of the Who in *Rolling Stone* Magazine's "100 Greatest Artists" feature of 2004, Vedder wrote, "What disturbs me about the Who is the way they smashed through every door of rock & roll, leaving rubble and not much else for the rest of us to lay claim to." Eddie Vedder never seemed too concerned about such matters, greedily scooping so much of the Who's rubble into his own music. Vedder shared Townshend's concern with the traumas of youth, which informed Pearl Jam's breakthrough records "Jeremy" (about a boy who commits suicide in class) and the semiautobiographical "Alive" (about sexual abuse and identity confusion). Vedder even identified the latter song as a chapter of "our own little mini-opera," a trilogy of songs about incest and murder he called "Mamasan" (it also incorporated "Once" and "Footsteps"). Pearl Jam have further pledged allegiance to the Who through the frequent covers they've performed in concert, including "Baba O'Riley," "Blue, Red, and Grey," "I'm One," "The Seeker," "My Generation," and "The Kids Are Alright."

Green Day

"I love the Who," Billie Joe Armstrong told *Spin* magazine in 2009. Well, duh. By that point, his band, Green Day, had released a cover of "My Generation" as a bonus track on their sophomore album, *Kerplunk*; had their breakthrough hit with "Longview," a bubblegum-punk ode to the Townshend-esque topics of teen frustration and masturbation with a bouncy Entwistle-esque bass line; and released not one but two rock operas, *American Idiot* and *21st Century Breakdown*. The main character of *Idiot* is one St. Jimmy, the name itself implying Tommy Walker's messianic rise and explicitly recycling the name of *Quadrophenia*'s protagonist. Green Day's first maxi-opera also included *two* multisectional mini-operas: "Jesus of Suburbia" and "Homecoming," which ends with a vamping refrain of "We're coming home again," fusing the final two sections of "A Quick One While He's Away" (a cover of which is included as an iTunes-only bonus track on *Breakdown*). Yes, Green Day, we know that you love the Who.

Alternative Rock

The grunge scene only dominated the nineties rock scene for a few years before its gray-toned sludge melded with the weedy indie scene to expand into a more eclectic, more colorful movement the media dubbed "alternative rock." This was essentially a catchall term for any band that didn't play hair rock or metal (a scene that had its own links to the Who, but almost exclusively limited to the heavy *Live at Leeds*). "Alternative" could mean anything from grunge to indie to hippie-ish jam bands to nouveau power pop to punk to new-wave godfathers such as Iggy Pop and Elvis Costello to the more angular, arty groups that followed in the footsteps of the eighties college bands the Pixies and Throwing Muses. One such band was the Breeders, a group that had direct links to both of these New England groups (leader Kim Deal was a founding Pixie and guitarist Tanya Donelly was a Muse). The Breeders' biggest claim to fame was the post-Donelly "Cannonball," a record that sounds like someone stacked up discs by the Jesus Lizard, the Beach Boys, and Bootsy Collins, smashed them with a sledgehammer, and pasted them back together willy-nilly. At their less avant garde, the Breeders revealed a reverence for sixties power pop, particularly that of the Who, which shines through in their joyous cover of "So Sad About Us," as well as the stormy originals "Divine Hammer" and "Overglazed." Elsewhere, the Alternative Nation gave us such disparate Who-influenced groups as Sloan, the glorious Canadian power-poppers whose "Anyone Who's Anyone" recreates the bouncy march of "Armenia City in the Sky"; Cincinnati's Afghan Whigs, mighty melders of angsty grunge, seventies soul, and *Quadrophenia*-era bombast and conceptualism (check out "Summer's Kiss" on *Black Love*, which singer Greg Dulli acknowledged as a Who homage); Japan's Puffy, who appropriated a "Won't Get Fooled Again"-style organ line for "Jet Keisatsu"; and Vermont's jammy hippies, Phish, whose lightweight sound recalls none of the Who's heft and depth, but revered the group enough to cover *Quadrophenia* in its entirety during their Halloween concert of 1995.

Britpop

Perhaps no postsixties movement has been more directly indebted to the Who than nineties Britpop, yet this has often been more a matter of image than sound. While Blur picked up on the collegiate look of mod-era Who and Oasis would appropriate the Union Jack insignias of their pop art phase, these bands didn't necessarily sound much like the Who, Blur sounding more like the Kinks and Oasis favoring the Beatles. Britpop's two leaders did have their moments (Blur's "It Could Be You" has a bit of a "Happy Jack" feel; Oasis's "I Hope I Think I Know" is built on a bedrock of Who bedlam), but to suggest either group was overly indebted to the Who would be wrong even as there are some strong, direct links between them and the topic of this book. Blur's anthemic "Parklife" features a lead oration from *Quadrophenia* star Phil Daniels. Zak Starkey split duties between Oasis and the Who for a while. Representatives of both bands have sung the Who's praises enthusiastically in interviews. Elsewhere in the Britpop pantheon, Who-esque tracks such as the Stone Roses' "This Is the One," the La's "I Can't Sleep," and Supergrass's "Sun Hits the Sky" speak for themselves.

The Twenty-First Century

The century that birthed rock 'n' roll ended, and a new digital era dawned. Bye-bye vinyl. Bye-bye compact disc. Here comes the MP3, the FLAC, the WAV, and a variety of other intangible ways of collecting music (thankfully, proponents of the LP and the CD wouldn't disappear completely). Digital recording has also made expensive studio time virtually unnecessary. Some home computers even come with the good-quality home-recording program GarageBand already installed, offering a variety of public-domain loops that make the challenge of finding a competent drummer or keyboardist a thing of the Stone Age. Tone-deaf, would-be singers get a leg up with Auto-Tune, and young people just need to flounce around with a guitar-shaped hunk of plastic while playing Guitar Hero or Rock Band to work their musical ambitions out of their systems. American public schools became more and more obsessed with boosting the English and math skills necessary to perform well on standardized tests, thus helping them get the funding they need to survive. Consequently, school music programs were often casualties. Rock 'n' roll seems to have become a casualty, too, with BBC news reporting how, in 2010, the genre made its worst showing in the charts since 1960.

The Who's influence has been tougher to kill.

Rock 'n' Roll

We have seen the fruits of twenty-first century technological "advances" in the pop music scene. Instrument-dependent rock 'n' roll is a dying art. There has been a fair share of new rock artists, but none have made the seismic impact of such generation-definers as Elvis Presley, the Beatles, the Sex Pistols, U2, or Nirvana. By the end of the 2010s, guitar-based music had all but vanished from the charts, allowing hip-hop artists and teen pop antiartists to become the most popular purveyors of pop music.

Relegated to the back row, rock bands have become more self-conscious than ever, relying on the tropes of old to make their fealty to a dying religion as clear as possible. Those who've remained true to real guitars and real drums regularly bow down to the old gods, which means the Who most definitely have not been forgotten. Sweden's Soundtrack of Our Lives may be the greatest cover band to ever play original material, unapologetically appropriating such past idols as Pink Floyd, the Rolling Stones, the Stooges, Love, Procol Harum, and the Who to make rock 'n' roll instantly recognizable in both sound and sight. Guitarist Mattias Barjed slipped into a Union Jack jacket for the music video advertising the awesome "Sister Surround." The even more defiantly retro Len Price 3 essentially rerecorded "Substitute" and called it "Rentacrowd." The Raconteurs—featuring the twenty-first century's most authentic bid for a real rock star, Jack White—hooked up with Pete Townshend to jam a version of "The Seeker" widely circulated on YouTube. Elsewhere, the Who's influence could be felt in the Mary Timony Band's bone-breaking rumble and Arcade Fire's impenitent pomp.

As for music you might not actually want to hear, there's the ironically titled "Best Song Ever" by the teeny-bop quintet One Direction, which shamelessly gobbles up "Baba O'Riley" and farts it back out again. When millions of tiny One Direction fans learned that a band called the Who once recorded a song with an intro nearly identical to their favorite tune, they became convinced the old geezers might deprive them of literally the best song ever. These not-quite-alright kids rushed to the home of ignorant opinions expressed ignorantly, flooding Twitter with comments like "never even heard of the who like who r they?," "The Who is just jealous of 1D bc they won't become as legendary as them," and "50+ million girls gonna attack you, The Who." In a petrified effort to stave off that murderous onslaught of 50+ million girls, Pete Townshend quickly issued a statement in which he confirmed that the Who had no intention of putting the kibosh on "Best Song Ever" and that he likes both the song and One Direction but is "relieved they're all not wearing boiler suits and Doc Martens, or Union Jack jackets." If nothing else, this bizarre episode proves that rock 'n' roll may be dying, but as long as there's a breath left in its nicotine-stained esophagus, it will continue exhaling the Who.

Samples

When rock 'n' roll dies for good, when it goes as deep underground as Pete Townshend predicted it would in *Lifehouse*, will the Who be gone for good? There is quite a lot of evidence to the contrary, first heralded way back in 1991 by Big Audio Dynamite, an all-genre-encompassing group founded by Mick Jones of the Clash. Their hit single "Rush" is built on synthesizer sampled from "Baba O Riley." The greater acceptance of sampling also saw Who snippets being swiped by the genre-jumping club band Pop Will Eat Itself ("Dance of the Mad Bastards" bites a bit of "Helpless Dancer"), rappers 3rd Bass ("Eminence Front" pops up in "Pop Goes the Weasel"), and hip-hop duo Downtown Science (ditto "This Is a Visit") in the early nineties.

In the twenty-first century, Who samples have exploded over a vast variety of sound collages by DJs, hip-hop, rap, and house artists. They've particularly favored the sci-fi keyboards of "Baba O'Riley" ("The Road Goes On Forever" by High Contrast, "Baba O Riley" by Cube Guys, "Dream Big" by Blueprint, who recorded an entire EP tribute called *Blueprint Who*) and "Won't Get Fooled Again" ("1,000 Whispers" by Illogic, "Never Fooled" by Mantis, "Pain" by Blueprint). Snatches of the Who could also be heard in "The Bad, the Sad, & the Hated" by Lil Wayne and DJ Cinema (utilizing "Behind Blue Eyes"), "See Me" by Herve (the *Woodstock* version of "See Me, Feel Me"), "Downloading" by Negativland ("Pure and Easy"), "Orgull Pastoril" by Herois De La Katalunya Interior ("I Can't Explain"), and "The Song Is Over" by Ayatollah (you can figure this one out on your own). Is this rock 'n' roll? Perhaps not, but it is strong evidence that the Who will continue to adapt to music as it evolves, devolves, and revolves throughout the new century.

25

The Punks and the Godfathers

The Who as Punk Pioneers

No Beatles, Elvis, or the Rolling Stones in 1977!" tolled the town criers of a new form of music ripe to rattle the old guard's cages. When the Clash sneered this statement, they failed to mention one of rock's other elder statesmen. That's because the punk revolution did not seek to overthrow the Who. After all, the Who were their forefathers.

Were the Who really a punk band? When the new movement had its heyday in 1977, there sure wasn't much about the Who's music anyone could call punky. In fact, that year Pete Townshend recorded and released *Rough Mix*, his most placid selection of music to date. The album even included a country-time parody of Johnny Rotten called "Misunderstood" (many have "mistakenly" assumed Townshend himself was the song's misunderstood character). The wealthy and synthesizer-dependent Who of the late seventies sounded nothing like the Clash or the Ramones, but the guys still had a lot of currency in the punk bank from their rabid and raw early days. The Who that defiantly destroyed their expensive equipment while barking about their generation were key punk role models.

In truth, their music wasn't a perfect punk predecessor. Most punks traveled at high speeds. The Who tended to move at mid-tempo. The punks generally kept the musicianship simple. John Entwistle and Keith Moon were notorious show-offs. But the essence of punk has more to do with attitude than execution. The early Who's combativeness, disparaging humor, contempt for the older generation, and hope for early death was as punk as Joe Strummer's Mohawk. Appropriately, when punks selected Who songs to cover, they tended to steer clear of anything recorded later than 1966.

Unlike some other classic rockers who recognized punk as a threat, the Who were more open to their deranged spawn even as they never incorporated those violent sounds in their current music. That may have been a mistake, since youthful fire was painfully lacking in *Who Are You* and *Face Dances*. Townshend's punkish solo tracks "Rough Boys" and "Jools and Jim" (from an album he dedicated in part to the Sex Pistols) absolutely annihilated all of the Who's rockers from that period. Other artists without the Who's punk pedigree managed to make such reasonable facsimiles as "Respectable" (the Rolling Stones), "Wearing and Tearing" (Led Zeppelin), and "Spin It On" (Paul McCartney and Wings). The Who were content to settle for their status as punk progenitors. These are some of their progeny.

The Sex Pistols

The Sex Pistols were not the first punk band, but they were the one that hooked the movement for the media. Their splashy appearance on London's *Today* show on December 1, 1976—you know, the one where thick-skulled host Bill Grundy goaded Steve Jones into calling him a "fucking rotter" on live TV—ensured the Pistols' place as public enemy number one. While Jones can lay claim to that particular faux pas, Johnny "Rotten" Lydon was the band's face and spokesman, and his disgust for rock's old guard is legendary. Future Clash manager Bernie Rhodes discovered Lydon bopping down the King's Road wearing his famous "I Hate Pink Floyd" T-shirt (in truth, Lydon was so gaga over the Floyd that he named his hamster—and renamed his best buddy—"Sid" after Syd Barrett). Another well-traveled yarn informs us that Lydon booted bassist Glen Matlock from the Pistols for being a Beatles fan. Actually, the two guys simply didn't get along, and when EMI offered Matlock the opportunity to make his own music with his own band, he escaped to put together the Rich Kids, a band that better showcased Matlock's adoration of British pop forefathers like the Beatles and the Who than the Sex Pistols did.

Lydon never had to feel embarrassed about his love for the Who. They had an anarchic and violent enough reputation to serve as a proper influence on the improper Sex Pistols. "Substitute" was a regularly featured cover in their live sets. Chris Thomas, who produced *Never Mind the Bollocks, Here's the Sex Pistols* (and mixed Pink Floyd's *Dark Side of the Moon!*) said the album sounded more like the Who than the more archetypically punk Ramones. This was a valid statement, as *Bollocks* is heavier, slower, less concise, and more polished than the records usually associated with punk.

The Sex Pistols' role in Who history runs deeper than matters of mere appreciation and influence. Most famously, Steve Jones and Paul Cook were present on the night Pete Townshend was inspired to write "Who Are You." Townshend was disgusted that he had to suffer through a fourteen-hour meeting moderated by the disagreeable Allen Klein just to get some delinquent royalties from publishing partner David Platz. After the ordeal, Townshend and Chris Stamp retired to the Speakeasy to drown their sorrows. There they encountered Jones and Cook (whom Townshend thought was Johnny Lydon). All worked up, Townshend railed about the money-grubbing record industry, ripped up the check for which he'd wasted the entire day negotiating, and praised punk Cook and his ilk for washing away warhorses such as himself. Cook was crestfallen, fearing that Townshend's ranting meant the Who, his favorite band, was breaking up.

Of course, the Who didn't break up, and soon threw themselves into work on a big-screen adaptation of *Quadrophenia.* The film is both a period piece looking back on the mods vs. rockers clashes of the early sixties and a very relevant reflection of the contemporary state of England. Grim, gritty, and despairing, *Quadrophenia* is a perfect snapshot of late seventies Britain's flailing economy, violent tensions, and classism, which left punks like Johnny Lydon feeling like they had "no future." Lydon was director Franc Roddam's first choice to play Jimmy the Mod in the film. He even auditioned for the part in the summer of 1978, after which Townshend took him and Roddam for a drunken joyride. Roddam says the film's distributor put the kibosh on the plan because it didn't want to insure the little menace with the bad reputation. There were no hard feelings, though. Lydon even gave Roddam a T-shirt Sid Vicious once puked on to say, "thanks for everything."

The Clash

Johnny Lydon's plans to work in their camp were abortive, but the Who did manage to score some genuine punk cred when they invited the Clash to tour with them in 1982. Three years earlier, the band played at a Rock Against Racism benefit gig Pete Townshend organized. Townshend loved the subversion of a group who could sneak an anticapitalist message into a tune as catchy as "Clampdown" and get it played on the radio. The Clash were not as noisy or plodding as the Sex Pistols. Joe Strummer and Mick Jones knew the value of disseminating their revolutionary viewpoint in tunes you could hum. The Who were a key influence on that tunefulness and the hard-hitting rhythms beneath the melodies. Nicky "Topper" Headon credits Keith Moon with inspiring him to play the drums, and Paul Simonon says Pete Townshend was his guitar hero before he moved to bass in the Clash. The guys would unwind to *The Who Sell Out* during rehearsals, though Mick Jones says that regularly rotating that very album may have inspired the Clash's most famous antirock institution statement. The song "1977" imagines a year without the Beatles, Elvis, or the Rolling Stones (they'd get their wish, as '77 produced no new studio product from the Stones and saw the end of Presley. The Beatles had been broken up for years, so no worries there). The Who escaped Strummer and Jones's wrath, while another band of oldsters, the Kinks, inspired the records' power-chording riff. The riff that gets "Clash City Rockers" going, however, is pure Who.

Townshend actually seemed to get off on the idea of punks wishing him into the cornfield, so maybe he would have preferred it if the Clash lumped the Who in with the other oldsters dispatched in "1977." Nevertheless, he struck up an association with the band and continued digging their music into the eighties. Townshend says he copped his early-eighties stage look and dance moves from Strummer, Jones, and Simonon, and in a typically magnanimous move, funded Headon's stint at an LA clinic where he underwent the "electric box" treatment to help him kick heroin. The Clash returned that respect to Townshend, who was always up for a bit of goofing around backstage on tour. Paul Simonon, however, said that Daltrey and Entwistle were "miserable gits" who "wouldn't talk to us" in the Clash's 2008 oral history.

The Damned

With a reputation that wasn't as threatening as the Sex Pistols' or as righteous as the Clash's, the Damned have often been dismissed as the least potent of England's original punk bands. Bollocks to that. The Damned just didn't put on airs. They had no self-conscious aversion to being called "punks," as so many of the movement's original bands did. They weren't afraid to write funny songs or act silly on- and offstage. They were destructive and reveled in antagonizing their audiences. They sang about monsters and the joys and frustrations of being young, and on occasion, they even sneaked some righteously blunt political statements into their songs. They said "sod it" to the dogmatic austerity of punk and recorded a gloriously pretentious, seventeen-minute magnum opus called "Curtain Call." They could also really play, drummer Rat Scabies being a madman who sounded like he was battering his kit with as many limbs as an

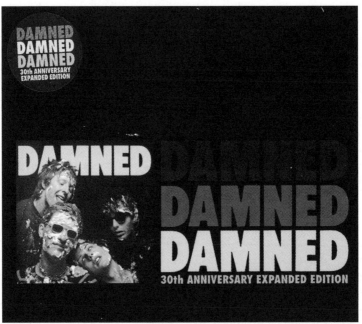

The thirtieth anniversary edition of the Damned's blistering debut album contains a hyper—and totally out of tune—version of the Who's "Circles" recorded at London's 100 Club on July 6, 1976. Will Rippingale captured the performance on a shitty Sony cassette recorder. He later cofounded the wacky pop group I, Ludicrous.   *Author's collection*

octopus. Destructive, funny, youthful, pretentious, revolutionary, and housing one of rock's greatest, wildest drummers. Sound like any other band to you?

The Damned love the Who. Scabies was a big Keith Moon fan, which should be obvious to anyone who's heard him play. Bassist/guitarist/keyboardist/singer/songwriter/all-around outrageous bloke Captain Sensible has often praised the Who among the other garage and psychedelic groups that profoundly affected the Damned. The band was known to mangle "Circles" in their early sets, and when they went in a more pop/Goth direction in the mid-eighties, they recorded a bouncy number called "Grimly Fiendish" that directly appropriates the falsetto "love, love, love long" passage from "Our Love Was." The Who's instrument smashing was also instrumental in winning the Damned's dirty little hearts, and when the Captain wrecked his malfunctioning organ and Ratty trashed his kit during a 1979 appearance on *The Old Grey Whistle Test*, host Annie Nightingale observed that the studio was "haunted by the Who."

The Jam

The Who had a sweeping influence on punk, but one band so completely patterned themselves after the bruisers that some critics would have you believe the Jam were a Who cover band. Yes, they were a combative three-piece band with a punchy, three-letter name. They donned sharp mod suits—and the occasional Union Jack jacket—and appropriated target and arrow imagery. They sang about "Numbers," had original songs called "I Need You" and "In the City," and covered "Disguises," "So Sad About Us" (released as a single with a photo of Keith Moon on the sleeve), and the Who's arrangements of "Batman" and "Heatwave." Paul Weller could be as prickly in interviews as his hero, Pete Townshend. All that being said, the Jam never really sounded much like the Who. They delivered everything on their debut album, *In the City*, at breakneck speeds the Who never attempted. The Jam's musicianship was strong, but only Weller seemed overly influenced by the band, mimicking Pete Townshend whenever he fired off a sudden slash chord, streaked his pick down the strings of his Rickenbacker, or flicked its pickup on and off to elicit Morse-code beeps. His deadpan Cockney vocal, however, was nothing like Roger Daltrey's bluesy bellow. Bruce Foxton played bass with a downstroke simplicity unrelated to John Entwistle's wild excursions. Rick Buckler was not against a big, mad drum fill, but he generally stuck to driving the beat with a straightforwardness alien to Keith Moon.

That the Jam were Who clones is highly questionable. That they were fans is undeniable. Pete Townshend returned his admiration, and the two struck up a tentative association, even though Weller told *Rolling Stone* in 2012 that they had "fuck-all in common, absolutely zero . . . Pete's an intellectual, you know, and I most definitely ain't."

Just as the Who had a positive influence on the Jam, the late-seventies mod revival the Jam sparked in England drew additional attention to *Quadrophenia*. Mod revivalists could often be spotted with the two bands' names buttoned to their parkas. Two decades later, Weller would appear onstage with Pete Townshend for a lovely, acoustic duet of "So Sad About Us" during the Who's 2000 Teenage Cancer Trust benefit at the Royal Albert Hall.

Generation X

Generation X was another band that longed for the days when mods roamed the earth and rushed home every Friday night to groove along with *Ready Steady Go!* That TV show was the subject of their best-remembered song, which contradicts the Clash's "1977" with a litany of love for the Beatles, the Stones, and "Bobby Dylan." Among the name-checked are the Who, whom singer Billy Idol mentions with a near-mumbled reference to the *Ready Steady Who* EP. Like a pop-punk "Long Live Rock," "Ready Steady Go" is a humorous, awestruck (though far less bittersweet) look back on rock 'n' roll history. Less reverent was the group's debut single. "Your Generation" was a pointed response to Generation X's former heroes in 1978, who'd failed to die before they got old and now needed to clear the way for the more youthful crew. "There ain't no time for substitutes / There ain't no time for idle threats," sang Billy Idol in

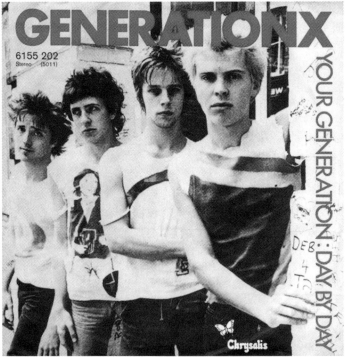

Billy Idol made rock 'n' roll for his own generation with Generation X.

Author's collection

reference to another early Who hit. Like Roger Daltrey, Gen X's lead singer was a diminutive yet buff blond who became one of the key rock 'n' roll sex symbols of his era. Two decades after Generation X snarled their disapproval in "Your Generation" and paid their respects in "Ready Steady Go," the Who invited Idol to their all-star *Tommy* concert at Los Angeles' Universal Amphitheater. He did a convincing job as punky thug Cousin Kevin, tossing in some choice expletive-laden improvisations to make the character that much less savory.

Buzzcocks

Perhaps the poppiest clan to vibrate out of the United Kingdom's first punk wave, Buzzcocks were rabble-rousers for the romantics. Less political than most of their young countrymen, Buzzcocks shared Pete Townshend's fascination with growing pains and sexual identity. Their breakthrough single "Orgasm Addict," a sweaty statement of wankery, dealt with one of Townshend's pet topics but in a graphic way that wouldn't have been permissible in 1967. Though the group wasn't as self-conscious in their Who fandom as someone like Paul Weller, they often found themselves unconsciously drifting back to that influence, as when guitarist Steve Diggle would toss off an impromptu windmill while thwacking his axe. The admiration apparently went both ways as Roger Daltrey took part in an all-star charity cover of the Buzzcocks' classic "Ever Fallen in Love (With Someone You Shouldn't've)" for Amnesty International in 2005.

Siouxsie and the Banshees

Dark, abrasive, and haunting, Siouxsie and the Banshees are best known as originators of Goth style and sounds, but the band arose from the same scene that produced the Clash, the Damned, and the Pistols. Siouxsie Sioux can be seen hovering over Paul Cook in that infamous appearance on Bill Grundy's *Today* show. The Banshees' first gig found Sid Vicious perched on the drum stool to thrash out an endless jam on "The Lord's Prayer." Siouxsie and the Banshees made several exquisite albums, including the icy and foreboding *Hyaena*, recorded at Pete's Eel Pie studios. The group also did some postproduction work on their live album *Nocturne* at Eel Pie, and during one session, Siouxsie slammed her finger in a heavy studio door and had to get stitches. "Pete was a very sweet man. He sent me flowers, and I think he even got the doors changed soon afterwards," she said in *Siouxsie & the Banshees—The Authorised Biography*.

Townshend was also a big fan of Siouxsie's music, though she and the Banshees have less in common with the Who than any other band in this chapter. Roger Daltrey, however, believes they share a strong link to at least one member of his band. Talking to *Goldmine* in 1994, he insisted, "Siouxsie and the Banshees made a whole career out of [John Entwistle's] *Smash Your Head Against the Wall*. Listen to the melodic form of that music. Exactly the same as Siouxsie and the Banshees 10 years later." True that both the Banshees and Entwistle shared a dark sensibility, and the Banshees' early records have some of the murky alchemy of *Smash Your Head*, but Rog was still overreaching.

The Pretenders

Bridging the divide between UK and US punk, the Pretenders may seem a bit too refined, a bit too poppy, to qualify as the real raw deal. However, Ohio-born Chrissie Hynde's punk credentials are pretty solid. She was a fixture at Malcolm McLaren and Vivienne Westwood's SEX boutique on the King's Road. She played with members of the Clash and the Damned during her brief stint in a group called London SS, and briefly screwed around in Masters of the Backside, a McLaren-masterminded combo with Rat Scabies, Captain Sensible, and Brian James. When Hynde left the group, which she wanted to call Mike Hunt's Honourable Discharge, singer Dave Vanian took her place and the Damned was born.

A couple of years later, Hynde hooked up with three natural-born Brits to form the Pretenders. Their debut single, "The Wait," is as rough and ready as any significant punk debut, though they'd slap a dash of polish on the number when rerecording it for their eponymous debut LP. Some of the grit had flaked off the band's sound, but *The Pretenders* is still one of the most exciting artifacts of the era, "The Wait," "Precious," and "Tattooed Love Boys" being particularly ferocious.

Such tracks impressed Pete Townshend, who gushed to *Rolling Stone* about how Hynde's lyrics were "full of the most brutal, head-on feminism that has ever come out of any band, anywhere!" A diehard British Invasion fanatic who was even involved in a stormy relationship with Ray Davies, Hynde found herself sharing a stage with her forefathers more than once. The Pretenders were opening for the Who as early as 1980, when they both contributed their talents to the Kampuchea benefit (see chapter 33). Pete and Chrissie performed together at a 1986 benefit for victims of a Colombian volcano eruption, which resulted in a live double album called *David Gilmour, Pete Townshend, Chrissie Hynde, & Friends* the following year. Twenty years later, the Pretenders supported the Who on a seventeen-date US tour.

Patti Smith

Now we cross the ocean completely to a place where punk did not stick to the dogmatic rules of its UK counterpart. In America, the term "punk" was so elastic that the jammy Television, the poppy Blondie, and the collegiate art rockers Talking Heads were all considered punks just because they were regulars at CBGB, Manhattan's fetid cauldron that conjured the American punk scene. One of its unlikeliest products was Patti Smith, a Rimbaud-obsessed poet whose songs were as likely to be epic and ethereal as short, sharp, and shocking. Smith remains a major punk icon for her gutter imagery, her ravaged voice, and her uncompromising rejection of anything approaching the popular music of her time. When *Horses* appeared in 1975, a year before punk's official arrival, it was a completely radical alternative to the lukewarm pop polluting the airwaves. When its opening cut, a stream-of-consciousness reworking of Van Morrison's "Gloria," was pulled for a single, an out-of-control live version of "My Generation" sat on the B-side.

Smith seems to have drawn inspiration from the Who beyond that cover. She shares Pete Townshend's reverence for rock 'n' roll, his poeticism, his pretensions, his prickliness, and his penchant for spiritual seeking. She is no all-forgiving fan, famously asking, "How can somebody like Townshend follow Meher Baba and be such a miserable bastard?" (as quoted by the miserable bastard himself in a 1978 interview with the *NME*). On March 2, 2010, she confirmed her love for the old curmudgeon when she gave a rip-snorting rendition of "My Generation" at the "Music of the Who" benefit concert at Carnegie Hall.

Richard Hell and the Voidoids

Like Patti Smith, Richard Hell was a CBGB-bred punk poet. An original member of Television, Hell branched off to front his own band, the Voidoids. Their anthem—and one of the major anthems of American punk—was "Blank Generation." With a chord progression nicked from Ray Charles's "Hit the Road Jack" and a message ripe for multiple interpretations (was Hell expressing nihilism? Was he inciting seventies youths to fill in the "blanks" with their own personal positions?), the song was a direct descendant of the Who's anthem for their generation. Hell has said that his obsession with the Who's debut album inspired him to write his very own "My Generation."

The Ramones

So you want to know the precise moment punk dropped its giant Converse All-Star on America? That, my friend, would be April 23, 1976, the day *Ramones* hit record stores like an A-bomb. This was the purest sound of punk imaginable: minute-and-a-half blasts of high-velocity adrenaline played with an utter absence of frills. No drum solos; no guitar solos. Sometimes there wasn't even anything more than a chorus repeated over and over. Quite a contrast to the Who, yet both bands were similar in their extreme intensity and their four distinct and often clashing personalities. The Ramones only covered "Substitute" (with backing vocals by Pete Townshend), which appeared on their psych tribute album *Acid Eaters*, but one could easily imagine them putting their personal stamp on "I Can't Explain," "Anyway, Anyhow, Anywhere," "Out in the Street," or "My Generation" (the idea of bassist Dee Dee Ramone attempting John Entwistle's solo, however, is laughable). Joey Ramone and Pete Townshend also shared more than a microphone on that version of "Substitute": they were both born on May 19. Draw whatever conclusions about that you want to.

Blondie

Plenty of Mohawk sporters feel uncomfortable filing a band as poppy and popular as Blondie in the punk drawer. They did the most un-punk thing imaginable when they had a number one hit with a disco song (albeit an awesome one). But because Blondie did their time at CBGB, journalists treated them as punks, even quaking in their loafers when faced with having to interview petite Debbie Harry. Terrifying! The frontwoman was not overly intoxicated with the Who, coolly resisting the advances of Keith Moon and Roger Daltrey, who had fantasies of shagging the Marilyn Monroe look-alike when she visited them backstage at their Madison Square Garden gig on June 14, 1974. Clem Burke was clearer in his Who worship, which is evident in his mighty, Moony drumming. Two nights after Moon died, Burke was so broken up that he broke up his kit at the Hammersmith Odeon in honor of his fallen idol. Since no one would lend him the axe and gasoline he wanted to use on his drums, Burke had to settle for the old-fashioned two-hands/two-feet method, chucking the pieces into the audience with the heartfelt declaration, "That's for Keith Moon."

Hüsker Dü

The poppy punk of the seventies transformed into to the faster, harder, more uncompromising sounds of hardcore in the eighties. While American punk was largely localized in New York City in the seventies, eighties hardcore was mostly stewed in South California. It soon spread across the country, reaching Saint Paul, Minnesota, home of Hüsker Dü. The murderous, light-speed thrash of Hüsker Dü's early records soon gave way to a more melodic sound that gave away singer/guitarist Bob Mould's obsession with Pete Townshend. In his autobiography, *See a Little Light: The Trail of Rage and Melody,* Mould wrote that he revered Townshend for his "ability to communicate what others feel but cannot fully express." He'd even craft his own highly influential rock opera in 1984. Like *Tommy* and *Quadrophenia, Zen Arcade* is a tale of a youth with a dysfunctional home life who embarks on a quest of self-discovery. When Hüsker Dü dissolved amidst personal turmoil in the late eighties, Mould formed the poppier Sugar, a group known to whip out "Armenia City in the Sky" in concert.

Mould received the thrill of ten lifetimes on March 4, 1996, during a solo show at Manhattan's Academy. Just as he was about to stride onstage to play the requisite encore, a stagehand gave Mould some big news: Pete Townshend was in the house and wanted to meet him. After finishing his set, Mould met Townshend, who told the former Sugarman he was "a big fan." The meeting led to Townshend inviting Mould to support him for a couple of gigs at the Supper Club later that year.

Minutemen

Like Hüsker Dü , San Pedro's Minutemen were one of the more eclectic punk groups to rise out of the hardcore movement. D. Boon, Mike Watt, and George Hurley broke from hardcore dogmatism to work such unthinkable elements as funk, jazz, and psychedelia into their freewheeling brew. One of their favorite items of the latter genre was *The Who Sell Out*. Boon and Watt loved to listen to the record together. Its adventurousness inspired them to take a similar tack with their own band.

On December 22, 1985, Minutemen suffered a devastating tragedy when D. Boon died in an auto accident. Mike Watt lost a bandmate and, more significantly, a friend. The bass player never forgot those times he and Boon spent digging *Sell Out*, and two decades after the accident, he masterminded what may be the strangest Who tribute on disc. Watt approached his friend, singer/violinist Petra Haden (formerly of That Dog), about putting her talents to work on an all a cappella remake of *Sell Out*. She was not familiar with the record, but Watt furnished her with a cassette of it and a Tascam eight-track recorder. He then left Haden to interpret the album at her own caprice, singing along to the vocals, the guitars, the bass, the drums, the—well, everything—on the original album, which she then wiped from the tape, leaving just her angelic tapestry of vocals. Watt was delighted with the results, and *Petra Haden Sings: The Who Sell Out* was released on Bar/None records to much acclaim in early 2005. Among its admirers was Pete Townshend, who told the *Boston Globe* that hearing the album was better than winning a Grammy.

PETRA HADEN SINGS: THE WHO SELL OUT
Petra Haden no longer sweats the small stuff since she's discovered the sweet smell of success. Petra faces the music under-armed with Odorono, the all-day deodorant that turns perspiration into inspiration.

PETRA HADEN SINGS: THE WHO SELL OUT
Saucy Petra cops a bean-there, done-that attitude. Her star shines with Heinz, and so can yours. Do like Petra and get baked.

Petra Haden's remake of *The Who Sell Out* extended to the iconic album cover. Pete Townshend counted himself among this quirky and lovely disc's fans. *Author's collection*

26

There's a Rock 'n' Roll Singer on the Television

The Who on TV

olorful, dynamic, action-packed, and very, very fashionable, the Who were the perfect band to stand out on TV. Their bold look and stage act jumped from small screens in a way that seemed specifically designed to reach living room audiences. So it's no surprise that they maintained such a regular presence on the tube, even considering starring in their own series in the mid-sixties (see chapter 16).

When the Who ceased to be for all intents and purposes in the eighties, they continued to be a regular presence on TV through the use of their music in weekly dramas and sitcoms. By the turn of the twenty-first century, the Who were popping up on the telly in ever more unexpected ways.

Important Band Appearances

Before they became TV soundtrack fixtures, before Roger Daltrey became a TV star in his own right, the Who shot numerous personal appearances for teen music programs, chat shows, variety shows, and one-off specials. Here's a handful of the most unmissable ones.

Ready Steady Go! (1965–1966)

"The Weekend Starts Here!" A bold statement, but ITV's *Ready Steady Go!* delivered on its tagline by spotlighting the hippest new bands presented by the hippest host on television, mod goddess Cathy McGowan. While getting ready to go out and rave after five dreary schooldays, British kids could rev their engines watching the Beatles, the Rolling Stones, the Kinks, Small Faces, the Yardbirds, and Manfred Mann (who provided the theme tune, "5-4-3-2-1") and other hometown acts, as well as American soul stars such as Otis Redding, James Brown, Marvin Gaye, the Supremes, and the Temptations.

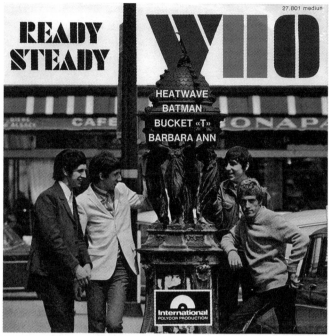

The French received an altered version of the *Ready Steady Who* EP.
Courtesy of the Rob Abramowicz Collection, digitized by Jeffrey Uleau

Ready Steady Go! had some stellar acts, but none were so closely associated with the program as the Who. Other artists appeared on it more often, but they'd all gotten their careers started a year or two before the Who. After Cathy McGowan caught them at the Harrow Technical College Christmas Dance on December 12, 1964, Lambert and Stamp invited producer Vicki Wickham and director Michael Lindsay-Hogg to a show at the Marquee that resulted in the Who being booked on *Ready Steady Go!* an impressive sixteen times over the program's final two years.

Unlike other pop shows of the time (*Top of the Pops, Thank Your Lucky Stars*), *Ready Steady Go!* took teen music very seriously. Relative youngsters McGowan, Wickham, and Lindsay-Hogg selected artists they personally liked. Not that the show lacked fun. *Ready Steady Go!* often provided brooding beatsters such as the Stones opportunities to let their hair down even further and get silly in ways they never would while sneering through "Satisfaction." During one priceless 1965 appearance, Brian Jones and Cathy mimed along to "I Got You Babe" as Charlie Watts planted flowers in Keith Richards's sousaphone.

This irreverence extended to how Lindsay-Hogg filmed the show. For the Who's July 2, 1965, appearance (taped the day before), he went bonkers, vibrating the camera wildly during the instrumental freak-out of "Anyway, Anyhow, Anywhere," zooming in on Keith Moon's target shirt during "Shout and Shimmy," capturing the guys in tight close-ups and from intimidating low angles, zipping in time to the raucous music with fast cuts, never shying away from Pete Townshend's nose or Roger Daltrey's zits as less honest music programs often would. It is hard to imagine anything more exciting on television in mid-1965.

This and their subsequent performance of "Shout and Shimmy" apparently constitute the only surviving footage of the Who on *Ready Steady Go!*, which is particularly tragic considering the enticingly odd nature of the Who's other appearances. On August 6, 1965, they appeared as a trio because Daltrey was recouping from glandular fever. On December 17, 1965, Moon took part in a silly Christmas pantomime based on "Cinderella." The October 18, 1966, "Ready Steady Who" special featured that rarest of occurrences: Entwistle smashing one of his precious bass guitars (a Hofner violin bass previously owned by Paul McCartney, no less). They regularly dug beyond their latest singles to feature such oddities as the Everly Brothers' "Love Hurts" (November 19, 1965), "Jingle Bells" (taped December 17, 1965, for the Christmas Eve show), Dion's "Runaround Sue" and their own risqué obscurity "Instant Party Mixture" (January 28, 1966), and Johnny Kidd and the Pirates' "Please Don't Touch" (taped December 16, 1966). That last performance was broadcast a week later during the show's final episode, *Ready Steady Goes!* The weekend ended there, but fans still had a pretty nice souvenir in the commemorative *Ready Steady Who* EP. Too bad it was mostly comprised of studio recordings of surf covers instead of actual recordings from the October 18, 1966, broadcast as intended before Reaction Records ran into legal issues with ITV.

A Whole Scene Going (January 5, 1966)

If *Ready Steady Go!* seemed reverent to rock 'n' roll compared to the other pop poppycock of the day, *A Whole Scene Going* was downright academic. Despite a goofy opening credits segment that found Eric Clapton doing the breaststroke on the floor while wearing scuba gear, Barry Fantoni's show went where no other shows of the day did by propping pop stars in "The Hot Seat" to answer probing questions about the state of culture and even drugs.

Show creator and host Fantoni was a fascinating character. He was a failed jazz musician who jammed with a pre-Kinks Ray Davies and spent some time homeless in Paris after being expelled from the Camberwell School of Arts and Crafts for drunkenness. Fantoni then found success writing for David Frost's topical satire *That Was the Week That Was* and creating cartoons for the satirical magazine *Private Eye*. A stint doing art design for *Ready Steady Go!* led to his own show for the BBC.

The Who's appearance on the premier episode of *A Whole Scene Going* on January 5, 1966, began like many of their TV appearances (other guests that week included Lulu, comedian Spike Milligan, and sex symbol Caroline Munro). They mime along to "Out in the Street" looking more static than usual. The program gets more interesting when it cuts to footage of the Who playing at the

Witchdoctor Club the previous August 4 while Townshend dishes on the band in voice-over. He talks about his band's appeal among mods, how the geezers dig the Who for their violence and the birds dig them for their style. He discusses pop art as an art form easily digested by young people and the Who as an even more palatable form of that art, while giving a nod to the older generation by acknowledging his dad's influence on his own music.

Less congenially, he calls out his audience as "thick" and reveals how his own hatred of pop music, particularly the Who's records, fuels his aggressive stage show. This would be a topic further explored when he took the Hot Seat to field questions from the shockingly long-haired Fantoni, cohost Wendy Varnals, and a selection of kids in the audience. In what must be a television first, the hosts are more defensive of pop music than the pop star they are interviewing. Townshend's whole contrarian stance is rather unconvincing. Obviously, he loved pop music as a hardcore Kinks, Stones, and Beatles fan. This does not stop him from dismissing the Fabs as "flippin' lousy" when asked about their obviously high quality. Oh, Pete!

More provocatively, he casually mentions how he and his bandmates are "blocked up all the time" on drugs. He acknowledges that the best way to perform is "stone cold sober," but the rest of the time is fair game for devouring all manner of stimulants. The hip hosts and audience do not react with the shock older folks certainly would have displayed in response to a celebrity admitting to his drug use on national TV—a full year and a half before Paul McCartney drew greater attention by admitting the same thing on Independent Television News. Townshend's openness so impressed producer Elizabeth Cowley that she called the Who back to mime to "Disguises" on the final broadcast of *A Whole Scene Going* the following June 15.

The Smothers Brothers Comedy Hour (filmed September 15, 1967, aired September 17, 1967)

While the Who were a nearly ubiquitous presence on British TV in the midsixties, they were less present in the United States, where they still hadn't slipped into the top twenty. Aside from a couple of appearances on *Shindig!*, the Who were tough to find on American TV. Not until "I Can See for Miles" peaked at #9 on the *Billboard* charts on November 25, 1967, did they develop real marketability in the States.

That peak was still two months away when comedian Tommy Smothers invited the Who to his and brother Dick's variety show on September 15. Tommy had been awed by the band at the Monterey Pop Festival the previous June, where he'd introduced Otis Redding and Paul Simon (just so Paul could then introduce the Blues Project). The Who were still three days from releasing "I Can See for Miles" when they plugged it on *The Smothers Brothers Comedy Hour*.

It was a strictly canned, strictly promotional mime job only enlivened by the guys' wild outfits (frilled blouses for Daltrey, Townshend, and Moon; gangster black for Entwistle) and a bit of psychedelic noodling from the lighting crew. No big deal.

The *Smothers Brothers* appearance is now regarded as a decisive moment in Who history because of the next performance. First Tommy engages the band in a bit of scripted banter. Townshend is forced to repeat a lame joke about how he adapted his windmilling from bowling. Entwistle is only in the lineup so Tommy can wave off Daltrey to chat with the bass player instead. Bad move. When Tommy turns back to Daltrey, the snubbed singer goes off script. Nothing major. He just says his homeland is "Oz" instead of "Duluth, Minnesota," as the writing staff devised. Thing is, you can't start improvising around Keith Moon without expecting him to take it too far. When Tommy talked to the rascally drummer, he was not expecting Moon to say more than two scripted lines: "I'm Keith. I'm from London too." Instead, Moon says he'd rather a non-friend like Tommy Smothers call him "John" and sneaks in a fart joke about the show's "sloppy stagehands." Everyone has a good laugh. Tommy seems mildly flummoxed but plays it off with standard comic professionalism.

Keith Moon's improv was a minor monkey wrench in the filming. He had a major one planned. Before the program, he'd convinced the pyrotechnician to load his bass drum with an inordinate amount of explosives to go "boom" during the smash-up planned at the end of "My Generation." This much was known by all. What wasn't known was that after the explosives went off "like a wet fart," as Daltrey would later say (there's those farting stagehands again), Moon decided he required a bigger bang. He slipped the pyrotechnician a bit of brandy in exchange for quadrupling (according to Daltrey again) the amount of flash powder. When Moon set it off at the intended climax, the explosion was so severe that the cameras quaked, the monitors went dark, and Daltrey was knocked off his feet. More severely, Moon received a concussion and an armful of drum shrapnel, and Townshend, who was standing right in front of the drum, ended up with a head of smoldering hair and twenty minutes of deafness. The legend goes that Bette Davis, who'd appeared as Elizabeth I in a sketch, fainted backstage, while fellow guest star Mickey Rooney leapt up and down begging for more.

The performance was shocking television: violent, showy, exciting—everything the Who were. Daltrey claimed the Smothers Brothers nearly lost their series over it—not the last time they'd run aground of the Powers That Be, as their increased focus on left-wing politics resulted in the show's untimely demise in 1969. The segment also provided Jeff Stein with a thrilling beginning to his film *The Kids Are Alright*. The repercussions may have been more serious than all that. Years later, Pete Townshend began citing this incident as the cause of his partial deafness and tinnitus. Recounting the incident in *Who I Am* thirty-five years later, he still considered Moon a "twat" for his little prank.

The Rolling Stones Rock and Roll Circus (filmed December 10, 1968, aired December 6, 1996)

"And now, ladies and gentlemen, dig the Who."

—Keith Richards

With their smoke bombs and loud outfits, the Who could reasonably be called a circus act. So when the Rolling Stones staged their own circus in December 1968, the Who were a natural choice to guest star.

As Pete Townshend told the origin story in 2004 on the Rolling Stones *Rock and Roll Circus* DVD, the concept was not solely the Stones'. Townshend recalled that he and Ronnie Lane had been singing backup on a Stones demo at Olympic Studio. What that song was remains a mystery. After the session, Townshend, Lane, and Mick Jagger began batting ideas about a traveling show back and forth. They imagined a US-traversing tour over railways, renting a Barnum and Bailey tent, and staging their own Rock and Roll Circus. Townshend remembers the bands as the Who, the Stones, and Faces. That last band would not exist until Small Faces officially dissolved in 1969, so the Faces involved must have been of the Small variety. When the logistics of railway travel proved unrealistic, Jagger suggested a one-off TV show.

Mick and Co. hired Michael Lindsay-Hogg to shoot the special, which would also feature Taj Mahal (a fave of Jagger and Townshend), Jethro Tull (the only group that mimed), Marianne Faithfull, and a one-time-only supergroup consisting of John Lennon, Keith Richards, Mitch Mitchell, and Eric Clapton called the Dirty Mac. Their working relationship in dire condition, Small Faces were not on the docket. The Stones' camp dropped £50,000 on the affair, which got underway in InterTel studios on December 10, 1968.

The Stones granted the Who a generous ten-minute slot in the hour-long special (only the Dirty Mac were afforded a similar length of time). They decided to fill that time with a single piece, "A Quick One While He's Away." The decision was a wise one, as the performance was arguably the most exciting thing they ever put to film. The Who had spent the better part of 1968 doing roadwork. It paid off in a tight but not uptight run-through of the mini-opera. They all looked in great spirits, full of smiles, Keith Moon gleefully singing along and flinging his drums about. The climactic vocal volley of "You are forgiven" is transcendent.

When *The Rolling Stones Rock and Roll Circus* failed to show up on TV in early 1969, rumors that the Stones had it blocked because the Who upstaged them started flying. True, the Who's performance is phenomenal. The Stones had been suffering from a lack of live performing. Faulty cameras caused interminable delays, so they didn't shoot their half hour until 2:00 a.m., by which point they'd been at it for fourteen hours and feeling worse for the wear (the Who, in contrast, were feeling fresh when they filmed their bit at 4:00 p.m.).

Who fans would not have to wait more than a decade to see that stunning performance of "A Quick One While He's Away," as it received pride of place in *The Kids Are Alright*. The rest of the *Rock and Roll Circus* would not see release until 1996, by which point the history books had decided the Stones' set was a shambles. In truth, they performed excellently, particularly considering how rusty they were. With plenty of great material from what may be their greatest album, *Beggars Banquet*, there's a lot to enjoy. Sure, they're no Who, but the Who is a live act no one can follow. Rumors that Jagger shelved the film because he didn't like the way he looked might be true. He certainly has the vanity to back up such charges, but to your author's eyes, he has rarely looked more beautiful or more commanding on film. Brian Jones, however, is in terrible shape. Ravaged by drugs and emotional problems (Townshend says Jones spent much

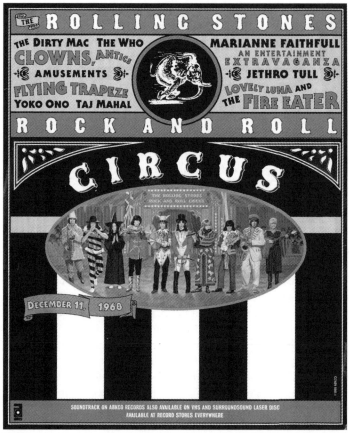

Released after a near three-decade delay, *The Rolling Stones Rock and Roll Circus* turned out to be well worth the wait. The Who's incendiary performance of "A Quick One While He's Away," however, had been available since the release of *The Kids Are Alright* in 1979.

Author's collection

of the day weeping), he would never perform with the Stones in public again and was dead in seven months. In his interview on the *Kids Are Alright* DVD, Daltrey concludes that the real reason the Stones held the *Rock and Roll Circus* back is that they didn't want the world seeing how wrecked Jones had become. Fortunately, the public would not remain sheltered forever. All fifty-four glorious minutes of *The Rolling Stones Rock and Roll Circus* were finally released on video and CD on October 15, 1996. The following December 6 it received its long, long overdue television airing on VH-1.

Russell Harty Plus (taped January 3, 1973, aired January 6, 1973)

The Who released "Relay" during a period of relative inactivity on December 22, 1972, in the United Kingdom. Two weeks later they casually promoted their final stand-alone single with an appearance on *Russell Harty Plus*. Like most chat show hosts, Harty was congenial yet square, and despite the Who's well-known reputation for improper behavior, he seemed somewhat unprepared for Keith Moon. There would be no hand-grenade-strength doses of flash powder this time, just an overenthusiastic clown with no patience for anyone steering the ship but him.

The reason Moon was in such rare form and this appearance is so special is that it is one of the very few times all four members of the band were interviewed together, thus providing Moon with the opportunity to step all over his colleagues' lines and prove who the Who's real star is. Jeff Stein threaded this appearance through *The Kids Are Alright* for that reason, but also because he felt it highlighted each musician's personality well. That's not too flattering to Entwistle and Daltrey, who say nothing more than how they paid the bills in the pre-Who days. Moon makes an infinitely larger impression.

Directed by Michael Lindsay-Hogg, the segment begins with a performance of "Relay" in which Daltrey's vocal is the only live element. Some primitive colored-video effects add minor interest. The group then retires to the front of the stage, Townshend deliberately elbowing an amp to the ground and Moon clacking away at his claves on the way. He seems to have the percussion just so he can keep making noise after the song, since "Relay" is totally clave-free. Townshend seems to have knocked over the amp for the same reason. Or perhaps it was a bit of genuine clumsiness brought on by the cup of brandy he sips throughout the appearance.

Anyone with enough interest in the Who to read this book should be well familiar with what follows from *The Kids Are Alright*. Townshend makes a crack about Entwistle being uninteresting when Harty dares to ask the Quiet One a question. Moon mocks Daltrey's admission about being a sheet-metal worker by saying he was a "rust repairer" and "full-time survivor." Townshend nudges Moon into some shtick in which they talk over each other as Entwistle and Daltrey laugh it up. Russell smiles his gnarly smile, runs his hands through his hair, and serves as a drying rack for Moon's sweaty socks. The drummer continues to strip down, revealing his tiny red y-fronts before setting his sights on Townshend.

Moon tears Townshend's sleeve as the guitarist slurs an ineffectual, "No, Keith." As if on cue, Townshend starts shredding Moon's silly military-uniform shirt. Then the two mad strippers start leering at Harty's neat suit, prodding the terrified host to warn, "If you touch my bleeding sleeve . . ." Moon takes a couple of pokes at Harty and barks, "Can't touch the interviewer, can we? He's in command, isn't he? He can make everyone else look a right twit as long as you don't have a go at him!"

Moon's rant is one of the funniest examples of his wit, but it's completely untrue. Harty was never in command, nor was he responsible for making anyone look a right twit. Only Keith Moon could be accused of such things.

His other great moment is his response to Harty's "You're all married, aren't you?" Without missing a beat, he responds, "I wouldn't marry this lot!" Very funny, but also revealing, because the Who had been in a ten-year marriage of sorts, and they interact with the good-humored comfort and slightly nasty honesty of old marrieds. One couldn't imagine the Stones, Beatles, Kinks, Beach Boys, or nearly any other major rock group interacting in such a way after ten years together. In that way, the *Russell Harty Plus* appearance is not just hilarious, it's kind of heartwarming.

On Their Own on TV

The Who made numerous other memorable appearances on the small screen throughout the world. There was their June 1966 spot on Sweden's *Pop Matters*, in which they awkwardly introduced and mimed to "Daddy Rolling Stone," "It's Not True," "Bald Headed Woman," "The Kids Are Alright," "Substitute," and "My Generation" after busting through a paper Union Jack. There was their farewell appearance on Germany's *Beat Club* in August 1969 when they showcased three-quarters of *Tommy* against a backdrop of Mike McInnerney's art. Their memorable TV moments were not always made together. Along with the individual guys' uncountable solo jaunts to chat shows there are the odder TV sojourns.

Our World (June 25, 1967)

For its contribution to the very first international live satellite broadcast, Great Britain chose to be represented by its favorite sons. John Lennon went to work on an appropriately unifying statement of universal love called "All You Need Is Love," which the Beatles would then "record" on live TV (in fact, the guitar, harpsichord, and drum tracks had already been cut). To contribute the keening "love, love, love" sing-a-long and spruce up the party atmosphere, the Beatles invited a selection of friends and colleagues. Among the guests were Mick Jagger, Keith Richards, Marianne Faithfull, Eric Clapton, Graham Nash, and Keith Moon. While the only kind of universal love that ever seemed to interest Keith

Moon was himself in bed with half a dozen groupies, he and wife Kim came along to clap hands, sing, and behave with an unusual degree of self-control. Never does he leap up, snatch the mic from McCartney, and start bellowing "Bucket T," although it may have made for more interesting TV if he had.

Surprise Partie (Taped November 27, 1968, aired December 31, 1968)

OK, so, the Who did appear together on the French New Year's Eve television special *Surprise Partie*. For the occasion they lip-synched to "I Can See for Miles," "Magic Bus," and the rare *Jigsaw Puzzle* version of "I'm a Boy." But later on in the program, two members appear unaccompanied by the rest of the band. The Who's old cronies Small Faces also appeared on the program to mime to the instrumental title track of their latest and last LP, *Ogden's Nut Gone Flake*. The astute viewer may have noticed a couple of long-haired weirdos freaking out on the drum riser behind Kenney Jones. Never do they turn to face the camera or draw attention to their presence. They're just there to have a good time grooving to some top-notch rock 'n' roll, so Pete Townshend and Keith Moon never distract from the performing band.

Roger Daltrey on TV

After Roger Daltrey's latent acting skills emerged in *Tommy*, he regularly pursued the bug on screens large and small. When the Who folded in the early eighties, he had an abundance of time to get in front of the TV cameras despite his insistence that doing so made him uncomfortable. Telly watchers got plenty of opportunities to watch Rog be uncomfortable on the BBC sitcom *Buddy*, in which he played the title character's dad; the fantasy series *Highlander*, in which he had a recurring role as the hero's buddy; and *Rude Awakening*, in which he stretched his skills as aging rock star Nobby Clegg. Daltrey played himself more explicitly while trying out obsolete survival techniques as host of the History Channel's *Extreme History with Roger Daltrey* and when he showed up on the BBC's über-surreal comedy *The Mighty Boosh* to tidy up after Julian Barratt and Noel Fielding, who'd met Rog after performing at a Teenage Cancer Trust benefit. At times, Roger Daltrey played characters quite unlike Roger Daltrey, as when he played a murderous photographer on *Tales from the Crypt*. Strangest of all was his voice work, as when a teenager lip-synched to his vocals in the 1984 TV movie *Pop Pirates* (Rog also appears in the flesh as a music-contest producer with bad facial hair) or when he voiced the puppet Argon the Dragon on the kiddie show *The Wheels on the Bus*. He would play a fantasy creature of a different sort on the fairy tale series *Once Upon a Time* when he voiced and provided visual inspiration for Wonderland's hookah-smoking Caterpillar. The appearance is extremely brief, little more than an excuse for Rog to repeat the insect's one line over and over: "Who are you? Who are you? Who are you?" Get it?

On the Soundtracks

The Who have always been a regular presence on TV, even during the two decades they essentially ceased to be a regularly functioning band. That's because small-screen producers recognized the power of their instantly recognizable music. It has been a handy way to establish the period for shows set in the sixties, as in an episode of *The Wonder Years* in which young Kevin Arnold goes shopping for his first guitar to the thundering strains of "My Generation," or the seventies, as when time-traveling cop Sam Tyler finds himself lost in that decade as "Baba O'Riley" blares on the soundtrack of *Life on Mars.* That tune was used over nearly identical scenes in both the British and American pilots for the series, the American one being titled "Out Here in the Fields" in homage to the most overused Who song on television. On *The Good Guys,* a seventies throwback cop who refuses to play by the rules chases down a perp to "Baba O'Riley."

Some series utilized Who songs to comment on the action directly, if only in superficial ways. The pastel-saturated cop show (what's with the Who and cop shows?) *Miami Vice* twice dipped into the Who's song bag: once using "Baba O'Riley" as background music for a boardwalk drug deal, suggesting the "teenage wasteland" of substance abuse, and later using "Eminence Front" for an episode full of "put-ons" (Detective Crockett goes undercover as a drug dealer; a jai alai player is framed for murder). On an episode of *Buffy the Vampire Slayer,* blue-eyed slayer-watcher Rupert Giles sings a teary rendition of "Behind Blue Eyes" at a coffee bar as his teenaged charges learn there's more to him than his constant tsking. A tough and insightful forensic pathologist tools onto a crime scene while blasting the tough "I Can See for Miles" on *Crossing Jordan.* On Steve Coogan's funny and insightful *Saxondale,* the title ex-roadie (who did some time with the Who . . . but *not* Led Zep, much to his shame) rides around in his muscle car rocking out to "Squeeze Box." On occasion, shows use Who songs for more inscrutable reasons, as when Louis C.K. serenades his toddler daughters with "Who Are You"—complete with screams of "Who the fuck are you?!?"—on *Louie.* Weird, yes. Funny too.

Sometimes the Who featured in select episodes of series beyond a mere tune or two on the soundtrack. Here are a few examples of such must-see TV for Who fanatics.

Freaks and Geeks: "Dead Dogs and Gym Teachers" (aired October 10, 2000)

Before Judd Apatow became the household-name filmmaker behind *The 40-Year-Old Virgin* and *Knocked Up,* he was having less commercial success on television with a short-lived series called *Freaks and Geeks.* Even earlier, he was a teenage Who freak, and he injected that obsession into an episode titled "Dead Dogs and Gym Teachers."

It's a terrible shame that *Freaks and Geeks* was not a big hit on TV. Apparently, audiences were not ready for such a truthful, bittersweet look at small-town high school life in the early eighties starring a cast of young unknowns (most of whom would go on to massively successful careers). It is also a shame that Apatow and Co. produced "Dead Dogs and Gym Teachers" after NBC started passing on episodes. Though it was scheduled to air on March 27, 2000, during its original run, NBC pulled the episode after deciding to cancel the series. "Dead Dogs and Gym Teachers" finally debuted during a syndicated run on Fox Family Channel the following October and can now be found on DVD, which you should own if you don't already. I'm dead serious. Stop reading this book right now, go to Amazon.com, and order *Freaks and Geeks: The Complete Series*. I can wait.

Are you back? OK then. So, "Dead Dogs and Gym Teachers" revolves around the "freaks" (denim-wearing, rock-devouring burnouts) attending a Who concert. Apatow says he consciously deprived another episode of songs just so he had the surplus budget to pack "Dead Dogs" with Who music (most likely, he was talking about the episode "The Little Things," which has an unusually scant two songs). This was not the first time Who music had been used on *Freaks and Geeks*: the "We've Got Spirit" episode used "The Song Is Over" to poignant effect and "Looks and Books" slipped in "Slip Kid." However, "Dead Dogs and Gym Teachers" uses an unprecedented seven tracks. The *Tommy* soundtrack version of "I'm Free" plays over a gym class basketball game. "I'm One" plays as freshman geek Bill Haverchuck (Martin Starr) fixes himself a grilled cheese sandwich and watches Garry Shandling doing standup on TV. "Boris the Spider" growls out as freaks Lindsay (Linda Cardellini) and Kim (Busy Philips) drive over (what they believe to be) a friend's dog ("He's come to a sticky end . . ."). "Love Reign o'er Me" brings gravity to a scene in which Bill learns his mom has spent the night with his dreaded gym teacher. Lindsay's parents (Beck Ann Baker and the great Joe Flaherty) scrutinize "Squeeze Box" while trying to determine if the Who's music is unfit for their young daughter's ears. "Goin' Mobile" plays over a go-cart race sequence, and "Drowned" drifts from the freaks' very own "magic bus" as they tailgate before the concert.

The Who references fly freely throughout the show. Freak Nick Andopolis (Jason Segel) composes a hilariously awful song for Lindsay called "Lady L," which he says was inspired by Pete Townshend. When Nick attempts to sing his composition for her at the tailgate party, pal Ken Miller (Seth Rogen) grabs Nick's guitar, shouts "I'm Pete Townshend," and smashes the instrument before his buddy has a chance to humiliate himself. With its pseudo ARP synthesizers and crashing guitars and drums, Mike Andrews's incidental music even pays tribute to the freaks' favorite band.

"Dead Dogs and Gym Teachers"—and *Freaks and Geeks* in general—draws from the Who at a deeper level than a few songs and references, reflecting the alienation, childhood humiliations, identity crises, fraught adolescent sexuality, and profound desire for love and acceptance that was always at the heart of the band's music. It is a funny, touching, and quite beautiful series, and the Who's music and influence are used to extraordinary effect in "Dead Dogs and Gym Teachers." The show is such a loving tribute to the Who that we can forgive the fact that one of the geeks is wearing a T-shirt depicting the cover of *Thirty Years of Maximum R&B*, which would not be released for more than a decade after this episode is supposed to take place. Oops!

The Simpsons: "A Tale of Two Simpsons" (aired November 5, 2000)

Like Judd Apatow, Dan Castellaneta is a longtime Who fan. However, while it is unlikely Roger Daltrey had even heard of Apatow when "Dead Dogs and Gym Teachers" aired in 2000, Castellaneta was so big that the Who's lead singer was actually starstruck when they met that same year. That's because Dan is behind one of the most recognizable voices on television. He is the man who says, "D'oh!" the voice of none other than Homer J. Simpson. Roger Daltrey was a fan of the long-running animated comedy, and knowing what a great time Peter Frampton had while doing voice work on the "Homerpalooza" episode, it probably took him all of four seconds to agree to appear on *The Simpsons*. Ever agreeable and unable to turn down a paycheck, John Entwistle got on board too. Ever disagreeable, Pete Townshend was a bit of a wild card. According to the show's producers, he initially signed off on an appearance on the show's 250th episode under the impression another actor would provide his voice *Yellow Submarine*-style, hence his failure to show up for his voice-over session. Daltrey says that Townshend just didn't want to do it, and after Daltrey finally convinced him to take a piece of the pop culture phenomenon that is *The Simpsons*, Townshend had second thoughts and bailed. That's probably the more realistic story.

When the guitarist proved a no-show, Daltrey suggested giving Pete's younger brother Paul a call. Enticed by the $2,000 payday, Paul showed up to voice his sibling. Although everyone involved in the "A Tale of Two Springfields" episode was apparently impressed by how much Paul sounded like his older brother, serious Who fans will immediately recognize that the closest thing the episode has to Pete Townshend is a yellow-faced likeness of the guy.

By its twelfth season, *The Simpsons* was several years beyond its golden age as the flat-out funniest thing on TV. "A Tale of Two Springfields" is no embarrassment, though. After Homer isolates his family on the wrong side of Springfield's version of the Berlin Wall, he schemes to get the Who to play on his side of the divider. This premise sets up a few opportunities for subtle Who references, as when a stock photo shown during a news report poses Homer, Moe, Lenny, and Carl in a parody of the *Meaty, Beaty, Big, and Bouncy* album cover. Moe later says of Homer, "That fat, dumb, and bald guy sure plays a mean hardball."

The Who eventually show up to bash out "The Seeker" and "Won't Get Fooled Again" atop the wall. The guys are depicted as they looked during the *Who Are You* era some twenty years earlier. John Entwistle is wearing his iconic skeleton suit and Boris neck pendant. The fellow behind the drums gets no lines, but it is no coincidence that he looks like a certain deceased madman. The Who requested they be shown playing with Keith Moon.

CSI: Crime Scene Investigation: "Living Legend" (aired November 23, 2006)

As the twenty-first century chugged on, TV watchers got more and more opportunities to hear old favorites from the Who when chestnuts such as "Bargain" and "Happy Jack" started popping up in commercials. Premiering in the first year of the decade, producer Jerry Bruckheimer's *CSI: Crime Scene Investigation* gave the Who another small-screen outlet for their back catalog. Roger Daltrey says that Bruckheimer was inspired to weave the Who into his crime drama after seeing an old advertisement for *Who Are You*. The ad depicted a cop holding back a crowd of onlookers gawping down at a chalk outline next to which the album title is also scrawled in chalk.

Bruckheimer selected the title track of that album for the theme song of his series. When *CSI* became a massive hit and turned into a franchise, he kept the Who theme going. For *CSI: Miami*, "Won't Get Fooled Again" served as title music. For *CSI: NY*, he used a remix of the ubiquitous "Baba O'Riley."

While Bruckheimer's show doesn't come within a light year of the quality of *Freaks and Geeks* or *The Simpsons*, Who fans may still want to check out an episode of *CSI: Crime Scene Investigation* called "Living Legend." The episode finds a gangster, long thought to be dead, murdering his way through some old enemies while wearing a series of outrageous disguises: a Mexican fisherman, a karaoke-singing yahoo, a gravel-voiced Italian American, and an African American woman. Most viewers will quickly figure out what it takes the CSI team half the episode to do: the man in disguise is Roger Daltrey. In their defense, it probably isn't easy doing forensics work under all of that neon, sex-pad lighting

It's all rather silly, but *CSI* may have one high-profile fan. During an interview for the *VH-1 Honors the Who* ceremony in 2008, Pete Townshend said of *CSI: Miami*, "I love that ginger guy and the girl whose voice is so high that it's beyond the range of human

Roger Daltrey says this ad inspired Jerry Bruckheimer to begin every episode of *CSI* with Who music.   *Author's collection*

hearing." Ginger guy David Caruso and high-voiced girl Emily Procter may want to familiarize themselves with Townshend's tendency toward sarcasm before patting themselves on the backs, though.

Other References

Shelling out the cash for some Who songs or even a Who band member is probably the preferred way to give the band its due on TV these days. Some shows have been cagier and more frugal in their homages. The tragic Riverfront Coliseum concert at which eleven Who fans were trampled to death inspired the awkward yet elegiac "In Concert" episode of *WKRP in Cincinnati* (none of the Who's music was used in the show, though the Stones' "Sympathy for the Devil" gets a spin). An episode of the British comedy anthology *The Comic Strip Presents . . .* featured an incompetent heavy-metal band called Bad News arguing over who "gets to be Pete Townshend" (apparently, none of them wanted to be poor Rog). The aging Swinging Londoners of *Absolutely Fabulous* reminisce about seeing the Who in their heyday and sneer at Daltrey for settling down to helm a fish farm in an episode called "Fish Farm." On the "For Cryin' Out Loud" episode of *Tales from the Crypt* (a show on which Daltrey would eventually guest star), a rock promoter murders his banker with a guitar he says he got from Pete Townshend while a facsimile of "Pinball Wizard" strums on the soundtrack. Dave Foley gives an acoustic guitar a less lethal bashing while declaring "Long live rock!" at the climax of a sketch on episode twelve of *The Kids in the Hall.* An episode of the bizarre and unbelievably funny "After School Special" spoof *Strangers with Candy* adopted the title "Behind Blank Eyes" in tribute to its stunted main character Jerry Blank. In the zonkers *Increasingly Poor Decisions of Todd Margaret*, David Cross's American energy-drink pusher decides to pretend he was born in Leeds after eyeing a copy of a certain live album. More substantially, every single episode of the sixth season of *That '70s Show* (another show on which Daltrey appeared) took its title from a Who song (Led Zeppelin had been afforded a similar tribute in season five, while season seven did the same for the Stones and season eight did it for Queen). The sixth season titles are: "The Kids Are Alright," "Join Together," "Magic Bus," "The Acid Queen," "I'm Free," "We're Not Gonna Take It," "Christmas," "I'm a Boy," "Young Man Blues," "A Legal Matter," "I Can See for Miles," "Sally Simpson," "Won't Get Fooled Again," "Baby Don't You Do It," "Who Are You," "Man with Money," "Happy Jack," "Do You Think It's Alright," "Substitute," "Squeeze Box," and "5:15."

27

Suddenly, It's the Silver Screen

The Who on Film

From the earliest notches on their timeline, rock's most musically and visually thrilling band was headed for the silver screen. Kit Lambert and Chris Stamp's first ambition was to make a movie starring the Who, not to manage the lunatics. When the Who made a promo film for "Happy Jack" in 1966, all of their latent movie star charisma came spilling from the screen. Potential dramatic feature-length vehicles started coming under consideration. The Who could have been seen yanking Stratocasters from the soil in Mike Myers's *Guitar Farm* or merging with the masses in *Lifehouse* or detailing their own history in *Rock Is Dead (Rock Lives)* or even playing dual parts as aliens and scientists in an unnamed, unfinished sci-fi film Pete Townshend and Keith Moon were allegedly scripting in 1967! Instead, Townshend, Moon, and John Entwistle were basically relegated to extras in *Tommy*, which only afforded a starring role to Roger Daltrey, the band member who made the lightest impact in that old "Happy Jack" promo.

Though the Who never made their own *A Hard Day's Night*, their presence in cinemas is substantial and ongoing in the documentaries and concert films, the movies utilizing the Who's music to enhance their drama or comedy and the ones that adapted their more conceptual works for rows of popcorn munchers. So please turn off your cell phone and no talking. The feature is about to begin.

Five Docs for the Big Screen and Home Video

Telling the Who's loony story is a challenge several filmmakers have attempted to take on. Some have been incredibly successful; some have not. Some couldn't even complete their film, taking management of the band as a consolation prize. At least one wasn't really concerned with the band at all, preferring the presence of naked girls. And so for a variety of reasons, the following five documentaries each have their own special importance in the history of the Who.

High Numbers (1964)

When they agreed to manage the High Numbers, Kit Lambert and Chris Stamp got permanently sidetracked from making the documentary for which they originally had the band in mind. Though a feature documentary was never released, the filmmakers did get a chance to shoot forty minutes of 16-mm film during a gig at The Railway Hotel on August 11, 1964. When they couldn't find distribution for their short doc, it languished on the shelf until Jeff Stein used a bit of footage sans sound in *The Kids Are Alright*. Early in the twenty-first century, seven minutes of footage from the unreleased documentary somehow turned up in the attic of a Dutch TV producer. The footage then found its way into Roger Daltrey's hands. In 2007, this footage of the boys performing Jessie Hill's "Ooh Poo Pah Dooh" and the Miracles' "I Gotta Dance to Keep from Crying" to a very serious mob of shimmying mods received its first official airing as an extra titled "The High Numbers at the Railway Hotel" on the *Amazing Journey* DVD. Perhaps in another forty years, clips of the High Numbers' performing "Green Onions," "Long Tall Shorty," or "Here 'Tis" will be found in some Tupperware at the bottom of the Indian Ocean.

Carousella (1966)

A documentary about a bunch of sweaty pop singers may have been a hard sell in 1964. One about women taking off their clothes, however, sells itself. Decades before he made *The Dogs of War* and *Hamburger Hill*, John Irvin made *Carousella*, an X-rated documentary short about strippers Katy Jordan, Tina Samuels, and Julie Lester. Buried amidst twenty-five minutes of interviews and nipple-less stripteasing are seven seconds of the Who performing at the Marquee in their very first big-screen appearance. A version of "It's All Over Now" by an unidentified group plays over that footage shot in early 1965.

The Kids Are Alright (1979)

It took fifteen years, and Kit Lambert was no longer in the family, but a feature Who documentary finally smashed screens across the world in 1979. Well, maybe "documentary" isn't the right word to describe *The Kids Are Alright*. It's a chronology-annihilating scrapbook of a decade and a half of TV footage, concert clips, promo films, and interviews new and old. It's a ridiculous comedy romp, a prayer to the rock 'n' roll religion, and a cheaper and more fun way to knock the crap out of your system than a high colonic.

The Kids Are Alright was not a film the Who were looking to make, though it might as well have evolved from one of their abandoned projects. As you may recall from chapter 16, *Rock Is Dead (Rock Lives)* would have been a semi-documentary about the band's history, and in screenwriter Nik Cohn's words, "a metaphor for rock in general." That is very much what *The Kids Are Alright* is, spitting on the most basic rules of documentary filmmaking—presenting its information in senseless order, staging artificial sequences—just as raucous rock 'n' roll spat on conventionally pretty pop music. Nik Cohn was not the mastermind behind *The Kids Are Alright*, nor was it even on Pete Townshend's ever-expanding list of potential projects. In fact, Jeff Stein had to do quite a bit of cajoling to get Pete Townshend involved.

Stein could hardly call himself a filmmaker when he first floated the idea in 1975. He was just another Who nut in his early twenties, though one with the ingenious idea to compile a decade of their footage into a fan love letter, a primer for the curious, and an enduring time capsule of their greatness. Townshend passed on the idea initially, but Stein pushed it relentlessly. The band finally came around after Stein screened a seventeen-minute sampler of what he had in mind, which included the *Smothers Brothers Comedy Hour* clip that would kick off the finished film. The scene in

The double album from their film, including unreleased live material and 20 page colour booklet.

The Kids Are Alright
THE WHO [polydor]
Musical Director John Entwistle   Film released through Brent Walker Film Distribution Limited   Album & Cassette

Pete Townshend puts the autodestructive theories of artist Gustav Metzger into practice in this iconic advert for *The Kids Are Alright*.   *Author's collection*

the screening room was as anarchic as what was going down on the screen. According to the filmmaker, Townshend and Keith Moon were rolling about on the carpet in hysterics. Heather Daltrey was laughing so hard she upended a coffee table. The fact that the Who was a really, really, really funny band hadn't been so on show since *Sell Out*.

Along with the amazing concert footage testifying to the Who's musical prowess and sublime showmanship would be snippets of Moon and Steve Martin tumbling about in a flood of soap suds during a staged hotel room smashing, Moon giving an interview from behind a leather mask while getting whipped by a dominatrix, Entwistle machine-gunning gold records (Daltrey's solo albums, he jested!), the boys getting up to Keystone Cops capering in promo films for "Happy Jack" and "Call Me Lightning" (though the audio track for the latter was replaced with the equally appropriate "Cobwebs and Strange"), and Townshend giving what must surely be the most hilarious recount of a doctor's diagnosis of a serious medical condition. Stein is funny too, juxtaposing Townshend's unconvincing explanation of how his band is devoid of glamour over footage of the guitarist applying mascara before a show.

There is also a melancholic undertone to the craziness. As it turned out, *The Kids Are Alright* would be an elegy to Keith Moon when it came out some nine months after his death. While Moon is in top clowning form throughout the footage Stein selected, he also undergoes a shocking transformation. One moment, he's a doe-eyed boy flailing away on "Shout and Shimmy" in 1965; the next he's a paunchy alcoholic looking decades older than his early thirties. Roger Daltrey remembered the drummer breaking down in tears watching his own deterioration on film. Considering the circumstances of his death, it can be difficult to find the humor in his wasted chats with Ringo Starr in the film, but for the vast majority of its 101 minute run time, *The Kids Are Alright* is everything Jeff Stein wanted it to be: an exhilarating, funny, get-up-on-your-seat-and-dance, toss-your-TV-out-the-window affirmation of the glory of rock 'n' roll and the Who's embodiment of it.

Thirty Years of Maximum R&B Live (1994)

The Kids Are Alright is the ultimate rock doc and the ultimate compilation of Who footage. Released on VHS in conjunction with the band's commemorative CD box set in 1994, *Thirty Years of Maximum R&B Live* didn't stand a chance of topping Jeff Stein's movie. That an hour of this 153-minute documentary is devoted to the post-Moon years is a huge flaw. One might wonder if Daltrey, Entwistle, or Townshend had their own moments of horrified reflections when witnessing their youthful vitality at the Marquee Club in 1967 or their peak proficiency at the Charlton Athletic Football Grounds in 1974 set against the bloated Who-on-ice spectacle at Giants Stadium in 1989. Certainly more sixties footage would have been a welcome alternative. Townshend's cynicism during the new interview he gave for the film can be dispiriting too (an hour-long condensation of *Thirty Years* aired on PBS on August 19, 1994, that included additional interviews with Keith Richards, Bono, Eric Clapton, Bryan Adams and Chris Barron of Spin Doctors).

There is also a bit of footage overlap with other video releases. "A Quick One While He's Away" can now be viewed in more complimentary context on the *Monterey Pop: The Outtake Performances* DVD. The clips of "Young Man Blues" and "I Don't Even Know Myself" have found a better home on the *Who at the Isle of Wight* DVD. *Thirty Years of Maximum R&B Live* is still worth owning for the delightful Marquee Club performance of "So Sad About Us" (too bad that the renditions of "Happy Jack" and "My Generation" shot at this same gig weren't included too) and the selection of four numbers from the landmark Charlton concert. But can a DVD of that entire show be far away?

Amazing Journey: The Story of the Who (2007)

Made with the full consent and cooperation of Roger Daltrey and Pete Townshend, *Amazing Journey: The Story of the Who* is the proper documentary *The Kids Are Alright* never aspired to be. It tells the Who's story chronologically from the guys' births up to *Endless Wire*. It gets the job done even as it feels like both not enough and too much. A lot of time is spent on the years preceding "I Can't Explain" and the years following Keith Moon's death, leaving the meat of the Who's career feeling underserved. While it isn't likely the Who would ever be documented as thoroughly as the Beatles were in the wholly satisfying eight-part *Beatles Anthology*, two hours of *Amazing Journey* just can't delve deep enough. The telling is overly conventional too, with director Paul Crowder's tone-deaf narration and Pete Townshend and Roger Daltrey's talking head interviews.

But maybe we shouldn't get too bogged down in what isn't here or the presentation. While the filmmaking doesn't strive to be high art, *Amazing Journey* is a valuable two hours spent with two old soldiers discussing a long and tumultuous tour of duty, coming away from the experience with a heartening mutual love and respect for each other they rarely expressed in earlier times. Hearing Townshend finally profess his respect for Daltrey is incredibly moving coming after decades of feuding and fisticuffs, the deaths of their friends and bandmates, and Townshend's pornography scandal (see chapter 30). Daltrey returns that affection with no small sincerity. If *Amazing Journey* is a bit lacking as a thorough and thrilling rock 'n' roll documentary, it delivers as an unexpectedly poignant love story.

LPs on Screen

The Who's knack for storytelling through song has made some of their records ripe for cinematic adaptation.

Tommy (1975)

Tommy was the obvious first serious choice for a Who movie. It had a plot, wall-to-wall terrific tunes, and potential roles for every member of the band (Pete Townshend as the narrator! John Entwistle as Cousin Kevin! Keith Moon as Uncle Ernie! *And* Roger Daltrey *aaaas* Tommy!). Kit Lambert was amped up to get the movie made, penning a script in conjunction with the album's recording. Joe Strick was being eyeballed for the director's seat, and his valiant effort to bring James Joyce's unfilmable novel *Ulysses* to the screen in 1967 made him an intriguing candidate to do the same for the Who's dicey rock opera, with its multiple scenes of the abuse of a disabled child.

Instead, we got Ken Russell's film.

Ken Russell had been digging a nook for himself as one of Britain's most outrageous filmmakers, having Oliver Reed and Alan Bates engage in a full-frontally naked wrestling scene in *Women in Love* and nude nuns molest a Jesus statue in *The Devils*. On paper, Russell's penchant for outré sexuality, surrealism, and iconoclasm seemed a perfect fit for *Tommy*, even though he thought the album was "awful" on first listen. Many critics have praised and continue to praise his film. There are certainly some effective sequences, particularly Elton John bouncing on stilt boots while screaming "Pinball Wizard" and the neat "Sally Simpson" film-within-a-film. Tina Turner is electrifying as the Acid Queen. The criticism of the crassness and commercialism of organized religion is on point too. However, the overall effect of *Tommy* is as numbing as having shades shoved over your eyes and corks shoved in your ears and mouth. The plot was

Roger Daltrey is surrounded by his all-star cast of costars on this *Tommy* promo poster. A few of them can even sing!

Courtesy of the Rob Abramowicz Collection, digitized by Jeffrey Uleau

never the strongest aspect of the rock opera; the Who's performances were. They are sometimes present on the soundtrack, but they've been asphyxiated by synthesizers and relegated to support for such rock 'n' roll ignoramuses as Reed, Jack Nicholson, and Ann-Margret. That trio's singing ranges from incompetent to ineffectual to unbearable, respectively. Ann-Margret should have been put on trial for reducing the mighty "Christmas" to tinkly cabaret. Although the acting may have suffered (*may* have), this movie should have been cast as Lou Reizner's orchestral *Tommy* album was. Imagine if Sandy Denny, the nurse on Reizner's album, had been promoted to Tommy's mom, Nora, or Steve Winwood had resumed his part as the dad. Imagine if Entwistle was allowed to voice Cousin Kevin instead of being used as a perpetually bored-looking background extra. Then you might have something. Instead, there are too many people who don't know the first thing about rock 'n' roll in this film. And even some of the genuine rockers should be held accountable. As The Hawker, Eric Clapton is at his most boring and lifeless. His vocal never finds the groove.

The film also has some serious plot, tone, and aesthetic issues. On the album, Tommy's disability is caused when he witnesses his father murder his mother's lover. In the film, the lover is the murderer, making his willingness to go along with Nora's efforts to help her son regain his senses less sensible. Shouldn't Uncle Frank be frightened that if Tommy is able to speak again he'll squeal to the authorities? The boy's real father might be frightened of the same thing, but at least we could better understand why he'd also want his own son to hear, speak, and see again.

On record, the beauty of the Who's performances ameliorated the opera's more tasteless plot points. The film revels in them, inflating a minute of "Fiddle About" into an extended set piece for Keith Moon to fondle Roger Daltrey. Moon is memorable, even funny, in the part, but despite the distancing absurdity of having him molest a nephew played by an actor two years older than himself, the fact remains that the movie is trying to milk laughs from the rape of a disabled kid. Nice. Then there's Ann-Margret's infamous swim in a puddle of baked beans and hot fudge. At least it stops her from singing.

The one real saving grace is Roger Daltrey, though we don't realize this until Tommy regains his senses an hour and ten minutes into the picture. To commemorate his rebirth, he sings "I'm Free," and getting to hear Daltrey take his rightful place as singer is liberating as Tommy is liberated from his disabilities and we the audience are liberated from all the wretched musical performances that preceded it. For the film's remaining forty minutes, Daltrey dominates the film and does a fine job it, and we only have to suffer through a few stray verses from Ann-Margret and Oliver Reed.

Tommy was certainly a valuable experience for the Who's singer. Daltrey learned he could distinguish himself artistically by stepping away from the mic and in front of the camera. In *Who's Back: The Story of the Who*, he described the opportunity to really play a character he'd been embodying in concert for half a decade as "an absolute dream . . . it was like taking the cork out of a champagne bottle." The film also received its share of accolades, earning three Oscar nominations (including one for Ann-Margret's fudge-curdling performance), enthusiastic reviews, and an official thumbs up from the man who matters most, composer Pete Townshend. Who fans with a shred of respect for rock 'n' roll might find it to be painful viewing, though.

Quadrophenia (1979)

All of the issues that left *Tommy* a camp relic of 1975 were stamped out for the strangely timeless period piece *Quadrophenia*. The key element of this deserved cult classic is director Franc Roddam. Unlike the grandfatherly Ken Russell, Roddam was born at the perfect time. He came of age in the rock 'n' roll era, was a year younger than Pete Townshend and five months older than Keith Moon. Roddam understood the value of electricity and the dangers of putting rock lyrics in the mouths of cabaret entertainers. When Townshend put forth the idea of rerecording the *Quadrophenia* album with full orchestral backing, Roddam put his foot down. There would be no more tinkering with the Who's music than a few superfluous additions (a bit of piano here, a touch of electric guitar there). Without having to wrestle with the surrealism of a story like *Tommy*, Roddam could take his approach and aesthetic in a totally different direction: dead realistic and grimy with London soot. The glitzy likes of Ann-Margret or Elton John would be completely distracting, completely out of place in this environment. A cast of newcomers, relative newcomers, and dependable character actors would be better suited to the verisimilitude. The closest the movie came to banking on a star was a minor role for Sting, and the Police hadn't quite taken the world into custody yet in 1979.

Franc Roddam only had a couple of directing credits for British television on his CV when he got the *Quadrophenia* gig. He'd made the proto-reality show *The Family* in 1974 and the gritty street drama *Dummy*, about a deaf and dumb (but not blind) girl who becomes a prostitute, in 1977. Both films displayed Roddam's affinity for the working and lower classes, which would come in handy while bringing *Quadrophenia* to life. He was as respectful of his subjects as he was of the Who's record. While also insisting on using the band's original music, he recreated a number of the scenes from the LP's booklet, making Ethan Russell's photos move and breathe: Jimmy tooling down the road in his Lambretta or lounging beneath his porn wall or slumping on the 5:15 out of his brain between a couple of bowler-bedecked geezers. Roddam selected Phil Daniels to play Jimmy because of his dynamic dramatic abilities, but also for his resemblance to a young Pete Townshend. The director was no dummy, recognizing that Jimmy was really a surrogate for the Who's leader. Surely Phil Davis partly got the role of Jimmy's mate Chalky because he looked like Roger Daltrey. Good actor too.

The Who's presence in their second cinematic rock opera is greatly reduced. Aside from a brief clip of them performing "Anyway, Anyhow, Anywhere" on

Ready Steady Go!, they never appear in the film outside of still photos or record sleeves. This was another smart move, not requiring these rock stars in their mid-thirties to look more youthful than any pre-CGI special effects could make possible. Their very seventies beards and bushy tresses might have created a problem too (remember how resistant John Entwistle was to getting a haircut back in the Pete Meaden days!), though period authenticity is not high on Roddam's agenda. *Quadrophenia* is lousy with anachronisms. The rockers wear their hair and beards hippie long. At one point in the film, the 1978 film *Heaven Can Wait* is visible on a cinema marquee. A copy of the 1974 twofer of *A Quick One/The Who Sell Out* can be seen sitting atop a hi-fi (the *original* versions of those records weren't even released until after the film's events!). There's no reason to believe such things are anything more than sloppy flubs, but they are not entirely inappropriate because *Quadrophenia*—with

Presumably, Cross Section were the winners of this *NME* contest to appear in *Quadrophenia*. The ad's promise of "INSTANT STARDOM!!" failed to specify that the stardom would come and go in an instant. Whether or not Cross Section's appearance in the film actually won them any GROUPIES!! is yet another frequently asked question that must go unanswered.   *Author's collection*

its economic despair and youthful unrest—was as relevant to 1970s Britain as it was to its own period setting. It is as much about the mods of 1965 as it is about the punks of 1978. Townshend never intended the *Quadrophenia* concept to be a strict period piece in the first place. He was more concerned with the phases young people go through than the specifics of mod, so synthesizers might find a place on his record, and mid-seventies signposts may pop up in the film to remind us that we are not just watching a long-gone England but one still viewable from any window.

Considerably less sensational than *Tommy* and more tied to the place it was created, *Quadrophenia* did not have anything near the international impact its forerunner enjoyed. There would be no Oscar nominations for Phil Daniels or Lesley Ash, no eight-figure rental returns in the United States. However, for a drama that truly embodies the Who's angst and romance, their everyman appeal, their violence and sensitivity, their artistry rather than their pomposity or pretentiousness, *Quadrophenia* is the classic.

Five Concert Films

There's no substitute for sitting in an actual concert hall and having your eardrums personally blown out by the World's Greatest Rock 'n' Roll Band. But if you simply cannot afford a concert ticket—or a time machine to take you back to when Keith Moon and John Entwistle still trod the boards—the following concert films are the best simulation you're going to get. Just be sure to set your volume knob to LOUD.

Monterey Pop (1968)

Those who didn't get a chance to see the next generation of stars at the Monterey County Fairgrounds in June '67 got an enticing sampler in late '68 when D. A. Pennebaker's *Monterey Pop* slipped into cinemas. For many Americans, this was their first full-color dose of Janis, Jimi, Ravi, and the Who.

Monterey Pop was not the first great multiartist rock 'n' roll concert film. That distinction belongs to 1964's *The T.A.M.I. Show*, an exhilarating cavalcade of pop and soul performers, including James Brown, the Beach Boys, The Supremes, and the Rolling Stones. However, *Monterey Pop* was the first to go for a more *vérité* style in the mode of 1960's *Jazz on a Summer Day*. Pennebaker didn't use any narration or employ cornball hosts like Jan and Dean from *The T.A.M.I. Show*. He filmed the hippie fans in all their babbling, zooted glory ("Have you ever been to a love-in? The vibrations are just going to be flowing everywhere!" Like, wow.), and provided no other orientation for each artist than popping their names on the screen and, maybe, including a snippet of their introductions from the festival. The Who receive neither, cutting directly from the Animals bowdlerizing "Paint It Black" to Pete Townshend's disembodied voice warning, "This is where it all ends." That's more than an idle threat. The preceding thirty minutes of good vibrations are violently splintered by his band's psychotic, instrument-demolishing performance of "My Generation." When it's all over, we know what we witnessed from the word "WHO" printed on the bass drum rolling across the stage.

The Who are sometimes painted as the bad-vibe merchants who gobbed on the love-in, but *Monterey Pop* isn't all peace and positivity. Janis Joplin's show-stopping performance of "Ball and Chain" is a raw expression of the pain that would propel her to an early death. Jimi Hendrix may bring more seductive sensuality to his destruction than the Who did, but his act is destructive nonetheless. Such moments make *Monterey Pop* more than a hippie time capsule. They offer a taste of the unrest at the heart of the counterculture and the revolutionary methods some of its members employed to enact change. *The T.A.M.I. Show* was thoroughly convincing in explaining why young people dug this boisterous new kind of music. *Monterey Pop* took that music and its audience completely seriously.

Woodstock (1970)

A depiction of the counterculture as frank and empathetic as *Monterey Pop* didn't find distribution easily, and D. A. Pennebaker had to resort to screening it at a porno cinema on the Lower East Side of Manhattan where it played to dope-puffing audiences for a year. What a difference fifteen months make. Michael Wadleigh's film of 1969's Woodstock Festival was a massive mainstream smash. Made on a paltry $600,000 budget, *Woodstock* earned some $23 million during its year of release (it would more than double that figure by the end of the decade) and garnered glowing reviews. It won an Oscar for Best Documentary Feature of 1970 and was selected for inclusion in the National Film Registry in 1996. *Woodstock* completed the Who's international takeover at the same time *Tommy* was doing its part for the cause.

Michael Wadleigh began his career as a cinematographer on Jim McBride's influential indie flick *David Holzman's Diary* and Martin Scorsese's first feature, *Who's That Knocking at My Door?* Scorsese served as assistant director when Wadleigh made his first film. Initially, the director was more interested in the festival's political implications than its musical entertainments. In 1911, the American Communist Party formed in Woodstock, and the area went on to become a gathering place for intellectuals and anarchists. Despite the concert's relocation outside of that town rich in leftist history, Wadleigh was enticed by the promise of bands reflecting his own ideology and even put up his own cash to ensure the movie would see completion.

Wadleigh tailored his approach for each act, from using a single ten-minute take for Canned Heat to a multicamera, multiscreen presentation to convey the grandeur of the Who. Their performance of "See Me, Feel Me" as the sun rises on acres of mud and hippies is a transcendent highlight of a three-hour movie with its share of them (Sly and the Family Stone's exhilarating pledge to "Take You Higher"; Hendrix's iconic exorcism of the national anthem). Never before had Roger Daltrey so commanded the stage, hitting his golden idol stride in fringed jacket and corkscrew locks. Pete Townshend communes with the crowd by presenting them with a sacramental S.G. If Woodstock was the miserable experience the Who always said it was, there is no evidence of that on the screen. Chalk it up to Wadleigh's canny talents and the Who's refusal to ever shortchange an audience.

Listening to You: The Who at the Isle of Wight (1998)

The Who owned their place as rock's greatest festival act once and for all at the Isle of Wight Festival of Music on August 30, 1970. Murray Lerner, who'd previously made *Festival*, a 1967 doc about the Newport Folk Festival, was on hand to film the event. There were plans to release the Who's set as a concert film in the seventies, but because sponsor Fiery Creations Ltd. lost so much money on the event, ownership of the footage ended up with the creditors. This was a tremendous shame as Lerner caught the Who playing a sublime set scattered with such oddities as "Water," "I Don't Even Know Myself," and "Spoonful." His approach was not as cinematic as Pennebaker or Wadleigh's. He just shot some straightforward footage of the Who at work. But what incredible work!

The legal issues were finally settled in time for the film to be released as *Listening to You: The Who at the Isle of Wight* in 1998 (a multiartist sampler of the festival called *Message to Love* was released the previous year and showcased the Who's performances of "Young Man Blues" and "Naked Eye," which didn't make the cut of *Listening to You*). It can now stand as the best sustained blast of the Who in concert on DVD.

The Who at Kilburn: 1977 (2008)

History may teach us that *The Who at Kilburn: 1977* would be the worst Who concert on film. Its reputation as a shambles preceded its release two decades after the fact. Everyone was in a shitty mood, and the performances were so dire that Jeff Stein had to reshoot the footage of "Baba O'Riley" and "Won't Get Fooled Again" he wanted for *The Kids Are Alright*. So it was quite a surprise when a DVD of the Kilburn show was released in 2008. Surely, this must be nothing more than a desperate money grab.

Yes, the Who were not in their finest form at Kilburn on that December day in 1977. John Entwistle's pitch isn't at its sharpest on "My Wife," nor is Pete's sure-handedness with the chords. Roger Daltrey discovers too late that he doesn't remember the words to "Dreaming from the Waist" (Townshend's critique: "A fresh turd"). "Who Are You" is little more than an inchoate jam. Townshend most certainly is not in the chipper mood he was in at the Isle of Wight, challenging "any big-mouthed little git" in the audience to take his guitar, grumbling that Stein should send the audience home, and taking out his rage on a paper cup. Keith Moon gets in on the griping when Daltrey nearly skips over his "Tommy's Holiday Camp" spotlight. However, moments such as these make Kilburn fascinating viewing. The previous concert films presented the Who as veritably flawless, virtually unstoppable, totally inspiring—regardless of the serious problems that plagued those gigs at Monterey, Woodstock, and the Isle of Wight (see chapter 22). The Who at Kilburn comes alive with its flaws, giving us a fully human look at these rock gods. And even if Townshend is in a shitty mood, he's still really funny about it, making his tantrums endearing instead of disheartening. We get to see Keith Moon for one last time, caterwauling his way through "Tommy's Holiday Camp" and parodying/embodying the extremes of rock star pomposity in his purple, glittery superhero costume. Plus there *is* some great music, particularly in the opening double punch of "I Can't Explain" and "Substitute" and Entwistle's staggering bass work that rescues "Dreaming from the Waist" from Daltrey's dodgy memory. If *Listening to You* is the concert film most likely to win over potential Who fans, then *Kilburn: 1977* is the one most likely to make them understand the Who.

The Who: Live in Houston, Texas, 1975 (2012)

Reaching deeper into the vaults, Eagle Rock Entertainment released a less historic but considerably tighter concert on DVD in 2012. Kicking off a North American tour, the Who required a bit of warming up at their gig at the Summit basketball arena in Houston on November 20, 1975. Once they got in gear, they were playing on peak through an intriguing set built around an extended *Tommy* tribute but spiced with a few numbers from the recently released *Who by Numbers* when the words of "Dreaming from the Waist" were still fresh in Roger Daltrey's head. Unfortunately, the presentation does not serve the performance well. Shot on video, *Live in Houston, Texas 1975* sounds tinny and compressed despite Jon Astley's valiant effort to restore the audio. The use of cheesy visual effects draws attention to the poor image quality and dates the movie badly (at one point we're forced to watch a freeze frame of Daltrey while the crowd screams for a full three minutes! *Three!*). When we're not watching the band in mood-murdering slo-mo or Keith Moon and Pete Townshend being superimposed over each other like they're costarring in a karaoke video, the picture is often completely static. Worst of all, we barely see John Entwistle—not a glimpse of his thunder fingers as he thunders through his "My Generation" solo. Still, what *Live in Houston* lacks as cinema it makes up for in music, because after all, we at least get to hear that solo. We also get to see Keith Moon firing at full velocity shortly before he lost the plot for good. For that alone, this would be an essential concert film.

On the Soundtrack

The Who made their grandest impression when they actually appeared on-screen, but sometimes it takes nothing more than a few power chords from "Baba O'Riley" to manipulate emotions to the precise level filmmakers desire. As we saw in the previous chapter, the Who's music has often been used as a valuable tool to get audiences weeping, raising fists, oriented in an era, or completely clear on a plot point. We've seen director Sam Mendes use "The Seeker" to clarify that Lester Burnam is on a quest of self-realization and not just fantasizing about humping teenage girls in *American Beauty*. We've also seen Bill Maher use it to illustrate his quest for sanity in a world fueled on religious superstitions in his potently hilarious documentary *Religulous*. We've seen Cameron Crowe use

"Getting in Tune" to show that Jerry Maguire is going to get his life and career on track. We've seen the paramedics taking "their bloody bag out" to the strains of "Bell Boy" in Martin Scorsese's *Bringing Out the Dead* and Julian Temple illustrating vintage sex-ed footage with a bit of "Pictures of Lily" in his Sex Pistols doc, *The Filth and the Fury*. When the Angels slip into disguises to go undercover in *Charlie's Angels: Full Throttle*, "Who Are You" plays on the soundtrack, while that same song was used to more artistic effect in Nicolas Roeg's *Bad Timing*, in which Art Garfunkel plays a psychiatrist who turns out to be a wacko obsessed with Pete Townshend's real-life obsession, Theresa Russell. In *Rushmore*, Wes Anderson came to use the *Rock and Roll Circus* version of "A Quick One While He's Away" following more atypical circumstances. Initially, he planned to load his soundtrack with Kinks songs because he intended the film's lead character, Max Fisher, to be a British exchange student wearing a blazer similar to those worn by Ray and Dave Davies in the early sixties. Although American Jason Schwartzman would end up playing Max, the school uniform remained, and Anderson diversified his soundtrack to include other British artists, such as the Who, the Rolling Stones, Chad and Jeremy, Faces, and the Creation.

At times, the Who figured into films more integrally than a song or two on a soundtrack. The first such instance was Michael Apted's *Stardust* from 1974, which not only used "My Generation" to help set its sixties scene, but costarred Keith Moon as J. D. Clover, the drummer behind David Essex's rock star Jim MacLaine (they'd first played their respective characters in 1973's *That'll Be the Day*). MacLaine later pens his very own rock opera, and in a far more obscure reference to Who lore, watches a bit of Dougal the Dog from *The Magic Roundabout* on the telly! Richard Curtis's 2009 film *The Boat That Rocked*, a fictionalized account of the mid-sixties radio pirates, would be unthinkable without a healthy slab of Who, and "My Generation," "I Can See for Miles," and "Won't Get Fooled Again" all featured on a soundtrack a lot better than the movie. Steven Soderbergh used "The Seeker" in *The Limey* because main character Wilson is seeking answers about his daughter's death. He also uses it as a sly nod to the fact that Wilson is played by Chris Stamp's brother Terence. In Spike Lee's *Summer of Sam*, a Brooklyn poseur jumps on the punk bandwagon but exposes his ignorance about it by selecting the Who as his favorite punk band. If only he'd decided to spin *My Generation* constantly instead of *Who's Next*, he might have gotten away with it. In Quentin Tarantino's *Death Proof*, there is no Who music to speak of, but the band does feature in one of its many monologues when DJ Jungle Julia explains that Pete Townshend once considered quitting the Who to join Dave Dee, Dozy, Beaky, Mick, and Tich, "thus making it Dave Dee, Dozy, Beaky, Mick, Tich, and Pete." Jungle Julia may have lost her job at the radio station for that bit of bullshit if she wasn't dismembered a few moments later.

28

Do It Alone

The Essential Solo Albums

By the seventies, the Who had achieved the international stardom they'd fought hard to win throughout the sixties. With that success came a certain complacency. Even as crazy ideas such as living with fans while composing a new album or reinterpreting the mod days as a prog rock opera still flitted hither and thither, there now was a strict formula in place. The smirking quirk of the psychedelic era had been replaced by heavy rock for good. John Entwistle got his two or three songs per album, Roger Daltrey and Keith Moon got their none.

For such a creative quartet, having to fulfill fan expectations in such a way was frustrating. Pete Townshend started resenting the Who's volume and aggression and longing for an outlet for the lighter side he'd abandoned. Entwistle started accumulating songs for which there was "no room" on his band's records. Daltrey wanted to see if there was life beyond being Townshend's vocal chords. Moon wanted to see if he could inflate his star any bigger.

And so came the solo albums. At a time when most of their thriving peers remained loyal to the team—not the Rolling Stones nor the Beach Boys nor Pink Floyd would start splintering off for solo discs until the mid-seventies, while Led Zeppelin, Black Sabbath, and the Kinks waited until the eighties—the ever restless members of the Who were exploring life outside the unit.

The Who's solo ventures are a mixed bushel. There is some incredible music to be heard on their records, but there is also a fair share of dross. To get an idea of where the solo-curious fan should start, I went the same route as I did when assembling the underrated songs of this book's sixth and thirty-fourth chapters. I roamed the reviews, blogs, and message boards. I put out calls for fans to vote for their favorite Pete, Roger, and John records (since Keith only put out one on his own, his place on the following list was preordained). After tallying the results I was able to extract three favorites for each of them, though the fact that some less-than-spectacular records slipped into the list says something about the limitations of my venture. So here they are, straight from the fans, the Who's ten essential solo albums . . . warts and all.

Smash Your Head Against the Wall—John Entwistle (1971)

Prolific Pete was the first member of the Who to release material outside of the band, distributing seven home recordings on the *Happy Birthday* record to Meher Baba followers in 1970, but John Entwistle was the first to chuck out a full-length LP. Before then he'd been "smashing his head against the wall trying to get songs on the Who albums," as he told Jud Cost in 1997. So Entwistle resolved to stop smashing his head and start rolling the tape.

Although he had a small backlog of songs, he actually didn't have enough for an LP and had to dash off some new ones to bring it up to size. He has said that his main impetus for making *Smash Your Head Against the Wall* was the desire to sing his own songs, an odd frustration considering that to date, Roger Daltrey had only taken the lead on one of his compositions, "Someone's Coming."

Recorded over a mere three weeks in late autumn 1970, *Smash Your Head Against the Wall* is everything one might want from a John Entwistle solo record. His lyrics remain gloomy, morbid, and deadpan funny in the tradition of "Boris the Spider" and "Whiskey Man." As it was on those tracks, the sound is murky and black, which establishes the cemetery atmosphere and unifies a diverse selection of songs. After getting the one heavy Who-like rocker, "My Size," out of the way, Entwistle samples a bit of brassy funk, a bit of acoustic balladry, a bit of pub sing-along, and a bit of tribal clatter. Entwistle rarely uses the record as an excuse to flex his finger muscles (which may have disappointed some fans), his bass often taking a backseat to the punchy and mournful horns, acoustic guitars, piano, and percussion that keep *Smash Your Head Against the Wall* interesting.

One thing that's never relegated to the shadows is Entwistle's fixation on death. The skull-crushing "My Size" reimagines "Boris the Spider" from the perspective of the arachnid before he gets squished. The tender and lovely "Ted End" is the tragicomic tale of all the people who couldn't be bothered to attend the funeral of a recently deceased schlub. "Heaven and Hell," in a more dirgelike arrangement than the Who's, thumbs its nose at the afterlife, while "You're Mine" voices a self-satisfied devil hollering warnings from the hot place. Elsewhere, Entwistle has a go at a barfly on "Pick Me Up (Big Chicken)," sneers at officious waiters and cops on "What Kind of People Are They?," and expresses his disdain for plastic surgery on the devastating "No. 29 (Eternal Youth)" and the overeagerly faithful on "I Believe in Everything." He even manages to let his guard down on the unexpectedly sincere road lament "What Are We Doing Here?" Loaded with superb songs veiled in alluringly Gothic gauze, *Smash Your Head Against the Wall* is the easy favorite among the fans, far outranking any of Entwistle's other records.

Whistle Rymes—John Entwistle (1972)

Entwistle put the best songs he had in storage on *Smash Your Head Against the Wall*, so it's only to be expected that his second effort isn't as substantial.

Whistle Rymes is no washout, though, nor is it a retread. He expands his sound with a newfound brightness, a conscious lack of guitars, and some well-placed synthesizer, even using it in place of his trademark instrument on the waltzing "Thinkin' It Over." The songs are tighter, poppier, and livelier, and there isn't nearly as much death. In fact, on the suicide-pondering "Thinkin' It Over," the guy actually decides against offing himself. Well, now, that isn't very Entwistley, is it?

Lest you fear The Ox had become a tea-sipping Pollyanna, take comfort in the petulant "I Feel Better" and the nihilistic "Who Cares?" There are also "Ten Little Friends," a bouncy funk about a deranged shut-in, and the propulsive and infectious "Apron Strings," on which the singer tells his overbearing mom he's glad she's dead (just to be clear, Queenie Entwistle was a fun-loving gal whom John loved dearly and who lived to the ripe old age of eighty-eight). He also gets off a few of his funniest character sketches, playing a perpetual dupe on "I Found Out," a guy who has mistaken a young woman for a hooker on "I Was Just Being Friendly," and a peeping tom on "The Window Shopper." John and Graham Lethbridge's storybook album art is totally far-out too.

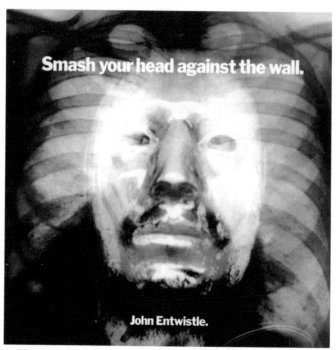

As if wearing a plastic serial killer mask wasn't gruesome enough, John Entwistle had his face superimposed over a chest x-ray on the cover of his debut album, *Smash Your Head Against the Wall.* The image complements the morbid music nicely.   *Author's collection*

Daltrey—Roger Daltrey (1973)

Roger Daltrey wasn't a frustrated songwriter, and he got to sing all the songs he desired with the Who. So why the hell did he need to make a solo album? Perhaps no one has asked that question more often than Roger Daltrey, who never had ambitions of splitting from the Who and knew how fortunate he was to be the voice of some of rock's most exceptional songs.

From Daltrey's perspective, making his first solo album was actually in the best interest of the Who. He saw it as a way to develop his vocal craft by voicing songs very different from Pete Townshend's. He'd then come back to his band refreshed and with some new tricks in his repertoire. When his single "Giving It All Away" went top five in the United Kingdom, he told *Crawdaddy* that he was happy that it "helped the group through a very dull period, the fact that someone has been successful outside of the group," but didn't seem overly impressed with the achievement otherwise. In fact, he was a lot more enthusiastic about John Entwistle's records and disappointed that they hadn't been more successful. Despite Daltrey's best intentions, his solo record caused a bit of friction at home base. Kit Lambert and Chris Stamp's dislike of it and lack of interest in putting it out hastened their ousting from the management position (see chapter 4).

Fans have been more accepting of *Daltrey*, appreciating it for one of the main reasons Daltrey made it: it sounds nothing like the Who. One would definitely be hard-pressed to come up with less Who-like collaborators than former cornball crooner Adam Faith ("What Do You Want," "Poor Me," etc.) and future cheeseball pop star Leo Sayer ("You Make Me Feel Like Dancing," "When I Need You"). That their songs cowritten with producer David Courtney conspired to remake the Who's front man into an MOR minstrel laid the groundwork for an embarrassment. Yet, somehow, it worked.

Daltrey is a refreshingly organic affair in the mode of some of Elton John's better albums, particularly *Tumbleweed Connection* and *Honky Château*. The songs are reasonably eclectic, though all of a similar singer-songwritery stripe (even though the singer didn't write a note on the record). While the string arrangements occasionally overwhelm, as they do on the schmaltzy "You Are Yourself," they can be incredibly effective, as they are on the stark and icy "When the Music Stops." Drummer Bob Henrit keeps the beat loose, almost sloppy, undercutting the polish pleasingly. Daltrey sounds like he isn't completely sure of the best way to interpret some of this material, hence the cracks in his delivery of the chummy oompah folk "One Man Band," but he's in great shape when the material is closer to his area of expertise, as the tough "The Way of the World" and the sensitive "Giving It All Away" are. The record's most serious flaw are its clichéd lyrics. After hearing Roger Daltrey sing Pete Townshend's inspired words, it's a drag to hear him mouth drivel like "It's a hard life when you feel down / And nobody understands you, they leave you hanging around." The best songs—"The Way of the World," "Giving It All Away," the wonderfully catchy "Thinking," "When the Music Stops"—rise above that issue.

Rigor Mortis Sets In—John Entwistle (1973)

The fans voted with concerted enthusiasm for *Smash Your Head Against the Wall* and came out fairly strong for *Whistle Rymes* too. After that, there's a steep drop-off. John Entwistle simply wasn't a prolific enough writer to keep a consistent solo career going. He'd tapped his keg when the time came to make his third album, hence the preponderance of other people's songs. Since his inspiration never quite recovered again, *Rigor Mortis Sets In* was voted the third most essential Entwistle solo album by default. This is not a great album, though the concept isn't half bad. Declaring rock 'n' roll dead during the days when stadium artistes such as Yes and ELP dominated the scene, Entwistle eulogized the simplicity of old with a bunch of classic covers and retro tributes. The problem is that he never stretches his imagination. His versions of the warhorses "Mr. Bassman," "Hound Dog," and "Lucille" are too faithful. "Mr. Bassman" would have been a great opportunity to twist Johnny Cymbal's doo-wop staple with a wild bass solo. Instead, Entwistle just copies the original as closely as possible. That he rerecorded his own "My Wife" just two years after the Who's definitive original shows how hard up for material he was. That the remake sounds so much less forceful, with its fatigued *boom-chick* drumming, highlights how pointless it is. Paging Dr. Moon.

Entwistle's originals redeem *Rigor Mortis Sets In*, though none are up to the level of the ones on his first two records. "Gimmie That Rock 'n' Roll" is a Little Richard–style raver on which Entwistle pulverizes opera, Dixieland, R&B, classical, opera, and everything else that neither rocks nor rolls. It is the album's mission statement, and though nothing that follows approaches its energy and commitment, there's still fun to be had. "Do the Dangle" is a "Bony Moronie" rewrite about a bunch of silly dances, culminating in the title step, which involves tying a rope around your neck, hopping on a chair, and kicking it away to leave yourself "dancing on air." At least you can't say Entwistle was lightening up. His conservatism shows on "Made in Japan," a xenophobic rant about how nothing's made in England anymore, but the tune is the album's best. On "Big Black Cadillac," a lazy sketch about an uneventful run-in with gangsters, he and drummer Graham Deakin shake themselves awake to whip off exciting solos. The song isn't great, but at least the band puts some elbow grease into their performance. The same cannot be said of the turgid "Roller Skate Kate," which sounds like "Earth Angel" and goofs on the dead-teen fad that gave us such best-forgotten hits as "Teen Angel" and "Tell Laura I Love Her."

That part of the original concept was to link the tracks with "a parody of children's character Andy Pandy spitting and vomiting" (*Anyway, Anyhow, Anywhere*) indicates just how seriously John Entwistle took his solo career in 1973. Unfortunately, his comedy songs were no longer as funny as he thought they were, and the decline would continue with his next album *Mad Dog*, on which the one decent song is the title track, a Phil Spector tribute on which he doesn't even sing.

Two Sides of the Moon—Keith Moon (1975)

Two Sides of the Moon is Keith Moon's best solo album. *Two Sides of the Moon* is Keith Moon's worst solo album. *Two Sides of the Moon* is Keith Moon's only solo album. *Hear* Keith destroy old favorites: the Beatles' "In My Life," the Beach Boys' "Don't Worry Baby," and the Who's own "The Kids Are Alright!" *See* Keith bare his ass on the inner sleeve! *Smell* the desperation of a great drummer attempting to sing! *Feel* your wallet get lighter as you waste several bucks on what surely must be one of the most misguided records ever made!

With too much time on his idle hands, too many perpetually crocked friends indulging his ego, two hundred thousand of MCA's dollars to burn, and enough coke and booze to give the population of China a pretty good buzz, Keith Moon went to work on a record of his very own. Who else would want to claim it? It has often been written that *Two Sides of the Moon* could have been a spectacular blowout showcasing his superhuman musicianship, a "drums-up-front album of instrumental classics," as John Atkins wrote in an eloquent "what might have been" scenario in his *Generations* fanzine. However, most Who albums do a pretty good job of celebrating the drums, and as *Rigor Mortis Sets In* hinted, covers of instrumental oldies don't always make for essential listening. Plus, Moon hated drum solos and wanted to spotlight another side of himself: his singing . . . I guess . . . *talents?*

Actually, in some of his earlier performances—"I Need You," "Girl's Eyes," "We Close Tonight," "Bell Boy"—Moon's singing isn't bad, but without a decent producer to steer him toward the right material (the Beatles' old roadie Mal Evans began the sessions, but was quickly replaced by Skip Taylor and John Stronach), he was doomed. Hearing Moon warble "Don't Worry Baby," one of Brian Wilson's most exquisitely sung pieces, isn't even good for a giggle. His voice cracks. Notes slide miles away from their intended targets. All the syrupy strings and corny backing singers in the universe aren't enough to smother his performance into acceptability. Only "Crazy Like a Fox," a pretty good blast of Bowie-esque glam, and the C&W Ricky Nelson duet "One Night Stand" bury him deep enough in the mix to be listenable.

Some people enjoy *Two Sides of the Moon* as a bit of kitsch, but there are too many stumbling blocks to appreciate it at this level. This is the work of a guy using self-aggrandizement and silly comedy to mask deep depression. It's a self-indulgent vanity project by a guy slowly murdering himself with extreme self-indulgence. In light of his death, it's tough to listen to "Teenage Idol," an absurd fifties parody on the surface, a disturbingly sincere admission of loneliness at heart. That Moon chose to sing this without any of his comedic gestures is telling. A similar sadness hovers over the utterly ridiculous, overorchestrated

"In My Life." The album is also an unfortunate waste of talent, though it's likely that Ringo Starr, Harry Nilsson, John Sebastian, Jim Keltner, Bobby Keys, Klaus Voormann, Flo and Eddie, and Miguel Ferrer—the future *Twin Peaks* supporting player who drummed on "Don't Worry Baby"—came along to get wasted, not use their talents. Yet, because of my desire to represent every member of the Who in this chapter, we still have to call *Two Sides of the Moon* "essential." Now let us never speak of it again.

One of the Boys—Roger Daltrey (1977)

Nineteen seventy-five was rough for Who solo albums. During the same year *Two Sides of the Moon* and *Mad Dog* were foisted on the world, Roger Daltrey followed his fine debut with *Ride a Rock Horse*, a collection of middling blues and ballads packaged in a totally tasteful sleeve depicting the singer as an airbrushed centaur.

Unlike Townshend and Moon, Daltrey was able to bring his solo career back on track, and he did so with a record many have rated as his best. *One of the Boys* is strong and eclectic, perhaps not as unified as *Daltrey*, but his voice is in top form throughout, and the lyrics don't suck. Daltrey expanded his stable of contributing writers to include such heavyweights as Paul McCartney and former Zombie Colin Blunstone (though their songs are among the weaker ones). He also got in on the creating, cowriting three numbers inspired by *McVicar by Himself*, the autobiography of an armed robber who so fascinated Daltrey that the singer would soon devote an entire film and album to the guy.

Once again, Elton John seems to be Daltrey's guiding light, which is particularly evident in the opening cut. "Parade" could be an outtake from *Captain Fantastic and the Brown Dirty Cowboy* with its piano-based slow burn and weary view of stardom. "Leon," another Elton-esque number (toss a "v" in the middle of the title and it becomes one!) is buoyed by John Entwistle's expressive bass playing. Daltrey started embracing the sound for which he is best known, and the two best songs on *One of the Boys* are its most Who-like. Murray Head's "Say It Ain't So, Joe" is a glorious power ballad with a haunting refrain. Andy Pratt's "Avenging Annie" is mighty and anthemic. Pratt composed the tune after listening to the Byrds' version of Woody Guthrie's "Pretty Boy Floyd," hence the melodic similarity. Pratt's wife inspired its outlaw protagonist, though his message is muddled: if Annie is the "avenger of womanhood," why would she consider getting back together with her abusive asshole boyfriend at the end of the song? Nevertheless, the song is inspiring. Pratt took some interesting chances on his original version by singing it in falsetto and from Annie's perspective. Unsurprisingly, big, macho Rog did neither, and though the shift in point-of-view might have been a bit cowardly, I doubt anyone would miss Pratt's piercing Bee Gees impression.

Elsewhere there's the dynamic country of "The Prisoner," the "My Generation"–quoting title track (which spawned a promo film often screened as a short feature before *Star Wars!*), and "Doing It All Again," an extraordinary, airy ballad. With its massed choral harmonies, absence of drums, and synth bass line, it sounds like *Carl and the Passions*–era Beach Boys.

Daltrey's view of *One of the Boys* was as dim as that of his other solo records (with the exception of *Daltrey*). The critics differed. Upon its 1977 release, Tony Stewart of the *NME* called it "the best album I have heard this year." In *The New Rolling Stone Record Guide*, Dave Marsh praised it for being "nearly as hard-rocking as a Who LP." Those were both exaggerations, but *One of the Boys* is still a convincing contender for Roger Daltrey's best record.

Empty Glass—Pete Townshend (1980)

While his coworkers were diversifying with widely released solo albums throughout the seventies, Pete Townshend was dabbling. He only made his work on the collaborative mini-albums *Happy Birthday* and *I Am* (which found an unlikely superfan in Keith Moon) available to Meher Baba devotees. The excellent *Who Came First* (1972) was afforded wider release on Track Records, but Townshend once again called on friends—Billy Nicholls and Ronnie Lane—to fill it out. Townshend and Lane split duties evenly on 1977's *Rough Mix*, another superb album bearing Townshend's name. He didn't consider himself a true solo artist until that name appeared unaccompanied on the cover of *Empty Glass*.

Most of the others' solo albums tended to suffer in comparison to the Who records that immediately preceded and followed them. For the first time, the reverse was true, and as early as 1974, Townshend told the *New York Times* that he'd be keeping his best material for himself. Sandwich *Empty Glass* between *Who Are You* and *Face Dances* and you'll hear exactly what he was talking about and why Daltrey was so irritated by Townshend's new distribution of songs. *Empty Glass* is a masterful collection of songs: commercially astute ("Let My Love Open the Door" charted as high in the United States as any Who single ever did), artistically wholesome, and carrying a profound personal stake.

Nineteen seventy-eight to 1980 was one of the most difficult periods in Pete Townshend's life. After Keith Moon's death, he was trapped in a cyclone of self-abuse, consuming booze with no consideration for the future, drifting from his marriage, partying as if it was his duty to keep the torch of Moon's self-destruction lit. *Empty Glass* chronicles his efforts to put himself back together. In 1994, he told *Playboy* the album was like "a war medal" earned after two years in "hell." While it is an exorcism of sorts, it is not an abrasive one in the vein of John Lennon's *Plastic Ono Band*. Even the punkiest tracks, "Rough Boys" and "Jools and Jim," are examples of Townshend's song craft at full maturation and complexity. "Rough Boys" can be read as both an incitement of violence and a celebration of rough gay sex at a time when most artists of Townshend's popularity kept those kinds of thoughts under wraps. "Jools and Jim" spits daggers at the *NME*'s Julie Burchill and Tony Parsons for denigrating Keith Moon as soon as he was safely in the grave, while also being equitable enough to recognize that the rift between himself and the journos could probably be talked out over drinks. "Let My Love Open the Door" (a song about God regularly mistaken for a valentine), "And I Moved" (which Townshend wrote for Bette Midler, whose management rejected it as "smutty"), "Keep on Working," "A Little Is Enough," and "Gonna Get Ya" are plain irresistible. The alternately delicate and triumphant "I Am an Animal" is a naked self-portrait while the title track is a taut, harrowing, multisectional epic overflowing with all the self-doubt, despair, anger, love, and joy saturating the rest of the record. This is music as exhilarating as anything the Who ever recorded and as potent as any other artist's. As personal as *Empty Glass* is, it so sweepingly sums up the human experience—the passion and exhaustion, the sex and love, the friendship and antagonism, the excess and reflection, the impulse to give up and the resolution to keep on working—that it never becomes inaccessible. No wonder Daltrey was miffed.

McVicar—Roger Daltrey (1980)

Although Roger Daltrey kept churning out solo records on a regular schedule, he never really put his heart into them, perhaps because he knew they'd never trump his work with the Who. Instead, he invested himself in an activity that would never suffer any such comparisons. After his acclaimed turn as the title character of *Tommy*, Daltrey became the Who's resident actor (Keith Moon had designs on that title himself, but he didn't have the discipline). After gaining confidence with a couple of other gigs in Ken Russell's crazy Franz Liszt fantasy-biopic, *Lisztomania*, and the forgettable horror flick *The Legacy*, Daltrey custom built a vehicle for himself called *McVicar*.

Like Daltrey, John "Muscles" McVicar was a smart guy from the rough side of town, a man knotted with anger and ambition. While Daltrey put those feelings to constructive use in a rock 'n' roll band, McVicar became a criminal. Given a twenty-six-year sentence for armed robbery and using firearms, he escaped from Durham Prison in 1969 only to be recaptured after a 744-day manhunt. While completing his prison sentence, he wrote and published his autobiography, *McVicar by Himself*. After reading the book, Daltrey felt an instant kinship with the convict and approached him about adapting it for film. John McVicar made parole in 1978, and the film went into production the following year.

Daltrey recruited former Argent singer Russ Ballard (who'd produced and written several songs for *Ride a Rock Horse*) and Billy Nicholls to help cook up some songs for the soundtrack. When the *McVicar* LP was released in 1980, it was not designated a Roger Daltrey release even though he sings eight of its ten tracks (the remaining two are incidental instrumentals). Regardless, the record has come to be considered an official Roger Daltrey release, and when polling fans for their favorite of his albums, it is the one that came out on top.

The common explanation for why the kids prefer *McVicar* is that it's Daltrey's album that sounds most like the Who. Indeed, Pete Townshend, John Entwistle, Kenney Jones, and Rabbit Bundrick all guest starred on it. However, though the album's two best songs, "Waiting for a Friend" and the title track, bear a definite Who-ish stamp, the rest of it sounds nothing like Daltrey's old group. On *McVicar*, he started to stray from the organic sound of his first three records and into the wasteland of synthesizers and saxes he'd remain lost in for the rest of the eighties. Badly dated arrangements sink the monotonous "Bitter and Twisted" and the minor hit "Free Me." Daltrey's bellowing performances don't help much either. Throughout the album, the lyricism has reverted to the banality of *Daltrey*.

Still, unlike *Parting Should Be Painless* or *Can't Wait to See the Movie*, there is enough good stuff to recommend at least half of *McVicar*. "Waiting for a Friend," "White City Lights," and "McVicar" are all above-average songs impressively performed. "Just a Dream Away" and "Without Your Love" (another minor hit) are sappy, but the former has some nice George Harrison–style slide guitar work, and the latter gains interest from its strange, underwater synth sounds. "Escape, Part One," the first of Jeff Wayne's incidental pieces, sounds like one of Townshend's synthed-up home studio experiments, which means it's pretty neat.

All the Best Cowboys Have Chinese Eyes—Pete Townshend (1982)

Townshend's neat synthesizers dominate his second proper solo album. In contrast to *McVicar*, *All the Best Cowboys Have Chinese Eyes* has the strong material to balance its utter eighties-ness. It also has more of the buck-naked honesty we've come to expect from Pete Townshend, so no matter how much electronic instrumentation he lays on, and no matter how slick and icy the production is, the record never sounds less than completely organic. In 1981, Townshend was still struggling to pull himself out of the hole from which he howled *Empty Glass*. The songs he wrote for *All the Best Cowboys*, released the following year, are similar cries of despair and desire. Once again, he keeps a hold of his commercial instincts even when escorting his songs to unexpected vistas, experimenting with talky stream-of-consciousness on the breathlessly romantic "Stop Hurting People" and the jittery "Communication," crafting a perfect pop song called "Face Dances, Part Two" in herky-jerky 5/4 time, and building bold orchestrations for the majestic "The Sea Refuses No River," another of Townshend's cagily veiled God songs.

Sometimes the album gets so personal that it is almost uncomfortable to hear, as Townshend confesses his sexual failings and suicidal thoughts on "Somebody Saved Me," but this intimacy is a key facet of the wonderful gift that is *All the Best Cowboys Have Chinese Eyes*. As always, Townshend is granting us full access to his pain and his life-affirming joy, while never lapsing into the weepiness that can make such confessions hard to stomach. Though there is much pain in "The Sea Refuses No River," "Somebody Saved Me," "Slit Skirts," "Exquisitely Bored," and so on, the delivery is always invigorating. This makes the moments of sadness that much more devastating, the moments of joy that much more exhilarating, the moments of seeking that much more transcendent. In the

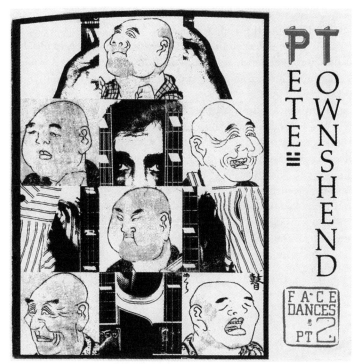

The music video for Pete Townshend's single "Face Dances Part Two" costarred some weird robots provided by former Bonzo Dog Doo-Dah Band member Roger Ruskin Spear.   *Author's collection*

year that the Who put out the fairly indifferent *It's Hard*, Pete Townshend made a much madder, much more interesting album on his own, and it stands the test of time even as it stands unmistakably in 1982.

White City: A Novel—Pete Townshend (1985)

Officially free of the Who, Pete Townshend started applying the ambition that sparked *Tommy*, *Lifehouse*, and *Quadrophenia* to a solo career in full swing. He designated his first post-Who music project not a rock opera but "a novel." Whatever the distinction is, he's probably the only one who understands it.

For the first time, Townshend brought one of his concepts up to date, eschewing tales of teens for a story a lot closer to where he was in 1985, even making himself (or a version of himself) the narrator. Rock Star Pete Townshend returns to the White City council estate in Shepherd's Bush, where he reunites with childhood buddy Jimmy (whom Townshend has hinted is *Quadrophenia*'s main character all grown up). While Townshend glides into town in his limo, Jimmy is stuck in an impoverished, violent microcosm where races clash and women flee from their drunken, abusive husbands to the local domestic refuge.

The distressed scene leaves the socialist star feeling guilty and hypocritical, but also rekindles a youthful spirit that rock 'n' roll can apparently no longer stoke. This tale was much sketchier than Townshend's operas of old, but he still brought the characters and environment to life by nourishing *White City* with his own childhood memories and experiences at Chiswick Family Rescue (see chapter 33).

Though antiseptic eighties production leaves his record sounding brittle and dated, his songs are once again exceptional, and as is always the case with his best conceptual works, they stand strong when pulled from the larger piece. "Give Blood" is a moody, yearning plea to cease fire propelled by an insistent Dave Gilmour riff. "Face the Face" is an ingeniously constructed jazzy show tune completely different from any of Townshend's past work. "Brilliant Blues" is a fun, extra-chewy wad of bubblegum. "Hiding Out" and "Crashing by Design" are sweet synth-pop morsels, while "Secondhand Love" and "White City Fighting" recapture a bit of the old Who aggression. His gnarly guitar only makes a few guest appearances, and it is missed, but *White City* is still another excellent Pete Townshend record, as your votes verify.

29

Our Love Was, Is

Girlfriends and Wives

Without a doubt, the Who was a boys club, a fact so glaring that Pete Townshend worked the male-signifying Mars symbol into his group's logo. Whereas no Beatles bio would be complete without Yoko or Pattie, and the absence of Marianne or Anita would leave a hole in any tale of the Stones, women are generally sidelined in Who history. Yet there were interesting, troubled, and almost unfathomably tolerant women behind the guys. These are the stories of their lives in the eye of that tornado known as the Who.

Jackie Rickman

Of all the wives and girlfriends glossed over in Who biographies, perhaps none are more mysterious than the first. When Roger Daltrey was still a spotty teen bellowing in front of Doug Sandom's drum kit, barely legal enough to drink in the hotels and social clubs he was serenading, he was married. Just five weeks after the Detours morphed into the Who, the eighteen-year-old singer married Jacqueline Rickman, only sixteen and quite pregnant.

In October 1963, the band began a semiregular stint at St. Mary's Hall in Putney. That is where Roger Daltrey first encountered Jackie. A rock 'n' roll rogue, Roger had no qualms about taking advantage of the girls frequenting his gigs, but when this particular tryst resulted in pregnancy, he was "decent" enough to propose. The two were married on March 28, 1964, his friend and Who roadie John Reader serving as witness.

The very next day, Roger was back on the road with the Who, often spending his nights in the touring van rather than making the long trek home to his new bride. Within a few months, he was basically living in the van as a more pleasing alternative to the domesticity waiting for him at his and Jackie's tiny council flat. By this point, Kit Lambert was helming the Who and pushing Roger to split from his wife so that female fans wouldn't write him off as unavailable. Roger actually required no serious pushing at all, valuing his emerging career and his penis far too much to keep himself tied down. To his credit, he continued to support Jackie and his son, Simon, born on August 22, but for all intents and purposes, the marriage was over long, long before a divorce was finalized in May 1970.

Kim Kerrigan

The Who's wives and girlfriends had to endure much in the way of infidelities and erratic rock star misbehavior. No one knew this better than Kim Kerrigan. She had the unfortunate experience of being married to Keith Moon. For outsiders, Keith's bizarre antics can make for hilarious anecdotes. Having to actually live with a guy who insisted on spending entire days as Hitler was an entirely different story.

They met at the Le Disque a Go! Go! Club in March 1965. Born Maryse Elizabeth Patricia Kerrigan, Kim was a gorgeous sixteen-year-old fashion model with the extraordinarily patient demeanor necessary for anyone in for long-term involvement with the troubled Keith Moon. Initially, Kim brought out a latent desire for domesticity in the hell-raiser. What she may not have realized is that desire did not extend to himself. Moon wanted to keep her holed up at home, taking care of the baby and making him supper on the nights he deigned to come home. Such a life was a sharp contrast to her globetrotting girlhood living in Malaysia, Uganda, and Tanganyika. A year after returning to England, her parents shipped her off to a convent in Bray, Ireland. Following that unpleasant stint, she worked as a hairdresser in Bournemouth. That's where Marie Fraser of the Dawn Academy discovered her. Going by her shortened middle name, Patsy, Ms. Kerrigan received her new name when Fraser decided she looked too much like a similarly named model, Pattie Boyd. So Patsy became Kim (and Pattie Boyd soon became Mrs. Beatle Pattie Harrison).

Marriage to a rock star might seem just another wild move in an already untraditional and unstable life, but as far as out-of-control rock stars go, Keith Moon was in a class of his own. At first, Kim enjoyed the wild lifestyle, and even shared Keith's enthusiasm for pills (though, to a much, much more moderate degree). Biographer Tony Fletcher makes a convincing amateur diagnosis that Moon suffered from borderline personality disorder, "a serious mental illness marked by unstable moods, behavior, and relationships" according to the National Institute of Mental Health. If he did suffer from that disorder, it manifested in his self-destructive behavior, his impulsiveness, his terror of abandonment, and of greatest concern to Kim, his uncontrollable anger. Keith was often physically abusive with his wife, breaking her nose on three separate occasions according to Fletcher. His jealousy of men he believed had designs on his wife was as irrepressible as his own serial adulterousness. As father to their daughter Mandy, he rarely made himself available, spent time with his friends' children instead of his own, and made no effort to hide his brutish behavior from her.

After seven insane years with Keith Moon, Kim collected Mandy and split in 1973. He was devastated when she left, wracked with guilt over his abhorrent behavior and often breaking down in front of friends. Unfortunate as her husband's serious mental problems were, she absolutely made the right decision for the sake of her own safety and the well-being of her child. A month after Keith's self-destruction caught up with him for good on September 7, 1978, Kim found a more stable life with new husband and former Small Faces/Faces keyboardist Ian McLagan. She enjoyed a relatively quiet life in Texas as a cosmetologist at the Lake Austin Spa resort until August 2, 2006, when she was killed in a car accident after reportedly jumping a stop sign in Travis County; a tragic end to a turbulent life. Kim was fifty-seven.

Alison Wise

How does a musician define true love? A girlfriend who agrees to carry his amplifier. John Entwistle and Alison Wise were just a couple of teenagers at Acton County Grammar School when they met. He was sixteen, she fourteen. They had their first date at a Scorpions gig, which is when Alison first lugged his amp. He must have been smitten, because when he started adopting stage names, an early one was "John Alison." Their budding romance, and need to sneak around behind Alison's protective parents' backs, would later inspire John's "Someone's Coming," by far the sweetest and most sincere composition in a songwriting career defined by its sarcasm and contempt for romance. Precisely one month after the Who recorded the track, John and Alison were striding down the aisle of Acton Congregational Church.

John knew marriage was inevitable ever since Alison first hauled his amplifier, but when he broke the news to Keith Moon, the drummer was emphatic in his disapproval. John suspected it was more from fear of losing his partner in partying than any particular objections to Alison. In fact, according to Tony Fletcher, Alison was one of the very few people steady enough to inspire relative good behavior in Moon. An adult amongst perpetual rock 'n' roll adolescents, Alison also volunteered for the undesirable task of informing Kim Moon that her husband had picked up a dose of VD while in America.

Meanwhile, John continued his own dual life as homebody lounging about a modest family home in Acton and raving rock 'n' roller taking advantage of the young women at his disposal while on tour. While she was installed at a Manhattan hotel during Woodstock, John and Keith were in the back of a parked car being pleasured by groupies.

John said that Alison was generally good-humored about her marriage, taking no offense when he cartoonishly portrayed her on a jealous murder mission in the song "My Wife." In a 1996 interview with *Goldmine*, he said his ex-wife always found the song funny and "had the ambition to come on and hit me over the head with a rolling pin halfway through it when I was doing it onstage." In *Who I Am*, Pete Townshend repeats a rumor that when John's personal assistant Mick Bratby gave Alison the full rundown of her husband's infidelities, she and Bratby commenced their own affair in the mid-seventies. Regardless, John and Alison remained together until he met a waitress named Maxene in 1978. Knowing their marriage had reached its end, John and Alison Entwistle divorced in 1981.

Karen Astley

Like John Entwistle and Alison Wise, Pete Townshend and Karen Astley met at school, Ealing Art College to be precise. On July 30, 1965, Karen attended a Who gig at the New Fender Club in Middlesex and ended the evening by impetuously kissing Pete before hopping into a taxi. However, it would be his constant impetuousness that would make their marriage a trying one.

Like Pete, Karen was the child of a musician who'd entertained the troops during World War II. Edwin "Ted" Astley made a name for himself after the war as a television and film composer, best known for writing the theme song to Roger Moore's spy series, *The Saint*. Karen was creative too, but she favored fashion over music. She worked as both a dress designer and a model before deciding upon a lower-profile life as a teacher. Rejection of the spotlight remained Karen's m.o. even after she married one of pop's highest-profile personalities on May 20, 1968. While Alison Entwistle, Annette Walter-Lax, and even Kim Kerrigan could be seen discussing their former husbands and boyfriends' band in various documentaries, Karen has remained mum on her husband and the Who, a band she never liked to begin with. Yet she still seems familiar to fans because of Pete Townshend's discussions of her in interviews and his autobiography.

From these sources, we can understand her intelligence, her patience, and her refusal to tolerate her husband's less savory behavior. Pete was not a physically, or apparently, verbally abusive husband. He just had a tendency to get carried away. In *Who I Am*, he discusses his multiple infidelities, not in the use-'em-and-discard-'em manner of Keith Moon, but as if every woman who entered his life was some great and passionate new love. That must have made his affairs all the more painful for his wife.

During the earliest days of their marriage, Pete made a genuine effort to remain faithful to Karen. She supported her husband as he tangled with his band and developed ambitious ideas they didn't always understand, while also instilling in him the pleasures of simple domestic life. He also struck up professional relationships with Karen's brother, Jon, who produced *Who Are You*, and her father, Ted, who orchestrated several of that album's tracks, as well as such solo compositions as "Street in the City," "Football Fugue," and "I Like It the Way It Is." That the latter is an account of Pete's infidelities on the road must have made for a pretty awkward recording session.

As stable and understanding as Karen seems to be, she still had a very difficult time acclimating to the rock 'n' roll lifestyle and kept her distance from it as best as possible. When Keith Moon died, and the Who's immediate future was in jeopardy, Karen hoped Pete would quit the business. Instead he signed a solo deal, continued working just as hard as ever, self-medicated with drugs and alcohol, and spent much of the eighties falling madly in love with other women. Karen busied herself with charity work, particularly as a chairperson of the domestic violence refuge Chiswick Family Rescue.

Karen and Pete often lived apart and regularly came to the precipice of splitting up throughout the eighties. They would always reconcile for their children's sake, and despite their marriage's ongoing madness, they still loved each other, even having another child in 1989. Karen and Pete were thrilled by the birth of their son, Joseph, but Pete's poor behavior, his affairs, and his drinking relapses, continued. They split up for good in 1999 and officially divorced ten years later. As of this writing, Karen runs Kestle Barton, an art gallery in Cornwall, no doubt enjoying some well-earned peace.

Heather Taylor

As the Who's popularity was peaking in early 1967, Roger Daltrey was enjoying his stardom and hardly on the lookout for another legally binding relationship. Of course, one never knows when the real thing is going to hit. The Who were playing their stint at the Murray the K concert series in New York City when Roger caught sight of Heather Taylor. She was a willowy redhead doing some modeling and dancing during the show. Heather was well acquainted with the pop world, having dated and run the fan club of a pre-Monkees Davy Jones and dated Gordon Waller of Peter and Gordon (she appears in appropriate undress on the cover of the duo's *Lady Godiva* album). Legend has it that she inspired "Foxy Lady" after a tryst with Jimi Hendrix.

Following their brief encounter in Manhattan, Roger Daltrey and Heather Taylor met again on the singer's home turf. Heather had traveled to London under the impression that Jimmy Page was up for a serious relationship. Not realizing that Page didn't know the meaning of the term, the dalliance ended abruptly, leaving Heather heartbroken and looking for a place to crash. Catherine James, a friend of Heather's who had her own share of experiences with rock stars, suggested she take refuge at Daltrey's pad.

Spending time with Heather in close quarters, Roger sensed he was falling hard. The emotions were not exactly welcome since he was still intent on maintaining his freedom and having his fun. Heather Taylor turned out to be the perfect woman for him. A veteran of rock star dating, she knew exactly what those little boys with their microphones and guitars were like. Roger was free to do as he pleased with other women as long as his heart belonged to Heather. She needn't worry, because it did. After four years of cohabitation, they decided to marry. Unfortunately, the couple hit a little snag on their big day: Roger was still married to Jackie. Oops! Agreeing that it would be bad form to tell their four hundred guests of the situation, the ceremony and reception went ahead as planned. On July 19, 1971, Roger and Heather made it completely legal.

Married life with a rock star could try even the most understanding women. Decades with Roger Daltrey was not always easy for Heather, though he has said that he affords his wife the same freedom . . . just as long as he doesn't have to hear about it. He could be moody too, and Heather considered separating on a number of occasions. However, she stuck it out, and their marriage is now the

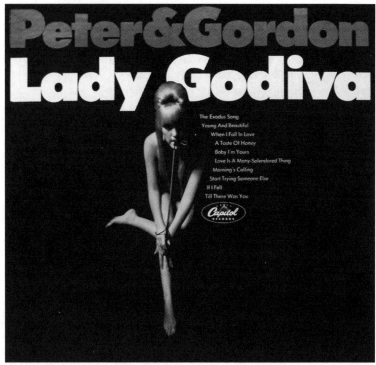

The Exodus Song
Young And Beautiful
When I Fall In Love
A Taste Of Honey
Baby I'm Yours
Love Is A Many-Splendored Thing
Morning's Calling
Start Trying Someone Else
If I Fell
Till There Was You

The future Heather Daltrey appeared in the buff on the cover of Peter and Gordon's LP *Lady Godiva* in 1967.   *Author's collection*

longest lasting in Who history. "Yes, rock and roll is totally destructive to a marriage," she told *People* magazine in 1994. "I don't know how it can work except that you have to make your decision to put up with the pros and cons." After more than four decades of marriage, Heather continues to put up with those pros and cons, for which Roger Daltrey is eternally grateful. In a 2011 article in the *Daily Mail*, he put his feelings for his wife plainly enough: "she is the most extraordinary woman I know."

Annette Walter-Lax

In 1974, Annette Walter-Lax had just moved from Stockholm, Sweden, to London when she first encountered human whirlwind Keith Moon. Their first meeting was uncharacteristically sedate. Their second, more typical. He was drunk, dangling from the chandelier at the Tramp Club, and missing a front tooth. When Annette stepped away from her date briefly for a loo visit, Keith seized the opportunity to slip the bouncer ten pounds to escort the poor guy out of the club. That night they retired to Keith's home, where Annette witnessed a screaming bout between him and soon-to-be ex-girlfriend Joy Bang. The only way the drummer could feature bringing an end to the ruckus was to have one last bang with Joy. When he was finished, he informed his new friend of this point blank. The revelation did not faze her unduly, and she spent the night. Annette Walter-Lax had passed the first test of dating Keith Moon.

Perhaps Annette was not so much unfazed as she was shell-shocked by Keith's bizarre behavior. The nineteen-year-old model knew nothing of his reputation and was only vaguely aware of the Who. She was, however, quite intoxicated by his extravagant lifestyle, found his pranks funny, and thought he was a genuinely sweet and kind guy. What she didn't realize was that Keith too was on a self-destructive bender that began when Kim went out the door. After a failed attempt to detox, Keith went ballistic in front of Annette for the first time. Fortunately, he didn't touch her, taking out his rage on a hotel room. Young and quite fearless, Annette took Keith's sudden mood swings and hard partying in stride. She liked to do a bit of partying herself. However, she soon realized that Keith expected her to be as homebound as Kim and was not only still obsessed with his ex-wife but would likely always be.

If Annette had any jealousy regarding Kim's hold over Keith, she could take comfort in one significant fact: she never suffered physically as Kim had. Annette surmised that Keith could only muster the self-control to keep his hands to himself for fear she would leave him as Kim had. Instead, he continued smashing furniture, appliances, and other household items. He also continued having very public sessions with groupies. Annette remained confident that she could rehabilitate him. In 1977, Keith overdosed and very nearly died. When he was released from the hospital, Annette had to monitor him for seizures. A short time later, he made a suicidal gesture by slashing his wrists, and she once again found herself dialing for medical assistance.

All of this was extremely wearing for a young woman with potential to be more than Keith Moon's nursemaid. When her former modeling agency offered her a job, Annette took it despite Keith's continued insistence that she remain home to mind him. She very nearly left him this time, but once again chose to believe his assertions that he would and could change. It was not long before he started acting up again, and Annette was once again considering whether enough was finally enough. She held out in the hope that doctor-prescribed Heminevrin would work magic on Keith Moon, assisting him through his latest attempt to withdraw from alcohol, but once he started taking the drug, it just made him seem drunk again.

On September 7, 1978, Keith Moon took his last dose of Heminevrin after he and Annette attended a screening of *The Buddy Holly Story*, where he enjoyed one last night of partying with friends. While Annette danced, he confided in friends his plans to marry her. He left the party early to go home and pass out on the couch while watching the Vincent Price horror flick *The Abominable Dr. Phibes* after taking a handful of Heminevrin. In the middle of the night, he woke up to take another dose of the drug. He passed out and never woke up again.

Annette's attempt to revive Keith with mouth-to-mouth came much too late. She was devastated by his death. She couldn't even bring herself to take advantage of his estate by declaring herself his common-law-wife, which she had every right to do according to the state of California. Annette Walter-Lax retreated from the pop world but not from celebrity, marrying TV actor Gareth Hunt, star of *Upstairs, Downstairs* and *The New Avengers*. Their marriage ended in divorce, and Hunt died of pancreatic cancer in 2007.

Maxene Harlow

When we last left John Entwistle, he'd just split up with Alison and taken up with a waitress he'd met several years earlier. Maxene Harlow was just twenty-two when she first met the taciturn bass player. Though not a Who fan, she enjoyed drawing the handsome older gent out of his shell. Maxene was taken aback when she learned John had a wife and child waiting for him in England. He persisted that they intensify their relationship, begging her to fly across the Atlantic with him so she could be close at hand. She refused to make the move but agreed to an ocean-crossing affair.

By 1980, John and Alison were all over but for the paperwork. That year, Maxene finally agreed to join him. Living in Pete Townshend's flat on the King's Road, their life was a nonstop string of partying, drinking, and drugging. In 1991, they finally resolved to settle down to some degree and marry, but John's attitude toward social unions had changed little since his days with Alison. More than once, she caught her husband with other women. Crestfallen by his infidelities, Maxene relied more and more on the bottle before realizing that rehab was the only way out. John admired his wife's effort to sober up, but didn't share the willpower to do the same.

Although a doctor had told Maxene that a bout with anorexia had left her infertile, a tryst with a man she met in Alcoholics Anonymous produced a son in 1994. By that point, her marriage with John had already been officially on the skids for some time, and it came to an end once and for all in 1997. Despite a seriously troubled relationship, and some lingering bitterness over her failure to obtain a sizable divorce settlement from her husband, Maxene says that she and John remained friends, so she was hurt when she was not able to attend his funeral in 2002. Maxene claims that Alison and John's final girlfriend, Lisa Pritchett-Johnson, barred her from entry.

Lisa Pritchett-Johnson

Lisa Pritchett-Johnson had been dating Joe Walsh when she met the man with whom he collaborated on the *Too Late the Hero* album. While married to Maxene, John Entwistle conducted an affair with Lisa that would come out in the open after his 1997 divorce. Lisa was still living with John when he died. With his mother and son, Lisa was reportedly the only other person to receive a slice of his fortune. Money did little to curb the pain and embarrassment that came with John's death. The public humiliation was exacerbated by tabloid claims she'd been carrying on an affair with a married vicar, who was subsequently forced to step down from his position in the church. Lisa started to exhibit self-destructive behavior and was arrested in 2003 under suspicion of possessing cocaine. She was barred from driving for two years after being discovered intoxicated behind the wheel of John's Rolls-Royce. Lisa Pritchett-Johnson was found dead of a drug overdose in her parents' Memphis, Tennessee, house in March 2005. Friends said she never got over her boyfriend's death.

Rachel Fuller

The landscape of Who history is littered with horribly failed relationships and an unacceptable deal of death. It is not all tragic, or even sad. Roger continues to enjoy a long and thriving relationship with Heather, and Pete seems to have similarly found stability and true love with Rachel Fuller. While Karen bristled at the spotlight, Rachel was already in it before meeting Pete Townshend. She'd been working as a musician, composer, and orchestrator when she met her future boyfriend while chatting with Zak Starkey on the last day of rehearsals for the 1996 *Quadrophenia* tour. At the time, Rachel was orchestrating sessions for German singer Ute Lemper down the hall at Nomis Studios. While Pete saw this as an in, he was also genuinely looking for an orchestrator and passed Rachel a note informing her of this.

Pete was first struck by Rachel's beauty, but on speaking to her, he also fell under the spell of her brassy personality. Completely contradicting clichés about snooty classical musicians, she was as funny and effervescent as she was smart and talented. She agreed to orchestrate three pieces that would end up on his *Lifehouse Chronicles* box set. The new relationship stuttered when Pete realized Rachel was having drinking problems just as he had in the past. He waited for Rachel to get help before resuming their relationship.

In Rachel Fuller, Pete Townshend had a partner in both love and creativity. They cohosted an Internet music series called *In the Attic* and cowrote "It's Not Enough," one of the best tracks on *Endless Wire*. Pete contributed guitar to Rachel's 2005 solo album *Cigarettes & Housework*, which All Music.com's Thom Jurek applauded as "head and shoulders above her peers . . . she exposes Sarah Brightman for the pretentious phony she is, and in her willingness to go further and wider, she makes Tori Amos and Sarah MacLachlan sound like they are spoiled children." Perhaps her greatest praise has come from her partner. In the acknowledgments of *Who I Am*, Pete Townshend saved his final thanks for the woman who "plays Chopin like Chopin, and sings like Baez to my Dylan."

30

This God-Forsaken Mess

The Pornography Investigation

On Saturday, January 11, 2003, the *Daily Mail* published an article that changed Pete Townshend's biography forever. "ROCK STAR BOMBSHELL; Police to quiz British multi-millionaire musician over internet child porn" the headline screamed. As Townshend wrote in *Who I Am*, when his business manager Nick Goderson called to relay the headline, Townshend responded, "That'll be me, then."

The following May 7, Pete Townshend was cleared of charges of possessing pornographic images of children. However, authorities officially cautioned him, and he was placed on Britain's Sex Offenders' Register for five years. Although an extensive forensics examination of his eleven computers confiscated in the investigation did not turn up a single child pornography image, the incident continues to haunt Pete Townshend to this day. It seems that not an article about the man can be posted on the Internet without at least one reader commenting that he's a "pervert" or "pedophile." As is often the case on the Internet, such comments are made by people who have not performed any research to support their claims. Many still do not understand all of the facts behind the child pornography investigation, so "Was Pete really guilty?" remains one of the most frequent and unfortunate questions asked about the Who.

Childhood Traumas

To understand how this recent dark chapter came to be, we must first look way, way back. Pete Townshend was the son of a vivacious and talented couple. They were troubled, too. Father Clifford was a swing clarinetist and saxophonist. Because of his busy schedule as alto-saxophonist in the Squadronaires, Cliff Townshend was rarely home. When he was in town, he spent most of his time at the White Lion pub tossing back drinks with mates and fans. Cliff missed the birth of his first son on May 19, 1945, which understandably incensed his wife, Betty.

Cliff and Betty reconciled, but their marriage never got back on truly solid ground. Cliff continued playing in the band. Betty started drinking. This left young Pete without the proper adult influence he needed. In 1951, Betty came up with a way to ease her parental responsibilities. Her mother, Denny, had been behaving erratically of late, wandering the streets in her dressing gown. Betty thought a visit from Pete might help sort out his troubled grandmother. So, six-year-old Pete was shunted off to live with his apparently unstable grandmother.

In *Who I Am*, Pete is very vague about "the darkest part of my life." Denny would deny him meals as punishment for the usual childhood transgressions and deny him the affection any child needs. She regularly slapped him, and on one occasion, dunked his head under water "for a long time" while subjecting him to one of her heavy-handed scrubbings in the bath tub. He also had a suggestive encounter with one of Denny's boyfriends in the backseat of a car. Pete only recalls that the man was an American Air Force officer, wanted Pete to call him "uncle," and had a "Hitler" mustache. Although Pete never gets specific about what happened between himself and the man, the implication is that the man molested him.

Ghosts Appear

Townshend seemed to have buried his experience with the man with the Hitler moustache deep in his psyche for decades. He certainly never spoke of it during interviews. However, the incident often colored his music. His recent discussions of the mini-opera "A Quick One While He's Away" reshapes a comedic song about infidelity into a shadowy confession of abuse in which a child (gender revised to that of "a little girl") has been abandoned by the one she loves (Betty) and left in the care of an adult (Denny's boyfriend) who takes sexual advantage of the child. When the love returns in the end, the abused child offers a prayer of forgiveness, one that Townshend says so enraged him onstage he would start thrashing away at his guitar with unprecedented fury.

More explicitly, *Tommy* places its title character in sexual danger at the hands of perverted Uncle Ernie. While several sloppy reporters cited "Fiddle About" as evidence of Townshend's alleged pedophiliac tendencies, John Entwistle was the song's composer. The subject was too tender for Townshend, so he farmed it out to his bandmate. Had Townshend written it himself, he may not have done so with such macabre, perverse glee. Granted, "A Quick One" wasn't a sober examination of child abuse either, but Townshend's refusal to face up to the abuse in his past may have led him to revisit it in song with an inappropriately comedic touch. As he wrote in *Who I Am*, "I wasn't sure enough of myself to tackle" the subject of his abuse yet.

A Different Bomb

Pete Townshend started confronting his childhood traumas in 1982. Long packing his share of psychological baggage, he was attending psychotherapy sessions when he finally spoke of his encounter in the mustachioed man's car.

His therapist urged Townshend to write out the incident, but he was not ready to deal with it yet, and his "memory just shut down" (*Who I Am*). A couple of years later, he was more willing to deal with his past, and consciously explored the abuse he suffered as a child during therapy. However, he continued to only deal with the subject indirectly in public, as he did in his 1993 rock opera, *Psychoderelict*, in which rock critic Ruth Streeting schemes to frame aging rock star Ray High as a pedophile. In ten years' time, this story line would play a part in a shocking example of life imitating art. In five years' time, Pete Townshend would see child pornography images online.

In 2003, Townshend was investigated under allegations he'd paid for and accessed sexually explicit images of children online. In 1998, he saw such images, though apparently, not by conscious design. His friend Ethan Silverman, who would collaborate with him on a stage production of *Psychoderelict* to star Peter Gallagher the following year, had recently completed *The Waiting Children*, a short documentary about a Russian orphanage. The film moved Townshend to seek out such an orphanage to make a donation. He began by typing some words into a search engine: "Russia," "orphanages," "boys." The search led him to a page boasting that pedophilia "is not illegal in Russia." To illustrate this, the page offered a free image of a small child (about "two-years old" by Townshend's estimation) being raped by a man. In *Who I Am*, Townshend wrote that the image left him "stunned" and unlocked memories of his own boyhood abuse that transformed that feeling into "rage."

Townshend considered calling the police to report the site. Then he thought again. On November 19, 1997, Gary Glitter had been arrested after taking his computer to PC World for servicing, and the technician discovered child pornography on its hard drive. The following March, Glitter was charged with fifty offenses. Incidents of more direct sexual abuse soon came to light. With stories of Glitter's criminal past all over the news, Townshend grew wary of associating himself with child pornography, particularly since Glitter had appeared as the Godfather in the Who's *Quadrophenia* stage show a couple of years earlier.

Instead of contacting the authorities immediately, Townshend placed a more pragmatic call to a lawyer, who told him to do nothing about what he'd seen. Speaking to a few people about the images he saw on the Internet, he discovered that not everyone was convinced his search was innocent. So he resolved to remain mum on the Internet child pornography issue for almost four years.

In January 2000, a friend of his from group therapy who had been a victim of child abuse died of an overdose. Two years later, another friend whose father had ritually abused her since infancy committed suicide. The following week, Townshend broke his silence on child abuse and Internet child pornography. He posted a lengthy essay titled "A Different Bomb" on his personal website (www.petetownshend.co.uk) in which he did exactly what his lawyer had advised against back in 1998: he publically explained that he had seen child pornography online, the nature of the image, how he'd come across it, and why he waited so long to write of the incident. The essay appeared a full year before Townshend had any reason to defend himself against charges that he, too, was a pedophile.

Operation Ore

Two weeks after he first posted "A Different Bomb," Townshend made it unavailable when he temporarily shut down his website to keep him from distractions while working on other writing projects. When he relaunched petetownshend.co.uk on June 10, 2003, he did not repost "A Different Bomb" right away. He finally reposted it a month later, including an addendum about a recently announced probe called Operation Ore. In his revision, he concluded that locking up child-porn addicts was futile when the credit card companies collecting charges for accessing child porn sites were allowed to skirt the law.

In 1999, US Attorney General John Ashcroft and Chief Postal Inspector Kenneth Weaver commenced an official investigation into a Fort Worth, Texas–based "portal" run by Thomas and Janice Reedy called Landslide.com. The site was a gateway, a middleman providing access to affiliated pornography websites, including ones offering images and videos of underaged people largely based in Russia and Southeast Asia. When a user purchased access to a site, the Reedys took 35 percent of the charge and dealt with the credit card company. On September 8, American authorities conducted a raid on Landslide.com that resulted in the arrest and 2001 conviction of the Reedys. Thomas Reedy initially received 1,335 years in prison—a 15-year sentence for each video and picture Detective Steven Nelson downloaded through the portal. American authorities also turned up credit card information on people throughout the world who'd apparently used their cards to access Landslide.com. When they provided British authorities with the names of their citizens under suspicion, National Crime Squad head Jim Gamble launched Operation Ore in the United Kingdom in 2002. A total of 7,272 British citizens were investigated for allegedly purchasing and accessing child pornography through Landslide.com. Among those whose credit card information appeared in the incriminating database was Pete Townshend.

Townshend was not named in that *Daily Mail* article of January 11, 2003. However, his frankness in the various versions of "A Different Bomb" led many shrewd reporters to the correct assumption that he was the "British multi-millionaire musician" in question. As they convened around his home, Townshend asked girlfriend Rachel Fuller to make a statement to the press. He later issued a written one. The statement begins strongly with his declaration "I am not a paedophile," and he goes on to make clear that he had already expressed how "shocked" and "angry" he was about child pornography on his website (referring to "A Different Bomb"). He continued to reveal publically his belief that he'd been abused while "in the care of my maternal grandmother" for the first time and lashed out about "the millions being made by American banks and credit card companies for the pornography industry." Less wisely, he admitted, "On one occasion I used a credit card to enter a site advertising child porn. I did this purely to see what was there. I spoke informally to a friend who was a lawyer and reported what I'd seen."

Anyone who had not been tracking Pete Townshend's campaign against Internet child pornography could reasonably read that last statement as a self-incriminating one, the lame defense of a guy who knew he'd been caught. Supposedly, "I was just doing research" is a common excuse among those who've been caught with child pornography. But he *had* written openly and honestly about his experiences in "A Different Bomb" long before he had a reason to defend himself. Nevertheless, the admission that he'd used his "credit card to enter a site advertising child porn" was a new twist.

As the investigation of Townshend began in earnest, the police confiscated eleven of his computers on January 13. Meanwhile, his name was being smeared all over the media in lurid reports of the superstar pedophile. Gary Glitter was small potatoes compared to a major international rock star like Pete Townshend. Seeing the reaction against him in the press, on the receiving end of hate mail and death threats, Townshend was distraught. In December 2003, he told *The Observer*, "If I had a gun, I would have shot myself."

Fortunately, he hung on, and on May 8, 2003, Scotland Yard made the following statement: "After four months of investigation by officers from Scotland Yard's child protection group, it was established that Mr. Townshend was not in possession of any downloaded child abuse images. He has fully cooperated with the investigation" (*The Guardian*).

Yet Townshend had still admitted to using his credit card to access Landslide. com. The previous day, authorities gave him a choice: he could either defend himself before a judge or agree to be placed on the Sex Offenders' Register for the next five years. Wishing to bring the nightmare to an end, he accepted his half-decade status as a "sex offender." Ignorant of the specifics of the situation, a lot of other people accepted that status too. From this point on, Pete Townshend could scarcely see his name appear in print without mention of the investigation. When the Who were invited to perform during the Super Bowl halftime show at Miami's Sun Life Stadium on February 7, 2010, the Florida-based anti–child abuse group Protect Our Children urged the National Football League to rescind its invitation. Similar outcry continues to dog him to this day.

Who I Am

Pete Townshend hesitated speaking about the investigation for close to a decade. While it would have been absurd to pretend it never happened, he shied away from discussing it in depth. At the same time, he was hard at work on his long-anticipated autobiography, and he knew he could not avoid the child pornography issue on its pages. When *Who I Am* finally hit the bookstores in

October 2012, the 2003 investigation was back in the headlines. This time, there was none of the vagueness that surrounded the story nine years earlier. For the first time, Townshend got specific about accessing Landslide.com. Realizing the issue was too significant to save for those who purchased his book, he explained his actions to the press openly.

In an attempt to bring the credit card companies quietly profiting from child pornography to justice, Townshend paid seven US dollars with his Barclaycard to gain access to a site advertising child pornography on Landslide.com in the spring of 1999. He claims that he canceled the charge as soon as he paid it, "not wanting even this small charge to benefit banks and credit-card companies that allowed the transaction in the first place" (*Who I Am*). He also wrote that he chose that particular site because he suspected, correctly as it turns out, that police were using it as part of a sting operation, which further ensured his seven dollars would not end up in the pockets of anyone profiting from child pornography. A friend in Boston, who was also undertaking the same home investigation, tipped him off on which sites were most likely being used in the sting. Townshend's goal was to use his credit card statement to follow the money trail he hoped would lead back to banks benefitting from the transaction and expose the financial institution in an article on his website.

By his own admission, the scheme was "insane," and its results prove him correct on that point. Why he'd done something so impetuous after displaying such caution in 1998 is a mystery. Why hadn't he contacted his lawyer before conducting his investigation as he had after stumbling across that image of rape in 1998? Surely, the lawyer would have steered him clear of such folly.

Only Pete Townshend knows what lies in the heart and mind of Pete Townshend. He has a history of honesty when discussing his foibles in the press, but even one as honest as he probably doesn't have so much self-disregard that he'd admit to being a pedophile just for the sake of honesty. Nevertheless, there simply isn't any evidence he's a pedophile. All the speculation from all the pundits in the world doesn't constitute proof that Townshend was interested in seeing or downloading child pornography. That he's written songs or rock operas about sexual abuse is not proof that he is a pedophile, a "pervert," or that he has ever sexually abused anyone, nor is the possibility that he may have been abused himself. No one has ever stepped forward to accuse Townshend of abuse, as Gary Glitter's victims have. Forensics experts declared his eleven computers clean. He'd proven himself an enemy of Internet child pornography in "A Different Bomb" a full year before authorities pinpointed him. The essay appeared months before Operation Ore even existed. As for that operation, it has since been subjected to its own controversies for failing to check whether or not the credit card owners had actually accessed any pornography websites. As it turns out, 54,348 of the credit card numbers found on Landslide.com's computers had been stolen and the portal provided access to legal sites as well as child pornography ones. The ramifications of Operation Ore have been severe. As of 2005, thirty-three people fingered by the operation had killed themselves.

I have presented this information for you as completely and concisely as I could. It's all out there on the Internet if you're interested in conducting your own research, and I do urge you to conduct research whenever a story like this appears in the press. There will always be those who insist Pete Townshend is a pedophile despite the lack of concrete evidence because they are too lazy to investigate the issue, want to believe the worst about people, are disgusted by the notion that rich celebrities are "above the law," or just enjoy talking a little smack on the Internet. Remember that suicide count might have been increased by one had Townshend succumbed to the embarrassment and pain of being classified a pedophile in the press, on the Internet, and possibly among his own associates. Yes, he is a major rock star, a celebrity we may believe to be completely disassociated from the comments of us mere mortals, but celebrities are human beings who use the Internet and read much of the very same things that you and I do. They are people just as capable of being hurt by the words of strangers as anyone else. Be sure you have your facts straight before casually accusing anyone of anything on the Internet. They just might be reading what you write.

31

The New Constitution

The Politics of the Who

T he Who were always more about introspection than worldviews. They generally avoided flipping in their two pence on social and political matters in song. While John Entwistle rarely broached such topics because he didn't seem to care much, Pete Townshend avoided tackling issues overtly because he did not want to dilute the universality of the Who's music. Yet sometimes his opinions did slip into his work, and they often spewed out during the multitude of interviews he has given. His bandmates too have indicated their political leanings, though with less frequency and less contradiction and complexity.

Pete

As the Who's lead songwriter and spokesman, it is necessary to examine Pete Townshend's politics closer than his bandmates'. It is also necessary because they are so difficult to define. Townshend has labeled himself a socialist perched on the far left of the political spectrum. He has called himself a conservative tucked on the right. I will not pretend to know exactly where Pete Townshend stands politically. Only he, and perhaps those closest to him, know that. Here, we will merely look at a selection of statements he has made throughout his career to give a taste of how he has presented himself politically.

In the Who's early days, Townshend's stance was that of the young: rebellious, revolutionary, and wary of the younger generation's susceptibility to succumb to the older generation's conservatism. When he wrote "Hope I die before I get old," he was speaking of his own fear that he would one day become one of the old richies who scoffed at him in his affluent neighborhood of Belgravia. In *Who I Am*, he writes of conservatism less as a belief than a "disease" of the old, the inevitable mindset of the complacency that comes with age. Ostensibly, young Pete would have preferred dying before reaching that age.

As a political work, "My Generation" is hardly overt rhetoric as, say, Dylan's "Masters of War" is. It works simply as standard anti–older generation rock 'n' roll rebellion, a "Roll Over Beethoven" for the sixties. In Townshend's numerous discussions of the song throughout the years, he very rarely even acknowledged that its title was inspired by *Generations*, an anthology of socialist dramatist

David Mercer's work. Onstage, "My Generation" would take on further political implications when Townshend would finish the song by ritualistically demolishing a very expensive Rickenbacker guitar, indicating what he thought of rock's most sacred symbol of capitalist materialism (Keith Moon's destruction of his drum kit, however, symbolized nothing more than his refusal to be upstaged by anyone).

Townshend made his first overtly political statements in one of those "Think In"-type interviews *Melody Maker* conducted in the sixties; a sort of word association game for pop stars. When the interviewer dropped "Vietnam" in his lap in 1966, Townshend said he "always stand(s) by Young Communist principles" (he was a member of the Young Communist League at the time), but stressed his desire for cessation of the conflict between communist North Vietnam and US-backed South Vietnam. Having had a friend die in the fighting, he was more concerned with an end to the violence than one side prevailing over the other. Townshend made a typical contradictory move the following year when he agreed to record a radio endorsement for the United States Air Force while the conflict in Vietnam was intensifying. This is the first evidence of his two poles at war with each other: on the one hand, he was a post–World War II child "brainwashed" to value military heroism as a key ingredient in personal growth (as he said in the 1985 short documentary *Pete Townshend Talks About White City*); on the other hand, he was a young man of mid-sixties antiwar idealism.

In the same 1966 *Melody Maker* interview, Townshend further revealed his conflicted political inclinations, expressing admiration for Communist China leader Mao Tse-tung while saying "China frightens me and it's the only thing that threatens my life . . . the Chinese are like a stampede of people and ideas. They are being taught to hate." This fear would manifest in his rock opera "Rael" (see chapter 15), and he would even describe its religion-conquering Red Chins as "fairly evil" in *The Story of Tommy* even as he continued aligning himself with communist principles. In a 1969 interview with Derek VanPelt of *Cleveland After Dark*, he said, "in European universities Communist Russia and Mao have more respect than American youth. Chairman Mao has done quite a lot for change in his country." Townshend's issue with America seems to have been that he felt it lacked the structure and discipline of Mao's communist constituents, that many Americans spouting communist rhetoric were spoiled and privileged, that their revolutionary actions were malformed incitements rather than organized plans. Townshend may have been a rock 'n' roll disciple, but he realized a song was not enough to enact true or positive revolution. When VanPelt asked him, "Do you feel rock has anything to do with revolution?," he responded, "It hasn't anything to do with it." Townshend had made this clear the previous summer when Abbie Hoffman leapt onstage during the Who's set at Woodstock to shout protestations about John Sinclair's recent drug arrest. Townshend reacted by bellowing, "Fuck off my fucking stage" and whacking Abbie with his guitar, an action he would call his most political on some occasions. On others, he said he regretted doing it and wasn't thinking clearly, that he was in the worked-up state he always got into onstage.

Townshend had become further skeptical of the hippie brand of revolution while living near the United Kingdom's biggest commune on Eel Pie Island in the Thames. He was open to engaging commune dwellers such as Gavin Kilty and Peter Crisp, but the ones that seemed more interested in tripping out than political ideology dismayed him. Their insistence that he join a cause he believed lacked organization and might rashly leap into violent confrontation irked him too. The last straw may have arrived when he reportedly caught one Eel Pier attempting to "liberate" his baby daughter. Maybe this wasn't a brand of communism worth dying for.

Townshend's experiences on Eel Pie Island inspired what many have labeled his most political song. He labeled "Won't Get Fooled Again" an antipolitics song. It is not counterrevolutionary, as pundits often believe; otherwise, he wouldn't be tipping his "hat to the new constitution" or smiling and grinning "at the changes all around." "Won't Get Fooled Again" is merely cautious. Not all revolutions are good ones, and the sloppily formed one—the kind that might be launched by a bunch of hippies who spend the day dropping acid and snatching babies—will just leave a lot of people hurt or dead without any positive change enacted. The song was most notoriously misinterpreted by John J. Miller in his asinine "Rockin' the Right: The 50 Greatest Conservative Rock Songs" published in *The National Review* in 2006. Some of the songs were easy picks: the Beatles' "Taxman" and Oingo Boingo's "Capitalism," for example. Most of Miller's picks ranged from overreaching (the Everly Brothers' "Wake Up Little Susie" is conservative because the teens in the song don't actually have sex?) to flat-out baffling (Led Zeppelin's "The Battle of Evermore" is "conservative" because Robert Plant sings of a frustrated tyrant's face turning red? So Miller thinks the tyrant's face has turned into a Russian flag or something? What?).

Guess Who's number one on this list. Miller argues that "Won't Get Fooled Again" is the ultimate conservative rock song because it "swears off naïve idealism once and for all." Townshend responded on his blog, writing that the song neither aligns with any political party nor decries revolution. In fact, he wrote that the song asserts that "we will indeed fight in the streets," but the outcome of any revolution is unpredictable, and those who wish to use him and his music to further their own political agendas should let him be to enact change as he wants to (incidentally, Townshend did write an emphatic prorevolution song for the Who, but since "Relay" has not endured as "Won't Get Fooled Again" has, it tends to get left out of the discussion).

In recent years, Townshend has become increasingly hard to pin down to a particular political wing. He famously denied Michael Moore use of "Won't Get Fooled Again" for his anti–George W. Bush film *Fahrenheit 9/11*. Moore wanted to end his film with the song to remind us of when Bush bungled the adage "Fool me once, shame on you; fool me twice, shame on me" as "Fool me once, shame on you; fool me . . . can't get fooled again" (it would have been a perfect finale to the film). Townshend did not say he refused the request because he disagreed with Moore's politics. He just didn't want his song to be used for political purposes of any stripe (though back in 1987, he considered allowing the Labour Party to use it during an election campaign, and even said he wanted to rewrite it to better suit the party's stance). He said he then referred Moore to the more dedicatedly political Neil Young, and "Rockin' in the Free World" took the place of "Won't Get Fooled Again" in *Fahrenheit 9/11*.

In a subsequent video interview, Townshend identified himself as a conservative for the first time, and the former member of the Campaign for Nuclear Disarmament began speaking in favor of nuclear arms as a deterrent and military action to combat terrorism. He also took issue with those who tried pushing him to denounce Bush, saying in a 2006 interview with *Rolling Stone* that he does not think Bush is "a bad man." Of course, that is not the same thing as saying Bush is a good president, and when the conservative finally lost his seat to the more liberal Barack Obama—a man whom many conservatives misclassify as a socialist—*Uncut* magazine reported that Townshend called Obama's win "the most wonderful result" during a postelection solo gig at the Troubadour in West

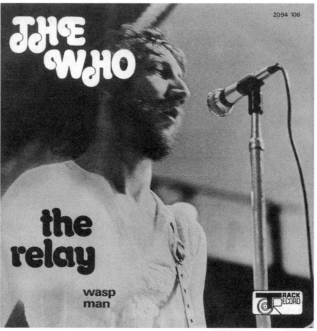

Although "Won't Get Fooled Again" conveys a cautious message, Pete Townshend aligned with revolutionary politics more assuredly with "Relay" . . . or as it was known in the United States and France, where this picture sleeve was released, "The Relay." *Courtesy of the Rob Abramowicz Collection, digitized by Jeffrey Uleau*

Hollywood. When he performed "Won't Get Fooled Again," that night, he gave the song a specific political slant for the very first time, amending "Meet the new boss, same as the old boss" with a cheeky "Maybe not."

Yet Pete Townshend continued to confound those seeking the real politics of Pete Townshend. After Obama defeated Republican Mitt Romney in the 2012 election, he wrote on his blog that he would have been happy had the result gone either way. That same month, he made headlines by telling interviewer Jonathan Karl of ABC's *Spinners and Winners*, "I'm a bit of a neocon . . . I like the idea of America as the world's police force, and then we [England] don't have to do it." Conservative commentators went into a frenzy claiming Townshend for their own, though most failed to note the wry smile on his face when making this declaration. In the more straight-faced *Who I Am*, published just one month earlier, he wrote quite the opposite: "although I am wealthy and privileged, in my heart and my actions I am still a socialist and activist, ready to stand by the underdog and the beaten down, and to entertain them if I can."

Roger

As he is regarding most matters, Roger Daltrey is not as inscrutable as Pete Townshend when it comes to politics. Daltrey is a lifelong voter of Labour, Britain's left-of-center party, more socialist leaning than US democrats. In the sixties he opposed the Vietnam War, in the seventies he turned his attention to environmentalism, and in the twenty-first century voiced his support for Obama.

Like Townshend, Daltrey is not a strictly party-line guy. He has been critical of his preferred party for failing to protect workers, railing against it in the seventies as self-serving and watered down compared to the purer socialism of former Labour deputy leader Aneurin "Nye" Bevan, a staunch ally of workers and seeker of social justice. More recently, Daltrey took a more conservative angle of attack, slamming former prime minister Tony Blair for loosening Britain's immigration controls in 2004. In 2011, Daltrey told *The Daily Mail*, "I was appalled at what Labour did to the working class —mass immigration, where people were allowed to come here and undercut our working class."

Keith

Keith Moon was even less ideologically complex, concerned with little more than his nonstop pursuit of a good time. Making and spending money on cars, toys, a big house, booze, etc., seemed the best way to achieve this, which got his friends calling him "a Capitalist pig," a label he wore more proudly than Pete Townshend, who is, when all is said and done, a rich rock star who does enjoy his money. When Moon fled to California in the seventies, it was both to immigrate to the sunshine and emigrate from England's steep taxes. "They're driving out all those people who make the money—whether it's on a long or short-term basis," he told the *NME* in 1976. "How on earth can a professional man afford to work and live in Britain? He can't. He's penalised because of his talent and because of his business acumen and individual enterprise." No socialist leanings there.

John

John Entwistle was another guy who had no guilt about his materialism and had little love for the British tax system. In a 1995 Internet interview with Alan McKendree, he was as plainspoken as could be about his personal politics. "I don't believe in socialism, no. Nor would socialists if they had money. I vote Conservative 'cause it's less income tax. I was paying something like 94 percent when the Labor [sic] government were in, so sod Labor."

32

Heaven and Hell

The Who on Religion

P ete Townshend had fewer reservations about blending religion with rock 'n' roll than he did about blending it with politics. Maybe it is the similarity between rock 'n' roll and religion. Both have their gathering places where people congregate to worship at the feet of larger-than-life icons: rock has its clubs and arenas; religion has its temples and cathedrals. For those of us who do not choose to believe in some sort of sentient higher power, rock 'n' roll can serve as an inspirational substitute for the sense of belonging and transcendence believers get from religion. The Who understood this well, even as the band's individual members had and have their own beliefs.

Pete

As discussed in chapter 7, abstract religious themes recur in the Who's music, but preachiness does not. Despite having a pulpit capable of reaching millions of potential converts, Pete Townshend has taken the same tack with religion as he has with politics. He has spoken freely of his own beliefs and how he came to them, yet he has never used the Who's music to force them on his fans. As quoted in *Behind Blue Eyes*, Townshend said of his role in religion, "I'm not a soldier of God. I'm a servant as much as I can be with his grace, but no soldier." He has been critical of both the pageantry of organized religion and its method of controlling devotees with guilt.

Townshend was not raised to be religious. His parents never went to church. However, he attended his local Congregational Church both for the social aspect and because he had "this Sunday school image of Jesus Christ as a pathetic character who needed my support" (*Playboy* 1994). He also attended for the music, joining the choir at the age of eight. Fourteen years later, his devotion would start deepening to a new level, and his ideas about God and religion would commence a radical change.

In *Who I Am*, Townshend described his conversion in a strange story. In early August 1967, the Who were in Illinois, playing Chicago's International Amphitheatre while on tour supporting Herman's Hermits. At a Holiday Inn in Rolling Meadows, he "heard the voice of God." Regardless of whether this was a hallucinogenic flashback or a legit call from some higher power, he resolved that he'd heard the real deal. As was the case with several sixties pop stars trading in their acid tabs for prayer (George Harrison, Donovan, Roger McGuinn, etc.), Townshend did not gravitate toward western Christianity. Rather, he reflected on a book called *The God-Man: The Life, Journeys & Work of Meher Baba with an Interpretation of His Silence & Spiritual Teaching*, which his pal Mike McInnerney had passed to him earlier in '67.

Merwan Sheriar Irani was born on February 25, 1894, in Poona, India. At the age of nineteen, he met the Muslim Saint Hazrat Babajan, a so-called perfect master. As the story goes, when Hazrat Babajan kissed Merwan on the forehead, he achieved enlightenment. Merwan Irani's followers came to know him as Meher Baba, meaning "compassionate Father."

On July 10, 1925, Meher Baba commenced a vow of silence he would not break for the remaining four decades of his life. He would use hand gestures and the letters on an alphabet board to communicate with his adherents. From 1931 to 1937, Baba traveled the world on his campaign of enlightenment. He then spent the next twelve years working with the poor and infirm. Baba took his own three-year vow of poverty on October 16, 1949, isolating himself from his followers until 1952 when he resumed his role as a spiritual leader unaffiliated with any one religion. Two years later, he announced that he was an "avatar": the personification of God on Earth.

For one claiming such an exalted state, Baba was surprisingly down to earth in his personality and loves. He was a jolly character whose favorite philosophy was "don't worry, be happy." He smiled perpetually and had a taste for American music. As a solo artist, Pete Townshend would record two of Baba's favorite songs: the Jim Reeves country and western lament "There's a Heartache Following Me" and the Cole Porter standard "Begin the Beguine."

After suffering through two car accidents in the fifties, Baba's health faltered, and on January 31, 1969, he died. At the time, Townshend was planning on visiting his new spiritual leader.

He initially gravitated toward Baba because of his respect for Baba's followers, which included his friends Mike McInnerney and Ronnie Lane. In his 1994 interview with *Playboy*, Townshend articulated why he stuck with Baba. "It is the idea that the main purpose of the human animal is to try to rise, to stand taller. It is the energy to aspire to more, to create, to discover or to invent. Meher Baba gives me an idea of what the target is. It is very simple: Thinking of him makes me aspire to more for myself and my family and the planet. It is not a religion, which often has more to do with guilt than with anything inspired."

Baba may have felt his own affinity for Townshend. According to a possibly apocryphal story repeated in *Behind Blue Eyes*, Baba found a photo of Townshend in the *Observer* in 1968. He then dropped his thumb on Townshend's nose, suggesting that it was a match for his own exceptionally sized schnoz.

You don't have to be a Meher Baba devotee to dig "Don't Let Go the Coat," one of Pete Townshend's loveliest and most subtle spirituals.

Author's collection

Despite his enthusiasm for Baba at a time when desperate for some sort of spiritual direction, Townshend often had to struggle with his leader's condemnation of alcohol and drugs, not to mention his "don't worry, be happy" edict, a line antithetical to the rocker's well-documented anxiety and anger if ever there was one. But it was Townshend's own desire for happiness that made him so determined to rise to Baba's wish for his followers. He flung himself fully into Baba worship, penning a piece called "In Love with Meher Baba" for *Rolling Stone* (not a soldier of God, eh?) and even converting a large boathouse on the Thames into the Meher Baba Oceanic Centre, a meeting and lodging ground for followers.

Townshend was never shy about his love for Baba, whose teachings were subtly reflected in Who songs such as "Bargain," "Let's See Action," and "Don't Let Go the Coat." The rest of the band gamely played such songs, and apparently had little to say when Baba was credited as contributing "avatar" on the *Tommy* album cover. Still Townshend's devotion never crossed over to his bandmates. Roger Daltrey supposedly liked to rib Townshend by calling his avatar "Ali Baba."

Roger

Roger Daltrey may not be a Baba believer, but he is a believer. At the same time, he has openly expressed disdain for organized religion, dismissing it as "big business" in a quote repeated in *The Who in Their Own Words*. He has been known to dangle huge crucifixes around his neck onstage, and according to Townshend in *Who I Am*, sign letters with "Allhamdulia"—a misspelling of *Alhamdulillah*, Arabic for "Praise be to God"—in private. He apparently believes in an afterlife, often referring to how John Entwistle and Keith Moon are now in heaven (or, jokingly, in hell). Unlike Townshend, he has had little interest in discussing his religious philosophies in depth.

John

The same goes for John Entwistle, who approached the subject with his skepticism as firmly lodged in his sentiments as his tongue was lodged in his cheek. "Heaven and Hell" assesses both afterlife options and concludes they're equally boring. In "Success Story," he took a subtle swipe at pop star religiosity that may have been aimed at Pete Townshend. His solo composition "I Believe (in Everything)" rakes the very notion of belief in everything from afterlives to telepathy to Mickey Mouse over the coals. Talking to Alan McKendree in 1995, he said he was not religious but believed "in some kind of entity but it's more a matter of fate than an old man with a gray beard."

Keith

As for Keith Moon, when Joe Collins of the *King Biscuit Flower Hour* asked him for his religion in 1974, he responded succinctly, and quite convincingly, "Courvoisier."

33

Give Love

Charity Work

Wealthy the Who are, but they have always given their time and money freely to favorite causes. Pete Townshend's very first solo performance happened in the name of charity. After folk singer Tim Hardin canceled on a benefit to raise money for a bus to transport needy children, Townshend stepped in to play the gig at London's Roundhouse on Easter 1974. In standard Who fashion, this act of charity climaxed with Townshend threatening to thump a bonehead in the audience who kept shouting requests for "Underture."

From playing benefit concerts to hands-on volunteering to establishing their own charities, the Who has made philanthropy nearly as much a priority as busting eardrums. This is just a selection of the band's pet causes.

The Stars Organisation for Spastics

Founded by revered singer Dame Vera Lynn and actor Wilfrid Pickles, the Stars Organisation for Spastics arranged various celeb-loaded events—golf tournaments, dinners, balls, movie premieres—to raise money for people with cerebral palsy. On December 9, 1972, producer Lou Reizner organized two performances of the version of *Tommy* he recorded with the London Symphony Orchestra to benefit the organization. All members of the Who were onboard. As he did on the album, Roger Daltrey voiced the title role while Pete Townshend resumed his part as narrator and John Entwistle embodied Cousin Kevin. Keith Moon subbed for Ringo Starr, who'd sung the part of wicked Uncle Ernie on vinyl (other guests included Steve Winwood, Sandy Denny, and Rod Stewart). Reizner originally had the Royal Albert Hall in mind for the performance, but when the hall's manager denounced the rock opera as "unsavory," Reizner moved his operation to the more sympathetic Rainbow Theatre. Unsavory or not, *Tommy* raised more than £15,000 for the Stars Organisation for Spastics . . . which has since changed its name to the more savory Stars Foundation for Cerebral Palsy.

Double 'O' Charity, Ltd.

In 1971, Erin Pizzey established Chiswick Women's Aid, the world's first refuge for battered women. To help raise money for Pizzey's organization, the Who set up Double 'O' Charity, Ltd. in 1976. After the band officially dissolved in 1983, Townshend assumed control of Double 'O,' and as the Aid morphed into Chiswick Family Rescue, and then simply the Refuge, he remained devoted to helping abused women from his hometown. He served on the management committee in the eighties and performed numerous benefit concerts for the Refuge with and without the Who. As recently as July 8, 2013, the Who performed at the Wembley Arena to raise money for the Refuge's now seventy UK locations, which "are suffering from cutbacks," as Townshend told the Samaritan Mag website in 2013. He has also expanded Double 'O''s interests to include rehabilitation for drug addicts and alcoholics; the Prince's Trust youth charity; Rock Against Racism; disaster relief; Nordoff Robbins, which provides rehabilitative music therapy for the disabled; and prison reform for young people. "I look at issues like, particularly to begin with, the syndrome of unmarried moms, with children growing up without active fathers, those fathers being the ones that I think I can help best," Townshend told Samaritan Mag. "So I'm interested in prison reform, particularly for young offenders."

Amnesty International

The Secret Policeman's Balls are among entertainment's most celebrated charity events. Peter Luff and Martin Lewis founded the series to benefit the human rights organization Amnesty International. Comedian and Monty Python icon John Cleese, who'd been involved in the events from the beginning, directed the first to go by its best-known title. Taking place at Her Majesty's Theatre on four nights from June 27 to June 30, 1979, the Secret Policeman's Ball featured such talents as Cleese's fellow Pythons Michael Palin and Terry Jones, a pre–Mr. Bean Rowan Atkinson, Peter Cook, singer and gay rights activist Tom Robinson, and Pete Townshend. For the occasion, Pete Townshend performed acoustic versions of "Pinball Wizard" and "Drowned" (ably supported by guitarist John Williams) before retiring to his dressing room to polish off a bottle of Rémy Martin. Returning to the stage for his encore, he briefly drifted off to sleep in the middle of "Won't Get Fooled Again" during the opening-night performance. The excellent version included in the film was wisely taken from another night.

Rock Against Racism

Townshend mounted his own righteous campaign on July 13, 1979, when he co-organized a benefit in conjunction with Rock Against Racism. Rock photographer Red Saunders established the organization in 1976, both to counter the rise of the young racists in the National Front and to take a stand against the drunken, hateful, anti-immigration, pro–Enoch Powell (the conservative Defence Secretary whose infamous "Rivers of Blood" speech helped spark the new wave of racism) tirade Eric Clapton unleashed at the Birmingham Odeon on August 5, 1976. Saunders gathered together an army of rock 'n' rollers to make it clear they did not share Clapton's sentiments. Ironically, one of these was

Clapton's close friend, Pete Townshend, who organized his own Rock Against Racism at the Rainbow Theatre to benefit the Southall Defence Fund. On April 23, 1979, the National Front descended on Southall in West London for an election meeting. The largely Asian community protested this trespass, and a violent clash ensued. In the melee, police murdered activist and teacher Blair Peach and arrested 350 people. Onboard to help raise money for the defense of arrested protestors were the Pop Group, Misty, the Ruts, and headliner Pete Townshend on the 13th. The benefit continued the following night with performances by the Enchanters, Aswad, the Clash, and the Members.

Concert for Kampuchea

Amidst its rise to power in 1970s Cambodia, the communist regime known as the Khmer Rouge murdered millions of people. UN Secretary-General Kurt Waldheim approached Paul McCartney to play a benefit concert to aid the suffering Cambodians. Macca one-upped Waldheim by developing a four-night series with an impressive roster that included Wings, Queen, the Clash, the Pretenders, the Specials, Elvis Costello and the Attractions, and the Specials.

Before performing "Rockestra Theme" live with Paul McCartney's Rockestra at the Concert for Kampuchea, Pete Townshend contributed guitar to the studio version on Wings' final album, *Back to the Egg*. Presumably, he was soberer for the recording session than he was for the concert.   *Author's collection*

Headlining night three on December 28, 1979, were the Who. As was sometimes his case, Pete Townshend's generosity went hand in hand with bad behavior. On the 29th, he was back onstage to join McCartney's "Rockestra," a conglomerate of musicians that included McCartney and Wings, Bruce Thomas of the Attractions, Ronnie Lane, Robert Plant (on Paul's Hofner bass!), and a quite inebriated Pete Townshend. Naughty Pete refused to wear the tacky spangled top hat and jacket McCartney insisted his musicians wear. McCartney retaliated by introducing him as a "lousy sod" and a "poof" (hope you regret that last one, Paulie). Townshend counterattacked by pulling faces through the entire overblown performance.

Live Aid

When the Who played their "final" concert in 1982, the likelihood they'd ever join together again was pretty grim. Less than three years later, they were back together, if for just one night, to play Live Aid. Boomtown Rat and noted activist Bob Geldof put together the show to benefit Ethiopian famine victims. The roster was massive, with Elvis Costello, U2, David Bowie, Elton John, the Four Tops, the Beach Boys, the Pretenders, Madonna, Tom Petty and the Heartbreakers, Paul McCartney, Mick Jagger, and Bob Dylan being just a small sampling of the more than fifty artists who took the stages at Philadelphia's JFK Stadium and London's Wembley Stadium on July 13, 1985. The biggest news items were the reunions of Led Zeppelin's Page, Plant, and Jones (of the John Paul variety), and a one-off appearance by Townshend, Daltrey, Entwistle, and Jones (of the Kenney variety). Following their transatlantic introduction by *Tommy* costar Jack Nicholson, the Who took the Wembley stage for a twenty-minute set of "My Generation," "Pinball Wizard," "Love Reign o'er Me," and "Won't Get Fooled Again." Townshend wanted to help Geldof but wasn't keen on playing again with his old band. Daltrey appreciated the gig as a proper ending to the Who's career. Little did they imagine they'd be back onstage together twenty years later for Live Aid's sequel Live 8.

Freddie Mercury Tribute Concert for AIDS Awareness

So, once again, a final Who concert would not really be a final Who concert, but they did perform together less often between Live Aid and the Quadrophenia tour of 1996 (the one big exception was the extensive "Kids Are Alright" tour of the United States in 1989). During his time off from Who business, Roger Daltrey appeared at the Freddie Mercury Tribute Concert at Wembley Stadium on April 20, 1992. To help raise funds to establish the AIDS-combating Mercury Phoenix Trust, Daltrey sang Queen's "I Want It All" accompanied by the band's surviving members and Black Sabbath's Tony Iommi.

Children's Health Fund

Pete Townshend kept up his charitable performances too. On September 10, 1995, he joined Paul Simon at New York's Paramount Theatre at Madison Square Garden for the benefit of the Children's Health Fund. Simon and pediatrician Irwin Redlener founded the cause to provide health care for underprivileged kids. The concert provided a very rare opportunity to see one of the sixties' most explosive artists duet with one of the decade's most sedate as Townshend and Simon harmonized on "The Kids Are Alright." For the finale, Townshend joined the lineup of Simon, Annie Lennox, and Wynton Marsalis for a version of "You Can Call Me Al" so rousing he broke into an impromptu jig. The concert drew $850,000 for the Children's Health Fund, and attendees were treated to a deep-digging set that included such delicacies as "Slit Skirts," "Cut My Hair," and "I Am an Animal," and covers of the Beat's "Save It for Later" and Screamin' Jay Hawkins's "I Put a Spell on You."

Children's Defense Fund

One of Roger Daltrey's more unusual charity appearances occurred on November 5, 1995, at the Avery Fisher Hall in Manhattan's Lincoln Center. That day, kiddies could watch the man who demanded to know "Who the fuck are you?" skipping down the yellow brick road with Toto. To benefit the Children's Defense Fund—a group advocating education and affordable health care, and battling child abuse and neglect—Daltrey played the Tin Man in the "Wizard of Oz Concert." At his side as he crooned a Who-like arrangement of "If I Only Had a Heart" were Jewel Kilcher as Dorothy and Jackson Browne as the Scarecrow. They were later joined by Nathan Lane as the Cowardly Lion . . . a role for which the golden-locked Daltrey seems better suited. Right?

The Concerts for New York City

On October 20, 2001, the Who convened in New York for a benefit concert organized by the Robin Hood Relief Fund. The circumstances were particularly solemn, as little more than a month had passed since Islamist terrorists flew two passenger airplanes into Manhattan's Twin Towers and crashed two others into the Pentagon and a Pennsylvania field. A large and diverse assortment of entertainers showed up to raise money for victims and survivors of the attacks. Paul McCartney, Susan Sarandon, Mick Jagger and Keith Richards, Adam Sandler, Macie Gray, David Bowie, Melissa Etheridge, Billy Crystal, Jay-Z, and Elton John were among the performers, but by most assessments, it was the Who that provided the most powerful moment of catharsis when they delivered a triumphant "Won't Get Fooled Again."

The Concert for Sandy Relief

The Who's presence was once again required at Madison Square Garden on December 12, 2012. The previous October 28, Hurricane Sandy slammed down on the American East Coast after wreaking havoc in the Caribbean. Approximately 160 people were killed in the US, with $71 billion of damage in New Jersey and New York alone. To relieve some of that burden, the Robin Hood Relief Fund assembled another roster of big names, including the Rolling Stones, Alicia Keys, Roger Waters, Kanye West, Bruce Springsteen, and McCartney (who performed with the surviving members of Nirvana!). For the event, Pete Townshend amended the bridge of "Baba O'Riley" to "It's only Sandy wasteland," and Keith Moon made a holographic appearance for his solo singing spot in "Bell Boy." The concert reportedly raised more than $30 million for the cause.

Teenage Cancer Trust and Teen Cancer America

Roger Daltrey is familiar with the devastating effects of cancer. His sister Carol succumbed to breast cancer. He lost his parents, dedicated smokers both, to lung cancer. In December 2009, Daltrey had a precancerous growth removed from a vocal cord. Fortunately, he recovered speedily enough to scream again at the Super Bowl the following February 7. At that point, he'd already been working closely with the Teenage Cancer Trust since 2002.

Daltrey learned of the Teenage Cancer Trust from his doctor, Adrian Whiteson, who served as copresident of the organization with wife Myrna. Whiteson informed Daltrey that teenagers tended to fall through the cracks when it came to adequate cancer care, relegated to pediatric care under the age of fifteen, and treated in wards for adult—many of whom are dying—at sixteen and older. As the singer in one of rock's great champions of disfranchised teens, Daltrey felt it was his duty to put some of his star power behind the Trust's efforts to raise money for cancer treatment wards tailored to teenagers. Since 2002, he has organized annual benefit concerts starring the Who at the Royal Albert Hall. The band has raised some £3 million for the Trust, and in November 2012, Daltrey and Townshend announced Teen Cancer America, which would do for US teens what the Teenage Cancer Trust had been doing for British ones.

John Entwistle Foundation

While John Entwistle did everything in his power to project the image of the blasé rock star, he was apparently more compassionate in private than he let on. According to friends and family, he dipped into his millions to help the less fortunate often enough that his loved ones deemed it appropriate to establish a charitable foundation in his honor. The John Entwistle Foundation attends to an array of causes, having raised money for those left homeless by Hurricane Katrina, the Children's Cancer Hospital, the March of Dimes, and the Alliance of the Arts. The foundation has also directed much energy into developing music education programs at American Public Libraries for underprivileged kids and providing scholarships for young and gifted musicians. Considering the pedigree of the foundation's namesake—and its advisory board, which has counted Peter Frampton, Leslie West, Cheap Trick's Robin Zander, original MTV VJ Martha Quinn, AC/DC's Brian Johnson, and the late Chris Stamp among its members—that is a most appropriate use of funds.

K9 Connection and the Brain Tumour Research Campaign

The Who were once again helping to pull lost souls out of the teenage waste-land when they joined forces with K9 Connection in 2008. The Santa Monica, California–based charity benefits both homeless dogs and "at risk" teenagers (those suffering from drug problems, depression, and domestic abuse, exhibiting criminal, violent, and otherwise antisocial behavior, etc.) by having them train and care for stray pups to help them learn responsibility and self-discipline. In August 2008, the Who hosted an ebay auction to benefit K9 Connection in which the highest bidder won an exceptionally odd prize: a day of work as a roadie for the band. Hopefully the Who didn't overwork the winner, an unnamed fan from Canada who bid $25,100 for the pleasure of lugging speakers.

In May 2013 they ran a similar ebay auction for the benefit of the Brain Tumour Research Campaign, Wendy Fulcher's charity determined "to assist the emergence of the UK's first multi-disciplinary Brain Tumour Research Centre of Excellence at Charing Cross Hospital in West London."

Consult the URLs below to make a donation to the Who-endorsed charity of your choice:

Amnesty International	www.amnestyusa.org
Brain Tumour Research Campaign	www.wayahead-btrc.org
Children's Defense Fund	www.childrensdefense.org
Children's Health Fund	www.childrenshealthfund.org
John Entwistle Foundation	www.johnentwistle.org
K9 Connection	k9connection.org
Mercury Phoenix Trust	www.mercuryphoenixtrust.com
National Association for People Abused in Childhood	www.napac.org.uk
National Society for the Prevention of Cruelty to Children	www.nspcc.org.uk
Nordoff Robbins	www.nordoff-robbins.org.uk
The Prince's Trust	www.princes-trust.org.uk
Refuge (formerly Chiswick Family Rescue)	refuge.org.uk
Robin Hood Relief Fund	www.robinhood.org
Stars Foundation for Cerebral Palsy	www.starsfoundation.co.uk
Teen Cancer America	www.teencanceramerica.org
Teenage Cancer Trust	www.teenagecancertrust.org

34

The Simple Secret

A Dozen Underrated Songs of the Seventies

W hen we last left the Who, they were exiting the sixties with a punishing new sound sparked by their increasing confidence onstage, their resolution to get serious with serious concepts, Roger Daltrey's discovery of his voice through *Tommy*, Pete Townshend's discovery of synthesizers, and the overall move away from sixties-style pop quirk to a heavy-duty rock world now dominated by the likes of Led Zeppelin and Black Sabbath. In the seventies, the Who would release most of their best-loved albums: *Live at Leeds*, *Who's Next*, and *Quadrophenia*. Some great songs still managed to slip through the cracks. While nearly every track on *Who's Next* ended up as a classic rock radio staple, DJs have paid little mind to most of the complex *Quadrophenia*. Even when compiling the sprawling box set *Thirty Years of Maximum R&B*, Chris Charlesworth included a mere three songs from the original double album. I'm sure you'll agree that the leftovers constitute quite a body of underrated songs.

My one criterion for compiling these underrated seventies songs is exactly the same as it was when I collected a dozen from the sixties back in chapter 8: nothing from *The Ultimate Collection*. Once again, I relied on my fellow Who freaks to do the deciding, and once again, you've chosen wisely, representing all of the seventies LPs plus some bonus singles, odds, and sods. Here are your picks.

"Water"

The environmental crisis at the center of *Lifehouse* received early examination on "Water," a song the Who intended to include on their maxi single of 1970 (see chapter 16) and Pete Townshend possibly considered for their equally ill-fated opera (the band performed it at the Young Vic *Lifehouse* shows, though it is absent from *Lifehouse Chronicles*). This swaggering blues workout was a stage staple in '70, but it remained unreleased until appearing on the flips of "5:15" in the United Kingdom and "Love Reign o'er Me" in the United States in 1973. The song depicts a society losing its marbles amidst a worldwide draught. Townshend and Moon convey a sweltering landscape with their slow-rolling

The flipside of "5:15" is a big favorite among Who aficionados on vinyl and onstage.

Courtesy of the Rob Abramowicz Collection, digitized by Jeffrey Uleau

intro. Townshend intended to convey his own spiritualism (the desire for "water," an element he'd use to represent God in such other songs as "Drowned" and "The Sea Refuses No River"), while placating Daltrey's macho bullshit (the lust for "somebody's daughter"). The singer takes the mic, hip and emotive as a beat poet, leading a call-and-response between voice and guitar and drums. Then it all slams to a stop as Townshend lays down an authoritative lick that booms into a steamy mid-tempo groove. A bit short on melody, "Water" is still a great show-case for the band's instrumental interplay and a greater excuse for some epic improvisation onstage.

"Naked Eye"

The fans' overwhelming favorite underrated song of the seventies was not deemed fit for release during its own time. Like "Water," "Naked Eye" was one of the tracks the Who cut for their 1970 maxi single and was allegedly in the running for *Lifehouse*. In his *Odds & Sods* essay from 1974, Townshend noted that he developed the song from a chord figure the band often jammed onstage. In a who.com Q&A from 2008, he reversed that statement, saying that it was a "proper song before it was touched on the stage," but considering that he dates its composition to the spring of 1970 in *Who I Am*, and the Who jammed "Naked Eye" during "My Generation" at the Valentine's Day 1970 gig taped for *Live at Leeds*, his memory seems amiss on this matter. The song's jam origins are apparent in the improvisations that are its centerpiece and climax, and the shift to waltz time proves that Keith Moon was capable of extending beyond 4/4 time.

The magic of "Naked Eye" is not limited to performance. Despite its stage origins, this is a "proper song," perhaps Townshend's most serious to date. He peers uncomfortably behind the self-delusions that guide us through our relationships, pleading with us to communicate more openly and take responsibility for our own actions (while slipping in his belief that some sort of higher power is capable of shifting us around like pawns). In a reverse of stereotype, Daltrey sings the more sensitive passages while Townshend rages through the second verse, his voice cracking with a disarming lack of artifice as he shouts "press any *button*." The writer claimed this recording wasn't released in 1970 because the Who were hoping to cut a definitive live version. Fortunately, fans only had to wait four years to hear this spellbinding studio take of "Naked Eye" on *Odds & Sods*.

"The Song Is Over"

In *Anyway, Anyhow, Anywhere*, Neill and Kent mark "Naked Eye" as part of the original *Lifehouse* concept, though the fact that Pete Townshend did not include it in his *Lifehouse Chronicles* may contradict that claim. One song most definitely intended for *Lifehouse* is "The Song Is Over," which Townshend conceived as the aborted opera's epilogue (in one of his weirder statements, he indicated that this heart-wrenching song might have been performed by the Bonzo Dog Doo-Dah Band had the *Lifehouse* film come to pass). On *Who's Next*, it serves as centerpiece. Split from a larger story line, "The Song Is Over" still holds up as a wistful farewell. Townshend takes his resigned goodbye through iterations delicate as a breath and bold as nature, singing his song to "the wide open spaces," "the infinite sea," and "the sky high mountains." In doing so, he poetically indicates that a heart may break, but it will endure as nature does, a sentiment expressed without metaphor in his bittersweet farewells "So Sad About Us" and "Our Love Was." Taking a more traditional tack than they had on "Naked Eye," Townshend sings the lovely, piano-based passages and Daltrey cuts loose to shout at the mountains. Sad and hopeful and designed around an Eb maj.7 progression guaranteed to jerk tears, "The Song Is Over" is one of the Who's most beautiful songs and one of the few tracks on the hit-laden *Who's Next* that could rightfully be called underrated.

"Going Mobile"

Another is the contrastingly jocular "Going Mobile." Townshend's vocal on "The Song Is Over" is a tearful sigh. On "Going Mobile," it is an elated whoop. The happy freedom of hopping in a vehicle and hitting the road is palpable in every one of his hoots and hollers and each laser-beam blast of his ARP synthesizer–filtered guitar. In the middle of the soul-searching that dominates *Who's Next*, "Going Mobile" is a gust of responsibility-shirking fun (naughty Pete indulges in a momentary disregard for pollution and paying his taxes). It's also a spiritual throwback to the Beach Boys' great car songs of the early sixties, though the bulky motor home Townshend had in mind is a far cry from Mike Love's lean hot rods. As such, it is another *Lifehouse* leftover that remains perfectly relatable and self-contained—no plotlines necessary here.

"Relay"

Sometimes you have to break the rules a little, be a little irresponsible, and get your kicks, as Townshend does in "Going Mobile." But we all have greater responsibilities too, which he acknowledges on the inspirational rallying cry "Relay." Those who've painted our hero as a counterrevolutionary tool based on their misinterpretations of "Won't Get Fooled Again" (see chapter 31) clearly haven't heard the Who's final stand-alone single. Townshend writes of our interconnectedness and our power to join together and enact positive, grassroots change on the streets. The "relay" is his electronic system for marshalling hearts and minds: science fiction back in 1972, a reality called the Internet today. Townshend conveys that futurism by once again filtering his guitar through a synthesizer for a "wah-wah" effect. "Relay" is funkier than the usual Who freak-out, a

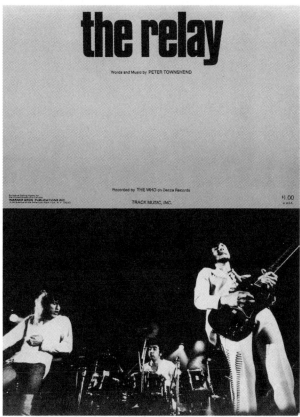

Although it sneaked into the top forty in the United States and came close to the top twenty in the United Kingdom, "Relay" tends to get swept aside by overly familiar hits like "Won't Get Fooled Again," "Squeeze Box," and "Who Are You." Fans believe it deserves wider appreciation.

Courtesy of the Rob Abramowicz Collection, digitized by Jeffrey Uleau

rubbery groove much closer in spirit to James Brown than the band's actual interpretations of the Godfather of Soul's repertoire. Perhaps that break from the Who's expected sound is why "Relay" didn't perform spectacularly on the charts and is regularly overlooked on compilations (the original single version has not been released in the United States or the United Kingdom since 1993's *Thirty Years of Maximum R&B*). It may also be why fans rate it as one the band's most underrated numbers.

"The Punk and the Godfather"

Quadrophenia began life as *Rock Is Dead . . . Long Live Rock*, an album/film project that would have surveyed the Who's career and history. "The Punk and the Godfather" feels like a remnant of that project, finding Jimmy (the punk) marching up to the Who (the godfathers) and calling out his idols for not living up to their supposed godliness. The Who "walked on the trail" the mods were carving instead of being the leaders they claimed to be. Rock 'n' roll failed to save the world and its "starving" masses. Their promise of radical change was a lie, and singing the part of the Godfather, Townshend takes a more cautious approach to his role, sheepishly resolving to no longer preach or pretend he can teach. The "My Generation" battle cry becomes a whimper in one of rock's most revealing one-man psychodramas.

If the Who come out defeated in the showdown that is "The Punk and the Godfather," they do not go down without a fight. Townshend's lick is one of his most direct: a three-chord cycle discharged with the violence of a razor-waving hooligan. Roger Daltrey sings the part of the punk with almighty outrage in one of his most commanding performances. John Entwistle's top-of-the neck shudders heighten the agitation of the opening riff, while the descending line mimicking Townshend's "M-M-My Generation" over the fade-out is his prettiest moment. If a bass line is capable of drawing tears, then this one surely will.

"Sea and Sand"

"Sea and Sand" is another great balancing act between melancholic resignation and indignant anger. After Jimmy touches down on the sands of Brighton Beach, he reflects on what brought him there: his dysfunctional, alcoholic parents, the unattainable girl, his perceived inability to live up to his sharp-dressed mod peers. Coming at the inconclusive center of *Quadrophenia*, "Sea and Sand" pivots off the arpeggios Townshend spins out like a succession of ellipses. Moon and Entwistle's sudden detonations are grand exclamation points as Jimmy's arrogance momentarily usurps his doubtfulness and he takes shallow solace in his fashionable clothes, regurgitating macho lines learned from a record by his favorite band ("I'm the face if you want it . . ."). "Sea and Sand" is mere interlude, not an instance of great revelation or drama . . . just the kind of underrated moment that might go unnoticed in the middle of bigger ideas.

"Doctor Jimmy"

The inattentive listener might skate over the subtle "Sea and Sand." "Doctor Jimmy," however, is a bombastic statement impossible to miss. Epic, confrontational, constantly shifting, and more "operatic" than anything else on *Quadrophenia* ("Wagnerian" by Pete Townshend's own description), "Doctor Jimmy" is our protagonist ping-ponging between the most extreme poles of his personality. At one end, he is a blowhard, a misogynist, an overindulgent monster—his ugly declaration of "Who is she? I'll rape it!" revealing the influence of *A Clockwork Orange* clearer than any other line on *Quadrophenia*. At the other end, Jimmy is a wistful romantic getting choked up at the sight of falling stars. He does this in the "Is It Me?" subsection, which Townshend earmarked as the John Entwistle side of Jimmy's quadrophenic personality. "Doctor Jimmy" works best as a portrait of Keith Moon alone, and Townshend has said he had the drummer in mind when composing it (let's not forget that five years earlier, Moon inspired Entwistle's own Jekyll/Hyde portrait of the drummer). "Doctor Jimmy" is also a complete summation of the *Quadrophenia* experience: the synths and horns, the grandeur and grace, the slashing guitar chords and avalanches

In France, the underrated "Doctor Jimmy" appeared on the flip of "The Real Me."

Courtesy of the Rob Abramowicz Collection, digitized by Jeffrey Uleau

of drums and bass, the field sound effects and recurring musical themes, the brutality and tenderness.

"Slip Kid"

In "The Punk and the Godfather," Pete Townshend imagined the younger generation railing at him for being an aging rock star as ultimately limited as all mortals. He'd continue that self-dissection on "Slip Kid" on the Who's next album, a self-dissecting bloodbath called *The Who by Numbers*. As there was in "The Punk," there is a dialogue here between members of the old and new guards, but it is hard to tell if they are separate people or a young man's missive to his older self, or vice versa. One man is youthful, enthusiastic, ready to go out and fight in the rock 'n' roll trenches with his kit bag and heavy boots. The other is a soldier at sixty-three, leaving behind a doctor-prescribed bungalow and toting a thermos of tea, stirring much mistrust in the hopeful kid. Townshend revealed the song was a word of warning for young people with dreams of rock 'n' roll stardom, but his youngster's angry response ("Keep away old man, you won't fool me . . .") suggests he didn't have much faith his advice would take root. The rhythm indicates a more restrained Who than the one we've known: a tight Latin shuffle topped with piano and grounded with groovy shakers. The beat forces Keith Moon to hold back his usual mad impulses, but Entwistle stills manages to find spaces to slip in tasty bass flourishes. Townshend brings the requisite violence with his stun-gun guitar, then simmers through the mid-section with ominous volume swells. Released as a flop single, "Slip Kid" is complex yet utterly accessible (the chorus unveils the slick harmonies that would be one of the most pleasurable ingredients of a largely bitter record). It deserved to be a hit.

"Dreaming from the Waist"

"Dreaming from the Waist" is one of the few songs from the Who's most unjustly underrated album to receive some play onstage. Maybe John Entwistle lobbied for its inclusion in the set lists because it's such a marvelous showcase for his genius. Roger Daltrey always made a special effort to give the bass player props at the number's conclusion. I wonder if it was a bit strange for Townshend to hear another man get the glory for such a personal composition. "Dreaming from the Waist" examines the plight of the aging rock star trying to work his mojo the way he did when he was a young buck. The song is overripe with frustration. The youthful urge to paint the town red is deflated by oversensitivity. Trying to put the moves on a "whorey lady," he ends up "quietly weeping" when she imparts her own "sad, sad story."

"Dreaming from the Waist" is one of Pete Townshend's most insightful songs about sex and one of his most brutally honest about aging. The musicians' virtuosity accounts for much of the song's popularity among fans, but they are also touched to hear such an intimate statement from such a big rock star. This is the kind of song that causes Who fans to feel such a close connection to a man they're never going to meet. I doubt Stones freaks feel the same way about Jagger. As a Stones freak myself, I can at least say that I don't.

"How Many Friends"

"Dreaming from the Waist" is a jolly nursery rhyme compared to this song. "How Many Friends" is such an unabashed monument to self-pity that Keith Moon burst into tears when he heard it and gave Pete Townshend a big hug to let him know that he has at least one friend. Roger Daltrey locates his feminine high register to sing words at direct odds with his macho persona. The singer sits at a bar and chats with a "handsome boy" he assumes only wants him for sex. He frets over his abilities between the sheets. Oddest of all for Daltrey must have been wailing the verse about how supposed friends talk "so much shit behind each other's backs" because the friend about whom Townshend was writing may have been Daltrey himself. There's a lot of history in "How Many Friends," and it is a song both moving and mighty. The chorus brings all of those churning emotions to a thrilling head. Once again, John Entwistle shines with his upper-fret bass work.

"Trick of the Light"

Now it's Entwistle's turn to question the power of the penis in this big, big favorite from *Who Are You*. He wouldn't be John Entwistle if he did so with Pete Townshend's melancholic introspection, and "Trick of the Light" can be viewed in a humorous light as it deals with an anxious trick concerned that he failed to bring a hooker to "the height of ecstasy." Genuine vulnerability makes the song more than a good giggle and undercuts the performance's cock-rock attitude. Entwistle slams down a bludgeoning riff on his Alembic 8-string bass. This is the closest the Who ever got to heavy metal in the studio, and the musicians sound happy to set the synths aside for a few minutes to get down to dirty business. Daltrey was less so, wishing it hadn't made the album's final cut and complaining that it went "on and on and on and on" to the point of blandness. But if everyone loved "Trick of the Light," it probably wouldn't be so underrated.

35

We Talk So Much Shit Behind Each Other's Backs

The Who as Mates and Foes

Oh yeah, it's the best way to get something out of your system. Roger gets talked about behind his back, and I think I get talked about behind my back, but I don't think Keith or Roger* get talked about because Roger and I, if we have a conversation, don't normally get brought down about things unless we're talking about money. But conversations with John and Keith are usually humorously scam.
—Pete Townshend (*New Musical Express*, March 3, 1973)
(* I'm pretty sure Pete meant to say "John" here.)

Is there a single major rock 'n' roll band in the history of rock 'n' roll bands that wasn't at least slightly dysfunctional? Even the Beatles, those four cherubic chums with the matching suits and matching hairdos, disbanded in acrimony. But they *had* started as chums, tight-knit allies in scaling to the "topper-most of the popper-most," as John Lennon promised they would. Mick Jagger and Keith Richards have always been known to take swipes at each other in the press, and had their own well-publicized split in the mid-eighties, but their brotherly love was at the heart of every nasty comment. Members of the Beach Boys or the Kinks really were family, and the lawsuits between cousins Mike Love and Brian Wilson or the vitriol between brothers Ray and Dave Davies were complicated by the baggage *and* the love that comes with blood relations.

That the relationships between the Beatles, the Stones, and the Kinks were of the love/hate variety is well known among pop followers. The relationships within the Who are usually thought of as hate/hate. The wars in the press. The punch-ups. The callous comments. The nearly constant threats of "I quit!" or "You're fired!" Where's the love?

Well, it is there. You just have to look beyond the headlines. Anyone who has ever been in a band understands the love/hate dynamic well. Being a bandmate may be the most intense kind of interpersonal relationship outside of romantic or familial ones. Like parents, you create something together: music.

Like siblings or parents and children, you aren't necessarily in the relationship because you like each other. There are more consequential matters, particularly musical compatibility. Not every group of musicians is able to bash out a good noise together no matter how well they may get along.

Pete, Roger, John, and Keith rarely got along, and their musical compatibility is why they played together. But they did love each other despite their combative reputation. Who fans just might have to dig a little deeper to understand how their idols felt about each other.

Pete and Roger

"I used to think he was a bit of a yob, a bit of a thug."
   —Pete Townshend on Roger Daltrey (*Six Quick Ones: Roger*)

"When you read things about what we did in the past and how many fights we used to have, you think, 'These guys used to hate each other.' Did we? Fuck. Well, I didn't, anyway. I loved him."
   —Roger Daltrey on Pete Townshend (*Amazing Journey: The Story of the Who*)

No two members of the Who shared a more complex relationship than Pete Townshend and Roger Daltrey. On the surface, their temperaments could not seem more different: Townshend the verbose intellectual, Daltrey the grunting everyman. Below the skin, they shared a deep connection that took them decades to understand. Most obviously, they both share an intense love of music. They are both fighters with strong ideas of what their band should be, and as it turns out, they are both fierce defenders of their often-misunderstood bandmates. That includes each other.

Pete Townshend first met Roger Daltrey at the age of thirteen under extreme circumstances. Daltrey was beating up one of Townshend's friends on a playground. When Townshend intervened, calling Daltrey a "dirty fighter," Daltrey let him know that if he didn't shut his trap, he would be the next to get pounded.

Daltrey ruled his band the Detours as a malevolent despot. This continued when the group evolved into the Who. Anyone who contradicted or displeased him was liable to end up with a jaw-full of knuckles. As the band's nascent songwriter and conceptual visionary, Townshend found his natural place as leader. This did not temper Daltrey's violence. At the same time, he remained typically diplomatic when discussing the guitarist in the press. In the September 24, 1966, issue of *Melody Maker*, Daltrey categorized Townshend as a "Very intelligent bloke" and said, "I like him a lot." Less honestly he claimed that punch-ups were "stupid" and he hadn't "had a fight since I left school."

In truth, Daltrey's role in the band had been in jeopardy just a year earlier because of his violent ways and his disapproval of his bandmates' drug use. When measures were taken to give him the boot, he finally relented, said he'd be "peaceful Perce" and keep his fists on ice. He kept his promise for some eight years, only breaking it when a drunken Townshend physically attacked him for voicing disapproval with a loitering film crew during a 1973 rehearsal. Daltrey regretted knocking Townshend out with a single punch. The Who's publicist Keith Altham told *Daltrey* biographers Tim Ewbank and Stafford Hildred that Daltrey actually cradled Townshend in his arms, telling the unconscious guitarist how much he loved him while waiting for the ambulance to arrive. The relationship did not mend as quickly as Townshend's head.

Discord between the two soon came back to a head. Townshend felt Daltrey was frustrated by his lack of input on *Quadrophenia*. Daltrey felt Townshend was getting unprofessional and too drunk. In the May 31, 1975, issue of *New Musical Express*, Townshend infamously unloaded a despondent torrent about his fans, his band, the state of rock 'n' roll, and his own role in it. Sneering, "When Roger says, 'We'll all be rockin' in our wheelchairs,' well, he might be, but you won't catch me rockin' in no wheelchair," Townshend provided the flint Daltrey would

use to spark a conflagration. Daltrey returned his fire in the August 9 issue of the *NME*, calling Townshend's interview "a load of bullshit" and saying "I've talked to a lot of fans and I think Townshend lost a lot of respect from that article. He's talked himself up his own ass." Daltrey took further issue with how he gets "laughed at" for daring to make artistic suggestions. He took particular issue with Townshend's suggestion that Daltrey would prefer rock 'n' roll to be about nothing more than "making records, pullin' birds, gettin' pissed and having a good time," saying, "don't talk to me about booze, because I've never been onstage drunk in the last seven years, Mr. Townshend! . . . I'm just getting' fed-up with these left handed attacks."

The Who squeeze together on the cover of this sheet music for "Squeeze Box."

Courtesy of the Rob Abramowicz Collection, digitized by Jeffrey Uleau

This *NME* back and forth has often been held up as exhibit A in the argument that Townshend and Daltrey hate each other's guts. Daltrey even acknowledged that "There's a terrible battle going on between me and him, ain't there?" In his otherwise self-critical "However Much I Booze," Townshend would wonder, "Are the problems that screw me up really down to him or me?" Daltrey refused to sing the song, supposedly because of its personal nature, but perhaps also because it might have been a bit too weird voicing the opposition's side in their ongoing battle.

In truth, this "battle" was not nearly as dire as the ones in which the Who had engaged in the past. Their current tussle was limited to the printed page. No one witnessed any verbal flare-ups between the two. There certainly was no resumption of their previous fisticuffs. The *NME* exchange has taken on mythic status as repeated in many Who biographies, though Townshend gives it no more than a few cursory lines in *Who I Am*, concluding, "Neither of us took this kind of thing to heart in the long run."

For all of the juicy lines scattered throughout the interviews, the overall effect of both is more weary than vitriolic. Think of what it must have been like for two such seemingly dissimilar people to be thrust together in the Who's close and tumultuous quarters, contending with a towering reputation and the near-unrealistic expectations of their fans and Keith Moon's ever-erratic behavior. Had Daltrey and Townshend really been through with each other, Moon's death would have been the ultimate excuse to split. But they stuck together for decades, even if it was an on-and-off relationship. When John Entwistle died, Daltrey and Townshend reached a new plateau in that relationship. These former adversaries realized they were all that was left of the Who. The bitterness and indifference they once expressed in the press turned into love. The two continued to acknowledge their differences while also giving heartfelt statements of devotion. Just listen to them talk about each other in *Amazing Journey: The Story of the Who* and try not to get choked up. "I recognize his genius and I love him dearly," Daltrey says. "He's like a brother." "He's my friend," Townshend says. "I love him."

Both men had strong reasons for expressing such strong emotions. Daltrey was always grateful that Townshends gave him those wonderful songs to sing. Surely he would never have achieved his stardom on his voice alone. It was that pairing of the perfect material and the perfect interpreter that made Roger Daltrey's fortune. Townshend, who always talked up the importance of rock 'n' roll while realizing there are more important things in life, was touched and impressed by the support Daltrey afforded him during his hardest times, particularly the way Rog went to bat for him during the child pornography investigation. "I stand by him and he stands by me," Townshend said in *Amazing Journey,* a sentiment he'd previously expressed on "You Stand By Me" from *Endless Wire.* In a commentary posted on his own website, Townshend admitted the touching song was inspired by both his new girlfriend Rachel Fuller and his old friend Roger Daltrey. In light of all this, a few snipes in an old music paper seem pretty insignificant, don't they?

John and Keith

"He goes along with my insane ideas and ventures."
—Keith Moon on John Entwistle (unknown 1967 article reprinted in *The Who Maximum R&B*)

"He was my best friend in the band."
—John Entwistle on Keith Moon (*Goldmine*, July 5, 1996)

From the band's two biggest adversaries to its two closest mates. Unless you followed the Who closely, you may not have been aware of that tight bond between John Entwistle and Keith Moon, Entwistle never being the effusive sort and Moon rarely remaining serious long enough to give a sincere opinion about anything. But make no mistake, they loved each other, and despite the polar opposition of their surface demeanors, they had a lot in common. The Quiet One and the Lunatic Clown shared passions for surf music, the Beatles, monster movies, spending money, clubbing, comedy, comic books, sex, drugs, booze, and playing with the Who. When the band's career seemed to be reaching a dead end in 1968, Moon and Entwistle schemed to form their own splinter group called Lead Zeppelin. They shared rooms on the road, and as Townshend suspects, they may have shared groupies too.

Things weren't always completely friendly between the two. Even one as seemingly unflappable as John Entwistle could be pushed to his limit by the Grand Looner. For a lark, Moon once put on a black wig and started copying Entwistle's every move. If Entwistle crossed his legs, Moon did the same. If he sighed, so did Moon. If he scratched his nose, as was his habit, Moon went to work on his own proboscis. Finally, Entwistle exploded and demanded Moon quit it. A big laugh was shared by all but poor John.

Moon's pranks were not always so benign. One night while on tour in Paris in 1972, he came knocking on Entwistle's hotel room door, hammered out of his mind. He staggered over to Entwistle's dinner, helped himself to a bit of steak and wine, splattered the rest on the carpet, and pissed in the corner, leaving Alison Entwistle beside herself and her husband livid. Entwistle marched to Moon's room and destroyed it Moon-the-Loon style. When Moon came to the next day, he naturally assumed he was responsible for the wreckage.

Such was friendship in the wacky day-to-day road life of the Who. Entwistle could destroy his friend's room, but he'd be damned if anyone else thought ill of the boy. His respect for his late mate ran so deep that he wanted to cut Moon's comment that cinematographer Peter Nevard "couldn't afford" the truth from *The Kids Are Alright*. In the movie, the comment plays like a silly pop-prima-donna parody, but I guess Entwistle knew Moon well enough to know when he was actually being a dick.

The respect went both ways. Moon loved Entwistle like a big brother. He loved Entwistle's songs, which appealed to his hankering for silly humor and creepy-crawlies. During a 1976 interview with *Trouser Press*, Moon took a break to put John's Entwistle's record *Mad Dog* on the turntable and dance around the room. One could assume he was mocking his mate, but even Keith Moon had his moments of sincerity and he seemed to love Entwistle too much to do anything so cruel.

Roger and Keith

"Roger—he hates me . . . I told him he can't sing."
—Keith Moon on Roger Daltrey (*New Musical Express*, December 10, 1965)

"He's the crying clown . . . I worry about Keith a lot."
—Roger Daltrey on Keith Moon (*Melody Maker*, February 9, 1974)

John Entwistle and Keith Moon were only superficially dissimilar. Roger Daltrey and Keith Moon were profoundly unalike. Aside from a mutual zeal for music and sex, there were not two more unlike people in the Who. Daltrey liked to quietly retire with a woman after a show. Moon liked to go out on the razzle all night, indulging in as many chemicals and females as he could consume. Daltrey was health conscious. Moon was the poster boy for idiotic self-destruction. Daltrey took whatever abstentious measures necessary to keep his voice in top shape. Moon was known to pass out in the middle of a concert. Daltrey envisioned the Who as a tight ship with himself at the helm. Moon had nothing but loathing for restrictions of any kind. And this is where the two most clashed.

Matters reached a head during a two-day, four-gig stint in Denmark in September 1965. Through no fault of the band, the crowd got a bit too rocking and rolling and rushed the stage. The melee brought an early end to their show in Aarhus Hallen. With the atmosphere already tense, Daltrey laid into his bandmates about their amphetamine use, which had caused some unintentionally chaotic performances and caused Daltrey to walk offstage on occasion. To punctuate his diatribe, Daltrey grabbed Moon's pills and plunged them down the loo. For the diminutive drug enthusiast, such an action was a declaration of war. Moon lunged at Daltrey with a tambourine. Bad move. Out-of-control he may have been, but he was no fighter. Daltrey beat him severely. The singer later said he felt terrible about the entire incident.

Moon rarely commented on Daltrey during interviews, but Chris Stamp insisted that Rog "was not liked by Keith at all" in *Moon*. This isn't surprising considering incidents such as the one described above. When Ringo Starr asked Moon his opinion of Daltrey in *The Kids Are Alright*, he merely cracked a drunken joke about Daltrey making a chopped salad with his swinging microphone prefaced with "I think he does a damned good job" onstage. By most accounts, Moon was not a fan of Daltrey's voice and resented his role as the band's front man/sex symbol.

Daltrey, however, has expressed nothing but love for Moon. He has expressed regret for the way he treated the drummer during those bellicose early years and his failure to rescue Moon from self-destruction (a task beyond the power of any mortal). "How could you not have fun around Keith Moon?," Daltrey asked during a bonus interview on the *Kids Are Alright* DVD. He certainly seemed to be having a good laugh at Moon's clowning on *Russell Harty Plus.* Daltrey later insisted that he was the only stable influence in Moon's life toward its end, so perhaps affection ran deeper between the two men than Moon let on.

John and Pete

"The only friction between me and Pete after that was on [A Quick One] *. . . a couple of people got interviews with him wrong or got the stuff wrong or he was flashing around and said, 'Of course I helped John to write* ["Boris the Spider" and "Whiskey Man"], *' which angered me a little."*
—John Entwistle on Pete Townshend (audio interview
with Roy Carr circa January 1974)

"I don't think he ever put a foot wrong in our relationship."
—Pete Townshend on John Entwistle ("John Entwistle"
essay on thewho.com, June 2012)

John Entwistle and Pete Townshend were the oldest friends in the Who. They would meet up in Townshend's bedroom and play music together after school. Entwistle treated his friend with great consideration, welcoming him into his trad jazz group the Confederates and his new pop band the Detours. When Townshend was unsure of his own musicianship, Entwistle offered reassurance that he was a great guitarist.

Townshend regarded Entwistle as his closest friend in the group and "a great musical ally" (*Amazing Journey*), but admitted he did not always return the support. Consequently, Entwistle seemed to resent Townshend to a certain degree. He did not like how Townshend's compositions dominated the Who's records or how he wasn't more generous with writing credits on songs Entwistle felt were collaborative enough that he should have shared the royalty wealth. Entwistle was suspicious of Townshend for allegedly claiming he'd had a hand in cowriting "Boris the Spider" and "Whiskey Man," and he resented the public perception that he and Keith Moon merely copied the bass and drums Townshend had recorded on his demos.

In his essay on thewho.com posted to commemorate the tenth anniversary of John Entwistle's death, Townshend implied that Entwistle's mother claimed her son never liked him. If this is true, Queenie may have been responding angrily to hurtful comments Townshend supposedly made about John's death. Or maybe she was telling the truth. Maybe John really did not return his love. Townshend said otherwise. In his essay, he wrote, "a couple of times John had actually told me he loved me. We were usually alone, and he might have been a bit drunk, but sometimes when we're drunk we tell the truth."

While we may never know how John Entwistle really felt about Pete Townshend, Townshend's love for his fallen bandmate is unquestionable. "For me, with John, the situation is clear cut," he wrote. "There are no difficulties, no blurred images. I loved John, I liked him, I respected him, and I miss him." He must have loved John; he named his pet Yorkshire terrier Wistle in honor of the late Mr. Entwistle.

John and Roger

"The story about me being the quiet one of the Who is not quite true. Roger is the hermit. When we're on tour, we never see him except on stage."
　　—John Entwistle on Roger Daltrey (*Rolling Stone*, December 5, 1974)

"He's very introverted . . . I find it very difficult to get through to John."
　　—Roger Daltrey on John Entwistle (*Melody Maker*, February 9, 1974)

John Entwistle and Roger Daltrey may have had the weakest rapport in the Who. Their reputation seems to have been largely professional, though not of any small consequence and not without its moments of friction. Daltrey recruited Entwistle into the Detours after seeing the bassist bopping down the street holding his homemade instrument while Alison Wise roadied his amp. Entwistle had been returning from a practice with his group the Scorpions when Daltrey convinced him to check out a Detours rehearsal. It was a decisive moment, ground zero for the Who falling into place, but hardly a warm and fuzzy "meet cute." It seems Daltrey and Entwistle never got much cuter with each other.

In his post "Peaceful Perce" interview with *Melody Maker* published on September 24, 1966, Daltrey spoke as highly of Entwistle as he did of everyone else in the group ("I like John a lot . . . He's amazing"). He remained as sociable with Entwistle as he did with Townshend and Moon, which is to say, not very sociable at all. Entwistle's drug use irked Daltrey as much as his other bandmates' did, and supposedly, Daltrey was not keen to participate in the bassist's first songwriting efforts. In future years, the singer and bass guitarist regularly clashed over volume. Daltrey would get annoyed at him for turning his amp up to eleven onstage. Entwistle got annoyed with Daltrey's complaining. With his usual low-key cheekiness, Entwistle would just turn up louder to get a rise out of Daltrey.

He seemed to take a certain pleasure in having a giggle at Daltrey's expense. He famously quipped that the gold records he used in the skeet-shooting sequence of *The Kids Are Alright* were Daltrey's. Daltrey seems to have taken Entwistle's jokes with good humor. He also humored his business partner when Entwistle's unfettered spending got him into dire financial straits in the nineties. Daltrey agreed to tour to help generate the revenue Entwistle needed to dig himself out of the hole. Entwistle played the genial sideman at Daltrey's "Music of Pete Townshend and the Who" gigs at Carnegie Hall in February

1994. Entwistle was never quick to reveal his true feelings about the singer to the press, but that did not deter Daltrey from praising him. In a 1994 interview with *Goldmine*, Daltrey gushed over Entwistle's songs and *Smash Your Head Against the Wall*. He also expressed his wish to sing those *Smash Your Head* songs and collaborate with Entwistle more.

Daltrey would get his wish for more collaboration when the Who resumed semiregular work a couple of years later. The collaboration ended for good with the bassman's death, which left him deeply saddened. "I miss him so much I can't tell you," Daltrey said in *Amazing Journey*, his emotion revealing the depth of their relationship, even if it may have been more of a musical than personal one.

Keith and Pete

"One of the greatest people I've ever met . . . I just hope we continue to have many happy years of creating wonderful mind-blowers for our dearly beloved audiences."
—Keith Moon on Pete Townshend (*Pop ThinkIn*, December 13, 1966)

"Keith was a very positive musician, a very positive performer, but a very negative animal. He needed you for his act, on and off stage."
—Pete Townshend on Keith Moon (*Oui*, March 1980)

One was the leader, the intellectual, the spiritual seeker. The other was the sultan of excess, the incorrigible joker, the gaping maw that could not devour enough drugs, booze, and sex. Opposites on paper, Pete Townshend and Keith Moon had some key similarities beyond music. They shared a confounding complexity and a mass of contradictions. They could also be very, very funny together. Just watch their dynamic on *Russell Harty Plus*. Moon seems totally out of control, but it is Townshend—one of the most vocal fans of Moonie's outrageous comedy—who instigates much of the mayhem. Daltrey and Entwistle just sit back and giggle. Harty looks a bit flustered, but he knows he's capturing some good TV. How could he not with two such ace performers?

But no one could escape the frustrations of friendship with Keith Moon, and that goes double for one as naturally frustrated as Pete Townshend. Moon seemed to love Townshend unequivocally, only voicing his displeasure during times when Townshend was too busy to work with the Who, which Moon treated as a lifeline (and even in these instances, he was reportedly quicker to blame Daltrey than Townshend). Toward the end of his life, he regularly phoned Townshend before bedtime to offer an emotionally overwrought, often tearful, "Goodnight" or "I love you."

Townshend often seemed angry with Moon, whom he always blamed for causing his hearing loss by exploding that bass drum on *The Smothers Brothers Comedy Hour*. Onstage and in the studio, Moon was a musical wild card whose skills were stunning and distinctive but hardly versatile, and as his health faltered, so did his skills. Townshend's comments following the drummer's death could come off as callous. Less than two years after he died, Townshend was telling *Oui* magazine that life in the Who without Moon was "great fun" and that the induction of Kenney Jones had given the group "a tremendous blood transfusion." Such insensitivity can be read as evidence of Townshend's raw feelings about his friend's death at a time when he was plummeting into his own cyclone of substance abuse and erratic behavior. Or maybe he was just being honest.

Nearing the end of this book, we should now understand that Pete Townshend's honest feelings could change from moment to moment. This holds true for his opinions of Keith Moon's drumming. In the 1989 MTV special *Who's Back: The Story of the Who*, he praised Moon's ability to tether his guitar playing and Entwistle's bass work in such a way that he "never felt limited musically." In the 2012 documentary *Can You See the Real Me*, he offhandedly mentioned, "I didn't think much of him as a drummer." Honest perhaps, but not the kind of thing fans want to hear about their dead idol.

That Townshend has a tendency to speak before he thinks is evident in countless controversial interviews. That he loved Keith Moon is evident too. Check out "Jools and Jim" on *Empty Glass*, Townshend's poison pen letter to the rock journos who disparaged Moon after his death. Check out the essay he wrote for *Thirty Years of Maximum R&B*, one of the more depressingly negative screeds in a career of many. Yet Townshend also relates a story that illuminates Moon's humanity, an incident in which the wild man was charmed and

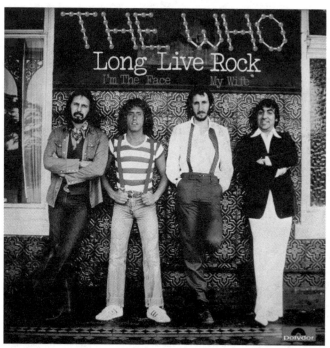

Long live the Who . . . fifty years and counting . . .   *Author's collection*

warmed by the kindness and hospitality of an average family in Little Rock, Arkansas. Townshend followed the story with the tart closing statement, "to critics of Moon and his diabolical certain-death style of rock 'n' roll nihilism, I say 'Fuck you.'" In other words, Pete Townshend could talk shit about Keith Moon because he knew him and loved him. Moon was his friend. The critics and commentators did not know Moon. We did not know the real man or how Townshend really felt about him and would be wise to shut the fuck up about it.

Fair enough.

Selected Bibliography

Books

Atkins, John. *The Who on Record*. Jefferson, NC: McFarland & Company, 2009.

Barnes, Richard (ed.). *The Who Maximum R&B*. New York, New York: St. Martin's Press, 1982.

Black, Johnny. *Eyewitness: The Who, the Day-By-Day Story*. London: Carlton Books, 2001.

Butler, Dougal, with Chris Trengove and Peter Lawrence. *Full Moon: The Amazing Rock & Roll Life of Keith Moon*. New York: William Morrow and Company, 1981.

Charlesworth, Chris. *The Who*. London: Omnibus Press, 1982.

Clarke, Steve (ed.). *The Who in Their Own Words*. New York: Quick Fox, 1979.

Ewbank, Tim, and Stafford Hildred. *Roger Daltrey: The Biography*. London: Piatkus Books, 2004.

Fletcher, Tony. *Moon*. New York: Spike, 1999.

Giuliano, Geoffrey. *Behind Blue Eyes*. New York, New York: Dutton, 1996.

Grantley, Steve, and Alan. G. Parker. *The Who by Numbers*. London: Helter Skelter Publishing, 2010.

Marsh, Dave. *Before I Get Old: The Story of the Who*. New York, New York: St. Martin's Press, 1983.

Neill, Andy, and Matt Kent. *Anyway, Anyhow, Anywhere: The Complete Chronicle of the Who 1958–1978*. New York: Sterling Publishing, 2005.

Perry, John. Classic Rock Albums: *Meaty, Beaty, Big, and Bouncy*. New York: Schirmer Books, 1998.

Schaffner, Nicholas. *The British Invasion*. New York: McGraw-Hill, 1983.

Townshend, Pete. *Horse's Neck*. Boston: Houghton Mifflin, 1985.

Townshend, Pete. *Who I Am*. New York: HarperCollins, 2012.

Unterberger, Richie. *Urban Spacemen and Wayfaring Strangers*. San Francisco: Miller Freeman Books, 2000.

Unterberger, Richie. *Won't Get Fooled Again: The Who from* Lifehouse *to* Quadrophenia. London: Jawbone, 2011

Wells, Simon. *Butterfly on a Wheel: The Great Stones Drugs Bust*. New York: Omnibus, 2011.

Wilkerson, Mark. *Amazing Journey: The Life of Pete Townshend*. Lulu.com, 2006.

Newspaper and Magazine Articles

Altham, Keith. "Keith Moon Interview." *New Music Express.* December 10, 1965.

Altham, Keith. "The Who in New York." *Hit Parader*, September 1967.

Bornino, Bruno. "Bruno's Big Beat." *Cleveland Press*, December 1967.

Buskin, Richard. "Classic Tracks: The Who 'Who Are You.'" *Sound on Sound*, May 2005.

Colapinto, John. "Giving Voice." *The New Yorker*, March 4, 2013.

Carr, Roy. "Is Keith Moon the Biggest Loony in the World? Or Is Denis Healey Even Dafter?," *New Music Express*, January 17, 1976.

Carr, Roy. "The Punk as the Godfather." *Creem*, May 31, 1975.

Carr, Roy. "The Who by Numbers—The March of the Mods Re-Visited." *New Music Express*, July 17, 1976.

Cott, Jonathan. "A Talk with Pete Townshend." *Rolling Stone*, May 14, 1970.

Crowe, Cameron. "The *Penthouse* Interview with Pete Townshend." *Penthouse*, December, 1974.

Du Noyer, Paul. "Pete Townshend: Forever's No Time at All." *New Music Express*, June 12, 1982.

Flippo, Chet. "John Entwistle Interview." *Rolling Stone*, December 5, 1974.

Gaines, Steven. "The Who Track Down Their 'Odds and Sods.'" *Circus*, December 1974.

Goddard, Simon. "Roger Daltrey's Track-by-Track Guide to the Who's Greatest Hits." *Uncut*, October 2001.

Goddard, Simon. "See Me, Feel Me." *Uncut*, April 2004.

Hopkins, Jerry. "Keith Moon Bites Back HAHAHAHAHA." *Rolling Stone*, December 21, 1972.

Lampert, Nicole. "Why My Wife Let Me Cheat on Her: Roger Daltrey on Why His Attitudes to Marriage Vows Are Far from Straightforward." *The Daily Mail*, July 15, 2011.

Ledgerwood, Mike. "Pete Townshend Interview." *Disc and Music Echo*, November 26, 1966.

Lennox, Richard. "WHO: Goodbye to the Pop Art Era." *Disc and Music Echo*, October 1, 1966.

Marcus, Greil. "The Rolling Stone Interview: Pete Townshend." *Rolling Stone*, June 26, 1980.

Miller, John J., "Rockin' the Right: The 50 Greatest Conservative Rock Songs." *The National Review*, May 26, 2006.

Rosen, Steve. "Townshend Talking." *Sound International*, April 1980.

Rothman, David. "A Conversation with Pete Townshend." *Oui*, March 1980.

Rudis, Al. "Roger Daltrey Interview." *Melody Maker*, February 9, 1974.

Scheff, David. "Interview: Pete Townshend." *Playboy*, February 1994.

Sharp, Ken. "Look Who's Talking: A Conversation with Roger Daltrey." *Goldmine*, July 8, 1994.

Sharp, Ken. "The Quiet One Speaks! A Chat with The Ox, the Who's JOHN ENTWISTLE." *Goldmine*, July 5, 1996.

Shaar Murray, Charles. "Four Way Pete." *New Music Express*, October 27, 1973.

Shaar Murray, Charles. "Townshend: The True Story of Clapton's Rainbow Gig." *New Music Express*, March 3, 1973.

Sheff, David. "Playboy Interview: A Candid Conversation with the Wizard of Rock About Life with the Who, Bisexuality in Music, 'Tommy' on Broadway, and, of Course, How to Smash a Guitar." *Playboy*, February 1994.

Stewart, Tony. "Who Said That?," *New Music Express*, August 12, 1978.

Stewart, Tony. "Who's Last?," *New Music Express*, August 9, 1975.

Swenson, John. "The Who: After Ten Years of Madness the Next Stage is 'Quadrophenia.'" *Crawdaddy*, January 1974.

Swift, Kevin. "New Who Grooves—Spiders—Runs—& Quick Ones." *Beat Instrumental*, January 1967.

Townshend, Pete. "Meaty, Beaty, Big, and Bouncy." *Rolling Stone*, December 9, 1971.

Uncredited. "Keith Moon Interview." *Pop ThinkIn*, December 13, 1966.

Uncredited. "Pete Townshend Interview." *Melody Maker*, March 26, 1966.

Uncredited. "WHO'S 'BIRDMAN' Pecks BEACH BOY." *Disc and Music*, September 17, 1966.

Van Ness, Chris. "An Interview with Pete Townshend and the Who." *Free Press*, December 1971.

VanPelt, Derek. "Townshend on 'Tommy,' Rock and America." *Cleveland After Dark*, November 19, 1969.

Welch, Chris. "Daltrey: Grandfather of Punk Rock." *Melody Maker*, April 30, 1977.

Wenner, Jann. "The Rolling Stone Interview: Pete Townshend." *Rolling Stone*, September 28, 1968.

Williams, Stephen. "Who Are They." *Newsday*, June 21, 1989.

Wilson, Jamie. "Pete Townshend Put on Sex Offender Register." *The Guardian*, May 8, 2003.

Websites

beta.thewho.net
www.rabbitwho.com
www.thewho.info
thewho.com

Internet Articles

Bliss, Karen. "Pete Townshend: Listen to Alarm Bells but Don't Be So Pessimistic." www.samaritanmag.com. Samaritan Mag. April 15, 2013. http://www.samaritanmag.com/1539/pete-townshend-listen-alarm-bells-dont-be-so-pessimistic.

Eccleston, Danny. ". . . Here's the Who Sell Out." www.mojo4music.com. Mojo. February 18, 2009. http://www.mojo4music.com/blog/2009/02/never_mind_the_psychedelics.html.

McKendree, Alan. "Interview with John Entwistle." www.recmusicbeatles.com. July 22, 1995. http://www.recmusicbeatles.com/public/files/bbs/entwistle.html.

Nevison, Ron. "Ron Nevison, March 2007." www.whochat.proboards.com. The Who Forum. March 17, 2007. http://whochat.proboards.com/index.cgi?action=display&board=nevison&thread=4672&page=1.

Raison, Mark. "Interview: Mark Raison Meets Dougal Butler-Keith Moon's Right Hand Man." www.Modculture.co.uk. Mod Culture. July 4, 2012. http://www.Modculture.co.uk/interview-mark-raison-meets-dougal-butler-keith-moons-right-hand-man/.

Townshend, Pete. "John Entwistle." thewho.com. TheWho.com. June 22, 2012. http://thewho.com/john-entwistle/.

Index

THE FAQ SERIES

HAL•LEONARD®
PERFORMING ARTS
PUBLISHING GROUP

FAQ.halleonardbooks.com